Essenti

Mathematics

Course

Book 2

Philip KG Baffour

Dip. Mech. Eng. BEd. MEd. (Cantab)

Ashanti Roses

Publishing

First published in 2011 by Ashanti Roses.

ISBN 978-0-9561798-1-4

Printed and bound in England by
CPI Antony Rowe Ltd.
Bumper's Farm, Chippenham
Wiltshire, SN14 6LH
England

Cover Design by Philip KG Baffour
Illustrations by Sherry Baffour and
Philip KG Baffour

Acknowledgements

My thanks to Shaun Reeder for proof reading the text.
My special thanks to Sherry Baffour who undertook the rigorous task of both illustrating and further proof reading the text.

The software used for typing and illustrating is Adobe Indesign Creative Suite 2 Premium Edition. I feel that in this text any incorrect answers will be due to my rearranging or typesetting.

Every effort has been made to contact all copyright holders. If any have been inadvertently omitted the author would be pleased to make full acknowledgement at the first opportunity.

The author and publishers are grateful to the following Junior High Schools involved in discussions and interviews about the type of textbooks pupils would like. These schools also took part in trials of the materials from the book:
A.M.E. Zion School, Kumasi
Assem Mixed School, Kumasi
Cambridge International School, Kumasi
Grace Baptist School, Kumasi
Martyrs of Uganda School, Kumasi
Mmofratro Junior High School. Kumasi
Presbyterian School, Kumasi
Roman Catholic School, Konongo
S.D.A. School, Kumasi
State Boys School, Kumasi
State Girls School, Kumasi
S[t] Thomas International School, Kumasi
T.I. Ahmadiyah School, Kumasi
Tweneboa Kodua School, Abuakwa
U.S.T. School, Kumasi
Wesley College Demonstration School, Kumasi

I dedicate this book to children to promote education in far-flung areas of the world. This book intends to help children experience success, pass examinations with integrity and to enhance their autonomous learning of basic mathematics and beyond.

To help all scholars I have provided thorough explanations and many opportunities to practise what you learn. My hope is that this book will lead you to a wider and more confident use of mathematics as you go on to create, design, invent and engineer in business, health, technology, agriculture, science and manufacturing. Together, we aim to make the world a better place.

2011   *Philip KG Baffour*

Preface

About this book

The second of the Essential Mathematics Course, this book is written for pupils in secondary schools and at the date of publication covers the junior high school syllabus of Ghana for year 2. It may be worked through chapter by chapter. On the title page of each chapter are some interesting facts to enjoy. These are supplementary to the syllabus and bring life to mathematics. Lots of examples are given to explain each topic and many exercises including those showing how mathematics is used in the real world. Pupils who study this book carefully will:

- Acquire mathematical skills to achieve success as a pupil and onwards into adult life.
- Recognise how mathematics is applied in real life.
- Enjoy mathematics as a source of interest in its own right.

Advice to pupils

You learn best by doing. To help you there are clear explanations at every stage and a summary at the end of each unit. To look for a topic turn to the contents page for key syllabus ideas or the index which lists the keywords and subjects.

Self Assessment

Continue to work through the exercises thoroughly once you have read and understood the text and examples. Take careful note of the summaries and revise summaries of book 1 to build up your knowledge base. Stretch your ability by doing the questions in the extension. Once you have done this go to the answers to assess how well you have done.

Using the Exercises

There are many worked examples for each topic which start with straightforward questions. These show how work can be set out. Using the same method will break down the more complex or difficult questions and help your success rate. An asterisk * shows a more challenging question.

Materials needed

You will need writing paper, 5 mm squared paper, ruler, protractor, a pair of compasses and a calculator. Be sparing in your use of your calculator. Detailed instructions on the use of calculator are not included in this book as there is no universal standard for the layout of the keys or of operation. You will need to consult your manual and I suggest that you keep the manual with the calculator for reference. The paper resource sheets at the back of the book can be photocopied and used as and when needed.

Answers and accuracy

Use every possible method to answer questions before turning to the answers. Get into the habit of checking your work yourself to see that the answer is reasonable. You should have some idea of the size of the answer expected. Refer back to the explanations or previous topics if you get stuck. The summaries will help you. Only check the answers at the back of the book to see how you are doing, carefully covering up future exercises.

Investigation and puzzles

Investigations answer the question "What happens if ..... ?" which encourages pupils to relate the topic to other areas of school curriculum and to people and careers that use mathematics. Great enjoyment can be had as they lead into deeper consideration of how numbers work. Note that no answers are given. Some investigations and puzzles are simple and others more difficult and some are open-ended while others lead to one result. They develop and use problem solving skills.

CONTENTS

Symbols and Abbreviations Used

$=$	is equal to	$\neq$	is not equal to
$>$	is greater than	$<$	is less than
$\geq$	is greater than or equal to	$\leq$	is less than or equal to
$\in$	is a member of	$\notin$	is not a member of
$\varnothing$	empty set or null set	1 d.p.	corrected to one decimal place
$\subset$	is a subset of	$\not\subset$	is not a subset of
$\cap$	intersection	$\cup$	union
$\therefore$	therefore	$\Rightarrow$	gives, giving, implies or implying that
∞	infinity	$@$	at
π	pi	$\sqrt{a}$	positive square root of a
$\sqrt[n]{a}$	n^{th} root of a	x^y	x to the power of y
$\perp$	is perpendicular to	$/\!/$	is parallel to
$\simeq$	is rounded to	$\approx$	is equivalent to
$\pm$	plus or minus	etc.	et cetera (and the rest)

International System of Units

The International System of Units - abbreviated **SI** - from the French
    Le Système Internationale d'Unités.
The SI dates from 1960. It is a system of physical units based on the metre, kilogram, second, ampere, kelvin, candela and mole together with a set of prefixes to indicate multiplication or division by the power of ten. It is now used all over the world more than any other system of measurement.

Commonly Used SI Prefixes

Prefix	Multiplication factor		Symbol
giga	1 000 000 000	$= 10^9$	G
mega	1 000 000	$= 10^6$	M
kilo	1 000	$= 10^3$	k
hecto	100	$= 10^2$	h
deca	10	$= 10^1$	da
deci	0.1	$= 10^{-1}$	d
centi	0.01	$= 10^{-2}$	c
milli	0.001	$= 10^{-3}$	m
micro	0.000 001	$= 10^{-6}$	μ
nano	0.000 000 001	$= 10^{-9}$	n

SI Convention

1 Symbols do not have period/full stop (.).
2 Symbols of units are written in upright, lower case except those larger than 10^3 (kilo).
3 A space separates the number and the symbols. The units are not written in plural.
   - 16 kg (not 16 KG); 12 cm (not 12cm); 33 ml (not 33ML)
4 Spaces may be used to separate thousands before or after a decimal point,
   examples are: 1 000 000 or 27 345 or 0.898 437.
5 Joined units such as metre per second can be written as m/s or m s^{-1} or m·s^{-1} or $\dfrac{\text{m}}{\text{s}}$.

Numeration systems

EXTENSION

SUMMARY

Just as the first attempts of writing came along after the development of speech, so the efforts at the graphical representation of numbers came after people had learnt to count. The earliest numerals were simple notches in a stick, scratches on a stone or marks on a piece of pottery.

Numerals from five early civilizations

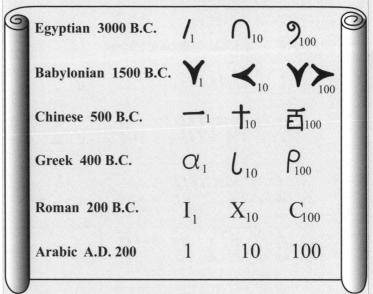

Egyptian 3000 B.C.	$/_1$	$\cap_{10}$	9_{100}
Babylonian 1500 B.C.	Y_1	$<_{10}$	$Y\!>_{100}$
Chinese 500 B.C.	$-_1$	$\dagger_{10}$	$百_{100}$
Greek 400 B.C.	α_1	L_{10}	P_{100}
Roman 200 B.C.	I_1	X_{10}	C_{100}
Arabic A.D. 200	1	10	100

Cuneiform numerals - In Babylonian times (4000 B.C. - 200 B.C.), symbols were impressed in damp clay tablets and then baked in the sun or in a kiln forming documents which were practically as permanent as stone.
Tablet - A small flat and thin piece of material used for inscription.
Papyrus - A material prepared in ancient Egypt from the pithy stem of a water plant used in sheets for writing or painting on.

1 Egyptian numeral system

Around 3000 BC the ancient Egyptians used **hieroglyphics** which is a kind of picture writing. They used to write on material made out of a reed plant called **papyrus**. Some reeds were mashed together into a flat sheet of pulp and then dried. They formed a very good writing surface. Soot was mixed to make ink and a sharpened reed used as a pen.

The system was based on 10. It did not include a zero symbol but it did use the principle of place value. The numerals were formed by putting the basic symbols together.

1	/	Stroke
10	 ∩	Arch - inverted wicket or a heel bone.
100	 ?	Coiled rope
1000	 𝓛	Lotus flower
10 000	 𝓡	Bent finger
100 000	 🐸	Tadpole
1 000 000	 🧎	Kneeling figure

Examples

a ∩∩//// = 24

b ?∩∩∩// = 132

c ???∩/// = 316

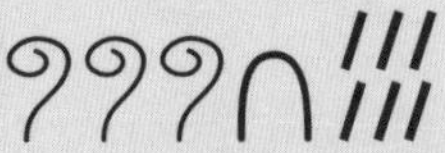

d 𝓛??∩∩/// = 1237

e 𝓛𝓛??//// = 2204

f 🐸𝓡𝓛/// = 111 003

g 𝓡𝓡𝓛𝓛𝓛?/// = 23 105

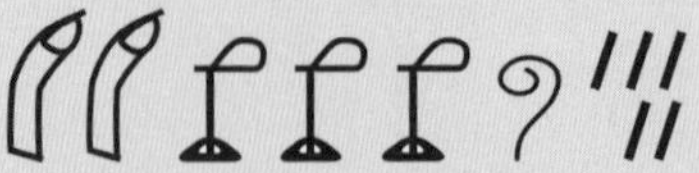

h 🧎🧎𝓛??/// = 2 001 203

i 🧎🐸🐸𝓡𝓡𝓡𝓛????∩//// = 1 231 418

Exercise 1:1

Use the Egyptian hieroglyphic numeral system to work out the value of the following symbols.

1  2

3  4

5  6

7  8

9  10

11  12

13  14

15  16

Exercise 1:2

Draw the hieroglyphic symbols for the following numbers:

1 15	**2** 23	**3** 48	**4** 50	**5** 96
6 120	**7** 200	**8** 274	**9** 381	**10** 467
11 490	**12** 539	**13** 771	**14** 1480	**15** 6072
16 10 266	**17** 324 400	**18** 604 054	**19** 1 212 424	**20** 2 131 246

Egyptian hieroglyphics: addition

The ancient Egyptians used special symbols for addition.

The symbol for addition was   The symbol for equal to was

Examples   **a**

| (22) | added to | (32) | equals | (54) |

b   121   added to   200   equals   321

Exercise 1:3

Do these additions using Egyptian hieroglyphic numerals.

1   **2**

3   **4**

Sometimes they ended up with more than ten numerals the same.

Example

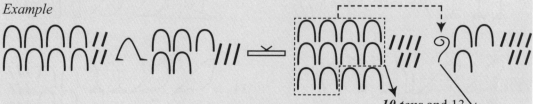

10 tens and 13 exchanged for **1 hundred** and 13.

They had to exchange these for the numeral that was the number ten times bigger.

Example

Find the answers to these hieroglyphic additions. You need to exchange for a numeral that is worth ten times more.

5   **6**

7   **8**

Egyptian hieroglyphics subtraction

Subtraction was the opposite to addition in that you just took away the numerals.

The symbol for subtraction was

Examples a

(67) (take away) (54) (equals) (13)

b

(1620) (take away) (210) (equals) (1410)

Exercise 1:4

Do these subtractions using Egyptian hieroglyphic numerals:

1

2

3

4

5

6

Subtraction involved having to exchange numerals.

Ten ∩ could be exchanged for ten ones ///// /////

Hundred could be exchanged for ten tens

Thousand could be exchanged for ten hundreds

Example (52) (take away) (25) equals (27)

Exchange ∩ for ///// ///// because there are not enough **one** numerals to take away **five ones**.

Work out the following:

7

8

9

10

11

12

6

Pyramid builders

Pyramids are big structures with square bases and four smooth triangular-shaped sides that come to a point at the top. They were built as tombs for Egyptian pharaohs from around the third dynasty (2649 B.C.) until around 1640 B.C. The early step pyramid, with several levels and a flat top, developed into the true pyramid such as the three largest at Giza near Cairo. These include the **Great Pyramid** of Cheops built for King Khufu in 2528 BC. It took 20 years to build using 2.3 million limestone blocks. The blocks range from 2.5 to 15 tonnes in weight.

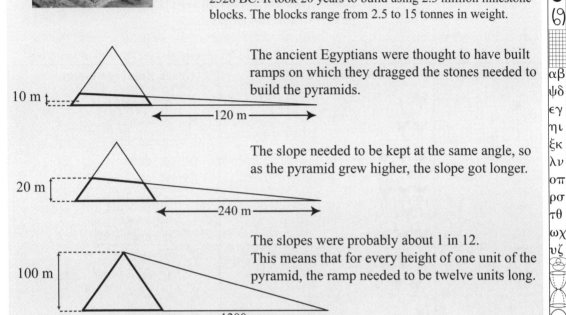

The ancient Egyptians were thought to have built ramps on which they dragged the stones needed to build the pyramids.

10 m

120 m

The slope needed to be kept at the same angle, so as the pyramid grew higher, the slope got longer.

20 m

240 m

The slopes were probably about 1 in 12. This means that for every height of one unit of the pyramid, the ramp needed to be twelve units long.

100 m

1200 m

Exercise 1:5

Copy and complete the following, assuming a slope of 1 in 12:

1 Pyramid 20 m high, ramp —— m long; **2** Pyramid 30 m high, ramp —— m long;

3 Pyramid 50 m high, ramp —— m long; **4** Pyramid 80 m high, ramp —— m long;

5 Ramp is 600 m long, pyramid — m high; **6** Ramp is 960 m long, pyramid —— m high;

7 Ramp is 2400 m long, pyramid — m high; **8** Ramp is 1980 m long, pyramid —— m high;

Work out what these slopes would be in these pyramid measurements:

9 Pyramid of 40 m high and ramp of 140 m in length;

10 Pyramid of 55 m high and ramp of 220 m in length;   .

11 Pyramid of 90 m high and ramp of 189 m in length.

12 King Khufu's pyramid at Al Giza near the west bank of the river Nile stood originally 147 m high. If the ramp is 1800 m in length, what is the slope?

13 The rhomboid pyramid at Dahshur in Egypt was erected by Pharaoh Snefru of the 4th dynasty. Using a slope of 1:12, if the ramp is 8.2 metres long, what is the height of the pyramid?

2 Other numeration systems

Zero 0 = nought = oh = nothing: Arabic: Sifr

Arabic numerals are numbers which correspond to numbers 0, 1, 2, 3, 4, 5, 6, 7, 8, 9

Hindu-Arabic number system is even now in common use using the ten digits with 0 as a place holder for numbers such as 20, 100, 0.604

Babylonian number system was used by the ancient Babylonians with mixed base of 10 and base 60. The methods of measuring time and angle used today probably came from this system..

Greek number system from ancient Greece used the letters of the alphabet to mean the numbers 1 to 9, 10 to 90 in tens and 100 to 900 in hundreds.

Arabic digits		Babylonian number system		Greek number system			
•	0	Y	1	A	α	alpha	1
		YY	2	B	β	beta	2
I	1	YYY	3	Γ	γ	gamma	3
		YYY Y	4	Δ	δ	delta	4
⟨	2			E	ε	epsillon	5
		YYY YYY	8	Ϲ	ς	digamma	6 *
⟨⟨	3	YY		Z	ζ	zeta	7
⟨⟨⟨	4			H	η	eta	8
				θ	θ	theta	9
Β	5			I	ι	iota	10
		⟨	10	K	κ	kappa	20
7	6	⟨YYY	13	Λ	λ	lambda	30
				M	μ	mu	40
V	7	⟨⟨⟨YYYY Y	24	N	ν	nu	50
∧	8			Ξ	ξ	ksi	60
		Y	60 (same as 1)	O	o	omicron	70
q	9			Π	π	pi	80
		Y⟨⟨⟨⟨	100 = (60 + 40)	Ϙ	ϙ	koppa	90
				P	ρ	rho	100
		YYY YYY YY	500 = (8 × 60 + 20)	Σ	σ	sigma	200
				T	τ	tau	300
				Y	υ	upsilon	400
				Φ	φ	phi	500
				X	χ	chi	600
				Ψ	ψ	psi	700
				Ω	ω	omega	800
				ϻ	ϡ	san or sampi 900 *

Roman number system is a number system used by the ancient Romans and up to the present day with repeated letters and a mixed base of 5 and 10.

I = 1 II = 2 III = 3 IV = 4 V = 5 VI = 6

VII = 7 VIII = 8 IX = 9 X = 10 XI = 11 XII = 12

XIII = 13 XIV = 14 XVI = 16 XIX = 19

XXXIV = 34 L = 50 LXVII = 67 LXXIX = 79

XCIII = 93 C = 100 D = 500 CM = 900 M = 1000

* These older letters are which are not in the usual Greek letters.

Greek numbers are produced by additive combinations.

Examples   **a** 18 = 10 + 8 = ιη   **b** 67 = 60 + 7 = ξζ

  c 125 = 100 + 20 + 5 = ρκε   **d** 234 = 200 + 30 + 4 = σλδ

In the Roman number system a single symbol of less value placed **before** one of greater value shows that it must be subtracted.

Examples   **a** 9 = 10 − 1 = IX   **b** 11 = 10 + 1 = XI   **c** 19 = 10 + 10 − 1 = XIX

  d 400 = 500 − 100 = CD   **e** 90 = 100 − 10 = XC   **f** 900 = 1000 − 100 = CM

Exercise 1:6

1 Interpret these Greek numbers into ordinary numbers:

  a λγ   **b** ιγ   **c** κβ   **d** πζ   **e** ξϛ   **f** νθ

  g ρκ   **h** ϙδ   **i** ͵ξε   **j** χϙϛ   **k** φοβ   **l** ωπη

2 Write these numbers using the Greek numerals:

  a 15   **b** 21   **c** 74   **d** 144   **e** 535   **f** 720

  g 805   **h** 999   **i** 678   **j** 267   **k** 450   **l** 953

3 Find out what these Roman numbers are:

  a LXVI   **b** DLV   **c** MLII   **d** MMV   **e** MDLVII   **f** CXXIII

  g XXXVIII **h** MDCLXV **i** CMXIX   **j** MCMXCIX   **k** MCDXXVII   **l** MMIX

4 Write these numbers in Roman numerals:

  a 18   **b** 29   **c** 42   **d** 67   **e** 70   **f** 89

  g 127   **h** 172   **i** 212   **j** 255   **k** 536   **l** 987

  m 1045   **n** 1600   **o** 1852   **p** 1927   **q** 2350   **r** 3436

5 Copy and work out answers to these Babylonian numerals:

  a   **b**   **c**

  d   **e**   **f**

  g ⟨image⟩ + ⟨image⟩ =   **h** ⟨image⟩ + ⟨image⟩ =   **i** ⟨image⟩ + ⟨image⟩ =

6 Copy these and write the answers in Babylonian numerals:

  a 52 − 22 =   **b** 100 − 16 =   **c** 6 × 10 + 10 =   **d** 60 + 30 =

  e 18 − 8 + 28 =   **f** 120 − 27 =   **g** 120 − 20 =   **h** 4 × 60 − 100 =

Modern arabic numerals سمشقةثقعى وهالشقش ىقثيخة

The table shows modern arabic numerals and their pronunciation.

Arabic numeral	Pronunciation	Digit
٠	sifr	0
١	wahid	1
٢	ithnan	2
٣	thalath	3
٤	arba'a	4
٥	khamsa	5
٦	sitta	6
٧	sab'a	7
٨	thamaniya	8
٩	tis'a	9
١٠	'ashar	10
١١	ahada 'ashar	11
١٢	ithna 'ashar	12
٢٠	'ishrun	20
٣٠	thalathun	30
٤٠	arba'un	40
٥٠	khamsun	50
٦٠	sittun	60
٧٠	sab'un	70
٨٠	thamanun	80
٩٠	tis'un	90
١٠٠	m'ia	100
٢٠٠	mi'ataan	200
٣٠٠	thalaath mi'a	300
١٠٠٠	alf	1000
١٠٠٠٠٠	mi'at alf	100 000
١٠٠٠٠٠٠	milyoun	1 000 000

Forming numbers in arabic numerals

For numbers from 13 to 19:
place a number before ten.

Examples

13 - ١٣ - three ten - thalatha 'ashar

17 - ١٧ - seven ten - sab'a 'ashar

For numbers from 21 to 99:
reverse the numbers and add *wa* (and) between the two numbers.

Examples:

21 - one and twenty
- ٢١
- wahid wa 'ishrun

38 - eight and thirty
- ٣٨
- thamaniya wa thalathun

92 - two and ninety
- ٩٢
- ithnan wa tis'un

Other numbers

174 - four and seventy and hundred
- ١٧٤
- mi'a wa arba'a wa sa'bun

561 - one and sixty and five hundred
- ٥٦١
- khamsu m'ia wa wahid wa sittun

1 700 000 - ١٧٠٠٠٠٠
- milyoun wa sab'a alf

Exercise 1:7

1 Write these in modern arabic numbers:

   a 14   **b** 15   **c** 16   **d** 18   **e** 19   **f** 20

2 Write these numbers in modern arabic numbers:

   a 25   **b** 27   **c** 31   **d** 33   **e** 36   **f** 44

   g 48   **h** 53   **i** 59   **j** 60   **k** 67   **l** 74

3 Write these numbers in modern arabic numbers and write their pronunciation:

   a 26   **b** 37   **c** 78   **d** 51   **e** 88   **f** 91

   g 120   **h** 237   **i** 350   **j** 400   **k** 645   **l** 700

4 Write these in modern arabic digits:

   a tis'a wa ishrun   **b** sab'a 'ashar   **c** thamaniya wa thalathum

   d thalatha wa sabun   **e** wahid wa thamanum   **f** khamsa wa khamsun

   g arba'a wa thamanum   **h** thalatha wa tis'un   **i** tis'a wa arba'un

5 Write these numbers in normal digits:

   a ٣٠   **b** ٥٥   **c** ٢٩   **d** ٢٦   **e** ٨١   **f** ٤٧

   g ٨٦   **h** ٩٣   **i** ٤٥   **j** ٧١٥   **k** ٣٩٤   **l** ٧٤٨

Arabic is written from right to left: 124 + 453 is written as 453 + 124.

Examples   **a** 453 + 124 → ١٢٤   **b** 905 + 378 → ٣٧٨   **c** 164 − 73 → ١٦٤

                       + ٤٥٣   + ٩٠٥   − ٧٣

                          ٥٧٧   ١٢٨٣   ٩١

---

6 Copy and complete these using modern arabic numerals:

   a 38 + 11 =   **b** 27 − 10 =   **c** 77 − 43 =   **d** 128 + 51 =

   e 208 − 77 =   **f** 381 + 195 =   **g** 661 − 428 =   **h** 783 + 857 =

7 Copy and complete these addition and subtraction sums:

   a   ٤٩   **b**   ٧٥   **c**   ٨٣   **d**   ٢٣٨

       + ٥٨   − ٤٨   − ٤٠   + ١١٦

   e   ٥٨٠   **f**   ١٢٨   **g**   ٤٠٤   **h**   ١٦٣

       − ٢٤٠   + ٣٠٤   + ٧٢٧   − ٧٣

8 Rewrite these magic squares using modern Arabic numerals:

a

21	26	19
20	22	24
25	18	23

b

1	15	14	4
12	6	7	9
8	10	11	5
13	3	2	16

c

21	2	8	14	15
13	19	20	1	7
0	6	12	18	24
17	23	4	5	11
9	10	16	22	3

9 Work out each of these and write yours answers in Roman numerals.

a XIV + CLX + MLII   **b** LXII − XXIV   **c** XIX + XL + XC

d IV + IX + LI   **e** V + X + L + C   **f** XX + CIV + LXV + XCV

g CCXXXII + CDXXXII   **h** MDCCCLII + MCCCXLVI   **i** MCCXIX − DCCCXLIII

For numbers between 900 and 10 000 an apostrophe is placed in front of the Greek letter from A to Θ as shown below. It represents 1000 times the unit value of the letter.

'A	'B	'Γ	'Δ	'E	'Ϛ	'Z	'H	'Θ
1000	2000	3000	4000	5000	6000	7000	8000	9000

The Greeks also used myriad (Μυριοι), the second "base" of the numeral to represent multiples of 10 000. They put an M (the first letter of the Greek word for "ten thousand") with the corresponding Greek letters over the top.

$\overset{\alpha}{M}$	$\overset{\beta}{M}$	$\overset{\gamma}{M}$	$\overset{\delta}{M}$	$\overset{\varepsilon}{M}$	$\overset{\iota\alpha}{M}$	$\overset{\iota\beta}{M}$	$\overset{\chi\xi\theta}{M}$
10 000	20 000	30 000	40 000	50 000	110 000	120 000	6 690 000

Examples   **a** 'ζωμ = 7840 (7000 + 800 + 40)   **b** 'δωλα = 4831 (4000 + 800 + 30 + 1)

c $\overset{οβ}{M}$ = 720 000 (72 × 10 000)   **d** 'εϙημ + 'Ϛδκζ = (5098 × 10 000 + 6427)

e $\overset{α}{M}$ωιε = 8 150 000 (815 × 10 000)   **f** $\overset{'θχλα}{M}$ = 96 310 000 (9631 × 10 000)

10 Find these in normal numbers:

a 'δϛ   **b** 'θγ   **c** 'ηβ   **d** 'εοη   **e** 'δμα

f 'ζροε   **g** 'εϡξϛ   **h** 'θϡϙϛ   **i** 'ηφλε   **j** 'δχιβ

k $\overset{βο}{M}$ **l** $\overset{πδ}{M}$ **m** $\overset{σξα}{M}$ **n** $\overset{'επδ}{M}$ **o** $\overset{θ}{M}$τϙϛ

11 Write these numbers in Greek alphabetical numerals:

a 3200   **b** 4760   **c** 9205   **d** 13 500   **e** 65 840

f 80 000   **g** 79 300   **h** 110 800   **i** 499 000   **j** 105 080

k 566 700   **l** 772 000   **m** 1 000 000   **n** 3 105 500   **o** 22 696 739

3 Number bases

Oware is a board game played in Ghana. The board has two rows of six holes, and an additional hole, or "pot" at each end. The two players face each other and begin by placing four seeds in each of the six holes. A player's home territory consists of the six holes in the row on his side and the pot on the right. In his first move player one scoops up all the seeds from any hole on his side and "sows" one in each hole in an anticlockwise direction, beginning with the next hole. The object of the game is to capture at least 25 seeds, a majority of the total of 48, in one's own pot. If a player when distributing the contents of his cups, has dropped the last seed in an enemy cup which already contains one or two seeds, he may capture the 2 or 3 seeds in this cup, as well as the seeds in all the enemy cups having 2 or 3 seeds, going clockwise in an unbroken sequence. If a player finds that the opponent's cups are empty, he may try to feed his seeds into enemy territory, if possible. If this is not possible, he gains all the remaining seeds. A few final seeds circulating endlessly are divided between the players.

	1	2	3	4	5	10	11	12
Babylonian numbers	˅	˅˅	˅˅˅	˅˅˅˅	˅˅˅˅˅	＜	＜˅	＜˅˅
Roman numbers	I	II	III	IV	V	X	XI	XII

Base	The **base** of a number system is that number on which the system is built.

Base ten (Denary)

We have ten fingers. That is why we probably count in tens or base ten. The digit 0, 1, 2, 3, 4, 5, 6, 7, 8, 9 are used.

Consider the number 4726. It means

$$4726 = 4 \times 10^3 + 7 \times 10^2 + 2 \times 10^1 + 6 \times 10^0$$
$$= 4000 \quad + 700 \quad + 20 \quad + 6$$

Each column is ten times the value of its right-hand neighbour.
The base of this number system is ten and it is called the **denary system**.

Base five (Quinary)

Base five

If we had one arm with a five fingered hand things might have been different. We would have to record every group of five instead of every group of ten.

This number of dots ● ● ● ● ● would be counted as ▦ ●● or as 1 ●● .

The one stands for a group of five units. If we write using the number symbols we could put 13.

13 might be confused with thirteen, so we read it as 'one three' or we write it as

Fives Units
  1   3   or more precisely 13_{five}. 13_{five} is written in short form as 13_5.

We call this number system **base five** or **quinary**. Base 5 digits are: 0, 1, 2, 3, 4

Examples   **a**   ●●●● is grouped by ▦ ●●●● or written as 14_5

b   ●●●●●●● is grouped by ▦ ▦ ● or written 23_5

c   ●●●●●●●●●●●●●●●●●●●● is grouped by ▦ ▦ ▦ ▦ or written as 40_5

Exercise 1:8

1
a How many dots?
b Draw round groups of five.
c How many groups of five are there?
d How many dots are left over?
e Show the number of dots in base five.

2
a How many dots?
b Draw round groups of five.
c How many groups of five are there?
d How many dots are left over?
e Show the number of dots in base five.

3
a How many dots?
b Draw round groups of five.
c How many groups of five are there?
d How many dots are left over?
e Show the number of dots in base five.

Copy these patterns of dots. Group them and write your answers in base five.

4   5   6   7

8   9   10   11

12   13   14   15

Draw these base five numbers as groups of dots:

16 3_5 17 11_5 18 21_5 19 12_5 20 23_5 21 44_5

22 33_5 23 100_5 24 111_5 25 123_5 26 201_5 27 240_5

28 Tins of tomatoes are put into boxes of five. How many tins are in:

a 3 boxes   b 7 boxes   c 6 boxes and 4 tins left over

d How many boxes are needed and how many tins will be left over if I have:

i 47 tins   ii 78 tins   iii 99 tins   iv 137 tins   v 261

Operations with base five

As with denary 314 in base 5 can be written in columns as shown below:

Twenty-fives	Fives	Units		TwF	F	U
3	1	4		3	1	4

The table below compares the first few denary numerals written in quinary (base 5) form.

Base 5 numbers can be added as well as subtracted. Remember that you borrow 5 or carry 5 wholes.

Examples

a
$$\begin{array}{r} {}^{1}4 \\ + 2 \\ \hline 11_5 \end{array}$$

b
$$\begin{array}{r} {}^{1}{}^{1}2 \\ + 34 \\ \hline 101_5 \end{array}$$

c
$$\begin{array}{r} 4{}^{1}21 \\ + 34 \\ \hline 1010_5 \end{array}$$

d
$$\begin{array}{r} {}^{2}{}^{1}22 \\ 434 \\ + 343 \\ \hline 1404_5 \end{array}$$

e
$$\begin{array}{r} 24 \\ - 10 \\ \hline 14_5 \end{array}$$

f
$$\begin{array}{r} 104 \\ - 13 \\ \hline 41_5 \end{array}$$

g
$$\begin{array}{r} 302 \\ - 124 \\ \hline 123_5 \end{array}$$

h
$$\begin{array}{r} 400 \\ - 214 \\ \hline 131_5 \end{array}$$

Exercise 1:9

Work out these additions and subtractions in base five:

1
$$\begin{array}{r} 4 \\ + 4 \\ \hline \end{array}$$

2
$$\begin{array}{r} 3 \\ + 3 \\ \hline \end{array}$$

3
$$\begin{array}{r} 2 \\ + 4 \\ \hline \end{array}$$

4
$$\begin{array}{r} 33 \\ + 22 \\ \hline \end{array}$$

5
$$\begin{array}{r} 44 \\ + 31 \\ \hline \end{array}$$

6
$$\begin{array}{r} 13 \\ + 31 \\ 24 \\ \hline \end{array}$$

7
$$\begin{array}{r} 404 \\ + 303 \\ \hline \end{array}$$

8
$$\begin{array}{r} 134 \\ 442 \\ + 41 \\ \hline \end{array}$$

9
$$\begin{array}{r} 3421 \\ + 1034 \\ \hline \end{array}$$

10
$$\begin{array}{r} 3333 \\ 1004 \\ + 4441 \\ \hline \end{array}$$

11
$$\begin{array}{r} 12 \\ - 3 \\ \hline \end{array}$$

12
$$\begin{array}{r} 30 \\ - 12 \\ \hline \end{array}$$

13
$$\begin{array}{r} 101 \\ - 32 \\ \hline \end{array}$$

14
$$\begin{array}{r} 233 \\ - 40 \\ \hline \end{array}$$

15
$$\begin{array}{r} 200 \\ - 33 \\ \hline \end{array}$$

16
$$\begin{array}{r} 321 \\ - 123 \\ \hline \end{array}$$

17
$$\begin{array}{r} 4031 \\ - 3402 \\ \hline \end{array}$$

18
$$\begin{array}{r} 1111 \\ - 444 \\ \hline \end{array}$$

19
$$\begin{array}{r} 3004 \\ - 1220 \\ \hline \end{array}$$

20
$$\begin{array}{r} 4003 \\ - 2324 \\ \hline \end{array}$$

21
$$\begin{array}{r} 3101 \\ - 413 \\ \hline \end{array}$$

22
$$\begin{array}{r} 43 \\ 402 \\ + 24 \\ \hline \end{array}$$

23
$$\begin{array}{r} 111 \\ 204 \\ + 43 \\ \hline \end{array}$$

24
$$\begin{array}{r} 200 \\ 424 \\ + 31 \\ \hline \end{array}$$

25
$$\begin{array}{r} 222 \\ 333 \\ + 444 \\ \hline \end{array}$$

Conversion from base 5 to base 10

Consider these columns:

One hundred and twenty-fives	Twenty-fives	Fives	Units
		●	
	●	●	
	●	●	●
●	●	●	●

The dots here represent 1342_5

Note
$5^0 = 1$
$5^1 = 5$
$5^2 = 25$
$5^3 = 125$
$5^4 = 625$
$5^5 = 3125$

$$1342_5 = (1 \times 5^3) + (3 \times 5^2) + (4 \times 5^1) + (2 \times 5^0) = 125 + 75 + 20 + 2$$
$$= 222_{10}$$

The table below compares the first few base 10 numerals and the same numerals written in base 5 form.

Base 10	Base 5	Meaning of the base 5 numeral	
0	0		$= 0$
1	1	5^0	$= 1$
2	2	2×5^0	$= 2 \times 1$
3	3	3×5^0	$= 3 \times 1$
4	4	4×5^0	$= 4 \times 1$
5	10	$1 \times 5^1 + 0 \times 5^0$	$= 5 + 0$
6	11	$1 \times 5^1 + 1 \times 5^0$	$= 5 + 1$
7	12	$1 \times 5^1 + 2 \times 5^0$	$= 5 + 2$
8	13	$1 \times 5^1 + 3 \times 5^0$	$= 5 + 3$
9	14	$1 \times 5^1 + 4 \times 5^0$	$= 5 + 4$
10	20	$2 \times 5^1 + 0 \times 5^0$	$= 10 + 0$

Examples Convert these numbers from base five to base ten:

a $32_5 = 3 \times 5^1 + 2 \times 5^0 = 3 \times 5 + 2 \times 1 = 15 + 2 = 17_{10}$

b $204_5 = 2 \times 5^2 + 0 \times 5^1 + 4 \times 5^0$
$= 2 \times 25 + 0 \times 5 + 4 \times 1 = 50 + 0 + 4$
$= 54_{10}$

c $3412_5 = 3 \times 5^3 + 4 \times 5^2 + 1 \times 5^1 + 2 \times 5^0$
$= 3 \times 125 + 4 \times 25 + 1 \times 5 + 2 \times 1$
$= 375 + 100 + 5 + 2$
$= 482_{10}$

Exercise 1:10

Write in figures the numbers represented by the dots in base five and their equivalent in base 10.

	5^5	5^4	5^3	5^2	5^1	5^0
1					●	●●●
2				●	●●●	●
3	●			●●	●●●	●
4		●●		● ●	●	●●●
5	●●		●●	●	●●	

Convert the following numbers from base five to base ten:

6 43_5 **7** 111_5

8 324_5 **9** 321_5

10 4203_5 **11** 3143_5

12 12043_5 **13** 102030_5

14 223311_5 **15** 421341_5

Conversion from base 10 to base 5

To convert a number from base ten to base five find how many ..., 3125s, 625s, 125s, 25s, 5s, and units that the number contains.

Using the continuous division method divide the number through by 5 until there is no more remainder. **The remainders (rem) will form the final answer (start from bottom up).**

Examples   Convert these numbers from base ten to base 5:

$$\textbf{a } 7_{10} \qquad \textbf{b } 17_{10} \qquad \textbf{c } 139_{10} \qquad \textbf{d } 7483_{10}$$

a $7_{10} \Longrightarrow$ 5) 7
            5) 1   rem **2** (units)
                0   rem **1** (fives)

$\therefore 7_{10} = 12_5$

b $17_{10} \Longrightarrow$ 5) 18
              5) 3   rem **3** (units)
                  0   rem **3** (fives)

$\therefore 17_{10} = 33_5$

c $139_{10} \Longrightarrow$ 5) 139
              5) 27   rem **4** (units or 4×5^0)
              5) 5   rem **2** (fives or 2×5^1)
              5) 1   rem **0** (twenty-fives or 0×5^2)
                  0   rem **1** (one hundred and twenty-fives or 1×5^3)

$\therefore 139_{10} = 1024_5$

d $7483_{10} \Longrightarrow$ 5) 7483
              5) 1496   rem **3** (units or 3×5^0)
              5) 299   rem **1** (fives or 1×5^1)
              5) 59   rem **4** (twenty-fives or 4×5^2)
              5) 11   rem **4** (one hundred and twenty-fives or 4×5^3)
              5) 2   rem **1** (six hundred and twenty-fives or 1×5^4)
                  0   rem **2** (three thousand one hundred and twenty-fives or 2×5^5)

$\therefore 7483_{10} = 214413_5$

Exercise 1:11

Convert these numbers from base ten to base five:

1 9_{10}	**2** 11_{10}	**3** 59_{10}	**4** 88_{10}	**5** 100_{10}
6 137_{10}	**7** 365_{10}	**8** 399_{10}	**9** 500_{10}	**10** 830_{10}
11 789_{10}	**12** 1000_{10}	**13** 2222_{10}	**14** 5555_{10}	**15** 3423_{10}
16 900_{10}	**17** 2600_{10}	**18** 999_{10}	**19** 2010_{10}	**20** 3126_{10}
21 1111_{10}	**22** 6081_{10}	**23** 5107_{10}	**24** 1999_{10}	**25** 7766_{10}

Base Two (Binary)

Base two number system counts only two digits 0 and 1.

The number: 1 in base two is 1 written as 1_2 pronounced 'one base two'

2 in base two is 10 written as 10_2 pronounced 'one zero base two'

3 in base two is 11 written as 11_2 pronounced 'one one base two'

4 in base two is 100 written as 100_2 pronounced 'one zero zero base two'

The table below compares the first eleven base 10 (denary) numerals and the same numerals written in base two (binary) form.

Denary numeral	Binary numeral	Meaning of the binary numeral
0	0	0
1	1	2^0
2	10	$1 \times 2^1 + 0 \times 2^0$
3	11	$1 \times 2^1 + 1 \times 2^0$
4	100	$1 \times 2^2 + 0 \times 2^1 + 0 \times 2^0 \qquad = 4 + 0 + 0$
5	101	$1 \times 2^2 + 0 \times 2^1 + 1 \times 2^0 \qquad = 4 + 0 + 1$
6	110	$1 \times 2^2 + 1 \times 2^1 + 0 \times 2^0 \qquad = 4 + 2 + 0$
7	111	$1 \times 2^2 + 1 \times 2^1 + 1 \times 2^0 \qquad = 4 + 2 + 1$
8	1000	$1 \times 2^3 + 0 \times 2^2 + 0 \times 2^1 + 0 \times 2^0 = 8 + 0 + 0 + 0$
9	1001	$1 \times 2^3 + 0 \times 2^2 + 0 \times 2^1 + 1 \times 2^0 = 8 + 0 + 0 + 1$
10	1010	$1 \times 2^3 + 0 \times 2^2 + 1 \times 2^1 + 0 \times 2^0 = 8 + 0 + 1 + 0$

Exercise 1:12

Convert these numbers from base two to base ten:

1 1100_2　　2 1011_2　　3 1110_2　　4 10111_2　　5 1111_2

6 1000_2　　7 11011_2　　8 11010_2　　9 10001_2　　10 11110_2

11 101010_2　　12 111001_2　　13 10101_2　　14 10111_2　　15 10000_2

Larger numbers in base two can be converted to base ten.

Examples　　**a** $110101_2 = 1 \times 2^5 + 1 \times 2^4 + 0 \times 2^3 + 1 \times 2^2 + 0 \times 2^1 + 1 \times 2^0$
$$= 32 + 16 + 0 + 4 + 0 + 1$$
$$= 53_{10}$$

b $1100110_2 = 1 \times 2^6 + 1 \times 2^5 + 0 \times 2^4 + 0 \times 2^3 + 1 \times 2^2 + 1 \times 2^1 + 0 \times 2^0$
$$= 64 + 32 + 0 + 0 + 4 + 2 + 0$$
$$= 102_{10}$$

Convert these numbers from base two to base ten:

16 1110111_2　　17 100110_2　　18 110100_2　　19 100001_2　　20 1011001_2

21 1101101_2　　22 1101001_2　　23 1111111_2　　24 1111000_2　　25 11111111_2

Conversion from base 10 to base 2

Method 1

Use the **continuous division method** noting the remainders. *The remainders (rem) will form the final answer (start from bottom up).*

Examples   Convert these numbers from base ten to base two: **a** 18_{10} **b** 50_{10}

a $18_{10} \Longrightarrow$

$$
\begin{array}{r|ll}
2 & 18 & \\
2 & 9 & \text{rem } \mathbf{0} \\
2 & 4 & \text{rem } \mathbf{1} \\
2 & 2 & \text{rem } \mathbf{0} \\
2 & 1 & \text{rem } \mathbf{0} \\
  & 0 & \text{rem } \mathbf{1}
\end{array}
$$

$\therefore 18_{10} = 10010_2$

b $50_{10} \Longrightarrow$

$$
\begin{array}{r|ll}
2 & 50 & \\
2 & 25 & \text{rem } \mathbf{0} \\
2 & 12 & \text{rem } \mathbf{1} \\
2 & 6 & \text{rem } \mathbf{0} \\
2 & 3 & \text{rem } \mathbf{0} \\
2 & 1 & \text{rem } \mathbf{1} \\
  & 0 & \text{rem } \mathbf{1}
\end{array}
$$

$\therefore 50_{10} = 110010_2$

Method 2

To convert a number from base ten to base two, find how many ...., 512s, 256s, 128s, 64s, 32s, 16s, 8s, 4s, 2, and units that the number contains. The numbers can be written in columns as shown:

1024s	512s	256s	128s	64s	32s	16s	8s	4s	2s	1
2^{10}	2^9	2^8	2^7	2^6	2^5	2^4	2^3	2^2	2^1	2^0

Examples

512s	256s	128s	64s	32s	16s	8s	4s	2s	1s	
					1	1	0	1	1	$16 + 8 + 2 + 1 = 27$
			1	0	1	1	1	0	1	$64 + 16 + 8 + 4 + 1 = 93$
	1	0	1	1	0	1	0	0	0	$256 + 64 + 32 + 8 = 360$
1	1	0	0	1	0	1	0	0	1	$512 + 256 + 32 + 8 + 1 = 809$

$\therefore 11011_2 = 27_{10} \qquad 1011101_2 = 93_{10} \qquad 101101000_2 = 360_{10} \qquad 1100101001_2 = 809_{10}$

Exercise 1:13

Convert these numbers from base ten to base two:

1 7_{10} 2 9_{10} 3 11_{10} 4 15_{10} 5 23_{10}

6 27_{10} 7 30_{10} 8 36_{10} 9 40_{10} 10 70_{10}

11 99_{10} 12 101_{10} 13 150_{10} 14 200_{10} 15 124_{10}

16 222_{10} 17 300_{10} 18 323_{10} 19 250_{10} 20 350_{10}

21 244_{10} * 22 365_{10} *23 382_{10} *24 407_{10} *25 499_{10}

26 534_{10} * 27 600_{10} *28 799_{10} *29 909_{10} *30 1023_{10}

19

Conversion from one base to another

To convert a number from one base to another, first convert to base ten and then convert the result to the required base of the number.

To convert a number from base two to base five, first convert to base ten and then convert the result to base five.

Examples

a Convert 1101011_2 to base five

First express 1101011_2 in base 10

$$1101011_2 = 1 \times 2^6 + 1 \times 2^5 + 0 \times 2^4 + 1 \times 2^3 + 0 \times 2^2 + 1 \times 2^1 + 1 \times 2^0$$
$$= 64 + 32 + 0 + 8 + 0 + 2 + 1$$
$$= 107_{10}$$

Then change 107_{10} to base five using the continuous division method.

$$107_{10} \implies$$

5	)107	
5	)21	rem **2**
5	)4	rem **1**
	0	rem **4**

$$\therefore 1101011_2 = 412_5$$

b Convert 1340_5 to base two

First express 1340_5 in base 10
$$1340_5 = 1 \times 5^3 + 3 \times 5^2 + 4 \times 5^1 + 0 \times 5^0$$
$$= 125 + 75 + 20 + 0$$
$$= 220_{10}$$

Then change 220_{10} to base two using the continuous division method.

$$220_{10} \implies$$

2	)220	
2	)110	rem **0**
2	)55	rem **0**
2	)27	rem **1**
2	)13	rem **1**
2	)6	rem **1**
2	)3	rem **0**
2	)1	rem **1**
	0	rem **1**

$$\therefore 1340_5 = 11011100_2$$

Exercise 1:14

Convert these numbers to base 5:

1 10111_2 **2** 1110100_2 **3** 1011011_2 **4** 10101010_2 **5** 1000000_2

6 11111111_2 **7** 11011011_2 **8** 101110111_2 **9** 100000011_2 **10** 110001111_2

Convert these numbers to base 2:

11 40_5 **12** 1133_5 **13** 1440_5 **14** 2030_5 **15** 1234_5

16 3322_5 **17** 1212_5 **18** 2020_5 **19** 3014_5 **20** 4444_5

Addition and subtraction of number bases

In the binary system $1 + 0 = 1$ $0 + 1 = 1$ $1 + 1 = 0$ carry 1 (or 10_2)

Examples Work out these: **a** $101101_2 + 11111_2$ **b** $110111_2 + 10111_2 + 1011_2$

  c $1000_2 - 101_2$ **d** $110010_2 - 10101_2$

$$
\textbf{a} \quad \begin{array}{r} 101101 \\ + \ 11111 \\ \hline 1001100_2 \end{array}
\qquad
\textbf{b} \quad \begin{array}{r} 110111 \\ 10111 \\ + \ 1011 \\ \hline 1011001_2 \end{array}
\qquad
\textbf{c} \quad \begin{array}{r} 1000 \\ - \ 101 \\ \hline 11_2 \end{array}
\qquad
\textbf{d} \quad \begin{array}{r} 110010 \\ - \ 10101 \\ \hline 11101_2 \end{array}
$$

[*Always borrow 2*]

Exercise 1:15

Work out the following:

1 $101_2 + 101_2$ **2** $1011_2 + 111_2$ **3** $1101_2 + 1001_2$

4 $1011_2 + 1110_2$ **5** $10111_2 + 10101_2$ **6** $10111_2 + 11101_2$

7 $111101_2 + 1101010_2$ **8** $101111_2 + 11110_2$ **9** $111_2 + 100_2 + 11_2$

10 $11011_2 + 1101_2 + 1001_2$ **11** $10111_2 + 10111_2 + 10110_2$ **12** $101_2 + 1101_2 + 1001_2$

13 $100_2 - 11_2$ **14** $1000_2 - 111_2$ **15** $10111_2 - 1010_2$

16 $11011_2 - 1101_2$ **17** $110000_2 - 11111_2$ **18** $1111000_2 - 100011_2$

In quinary system $1 + 2 = 3$ $2 + 2 = 4$ $2 + 3 = 0$ carry 1 (or 10_5)

Examples Work out these: **a** $403_5 + 144_5$ **b** $4322_2 + 3404_5 + 244_5$

  c $343_5 - 144_5$ **d** $3402_5 - 2414_5$

$$
\textbf{a} \quad \begin{array}{r} 403 \\ + \ 144 \\ \hline 1002_5 \end{array}
\qquad
\textbf{b} \quad \begin{array}{r} 4322 \\ 3404 \\ + \ 244 \\ \hline 14030_5 \end{array}
\qquad
\textbf{c} \quad \begin{array}{r} 343 \\ - \ 144 \\ \hline 144_5 \end{array}
\qquad
\textbf{d} \quad \begin{array}{r} 3402 \\ - \ 2414 \\ \hline 433_5 \end{array}
$$

[*Always borrow 5*]

Exercise 1:16

Work out the following:

1 $33_5 + 21_5$ **2** $24_5 + 11_5$ **3** $14_5 + 121_5$

4 $40_5 + 30_5$ **5** $431_5 + 43_5$ **6** $140_5 + 241_5$

7 $240_5 + 311_5$ **8** $234_5 + 333_5$ **9** $1134_5 + 442_5$

10 $231_5 + 401_5 + 1333_5$ **11** $34301_5 + 2311_5 + 1442_5$ **12** $14111_5 + 2300_5 + 1044_5$

13 $40_5 - 33_5$ **14** $344_5 - 243_5$ **15** $400_5 - 241_5$

16 $1143_5 - 314_5$ **17** $14132_5 - 3443_5$ **18** $40332_5 - 23344_5$

Electronic information exchanges and processes with bits

A binary system is ideal for use in computer programs because the two digits can be represented by the two electronic states: 'circuit on' = 1 and 'circuit off' = 0.

A computer software program uses digital codes called ASCII to represent letters, symbols and numerals called "glyphs" as a standard format to transfer text between computers. (Note: ASCII stand for American Standard Code for Information Interchange)

When operating this keyboard on a computer if you press the glyph:

H the computer transfers it electronically to the ASCII code 1001000_2.

& the computer transfers it electronically to the ASCII code 0100110_2.

Exercise 1:17

1 Copy and complete the table. The first row has been done for you.

Glyph	Binary	Quinary	Denary	Glyph	Binary	Quinary	Denary
s	1110011_2	430_5	115_{10}	$	0100100_2		
%	0100101_2			@		224_5	
ι		413_5		t	1110100_2		
n	1101110_2		77_{10}	/			47_{10}
p		422_5		j		411_5	
r	1110010_2			o	1101111_2		
?			63_{10}	=			61_{10}
m		414_5		9		212_5	
]	1011011_2			P	1000111_2		
L			76_{10}	s			115_{10}

2 The table shows the results of a survey of a school dinner in a coded format.
Copy the table and decode all the numbers in:
a Quinary numbers   **b** Decimal numbers
c How many pupils took part in the survey?
(Give your answer in base 5 and base 10.)

Comment	Week 1	Week 2
Excellent	1111110_2	1100100_2
Good	1101101_2	10011001_2
Average	1110000_2	10000100_2
Damage Health	1111011_2	1010101_2

4 Numbers everywhere

Telephone numbers

Telephones use electricity to carry sound. They provide the commonest means of communicating with people at a distance.

Every telephone line has an identification number.
A typical telephone number used in Ghana reads like this:

$$00 \quad 233 \quad (0) \quad 21 \quad 6917$$

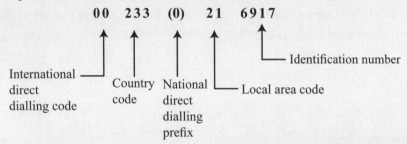

International direct dialling code

Country code

National direct dialling prefix

Local area code

Identification number

The international dialling and country codes are not necessary if a call is being made within the country on a land line. When using a mobile phone the area code must be used.

Here are some area codes in Ghana, shown with the national dialling prefixes.

Accra 021	Agona Swedru 041	Bolgatanga 072	Cape Coast 042
Ho 091	Koforidua 081	Kumasi 051	Sunyani 061
Takoradi 031	Tamale 071	Tema 022	

International telephone dialling codes

Amsterdam (Holland): 00 31 20   Cairo (Egypt) : 00 20 2   Lagos (Nigeria): 009 234 1
Hamburg (Germany) 00 49 40   London (England): 00 44 207   Moscow (Russia): 00 7 495
Montreal (Canada) 011 1 514   New York (USA): 011 1 845   Paris (France): 00 33 1
(All the countries have zero (0) as national direct dialling prefix. Ignore it when dialling abroad.)

Examples **a** Opoku makes a call from Sekondi to a local number 49264 in Cape Coast. He must dial 04249264.

   b Marfo who lives in London wants to make a phone call to his father in Kumasi on 028294. He must dial 002335128294.

Exercise 1:18

Write down all the digits to dial for making these telephone calls:

1 From Atta who lives in Accra to Ababio whose number in Accra is 72486.

2 From Kobi who lives in Bolgatanga to Atia on 66277 in Sunyani.

3 From Asiama who lives at Ho to Enyonam whose number is on 55266 in Koforidua.

4 From Hajia who works in Kumasi to Amina who lives in London on 0207 774224.

5 From Afra in Ghana who wants to call her sister whose number in Lagos is 01483344.

6 From Abukari who lives in Cairo to Agyiri whose local number in Sekondi is 03126626.

7 From Kofi in New York to Kwasi whose local number in Amsterdam is 048218007.

8 From Anton who lives in Montreal to Adjei whose local number in Paris is 049641254.

Mobile phones calls

When using a mobile phone to call another mobile abroad use the international code, otherwise dial only the mobile number. If phoning a landline, always use the national prefix and the area code in front of the person's own phone number.

Examples   **a** Busia in Accra wants to call Akua whose mobile phone number in Koforidua is 0542 261990. Busia needs to dial 0542261990.

                b Afful who lives in Montreal wants to call Larbi whose mobile phone in Ghana is 0243 554417. Afful must dial 00233243554417.

Write down all the digits needed to make these calls, from:

9 Jumah in Cape coast to his sister in London on a mobile number 07887824834.

10 Baba in Moscow to Takyi whose mobile number in Accra is 0242027779.

11 Ohemah in Tema to Nana in Amsterdam whose mobile number is 076215315.

12 Agengo in Lagos to Sikaena whose mobile number in Paris is 07579334016.

13 Dr Mintah in Sunyani to a hospital in Lagos whose telephone number is 016747742.

14 Iddrisu in Kumasi to Yigah in Moscow on mobile number 02439283376.

15 Owusu in Tamale to a pharmacist in London on a mobile phone number 079241729923.

16 Festus in Bolgatanga to Asante at Agona Swedru on 01438244.

17 Mr Anim at Ho to Ms Badawi in Montreal on 04893527.

18 Miss Obeng in Sunyani to Mr Bisi in Moscow on a mobile phone number 06724030429.

19 Mr Oteng who lives in Tema to Ms Kepako in London on 0208 8927234.

20 Write down the full telephone numbers to be dialled from Ghana to these countries:

    a London   07954328759 (mobile)   **b** Lagos   018014044

    c Montreal   892 1025   **d** Hamburg   07978903682 (mobile)

    e New York   742 2693   **f** Amsterdam   0206 488713

Vehicle registration plates

AT 483 Z GH
BA 77 X GH
GT 1108 S GH
NR 349 Y GH

Registration marks on vehicles must be fitted onto number plates at the front and rear of the vehicle. The marks must be displayed in accordance with road vehicle regulations. Vehicle registration plates in Ghana start with a group of letters indicating the region or city of registration followed by a number and ending with a letter. This letter represents the year of registration.

These are examples of vehicles registered in various regions in Ghana.

Greater Accra - AA, GT, AG, ACA, ACB, GS	Upper West - UR, UWR
Ashanti - AS, AT, AH, ARC, ASA, ARA	Upper East - URA
Central - CR, CF and CRA	Volta - VR
Brong Ahafo - BA	Western - WE, WP, WR, WRA
Northern - NG, NP, NR, NRA	Eastern - ER

The letters for the year of registration are for example:
R - 2000; S - 2001; T - 2002; U - 2003; V - 2004; W - 2005; X - 2006; Y - 2007.
Vehicles registered in Kumasi (Ashanti region) may have a typical registration number such as AS 7824 R, AT 42 3911 T, ASA 195 W.

The new type of registration starts with region, number and ends with the year e.g. BA 48 09.

Exercise 1:19

1 Write down where these vehicles were registered:

a WRA 241 P   b ARA 4499 R   c ACA 4 B   d NRA 555

e URA 903 S   f CF 67 S   g GT 1302 P   h BA 4010 G

i NP 4589 T   j UR 5884 H   k BA 9222 H   l VR 648 J

2 Make up vehicle registration marks from these cities. The numbers must be less than 10 000:

a Sunyani   b Bolgatanga   c Wa   d Kumasi

e Ho   f Accra   g Koforidua   h Cape Coast

3 Make up vehicle registration numbers which have prime numbers between 1000 and 9000 from these cities.

a Accra   b Cape Coast   c Tamale   d Kumasi

e Wa   f Ho   g Bolgatanga   h Sekondi

4 Make up vehicle registration marks from these cities. The numbers must be less than 10 000:

a Sunyani (2002)   b Bolgatanga (2005)   c Kumasi (2009)   d Wa (2008)

e Cape Coast (2007)   f Accra (2006)   g Koforidua (2010)   h Ho (2003)

i Tamale (2006)   j Sekondi (2010)   k Ho (2001)   l Kumasi (2006)

Radio frequency bandwidth

Individual broadcasting stations are assigned a portion of frequency scale called a bandwidth to operate so that the signal of one station does not interfere with another.

The fascia of a radio showing the transmission bandwidths FM, SW, LW and MW

	0	1	2	3	4	5	6	7	8	9	10		
FM ——	88	90	92	94	96	98 100	102	104	106	108	FREQUENCY MODULATION		MHz
CHANNEL	2 5	10	20		30	40	50	55				CHANNEL	
SW ——	—— 49m —— 41m ——					31m —25m —			—19m — 16m		SHORT WAVE ——		MHz
	6.0	7.0		8.0		10 12		14	16	18			
LW ——	150		170		190		210	230	250		LONG WAVE ——		KHz
MW ——520		600		700 800		1000		1200	1400	1600	MEDIUM WAVE ——		KHz

Bandwidth is the difference between the upper and lower cut off frequencies.
Frequency is the rate at which the radio signals are broadcast or transmitted.
Frequency is measured in hertz (Hz). Hertz is the number of cycles per second.
Kilo hertz - kHz   Mega hertz - MHz $1000\,kHz = 1\,MHz$
Radio wave is an electromagnetic wave of a frequency between 10^4 and 10^{11} or 10^{12} Hz.
Radio frequency bandwidth is the range of frequencies within a band used for transmitting a signal.

The table shows radio frequency bands.

Name	Symbol	Frequency range
Long Wave	LW	145 kHz - 350 kHz
Medium Wave	MW	530 kHz - 1600 kHz
Short Wave	SW	2310 kHZ - 30 MHz
Frequency Modulation	FM	88 MHz - 108 MHz

Examples   **a** Soul Classics radio station whose frequency wave band is 95.8 MHz operates on frequency modulation (FM) band.

b Jamo radio station which operates on 2020 kHz can be picked up on short wave or SW band.

Exercise 1:20

1 Using the table above write down the frequency designated in which these radio stations operate:
   a Atlantic Radio - 257.4 kHz   b BBC World Service - 6.195 MHz
   c Otec Radio - 99.9 MHz   d Garden City Radio - 4875 - 4995 kHz
   e World Music Radio - 672 kHz   f Ocean Radio 172 kHz
   g Talk Radio - 1548 kHz   h Akasonoma Radio 2.5 MHz

2 What is the range of these bandwidths : **a** LW   **b** MW   **c** SW   **d** FM

3 Stereo sound mode is normally clear on FM radio stations. Find three local radio stations in your area that operate in stereo mode. In each station state the FM band.

4 Find two radio stations in your area that are on: **a** MW   **b** SW   **c** LW

5 Copy the table and assign the correct frequency designation for the radio stations.

Radio station	Frequency band	Frequency designation
Africa No. 1	808 kHz	
Spiritual	89 - 91 kHz	
WQMD	1507 kHz	
West Coast	202 - 205 kHz	
Kids	90500 - 91500 kHz	
Oneworld	2050 - 2090 kHz	

The radio frequency spectrum is divided into a number of bands from very low frequencies to super high frequencies. Frequencies can be converted to **meter bands** or wavelength ranges. To concert frequency into metres you divide 300 000 by the frequency in kilohertz.

Examples **a** Convert 17 705 to metres

$$\text{Metres} = \frac{300\,000}{\text{Frequency in kHz}}$$

$$17\,705 \text{ kHz} = \frac{300\,000}{17705}$$

$$= 16.9 \text{ metre band}$$

b Convert 1548 kHz into metres

$$\text{Metres} = \frac{300\,000}{\text{Frequency in kHz}}$$

$$1548 \text{ kHz} = \frac{300\,000}{1548}$$

$$= 198.8 \text{ metre band}$$

Exercise 1:21

1 Convert these into metre bands:

  a 5 kHz   **b** 12 kHz   **c** 150 kHz   **d** 625 kHz   **e** 905 kHz

  f 1000 kHz   **g** 24500 kHz   **h** 70 MHz   **i** 85.65 MHz   **j** 128.5 MHz

2 The table below shows frequency band designations and where they are used. Copy and complete the table showing all your calculations. The first one has been done for you.

Frequency designation	Frequency range and their uses	Calculations	Wavelength range
Very low frequencies, VLF	3 - 30 kHz **time signals**	$\frac{300\,000}{3}$ to $\frac{300\,000}{30}$	*100 000 - 10 000 m*
Low frequencies, LF	30 - 300 kHz **radio broadcasting**		
Medium frequencies, MF	300 - 3000 kHz **aviation communication**		
High frequencies, HF	3 - 30 MHz **shortwave radio**		
Very high frequencies VHF	30 - 300 MHz **television bradcasting**		
Ultra high frequencies, UHF	300 - 3000 MHz **mobile telephones**		
Super high frequencies, SHF	3 - 30 GHz **satellite television**		

Library numbering system

Every book in the library is given a unique number known as "call number" which serves as an address for locating the book on the library shelf. Most library numbering systems are based on the Dewey decimal classification which was devised by the American Mevril Dewey in 1876. The system has 10 main classes which are:

000 - 099 General knowledge	500 - 599 Natural science and mathematics
100 - 199 Philosophy and psychology	600 - 699 Technology (Applied science)
200 - 299 Religion	700 - 799 The Arts
300 - 399 Social science	800 - 899 Literature
400 - 499 Language	900 - 999 Geography

This how the classification of a book on butterflies is sorted.

500	↓	Natural Sciences and Mathematics
590	↓	Zoological sciences
595	↓	Other invertebrates (worms and insects)
595.7	↓	Insects
595.78	↓	Lepidoptera
595.789	*end*	Butterflies

Exercise 1:22

1 Copy and complete the table by inserting these numbers in the appropriate place to complete the classification numbers of a book on the three planets. 523.41; 523 and 520.

500	↓	Natural Sciences and Mathematics	523.3	↓	The Moon
?	↓	Astronomy and allied sciences	523.4	↓	The Planets
?	↓	Specific celestial bodies and phenomena	?	↓	Mercury
523.1	↓	The universe	523.42	↓	Venus
523.2	↓	The Solar system	523.43	*end*	Mars

2 Arrange these numbers according to the Dewey classification:

	a	**b**	**c**	**d**
	331.01	311.0942	959.927	065.68783
	330	311.07	950	000
	331.02	311.2	900	065.6
	331.016	311.126	959	065.6878
	331.011	311.018	959.92	065
	331	311.116	959.9278	065.687
	331.026	310	959.92781	063
	331.04136	311	959.9	065.68

3 State which of the ten major subjects these numbers are classified under:
   a 523. 71   **b** 636.9   **c** 781.7161   **d** 012.345   **e** 375.632

4 Rearrange these numbers with their correct Dewey classification:
   a 523.78 Four Ways For Forgiveness   **b** 622.07 History Of Art
   c 709 The Study Of Mining   **d** 813.54 Eclipses

Identification codes

Reference numbers are created by people, companies or institutions for different reasons in various ways. These could be the registration of documents, identification of products, credit cards, wages and salary slips, tax codes or bank accounts.

The people who make up the reference numbers use the easiest ways possible to remember. References numbers are only applicable for specific purposes.

Example   A shoe manufacturer's product reference code could be:

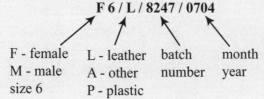

F 6 / L / 8247 / 0704

F - female   L - leather   batch   month
M - male   A - other   number   year
size 6   P - plastic

Exercise 1:23

1 From the above example create a reference code for the following:

  a A pair of leather shoes which was made in May 2008 for a woman who wears size 4. The shoes are included in batch 7073.

  b A pair of leather shoes which was made in January 2006 for a man who wears size 10. The shoes are included in batch 7002.

  c A pair of plastic shoes which was made in August 2006 for a woman who wears size 4. The shoes are included in batch 4915.

2 Find the meaning of these shoe manufacturer's product codes:

  a M 11 / A / 5250 / 1010   **b** F $6\frac{1}{2}$ / P / 3029 / 1108   **c** M 10 / A / 800 / 0105

  d F $5\frac{1}{2}$ / L / 7438 / 0407   **e** M 11 / A / 1055 / 0910   **f** F $7\frac{1}{2}$ / L / 606 / 0808

A reference number for a driver's licence could be written using this code.

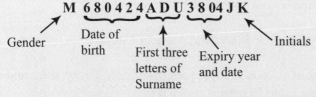

M 6 8 0 4 2 4 A D U 3 8 04 J K

Gender   Date of birth   First three letters of Surname   Expiry year and date   Initials

Example   Mrs Afua Sarpong Bimpey was born on 5th February 1971, her licence expires on her 70th birthday, her licence number will be: F710205BIM4102AS.

3 What is the driver's licence number of each of these people whose licence expires on their seventieth birthday?

  a Ms Ayesha Hajia Banta; (born - 18th July 1958)   **b** Mr Seth Kobi; born - 2nd May 1975

  c Miss Akua Ansom; (born - 1st October 1969)   **d** Mr Nii Ayew; (born - 20th June 1987)

4 Work out the gender, initials, birth/expiry date and the first three letters of each driver's surname from these licence numbers: **a** M690901ARM3909NK   **b** F751115SEK4511MB

                                         c F560530SUL2605ME   **d** M800711KUF5007IF

Work out the following sums using Egyptian hieroglyphics:

1

2

3

4

5 Copy and complete this table of Greek, Roman and decimal numeral interpretation.

Greek	Ϙα			σζε			υοζ		
Roman		CXXXIV			CCCI			DLXIII	
Decimal			58			177				2063

6 Add, in hours and minutes: 1 hour 30 minutes, 3 hours 45 minutes and 2 hours 25 minutes.

7 Add, in months: 5 years 6 months and 4 years and 11 months.

8 Add, in days: 5 weeks 2 days, 1 week 6 days and 3 weeks 5 days.

9 Write down the number of dots in each of these patterns of dots. Group them and write the answers in base two, base 5 and base ten.

a b c d

10 Convert these base ten numbers to base 5:

   a 1000_{10} **b** 2489_{10} **c** 3179_{10} **d** 4000_{10} **e** 5729_{10} **f** 8795_{10}

11 Convert these base ten numbers to base 5 and base 2:

   a 99_{10} **b** 199_{10} **c** 299_{10} **d** 399_{10} **e** 499_{10} **f** 599_{10}

12 Change these binary digits to quinary digits:

    a 1110_2 **b** 1010101_2 **c** 110110110_2 **d** 1111111111_2 **e** 10001000_2

13 Copy and complete this table:

	base ten	base five	base two
a	10		
b			1111110
c		2233	
d	102		
e			101001001
f		43210	

14 Copy and complete the crossnumber puzzle using the clues. The clues are in base five and base 2. Write the answers in base ten.

Across

  1 2331_5

  3 1011111_2

  5 241_5

  7 111010100_2

Down

  1 100110_2

  2 300_5

  3 340_5

  4 11111_2

  5 1001101_2

  6 303_5

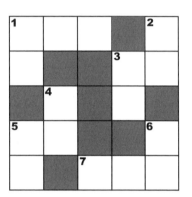

15 Work out the following:

  a $11010_2 + 1101_2$ as a number in base two   **b** $214_5 + 312_5$ as a number in base two.

  c $1011_2 + 2441_5$ as a number in base two.   **d** $432_5 - 110_2$ as a number in base two.

 *e $110110_2 + 10101_2 + 111_2 - 214_5$ as a number in base two.

16 Convert these numbers from binary to quinary:

    a 11111_{two} **b** 101010_{two} **c** 101110_{two} **d** 1010111_{two} **e** 100000_{two}

17 Eggs are packed into cartons of 6. Six cartons of 6 eggs fill a box.

  a How many eggs does each box hold?

  b How many eggs have I got if I have:

  i 4 cartons   **ii** 3 cartons and 5 eggs

  ii 1 box and 3 eggs   **iv** 3 boxes, 1 carton and 2 eggs ?

  c Write the number of boxes and cartons that I need and state the number of eggs leftover if I packed:

  i 27 eggs   **ii** 38 eggs   **iii** 147 eggs   **iv** 100 eggs   **v** 189 eggs

Using fixed scales to add and subtract. This device can be used to work in base five.

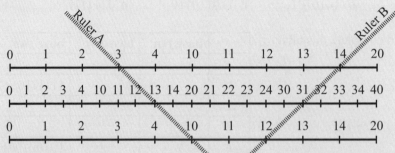

Copy these scales into your book.

To add two numbers, find one number on the top scale and the other on the bottom.

Lay a ruler across and the answer will appear on the middle scale.

Ruler A shows: $3_5 + 10_5 = 13_5$ Ruler B shows: $14_5 + 12_5 = 31_5$

18 Perform these additions with the aid of the adding scales:

     a $2_5 + 14_5$ **b** $14_5 + 4_5$ **c** $13_5 + 3_5$ **d** $13_5 + 11_5$ **e** $14_5 + 14_5$

19 Using the scale, 'work backwards' to do these:

     a $11_5 - 4_5$ **b** $20_5 - 14_5$ **c** $22_5 - 13_5$ **d** $30_5 - 12_5$ **e** $33_5 - 24_5$

20 Explain how you will use the scales to subtract.

21 Study the scale and make other scales which will work in: **a** base two   **b** base ten

When a key is pressed on a computer keyboard a signal is sent to the computer. The signal is in the form of a binary code called ASCII. The table shows various letters and numbers:

Lower case	Binary	ASCII	Upper case	Binary	ASCII	Number	Binary	ASCII
a	1	1100001	**A**	1	1000001	**1**	1	0110001
b	10	1100010	**B**	10	1000010	**2**	10	0110010
c	11	1100011	**C**	11	1000011	**3**	11	0110011
d	100	1100100	**D**	100	1000100	**4**	100	0110100
e	101	1100101	**E**	101	1000101	**5**	101	0110101
f	110	1100110	**F**	110	1000110	**6**	110	0110110
g	111	1100111	**G**	111	1000111	**7**	111	0110111
h	1000	1101000	**H**	1000	1001000	**8**	1000	0111000
i	1001	1101001	**I**	1001	1001001	**9**	1001	0111001

Code for lower case   Binary for letter position   Code for upper case letters   Binary for letter position   Code for numbers   Binary for the numbers

If the first two bits are 11 the character is lower case; if the first 2 bits are 10 the character is an upper case letter; if the first 3 bits are 011 the character is a number.

22 Using the codes in **exercise 1:17** write these words and numbers in ASCII code:

a mathematics	**b** Print	**c** emc@jhs2	**d** 9%
e BASIC	**f** 7289	**g** help	**h** PLEASE
i triangle	**j** Decimal	**k** Chief	**l** S/he
m SCALE	**n** dotcom	**o** 1957	**p** Angle

23 In each question below, the ASCII code for a word or number has been given.
Find that word or number:

a 1101101
1100101
1110100

b 0110110
0111000
0111001

c 0110011
0110100
0110101
0110111

d 1000011
1101111
1100100
1100101

e 1000100
1000101
1000001
1001100

f 1100110
1101111
1110010
1101101

g 1010100
1101001
1101101
1100101

h 1101010
1101111
1101001
1101110

24 Copy and complete these operation tables for the addition of numbers written in base five:

+	0	1	2	3	4
0					
1		2			
2					
3				11	
4		10			

+	11	23	42	131	442
2	13				
4					1001
12					
34					
432		1010			

25 Railway sidings tracks

This drawing shows some railway sidings tracks for loading and unloading in an underground mine. Every 100 m there is a set of points at which the line splits into two lines.

Copy and complete these sentences:

a At 100 m the line splits into [?] lines.

b At 200 m the line splits into [?] lines.

c At 300 m the line splits into [?] lines.

d At 400 m the line splits into [?] lines.

e At 500 m the line splits into [?] lines.

f At 600 m the line splits into [?] lines.

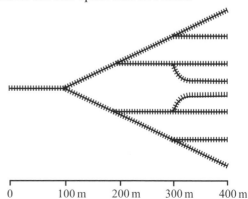

| 0 | 100 m | 200 m | 300 m | 400 m |

SUMMARY

Egyptians used **hieroglyphics** which is a kind of picture writing.

1 / Stroke   10 ∩ Arch   100 ⌒ Coiled rope   1000 ⌇ Lotus flower

10 000 ⌇ Bent finger   100 000 ⌇ Tadpole   1 000 000 ⌇ Kneeling figure

The system was based on 10. It did not include a zero symbol. It did use the principle of place value. Numerals were formed by putting the basic symbols together.

Base ten (Denary)   We have ten fingers. That is why we probably count in tens or base ten. The digit 0, 1, 2, 3, 4, 5, 6, 7, 8, 9 are used.

Base five (Quinary)   If we had one arm with five fingers on the hand things might have been different. We would have to record every group five instead of every group of ten.

Fives Units
   1   3   or more precisely 13_{five} . 13_{five} is written in short form as 13_5.

Base 5 digits are: 0, 1, 2, 3, 4

Base Two (Binary)

Base two number system counts only two digits 0 and 1.

The number: 1 in base two is 1 written as 1_2 pronounced 'one base two'
2 in base two is 10 written as 10_2 pronounced 'one zero base two'
3 in base two is 11 written as 11_2 pronounced 'one one base two'
4 in base two is 100 written as 100_2 pronounced 'one zero zero base two'

Other numeration systems

Arabic numerals are numbers which correspond to numbers 0, 1, 2, 3, 4, 5, 6, 7, 8, 9
Hindu-Arabic number system is even now in common use using the ten digits with 0 as a place holder for numbers such as 20, 100, 0.604
Babylonian number system was used by the ancient Babylonians with mixed base of 10 and base 60 from which the methods of measuring time and angle used today are probably obtained.
Greek number system from ancient Greece used the letters of the alphabet to mean the numbers 1 to 9, 10 to 90 in tens and 100 to 900 in hundreds. There is no zero.

Numbers are used in everyday life. These numbers could be vehicle registration plates, radio frequency bandwidths, library a numbering system, telephone numbers and other reference numbers.

Example of an international telephone number

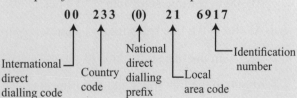

2 Linear equations and inequalities

EXTENSION

SUMMARY

The **equation** is one of the first mathematical achievements of mankind, dating back to the Middle Kingdom of ancient Egypt around 1800 B.C.

Equation: phonetic: I`kweIʒ(ə)n;   Latin: æquatio
        The action of making equal or balancing.
        Two expressions which are equal and are joined
        by the symbol $=$.
To solve an equation is to find the numerical value of the symbols representing unknown quantities.

Inequality: phonetic: inĭkwǫ·lĭti ;   Latin: inæqualitas
The relation between quantities that are unequal in value.

Signs of inequality: $>$ 'is greater than',

                 $<$ 'is less than'

                 $\geq$ 'is greater than or equal to'

                 $\leq$ 'is less than or equal to'

The symbols $>$ and $<$ were introduced by Thomas Harriot. (1560 - 1621) an Oxford university mathematician and astronomer, in his book *Artis analyticae praxis,* a treatise on algebra, that was published posthumously in 1631.

Solving linear inequalities is very similar to solving linear equations except that you flip the inequality sign whenever you multiply or divide the inequality by a negative number.

Rules of Algebra

There are some simple rules in algebra that everyone uses.

The language of algebra is the same in all languages.

To avoid any confusion mathematicians have agreed various shorthand rules.

Learn these rules and use them.

- $4a$ means $4 \times a$.
- ab means $a \times b$
- $\dfrac{a}{b}$ means $a \div b$
- $\frac{1}{2}ab$ means $a \times b \div 2$ or $\dfrac{a \times b}{2}$
- a^2 means $a \times a$
- $2ab$ means $2 \times a \times b$
- $5(a + b)$ means $5 \times a + 5 \times b$
- $-(a + b) = -a - b$
- Always write the number before the letters
- Normally write the letters in alphabetical order e.g. $6yzx$ is normally written as $6xyz$.

The formula for finding the perimeter, (P) of a rectangle is **2** times the length (l) plus **2** times the width (**w**) of the rectangle.

Therefore the formulae is written in short as : $P = 2 \times l + 2 \times w$
$$P = 2l + 2w$$
$$= 2(l + w)$$

In any formula we usually put what we are finding on the left hand side.

Examples   Write these formulas using the rules of algebra:

a $d = 2 \times r$	**b** $C = 2 \times \pi \times r$	**c** $s = 0.5 \times g + 3 \times 3$
$= 2r$	$= 2\pi r$	$= 0.5g + 3^2$

Exercise 2:1

Rewrite these algebraic formulas using the rules of algebra:

1 $D = S \times T$

2 $A = 2 \times t$

3 $E = m \times 6 \times b$

4 $y = m \times x + c$

5 $v = u + a \times t$

6 $c = 5 \times a \times b \times 3 \times c$

7 $k = 7 \times b \times 3 \div 2$

8 $g = G \times m \div 2 \times r$

9 $E = \frac{1}{2} \times m \times v$

10 $c = 3 \times a + 5 \times 5$

*11 $F \times s = m \times v \times 5 \div 2$

*12 $y = a \times 2 \times 2 + bx + c$

*13 $I = m \times v - m \times u$

*14 $v = 4 \times u - 2 \times a \times p$

2   Equations

Kwame went to the bushes to fetch red marbles for Ama and brown marbles for himself. Kwame put all the 127 marbles he found in a small sack. When Ama asked Kwame how many red marbles he fetched for her, all he could remember was she had 19 more than his brown marbles.

They could find out how many marbles each had by:

* guessing until they found two amounts that have a total of 127 and a difference of 19, or
* writing down the information using mathematical symbols.

To do this we can write: (amount Kwame had) + (amount Ama had) is 127 but
(amount Ama had) is (amount Kwame had + 19)
so (amount Kwame had) + (amount Kwame had + 19) is 127

$$A + (K + 19) = 127$$
$$\therefore \quad K + K + 19 = 127$$

This is called an **equation**.

Alternatively
$$A + (A - 19) = 127$$
$$\therefore \quad A + A - 19 = 127$$

Now we can see that Kwame had 54 brown marbles so Ama had 73 red marbles.

Exercise 2:2

Write down how you might solve these problems that arise in the following situations.

1   Kofi and Afua have been given 12 sweets between them. They must share them so that Kofi has two more than Afua.

2   Aba and Ekow have been given 65 marbles between them. They must share them so that Aba has 7 fewer than Ekow.

3   The length of a car and its trailer is 6.83 m. What is the length of the trailer if the car is 3.45 m long?

4   Two sisters paid ¢1.20 each on their bus fares to shop in town. They spent ¢10 in total on their shopping. How much did each person spend if both spent the same amount?

5   During a mathematics game a teacher had 68 cedis. Each pupil needed 9. She found two faulty cedis and had 3 left over. How many pupils played the mathematics game?

6   Mr Boahen's house number and Mr Allotey's house number total 73. If Mr Boahen lives at number 39, at what number does Mr Allotey live?

7   Kobi and Fifi went mango hunting in a fruit farm. They got 157 mangoes altogether. Fifi got 13 more than Kobi and Fifi was unwilling to share the mangoes equally. He wanted each to have his own. How many mangoes did each find?

8   Tetteh and Sakina went to eat in a restaurant. The total cost came to ¢86.70. Tetteh's meal came to ¢7.50 less than Sakina's. How much did each person pay?

9   Two hundred boxes of chocolates weigh 904 kg. If each empty box weighs 80g, what is the weight of: **a** each full box of chocolate   **b** each of the 24 bars in a box?

10   Think of five other situations where you can form an equation rather than guess and then check to see if the chosen solutions work.

3   Forming equations

Equation	Two expressions which are equal and are joined by the symbol '=' (equals) are called an **equation**. An equation is formed when a given expression is equal to a number or another expression.
Linear equation	A **linear equation** is an equation in which the unknown quantity is raised to the power of 1, i.e., linear equations must not have any terms like x^2, x^3 or $\frac{1}{x}$ in them. When you solve an equation you are trying to work out the value of a letter or variable. *Equations can be formed using algebraic expressions. Use the rules.*
Examples:	Show how equations can be formed with these expressions:

a Think of a number, multiply it by 5, add 3, the answer is 18

Let the number be x

Equation is: $x \times 5 + 3 = 18 \quad \Longrightarrow \quad 5x + 3 = 18$

b Think of a number, add 2, then multiply by 4, the answer is 32

Let the number be x

Equation is: $(x + 2) \times 4 = 32 \quad \Longrightarrow \quad 4(x + 2) = 32$

c Think of a number, multiply it by 3, then take away 4, the answer is 6.

Let the number be x

Equation is: $x \times 3 - 4 = 6 \quad \Longrightarrow \quad 3x - 4 = 6$

Exercise 2:3

Form an equation for each of the following. Make your number to be x.

1 Think of a number, take away 10 and the answer is 6.

2 Think of a number, add 3 and the answer is 15.

3 Think of a number, add 3, then multiply by 5 and the answer is 30.

4 Think of a number, take away 2, then multiply by 4 and the answer is 12.

5 Think of a number, multiply it by 4, then take away 10 and the answer is 26.

6 Think of a number, multiply it by 8, then add 5 and the answer is 13.

7 Think of a number, divide it by 8, then add 25 and the answer is 49.

8 Multiply a number by 4, subtract 1, then multiply by 3 and the answer is 33.

9 Think of a number, double it, then take away 5 and the answer is 20.

10 Asem is 15 years old and Prempeh is x years old and their total age is 27.

11 Adu has x sweets, Manu has three times that of Adu and their total number of sweets is 24.

Write sentences to show the meaning of these equations:

12 $2x + 13 = 19$ **13** $8(x + 2) = 16$ **14** $\frac{3}{5}x = 6$ **15** $\frac{x}{4} - 1 = 17$

*16 $3\left(\frac{x}{2} + 5\right) = 15$ ***17** $\frac{4}{7}x - 2 = 8$ ***18** $4\left(\frac{1}{2}x + 5\right) = 28$ ***19** $6\left(\frac{x}{2} - 4\right) = \frac{1}{2}$

4   Solving equations

Linear equations (sometimes referred to as **simple equations**) have only one solution.
Equations can be solved by using reverse operations and the balancing method.

'Add 6', 'subtract 2', 'multiply by 5' and 'divide by 7' are all examples of operations.
Each operation has a reverse or 'undo' operation.

The reverse of : + is −;   − is +;   × is ÷;   ÷ is ×

To undo 'add 6' we 'subtract 6'; to undo 'subtract 2' we 'add 2'; to undo 'multiply by 5' we
'divide by 5', to undo 'divide by 7' we 'multiply by 7'. This can be shown by using a flow
diagram. ***The unknown number can be any letter or symbol.***

Examples

a   If the question is written as an equation $5x - 4 = 6$ the flow diagram looks like this:

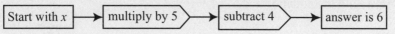

   In order to find the number we reverse the diagram :

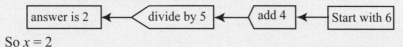

   So $x = 2$

b   To solve $4(x + 3)$ we would get:

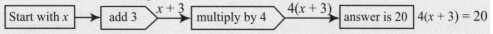

   The reverse flow diagram is:

| answer is 2 | ← | subtract 3 | ←⁵ | divide by 4 | ← | Start with 20 |

   So $x = 2$

Exercise 2:4

> To solve an equation means to find the value of the unknown letter or symbol.

Solve these equations by drawing flow diagrams:

1   Think of a number, x, then take away 10 and the answer is 6.

2   Think of a number, y, multiply it by 5 and the answer is 20.

3   Think of a number, z, take away 2, then multiply by 4 and the answer is 12.

4   Think of a number, d, multiply it by 8, then add 4 and the answer is 28.

5   Multiply a number q by 4, subtract 1, then multiply by 3 and the answer is 33.

6   Eight times double an unknown number gives 112.

7 $x + 6 = 17$	**8** $x - 5 = 1$	**9** $7x = 21$	**10** $x \div 9 = 25$
11 $a + 9 = 12$	**12** $b - 6 = 15$	**13** $5c = 22$	**14** $10d = 25$
15 $5 + e = 8$	**16** $5f - 2 = 33$	**17** $3g + 4 = 1$	**18** $\frac{h}{2} = 6$
19 $\frac{8j}{3} = 12$	**20** $5(k + 2) = 20$	**21** $\frac{3}{7}l + 10 = 25$	**22** $5m + 3 = 6m$
23 $\frac{n}{3} + 5 = 23$	***24** $3\left(\frac{p}{4} + 2\right) = 15$	***25** $\frac{2q}{7} + 1 = 5$	***26** $\frac{3r}{2} + \frac{r}{4} = 11$

Balancing method

In solving equations using the balancing method:

i the same quantity may be added or subtracted from both sides of the equation;

ii each side may be multiplied or divided by the same quantity;

iii the unknown letter or symbol is put on one side of the equation (usually on the left).

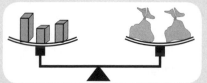

An equation is a balancing act!

'Do the same thing to both sides'

Examples **a** Solve the equation $x + 5 = 12$

Start with the equation $x + 5 = 12$

Take away 5 from each side to get x by itself

$x = 7$ (x must equal 7 because $7 + 5 = 12$)

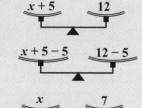

b Solve the equation $x - 8 = 26$

Start with the equation $x - 8 = 26$

Add 8 to each side to get x by itself

$x = 34$ (x must equal 34 because 34 minus 8 is 26)

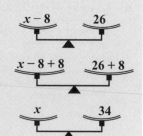

Exercise 2:5

Solve these equations using the balancing method:

1 $x + 2 = 3$

2 $x + 10 = 13$

3 $x + 1 = 8$

4 $x - 7 = 9$

5 $x - 31 = 6$

6 $a - 5 = 4$

7 $q - 3 = 8$

8 $21 + y = 30$

9 $7 = x + 2$

10 $8 = a - 12$

11 $10 = x + 4$

12 $n + 7 = 7$

13 $c - 12 = 27$

14 $l - 6 = 4$

15 $31 = f + 12$

16 $x - \frac{1}{2} = 5$

17 $4 + y = 19$

18 $31 - x = 51$

19 $17 - t = -38$

20 $\frac{2}{3} - n = \frac{1}{3}$

21 Ofori is 14. He is six years older than Barfi. If Barfi is b years old, write down an equation with b in it. Solve the equation to find Barfi's age.

22 The sum of x and y is 72. If y is 34.8 find x.

23 A cup of chocolate cost 19 pesewas more than a cup of milk. If a cup of milk cost x pesewas and a cup of chocolate cost 83 pesewas, form an equation. How much is a cup of milk?

24 A cup of tea cost 48 p less than a cake. Together they cost 142 p. How much is the cake?

Balancing method: multiplication and division

Two sides of an equation can be thought of as the contents of the two pans on a pair of weighing scales which are exactly balanced. The scales will stay balanced *provided that we do the same thing to both sides*.

| The reverse of: $\times$ is $\div$; $\div$ is $\times$ |

Examples **a** Solve $4x = 20$

(This means $4 \times x = 20$)

$4 \times x \div 4 = 20 \div 4$ (Divide both sides by 4.)

$x = 5$

b Solve $\dfrac{x}{2} = 9$

(Multiply both sides by 2.)

$\dfrac{x}{2} \times 2 = 9 \times 2$

$x = 18$

In solving an equation always align the equal sign to make it easier to read the solution.

Exercise 2:6

The aim is to end up with 'letter' = 'number'

Solve the following equations

1 $3x = 6$

2 $6x = 18$

3 $2f = 10$

4 $7t = 42$

5 $4j = 34$

6 $11y = 132$

7 $13x = 52$

8 $23p = 92$

9 $n \div 15 = 5$

10 $y \div 6 = 10$

11 $c \div 2 = 25$

12 $l \div 9 = 12$

13 $\dfrac{x}{3} = 15$

14 $\dfrac{a}{7} = 2.5$

15 $\dfrac{b}{10} = 3\tfrac{1}{2}$

16 $\dfrac{k}{13} = 4$

17 $2.6k = 26$

18 $\dfrac{v}{0.8} = 6.9$

19 $\dfrac{x}{2} = \dfrac{3}{2}$

20 $2.8l = 55.3$

21 $\dfrac{x}{4} = 2\tfrac{1}{4}$

22 $\dfrac{a}{5} = 5\tfrac{5}{8}$

23 $2\tfrac{1}{7}x = 30$

24 $\dfrac{2x}{0.5} = 48$

25 $\dfrac{4x}{20} = 2\tfrac{1}{2}$

26 $4p \div 8 = 7\tfrac{1}{4}$

27 $\dfrac{10p}{4} = 15$

28 $\dfrac{4x}{14} = \dfrac{1}{21}$

29 $1.7y = 51$

30 $q \div 10 = \tfrac{4}{5}$

31 $\dfrac{7s}{3} = \dfrac{42}{9}$

32 $\dfrac{1.5x}{4} = 10\tfrac{1}{2}$

Equation combining operations

Examples   Solve these equations: **a** $3x + 4 = 16$ **b** $\dfrac{51}{y} - 2 = 28$ **c** $\dfrac{7t}{2} + 3 = -5$

a $3x + 4 = 16$

$3x + 4 - 4 = 16 - 4$

$3x = 12$

$3x \div 3 = 12 \div 3$

$x = 4$

b $\dfrac{51}{y} - 2 = 28$

$\dfrac{51}{y} - 2 + 2 = 28 + 2$

$\dfrac{51}{y} = 30$

$\dfrac{51}{y} \times y = 30 \times y$

$51 = 30y$

$51 \div 30 = 30y \div 30$

$1\tfrac{7}{10} = y$

c $\dfrac{7t}{2} + 3 = -5$

$\dfrac{7t}{2} + 3 - 3 = -5 - 3$

$\dfrac{7t}{2} = -8$

$\dfrac{7t}{2} \times 2 \div 7 = -8 \times 2 \div 7$

$t = \dfrac{-16}{7}$

$= -2\tfrac{2}{7}$

Note: ■ Balancing is made possible by using y on both sides.
        ■ Two or more operations can be done together.

Exercise 2:7

Solve these equations:

1 $3x + 1 = 7$ **2** $6x + 4 = 22$ **3** $2f + 6 = 10$ **4** $40 \div t = 7$

5 $11x - 33 = 66$ **6** $\dfrac{2}{x} = 8$ **7** $2x - 1 = 5$ **8** $6x - 12 = 18$

9 $10y - 5 = 5$ **10** $\dfrac{2}{y} - 5 = 7$ **11** $\dfrac{5}{t} + 11 = 13$ **12** $\dfrac{6x}{5} - 13 = 2$

13 $\dfrac{5y}{2} - 8 = 12$ **14** $\dfrac{w}{7} + 18 = 67$ **15** $\dfrac{10t}{17} + 1 = 13$ **16** $\dfrac{3p}{4} + 66 = 14$

17 $11 = \dfrac{80}{x} + 10$ **18** $\dfrac{x}{4} + 25 = 26$ **19** $26 + \dfrac{x}{6} = 32$ **20** $\dfrac{3x}{8} + 6 = 9$

21 $3 - \dfrac{4x}{7} = 9$ **22** $5 = 25 - \dfrac{x}{3}$ **23** $\dfrac{9x}{4} + \dfrac{1}{2} = 5$ **24** $26 - \dfrac{7w}{3} = 12$

25 $4d + 10 = 6$ **26** $3 \div e - 3 = -3$ **27** $\dfrac{16}{2x} = 48$ **28** $30 \div g = 54$

29 $17 + h = 2h$ **30** $33 - 11j = 11$ **31** $12 - 5k = 17$ **32** $22l + 17 = 12$

33 $\dfrac{20}{4x} = 2\tfrac{1}{2}$ **34** $63 - 7n = 50$ **35** $\dfrac{8p}{5} - 10 = -5p$ **36** $\dfrac{51}{y} = 1.7$

37 $\dfrac{7.5r}{15} + 20 = 9$ **38** $\dfrac{s}{11} - 41 = -8$ **39** $16 - \dfrac{3v}{7} = 5$ **40** $\dfrac{12x}{5} + 34 = 28$

41 $36 \div 0.8w = 45$ **42** $7\tfrac{1}{5} - 8\tfrac{1}{2}u = 2\tfrac{1}{5}$ **43** $11.4 + 12v = 0$ **44** $\dfrac{2.8x}{11.2} + 60 = 13$

5 Equations with brackets

To solve an equation with brackets, **remove the brackets first** and solve the resulting equation using the methods already shown.

Example Solve these equations $2(3t - 5) = 8$

$$2(3t - 5) = 8$$
$$2 \times 3t - 2 \times 5 = 8 \qquad \text{Multiply out the brackets} \boxed{2(3t - 5) = 2 \times 3t - 2 \times 5}$$
$$6t - 10 = 8$$
$$6t - 10 + 10 = 8 + 10 \quad \text{Add 10 to each side}$$
$$6t = 18$$
$$\frac{6t}{6} = \frac{18}{6} \qquad \text{Divide each side by 6}$$
$$t = 3$$

Exercise 2:8

Solve these equations:

1 $3(d + 5) = 21$ **2** $5(b + 1) = 25$ **3** $2(f - 3) = 12$ **4** $3(t - 4) = 15$

5 $4(4 + y) = 17$ **6** $4(c - 2) = 14$ **7** $9(4v - 3) = 18$ **8** $6(3d + 3) = 15$

9 $9(3p - 5) = 9$ **10** $2(7j - 3) = 57$ **11** $4(5k - 4) = 54$ **12** $2(3m + 11) = 10$

13 $7(3n + 5) = -7$ **14** $2(3p - 8) = 7$ **15** $5(2q - 1) = -45$ **16** $11(3x - 5) = -11$

Another way of solving equations is to rearrange the terms to get all the variables on one side of the equation.

Example Solve the equation: $2(3x - 15) = 2(x + 3)$

$$2(3x - 15) = 2(x + 3)$$
$$6x - 30 = 2x + 6 \qquad \text{(multiply out the brackets)}$$
$$6x - 30 + 30 = 2x + 6 + 30 \qquad \text{(add 30 to each side)}$$
$$6x = 2x + 36$$
$$6x - 2x = 2x - 2x + 36 \qquad \text{(take away } 2x \text{ from each side)}$$
$$4x = 36$$
$$4x \div 4 = 36 \div 4 \qquad \text{(divide each side by 4)}$$
$$x = 9$$

Exercise 2:9

1 $2(e + 1) = 3(e + 3)$ **2** $3(g - 2) = 2(g + 1)$ **3** $6(5k - 3) = 4(3k + 9)$

4 $3(3d - 10) = 6(1 + d)$ **5** $8(2h - 7) = 2h + 7$ **6** $3(j + 1) = 3(2j - 9)$

7 $4(8m + 3) = 6(7m - 5)$ **8** $7(2p + 3) = 4(5p - 3)$ **9** $4(200 - q) = 50(q - 92)$

10 $7(2r + 3) = 2\left(\dfrac{5r}{2} - 3\right)$ **11** $3(80 - 2s) = 15(s - \frac{1}{5})$ **12** $7 - 3(z + 4) = 4 - 7(3 - z)$

6 Cross-multiplication

When an equation contains a single fraction on both sides it may be solved by the method of **cross-multiplication**. The method of cross-multiplication is multiplying the denominator of each side of the equation by the numerator of the opposite side of the equation.

$$\frac{a}{b} = \frac{c}{d} \implies a \times d = b \times c \implies ad = bc$$

Examples

Solve:

a $\dfrac{x}{8} = \dfrac{3}{4}$

$$4 \times x = 8 \times 3$$
$$4x = 24$$
$$\frac{4x}{4} = \frac{24}{4}$$
$$x = 6$$

b $\dfrac{x}{2} = \dfrac{x+3}{4}$

$$4x = 2(x+3)$$
$$4x = 2x + 6$$
$$4x - 2x = 2x - 2x + 6$$
$$2x = 6$$
$$\frac{2x}{2} = \frac{6}{2}$$
$$x = 3$$

c $\dfrac{x+1}{2} = \dfrac{2+x}{3}$

$$3(x+1) = 2(2+x)$$
$$3x + 3 = 4 + 2x$$
$$3x + 3 - 2x = 4 + 2x - 2x$$
$$x + 3 = 4$$
$$x + 3 - 3 = 4 - 3$$
$$x = 1$$

Exercise 2:10

Solve these equations:

1 $\dfrac{x}{3} = \dfrac{1}{2}$

2 $\dfrac{x}{4} = \dfrac{3}{2}$

3 $\dfrac{x}{2} = \dfrac{5}{2}$

4 $\dfrac{x}{5} = \dfrac{6}{5}$

5 $\dfrac{3}{4x} = 6$

6 $\dfrac{1}{2x} = \dfrac{4}{3}$

7 $\dfrac{5x}{3} = \dfrac{10}{3}$

8 $\dfrac{x+3}{4} = \dfrac{1}{2}$

9 $\dfrac{x-3}{3} = \dfrac{5}{3}$

10 $\dfrac{7-x}{10} = \dfrac{1}{2}$

11 $\dfrac{3x+5}{2} = 19$

12 $\dfrac{x}{4} = \dfrac{x-1}{3}$

13 $\dfrac{x-2}{3} = \dfrac{3x+5}{2}$

14 $\dfrac{x-4}{4} = \dfrac{x+5}{5}$

15 $\dfrac{x+2}{3} = \dfrac{x-1}{2}$

16 $\dfrac{1}{x} = \dfrac{6}{3x+10}$

17 $\dfrac{10}{5x-2} = \dfrac{5}{3}$

18 $\dfrac{7-x}{x-4} = \dfrac{3}{2}$

19 $\dfrac{12+x}{x} = \dfrac{9}{5}$

20 $\dfrac{x+5}{4} = \dfrac{x-8}{2}$

21 $\dfrac{8x}{x} - 2 = \dfrac{x-6}{4}$

22 $\dfrac{5(x-2)}{100} = \dfrac{20-x}{4}$

23 $\dfrac{3}{2} = \dfrac{15-x}{3(10-2x)}$

24 $\dfrac{x}{2} + \dfrac{1}{3} = \dfrac{x}{3}$

25 $\dfrac{x}{3} + \dfrac{2x}{5} = 4$

26 $\dfrac{2x-2}{7} + \dfrac{2-2x}{14} = 0$

27 $\dfrac{2x}{3} + 1 = \dfrac{7}{5}$

28 $\dfrac{6x-4}{9} - \dfrac{1}{3} = 5$

29 $\dfrac{2}{3x} - \dfrac{1}{2} = \dfrac{1}{6}$

30 $\dfrac{x+1}{2} - \dfrac{3}{4} = 2$

31 $16 - x = \dfrac{3x}{11}$

32 $\dfrac{4}{x-1} + \dfrac{4}{x-1} = 1$

Mixed questions on equations

Exercise 2:11

Solve these equations:

1 $1.5 - x = 0.7 - 3x$ **2** $7 - 5x = 4x - 11$ **3** $3 - 2(x - 2) = 10$

4 $1 - (6 - 4x) = 0$ **5** $-4 - 0.25x = 3$ **6** $6x = 4 - 3(x - 5)$

7 $\dfrac{10}{x} + 5 = 3.9$ **8** $4(x - 5) = 14 - 5(2 - x)$ **9** $0.25(0.4x + 6) = 8$

10 $23 - (3x - 16) = 4.5 - x$ **11** $7.2(x + 5) = -1.2x$ **12** $6.6 - 6.6(x + 0.6) = 6.6$

The perimeter of a shape is the distance around the outside.
If the perimeter, p, of this triangle is 57 cm, write an equation
for the perimeter of this shape and find x.

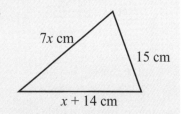

$$7x + 15 + x + 14 = p$$
$$7x + 15 + x + 14 = 57$$
$$8x + 29 = 57$$
$$8x = 28$$
$$\text{so} \quad x = 3.5$$

For each of these shapes form an equation for the perimeter and find each side.

13

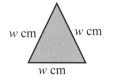

Perimeter = 38.9 cm

14

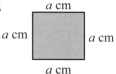

Perimeter = 25 cm

15

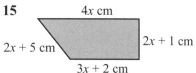

Perimeter = 74 cm

Solve each of these by forming an equation.

16 A number is divided by 4 and 5 is subtracted from the result giving 6.
What is the number?

17 The sum of three consecutive whole numbers is 117; find the three numbers.

18 Find the fraction which when added to $\frac{1}{7}$ gives $\frac{4}{5}$.

19 The sides of a triangle are x cm, $(x - 5)$ cm and $(x + 3)$ cm. If the perimeter is 25 cm, find the lengths of the three sides.

20 The perimeter of a rectangular sheet is 12 m and the length is $\frac{3}{4}$ more than the width. Find the length and width of the sheet by forming the equation and solving it.

21 Find the area of the rectangle
if the perimeter is 48 cm.

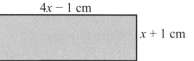

22 Express: **a** x metres in centimetres **b** n centimetres in metres

  c t kilometres in metres **d** y metres in kilometres

23 Simplify these: **a** $\dfrac{7y}{56}$ **b** $\dfrac{15pg}{60gx}$ **c** $\dfrac{49ab}{91a}$ **d** $\dfrac{30.6xyz}{49.3wz}$

24 Copy and complete these equivalent fractions:

a $\dfrac{1}{p} = \dfrac{}{pt}$ **b** $\dfrac{1}{y} = \dfrac{}{8y}$ **c** $\dfrac{1}{f} = \dfrac{}{9f}$ **d** $\dfrac{3}{d} = \dfrac{}{6d}$

e $\dfrac{11}{b} = \dfrac{}{12b}$ **f** $\dfrac{3b}{4c} = \dfrac{6ab}{}$ **g** $\dfrac{7}{uv} = \dfrac{}{12uv}$ **h** $\dfrac{2u}{9} = \dfrac{}{117t}$

i $\dfrac{5.3r}{} = \dfrac{21.2qr}{25pq}$ **j** $\dfrac{}{0.03y} = \dfrac{19.8xy}{0.33y}$ **k** $\dfrac{}{4.72m} = \dfrac{2.6ep}{6.136mp}$ **l** $\dfrac{0.7j}{1.8v} = \dfrac{}{27v}$

25 Solve these: **a** $\dfrac{x+1}{7} = \dfrac{x-2}{3} + \dfrac{1}{21}$ **b** $\dfrac{2h+5}{4} + \dfrac{h}{3} + \dfrac{4h-1}{12} = 0$

26 In a game, m marbles were shared equally among 4 players. Write down an expression for the number of marbles each player received. In another game the same m marbles were shared equally among 5 players. How many did each receive? If in this second game each received 2 less than each player in the first game, form an equation for m and solve it.

27 A boat travelled 23 kilometres in 2 hours. For the first x kilometres the speed was 10 kilometres per hour and the rest of the journey the speed was 15 kilometres per hour. Form an equation for x and solve it.

$$Speed = \dfrac{Distance}{Time}$$

28 A boy ran for y metres at a speed of 6 metres per second and then walked for y metres at a speed of 2 metres per second. Write down in terms of y:
a the time for which he ran. **b** the time for which he walked
c If the total time was 20 seconds, write down an equation for y and solve it.

29 Two cars started at the same speed on a journey of k kilometres. One travelled at 80 kilometres per hour and the other at 60 kilometres per hour.
a State, in terms of k, the time taken by each car.
b If one car arrived $\frac{1}{2}$ hour before the other, write down an equation for k and solve it.

30 On a journey to watch a football match, a motorist had an average speed of 45 kilometres per hour. On the return journey he used a highway and his average speed was 90 kilometres per hour. The return journey was 10 kilometres longer than the outward journey but it was 20 minutes quicker. Let the outward distance be x kilometres. Write down expression for:
a the return distance,
b the time in hours for the outward journey,
c the time in hours for the return journey.
d Writing $\frac{1}{3}$ hour for the difference in time, write down an equation for x and solve it.

Puzzling Algebra

The letters or symbols in each row or column add up to the numbers shown. Form an equation where you can solve it to find the values of all the characters and find the total represented by the question mark.

1

p	m	n	k	?
p	p	p	p	16
n	m	n	k	12
m	m	p	k	?
?	13	?	19	

2

t	a	u	a	16
t	q	t	q	28
t	a	u	u	?
t	a	q	t	?
24	?	22	?	

3

b	j	g	b	?
c	c	g	b	?
j	b	j	b	28
g	c	g	b	16
?	22	?	24	

4

y	f	y	v	?
y	f	y	f	16
v	d	y	d	22
v	y	y	d	?
28	?	20	?	

5

m	e	m	h	47
e	e	e	e	56
k	z	e	k	54
h	z	e	h	?
?	40	?	49	

6

f	f	f	f	44
s	s	u	f	?
x	x	f	u	34
p	u	u	x	28
?	36	36	?	

7

Σ	π	∞	ε	39
Σ	Σ	Σ	Σ	36
ε	π	#	#	46
∞	π	Σ	∞	40
?	54	?	?	

8

£	¢	$	£	?
¥	¢	£	¢	61
₦	¢	₦	£	44
$	¢	¢	$	72
?	84	?	54	

9

♣	◇	♡	♣	?
♣	◇	♤	◎	?
♣	♡	♣	♡	84
♣	♡	♤	◎	71
68	76	80	?	

10

⊕	◈	⊕	⊞	?
⊠	⊞	⊕	⊠	55
◈	✚	⊕	✚	59
⊞	⊞	⊞	⊞	96
63	?	45	?	

11

♀	¶	♂	∅	29
♀	♀	♂	♀	33
∅	♂	♂	∅	?
∅	¶	♂	♀	?
?	31	48	?	

12

δ	μ	σ	θ	η	63
σ	σ	σ	σ	σ	75
λ	ψ	β	β	λ	57
δ	μ	β	ψ	η	?
ψ	β	σ	ψ	σ	68
40	68	85	?	80	

7   Inequalities

Inequality   In **inequality** one side of the equation is not equal to the other side. It can be smaller than or bigger than the other side.

Suppose that fewer than 60 pupils enrol for a course in a university. The number of students enrolling is unknown but if we represent it by x, then using the symbol < to mean 'less than', we can write
$$x < 60$$

This is an inequality. It is true when x represents any number less than 60. This range of numbers is illustrated on this number line.

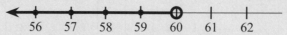

An open circle at the end of the range indicates that the point is not included. A closed circle at the end of inequality line indicates that the point is included in the range

These symbols are used when dealing with inequalities:

>	<	≥	≤
greater than	less than	greater than or equal to	less than or equal to

The 'arrow' always points to the smaller quantity

Examples: **a** The number line shows $x < 4$

$x < 4$

   b The number line shows $x > -2$

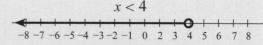

$x > -2$

   c The number line shows $x \leq -1$

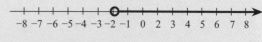

$x \leq -1$

Exercise 2:12

Draw a number line between −8 and +8 to show each of these inequalities:

1 $x > 3$	**2** $x > 4$	**3** $x < 5$	**4** $x < 0$
5 $x \leq -3$	**6** $x > -5$	**7** $x < 2.5$	**8** $x \leq 4$
9 $x \leq 3.5$	**10** $x > -4.5$	**11** $x \leq 1$	**12** $x \geq 2$
13 $x \geq -8$	**14** $x > -1$	**15** $x \leq 7$	**16** $x < 8$
17 $x \geq 0$	**18** $x \leq 2$	**19** $x \geq 5$	**20** $x \leq -7$

Combined inequalities

If $x < 5$ and $x > 2$, the inequalities can be combined to give $2 < x < 5$.
$2 < x < 5$ is pronounced as "x is greater than 2 or less than 5". This means that the value of x lies between 2 and 5. The region is shown on this number line.

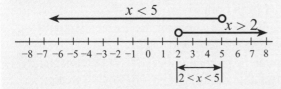

The region is the set $S = \{x : 2 < x < 5\}$

Example   Show the inequality $-4 < x \le 3$ on a number line.

$-4 < x \le 3$ is pronounced as x is greater than -4 and less than or equal to 3.

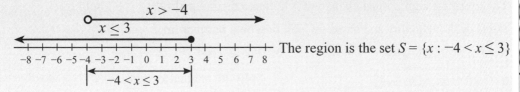

The region is the set $S = \{x : -4 < x \le 3\}$

Exercise 2:13

Use a number line to show each of these inequalities:

1 $0 < x < 4$	**2** $-3 < x < 1$	**3** $-1 < x \le 5$	**4** $-2 < x \le 2$
5 $-5 \le x < 0$	**6** $2 \le x < 6$	**7** $-5 < x \le 5$	**8** $-7 \le x \le 6$
9 $-5 \le x \le 1$	**10** $-8 \le x \le -2$	**11** $-8 < x < 8$	**12** $-6 < x \le -1$
13 $-4 \le x < 3.5$	**14** $-6.5 < x \le 7$	**15** $-4 \le x \le 0.5$	**16** $-1.5 \le x < 7.5$
17 $-8 \le x < -2$	**18** $-1 \le x \le 1$	**19** $-6\frac{1}{2} \le x < 6$	**20** $-3.5 < x < 4$

Write down the inequalities to describe each of these number lines:

21
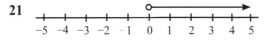

22
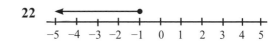

23
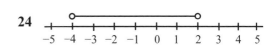

24
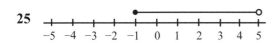

25
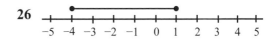

26
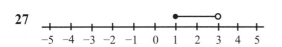

27
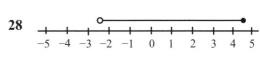

28

49

8 Solving inequalities

Rules for solving inequalities

Most inequalities are written in algebra. Inequalities are solved in a very similar way to equations. This means that:

* the same number can be added or subtracted from both sides
* multiplying or dividing both sides by the same positive number leaves the inequality unchanged
* multiplying or dividing both sides by the same negative number reverses the inequality sign. For instance $28 > 14$. Clearly this is true, but dividing both sides by -7 make:

$$\frac{28}{-7} > \frac{14}{-7} \quad \text{gives} \quad -4 > -2 \quad \text{(This is not true.)}$$

Therefore the sign $>$ must change to $<$ to make the inequality $-4 < -2$ hold true.

Solve each inequality and show the solution on a number line:

a $3 - 5x \geq 2x + 24$

b $3x - 8 < x + 2 \leq 2x + 1$

a
$$3 - 5x \geq 2x + 24$$
$$3 - 3 - 5x \geq 2x + 24 - 3$$
$$-5x \geq 2x + 21$$
$$-5x - 2x \geq 2x + 21 - 2x$$
$$-7x \geq 21$$
$$\frac{-7x}{-7} \leq \frac{21}{-7}$$
$$x \leq -3$$

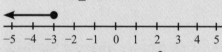

The values of x less than -3 satisfy the inequality $x \leq -3$

Split the inequality into two parts and solve each separately:

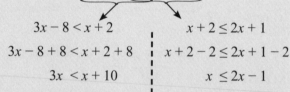

$$3x - 8 < x + 2 \quad | \quad x + 2 \leq 2x + 1$$
$$3x - 8 + 8 < x + 2 + 8 \quad | \quad x + 2 - 2 \leq 2x + 1 - 2$$
$$3x < x + 10 \quad | \quad x \leq 2x - 1$$
$$3x - x < x - x + 10 \quad | \quad x - 2x \leq 2x - 2x - 1$$
$$2x < 10 \quad | \quad -x \leq -1$$
$$x < 5 \quad | \quad x \geq 1$$

$$1 \leq x < 5$$

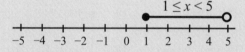

The values of x are numbers greater or equal to 1 but less than 5 satisfy the inequality: $1 \leq x < 5$

Exercise 2:14

Solve each inequality below and show the solution on a number line:

1 $x + 5 < 9$

2 $1 + 3x < 4$

3 $2 + 3x \leq 11$

4 $7 > 3 + 2x$

5 $8 - 5x > 5$

6 $5x - 6 \leq 9$

7 $\dfrac{x}{5} - 10 > 20$

8 $\dfrac{3x}{2} + 7 \leq -8$

9 $2x - 7 \leq 5x + 8$

10 $6x + 1 > 18 - x$

11 $3x + 25 < 8x - 15$

12 $3 < 2x - 1 \leq 5$

13 $6 < x + 5 < 9$

14 $x + 4 < 2x + 1 < 5$

15 $x + 1 < 2x + 6 < 10$

16 $x - 1 < 2x < 10$

17 $x - 1 < 2x - 3 < 7$

18 $55 \le 3x + 1 < 64$

19 $x + 6 \le 3x \le 26$

20 $5 - 3x < 6 + x \le 18 - 3x$

21 $-2 \le \dfrac{3x - 7}{3} \le 6$

22 $x \le \dfrac{2(3 + 4x)}{5} \le x + 7$

23 $2(x - 1) \le 3(x + 5) \le 12$

24 $5(6 - x) \le 3 - \dfrac{x}{2} \le -4x$

Placement of a number within a range

A piece of string is 43 cm to the nearest centimetre.
The smallest number that can be rounded up to 43 is 42.5, and the largest number that can be rounded down to 43 is *just less than* 43.5. Therefore the string can have any length from 42.5 cm up to but not including 43.5 cm. The range of numbers is shown on the number line.

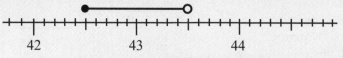

42.5 is called the **lower bound** of the range and
43.5 is called the **upper bound** of the range.

If the length of the string is denoted by l cm then we can say that $42.5 \le l < 43.5$

Exercise 2:15

1 Each of the following numbers is given to the nearest whole number. Show the range in which the number lies on a number line.

   a 6   **b** 9   **c** 35   **d** 50   **e** 69   **f** 100

2 Each of these numbers is given to 1 decimal place. Show the range in which the number lies on a number line.

   a 4.6   **b** 11.2   **c** 18.0   **d** 27.4   **e** 5.5   **f** 44.4

3 Each of these numbers is given to 2 decimal places. Show the range in which the number lies on a number line.

   a 1.23   **b** 7.00   **c** 10.46   **d** 19.91   **e** 50   **f** 26.66

4 Using your own letter draw an inequality to represent the information about the unknown quantity. State if your letter can only have whole number values.
   a The temperature (t) will remain above 24 °C.
   b No more than 36 passengers (p) on a bus.
   c The minimum weight (w) of popcorn that can be bought from a wholesaler is 12 kg.
   d Double a number (n), subtract five and the result is less than one hundred.

5 If n is an integer list all possible values of n:
   a $3 < 5n - 7 < 25$ **b** $-1 \le 4n + 15 < 23$ **c** $4 < 2n + 7 < 13$
   d $-5 \le 3n - 14 \le 0$ **e** $2 \le 3n + 8 < 40$ **f** $3 < 11 - n < 11$

9   Tolerances

It is impossible to manufacture a product to an exact size. To enable engineers to achieve success with their manufactured product they must show how much the item or component can vary (bigger or smaller) from a perfectly exact size. This is called **design tolerance**. For example $9.5 \leq A \leq 10.5$ is A: 10 ± 0.5 mm.

Tolerance   **Tolerance** is the range between the allowable maximum and minimum limits of size of distance between features on a component. These features could be hole centres, weights, roundness $\bigcirc$, parallelism $//$, flatness $\diagup\!\!\!\diagup$, perpendicularity $\perp$ and diameter $\emptyset$.

Tolerances are usually expressed as plus-or-minus values ($\pm$).

Nominal value The value stated or expressed on a component is the **nominal value**.

This metal plate has a thickness
(**T**) of: maximum: 5.001 mm
          minimum: 4.999 mm

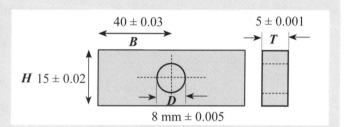

Exercise 2:16

1   Write down the maximum and minimum sizes of **B**, **H** and **D** in the section shown above.

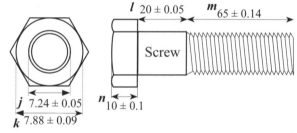

2   Sketch and write down the maximum and minimum geometric dimensions labelled **a - n** with the given tolerances of the screw and the metal vice.
All measurements are in millimetres.

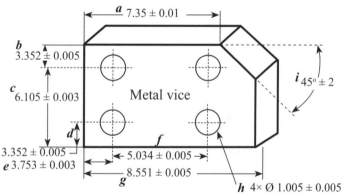

3   Write down the maximum and minimum geometric dimensions of the following:
   a 42.04 ± 0.005 mm   **b** 17.9 ± 0.05 mm   **c** 36.5 ± 0.0015 mm
   d 3.05 ± 0.005 mm   **e** 79.9 ± 0.0125 mm   **f** 93.95 ± 0.0005 mm

4   Write down the nominal value and the tolerance of each of these dimensions:
   a   6.027 - 6.033 mm   **b**   14.988 - 15.00 mm   **c**   24.585 - 24.815 mm
   d   17.075 - 17.325 mm   **e**   48.95 - 49.04 mm   **f**   82.245 - 82.755 mm

EXTENSION

1 For each of these questions construct an equation and solve it:

   a Start with x, multiply by 6 and divide by 7. The result is 9.

   b Start with y, divide by $1\frac{1}{2}$ and add 5. The result is 17.

   c Start with n, subtract 23 and divide by 4. The result is -2.

2 Solve these equations:

   a $3(4x - 5) = 7(x + 3)$ **b** $9x - 2 = 2(3x + 5)$ **c** $5 - 2x = 6(1 - \frac{1}{2}x)$

   d $\frac{1}{2}(4 - 8x) = 5 - 3x$ **e** $2(x + 3) = \frac{1}{2}(x - 5)$ **f** $\frac{1}{5}(x - 2) = \frac{4}{5}(x + 8)$

3 Solve these equations:

   a $\dfrac{x - 3}{6} = 5$ **b** $\dfrac{x}{5} + \dfrac{x}{6} = 2$ **c** $\dfrac{x}{4} + \dfrac{2x}{5} = \dfrac{13}{2}$

   d $\dfrac{3 - x}{5} + 4 = \dfrac{2x + 1}{10}$ **e** $\dfrac{5x}{4} = \dfrac{6x - 5}{3}$ **f** $\dfrac{2x + 1}{7} = \dfrac{x - 3}{2}$

   g $\dfrac{x + 1}{4} - \dfrac{x - 1}{3} = 4$ **h** $4(x - 8) = \dfrac{x - 8}{5}$ **i** $\dfrac{1}{10x + 15} = \dfrac{2}{3x - 4}$

4 The sum of three consecutive odd numbers is 147; find the numbers.

5 A rectangular lawn has a perimeter of 128 m. What is the width if the length is twice the width?

6 An increase of eight percent in Alloteys's weekly wage will give him an extra ¢1.30 a week. What is Allotey's wage?

7 The diagram shows the capacity in millilitres of a cup, a mug and a jug. The jug fills three cups and a mug.

   a Make an equation for the amount of liquid the jug holds.

   b How much does the cup hold?

   c How much does the mug hold?

   d How much does the jug hold

           Cup   Mug   Jug

           c $3c - 180$ $5c$

8 Solve each of these inequalities. Show your answer on a number line.

   a $\dfrac{5x + 2}{4} \le \dfrac{3x - 5}{3}$ **b** $8(x - 1) + 3(x + 3) < 16$ **c** $\dfrac{x}{2} \ge 7 - \dfrac{2x}{3}$

   d $\dfrac{2x}{3} - 6 \le \dfrac{x}{3} - 8$ **e** $\dfrac{2x - 2}{4} - \dfrac{2x - 2}{3} \le 1$ **f** $\dfrac{8x + 5}{9} - \dfrac{6x + 6}{5} \ge \dfrac{x}{3}$

9 The total mass of three stones A, B and C is 76 kg. Stone B is twice as heavy as stone A. Stone C is 40 kg heavier than stone A. Find the masses of stones A and B.

A   B   C

10 In an **arithmagon**, the number in a square is the sum of the numbers in the two circles either side of it.
  a Explain why the number in circle B is $15 - n$.
  b Explain why the number in circle C is $20 - n$.
  c Form an equation across the lowest side of the triangle.
  d Solve the equation for n.

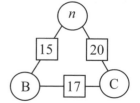

11 Use the method above to find n in these arithmagons.

  a 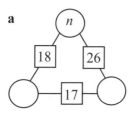   **b** 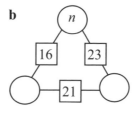   **c**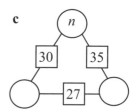

12 Solve these equations using 'look and see'.
Copy the diagram.
Shade the answer on the diagram.
What pattern have you got?

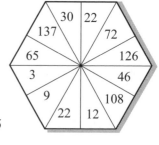

  a $t - 8 = 64$ **b** $11u = 132$ **c** $\dfrac{v}{5} = 13$

  d $w - 19 = 27$ **e** $8x - 47 = 25$ **f** $\dfrac{2y}{4} + 10 = 25$

13 Copy this cross number. Fill it in by solving the equations.

Across
  1 $4x = 48$
  3 $2n = 28$
  5 $3x + 7 = 22$
  6 $\dfrac{x}{99} = 6$
  8 $5y + 2 = 212$
  10 $12n - 24 = 72$
  11 $2b - 20 = 28$
  13 $2q - 49 = -7$
  15 $\dfrac{2x}{9} = 12$
  17 $2(p - 50) = 62$
  19 $2(3y - 17) = 20$
  20 $4(7 + \frac{1}{5}x) = 80$

Down
  1 $\frac{1}{7}a \times 7 = 2 \times \frac{1}{2}$
  2 $x + 11 = 36$
  3 $2y - 31 = -1$
  4 $9(2x + 2) = 900$
  7 $\dfrac{x}{8} - 1 = 5$
  9 $29\frac{1}{2} + p = 36\frac{1}{2}$
  12 $\dfrac{y}{5} = 9$
  13 $3(p + 7) = 27$
  14 $3(x - 8) = 30$
  16 $n - 23 = \frac{1}{2}n$
  18 $2(2p - 20) = 24$

14

Each bus takes p passengers

There are three full buses and one with 5 empty seats.

a   Write the total number of passengers as an expression in p.

b   If $p = 32$, what is the *total* number of passengers?

c   If $p = 40$, what is the *total* number of passengers?

d   The *total* number of passengers is 143. Write this as an equation involving p and solve it.

15   Yusuf, the plumber, charges ¢7.50 on every call out plus ¢2 per hour.

a   Write an expression for the *c*ost of work done in n hours.

b   Mrs Serwaah paid ¢25 for the plumber to visit.
Write an equation in n. Solve the equation to find the number of hours Mrs Serwaah paid for.

16   A tortoise is x years old. Her father is four times as old as she is. Her mother is 7 years younger than her father. Their ages add up to 101 years. Find the age of each tortoise.

Game

A line of four solutions

This game can be played by 2 - 3 players. You need a dice, counters and A3 paper. Copy this table onto A3 paper (about 290 × 420 mm). Each player rolls the dice and puts a counter on an equation that has that solution. The winner is the first player with four counters in a straight line.

$3p + 1 = 16$	$3(5 + d) = 18$	$3g = 12$	$\dfrac{w + 8}{5} = 2$	$3x + 15 = 21$	$t - 1 = 2$
$4k - 2 = 10$	$\frac{1}{2}(f - 1) = 2$	$5p - 15 = 5$	$8 - y = 7$	$\frac{1}{3}h - 1 = \frac{1}{3}$	$p + 5 = 11$
$101 - n = 98$	$\frac{1}{2}p + 1 = 3\frac{1}{2}$	$4w - 2 = 10$	$\frac{1}{2}(x + 6) = 4$	$7(3 - d) = 14$	$4k - 10 = 2$
$x(x - 1) = 2$	$2(d - 1) = 8$	$\dfrac{m}{2} + 3 = 5$	$7 - l = 6$	$\dfrac{a}{3} + 3 = 5$	$5(2e - 1) = 25$
$\dfrac{12}{u} + 1 = 3$	$x(x + 1) = 2$	$5(w + 3) = 25$	$\frac{1}{2}d + 3 = 5$	$2(h + 6) = 18$	$3k + 60 = 72$
$2y + 1 = 7$	$\dfrac{108}{4u} = 9$	$4(g - 2) = 16$	$5m + 3 = 8$	$5f - 3 = 22$	$\dfrac{15}{a + 1} = 3$

Equation	Two expressions which are equal and are joined by the symbol '=' (equals) is an **equation**. An equation is formed when a given expression is equal to a number or another expression.
Linear equation	A **linear equation** is an equation which the unknown quantity is raised to the power of 1. Linear equations must not have any terms like x^2, x^3, $\frac{1}{x}$ or in them. When you solve an equation you are trying to work out the value of a letter.

Linear equations (sometimes referred to as **simple equations**) have only one solution. Equations can be solved by using reverse operations and a balancing method.

'Add 6', 'subtract 2', 'multiply by 5' and 'divide by 7' are all examples of operations. Each operation has a reverse or 'undo' operation.

The reverse of : $+$ **is** $-$; $-$ **is** $+$; $\times$ **is** $\div$; $\div$ **is** $\times$

To undo 'add 6' we 'subtract 6'; to undo 'subtract 2' we 'add 2'; to undo 'multiply by 5' we 'divide by 5', to undo 'divide by 7' we 'multiply by 7'.

In solving equations using a balance method:

i The same quantity may be added or subtracted from both sides;

ii Each side may be multiplied or divided by the same quantity;

iii The unknown letter or symbol is put on one side of the equation.

> Solve $\dfrac{x}{2} = 9$
>
> (Multiply both sides by 2.)
>
> $\dfrac{x}{2} \times 2 = 9 \times 2$
>
> $x = 18$

To solve an equation with brackets, **remove the brackets first** and solve the resulting equation.

Inequality	In inequality one side of the equation is not equal to the other side. It can be smaller than or bigger than the other side.

Suppose that fewer than 60 pupils enrol for a course in a university. The number of students enrolling is unknown but if we represent it by x, then using the symbol $<$ to mean 'less than', we can write

$x < 60$

This is an inequality. It is true when x represents any number less than 60. This range of numbers is illustrated on this number line.

Combined inequalities

If $x < 5$ and $x > 2$, the inequalities can be combined to give $2 < x < 5$.

$2 < x < 5$ is pronounced as x is greater than 2 or less than 5. This means that the value of x lies between 2 and 5. The region is shown on the number line.

Tolerance	**Tolerance** is the range between the allowable maximum and minimum limits of size of distance between features on a component. These features could be hole centres, weights, roundness ◯, parallelism //, flatness ▱, perpendicularity ⊥ and diameter ∅. Tolerances are usually expressed as plus-or-minus values (±).

Nominal value The value stated or expressed on a component is the **nominal value**.

Angles

EXTENSION

SUMMARY

When two lines meet at a point they form an **angle**. The size of an angle is usually measured in degrees ($^\circ$). A simple device called a protractor is used to measure or draw angles.

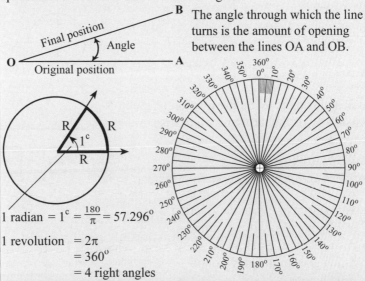

The angle through which the line turns is the amount of opening between the lines OA and OB.

$1 \text{ radian} = 1^c = \dfrac{180}{\pi} = 57.296^\circ$

$1 \text{ revolution} = 2\pi$
$= 360^\circ$
$= 4 \text{ right angles}$

One minute, denoted by $1'$, is defined as $= \frac{1}{60}$ degree. **One second**, denoted by $1''$ is defined as $= \frac{1}{60}$ minute or $\frac{1}{3600}$ degree. An angle of say, 40 degrees, 30 minutes, 10 seconds is written in short as $40^\circ 30' 10''$.

Types of angle:

An acute angle is less than 90°; a right angle is equal to 90°; an obtuse angle is between 90° and 180°; a reflex angle is between 180° and 360°.

1 Turning

Angle measurement is not just a classroom subject: around the world at this moment builders, engineers, surveyors, astronomers, pilots and sea captains employ angle measurement skills to do their job.

This instrument is called a **Sextant.** It is used to measure the angular distance between any two points, such as the sun and the horizon. Navigators use it to determine the position of their ships or aircraft.

Angle An angle is a measure of change of direction or turning about a point.
An object can turn around clockwise.
This is the same direction as the hands of a clock.

Symbol: ↻

An object can turn anticlockwise. This is the opposite direction to clockwise.
Anti-clockwise is also known as counter-clockwise.

Symbol: ↺

$\frac{1}{4}$ turn clockwise $\frac{1}{2}$ turn clockwise $\frac{3}{4}$ turn clockwise   full turn clockwise

Exercise 3:1

1 Write down the fraction of turn of each diagram.
State whether the turning is clockwise or anti-clockwise.

a   b   c   d

2 Look at this map. Write the fraction of each turn and say if the turning is clockwise or anti-clockwise:

a When Bimpeh goes to school;

b When Bimpeh goes home from school.

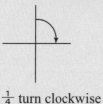

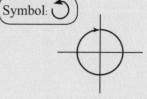

Bimpeh's house

School

3 Look at this map. Write the fraction of each turn and say if the turning is clockwise or anti-clockwise:

a Adjoa goes to the playground from home;

b Adjoa goes to the library from school;

c Adjoa goes from school to the library via the playground.

d Repeat **3 a, b, c** using symbols.

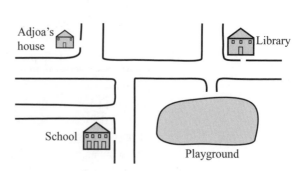

Adjoa's house

Library

School

Playground

Division of Cardinal points

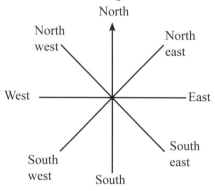

Clock face

One full turn is one revolution. Use the two diagrams to answer these.

4 If you stand facing east and turn clockwise through $\frac{3}{4}$ of a revolution, in which direction are you facing?

5 If you stand facing south and turn anticlockwise $1\frac{1}{2}$ revolution, in which direction are you facing?

6 If you stand facing south-west, in which direction will you be facing after making these turns: **a** a quarter turn anti-clockwise **b** a half turn clockwise

  c a three-quarter turn anti-clockwise **d** a three-quarter turn clockwise?

7 If you stand facing north and move clockwise to face north-west what part of a revolution have you turned through?

8 What fraction of a revolution does the minute hand of a round clock turn through when it:
   a starts at 12 and stops at 3   **b** starts at 6 and stops at 12

   c starts at 9 and stops at 6   **d** starts at 2 and stops at 8

   e starts at 4 and stops at 3   **f** starts at 12 and stops at 1

   g starts at 10 and stops at 8   **h** starts at 7 and stops at 2?

9 Describe these journeys in terms of clockwise and anticlockwise.

   a Osei travels from Prempeh college to Suntreso via the service station.

   b Musah travels from the Officers Mess via the Residency hotel and the SecTec school to Patase.

   c Kwaku travels from Bantama to the Police station via Santasi roundabout.

   d Abenah travels from the hospital (**H**) to the Golf course via Pine road.

   e Give three different instructions to travel from the zoo; Golden Tulip hotel; Residency hotel or Parks and gardens to any other place.

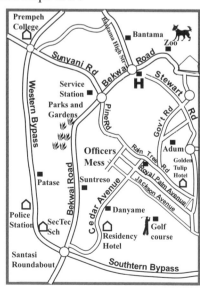

2   Measuring and naming angles

The size of an angle is usually measured in degrees (°). Made of transparent material, a **protractor** is used to measure and draw angles accurately.

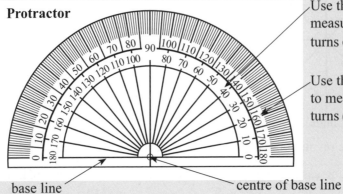

Protractor

Use the inside scale to measure anti-clockwise turns ↺.

Use the outside scale to measure clockwise turns ↻.

base line

centre of base line

To use a protractor:
* place the centre of the protractor exactly on the corner (vertex) of the angle.
* lay the base-line of the protractor exactly along the side of the angle.

Examples

a

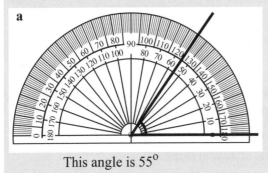

This angle is 55°

b

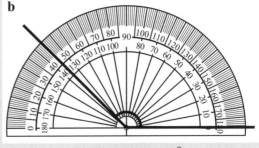

This angle is 136°

Exercise 3:2

Measure these angles

1

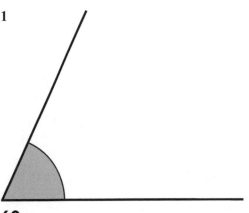

2

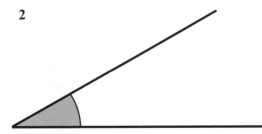

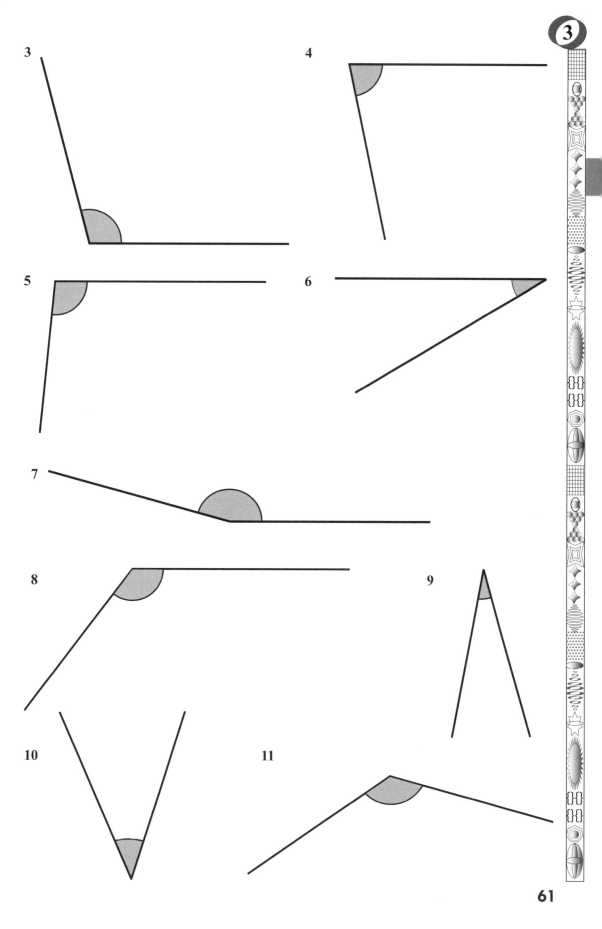

Letters can be used to name angles. Angle ABC or ∠ABC or AB̂C.
The angle is always on the middle letter.
In naming angles: ∠ABC = ∠CBA, the visual direction of ∠ABC starts from point A then
B and C; the visual direction of ∠CBA starts from point C then B and A.

Examples

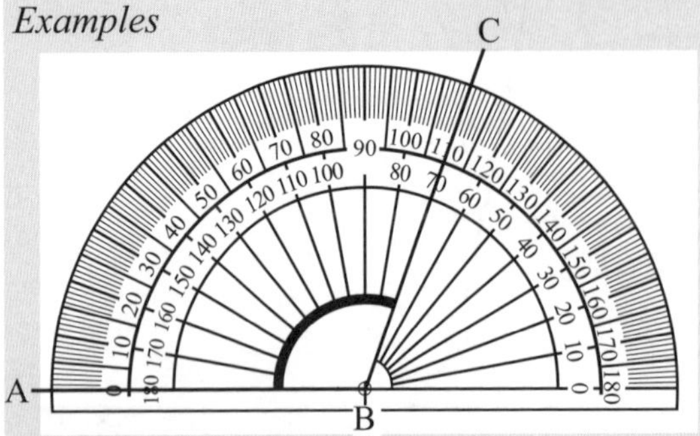

This angle ABC is 110°

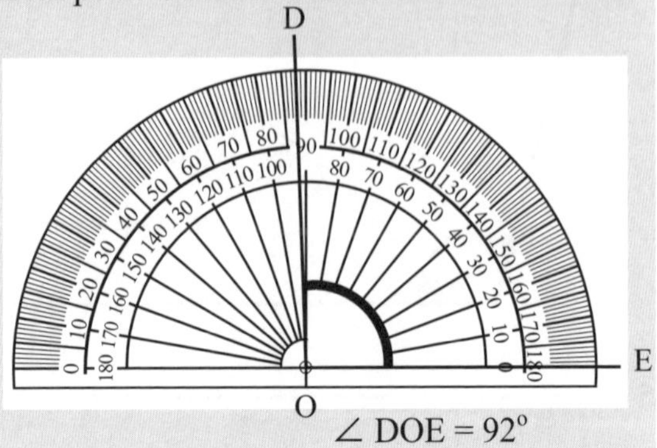

∠ DOE = 92°

Exercise 3:3

Measure and name these angles:

1

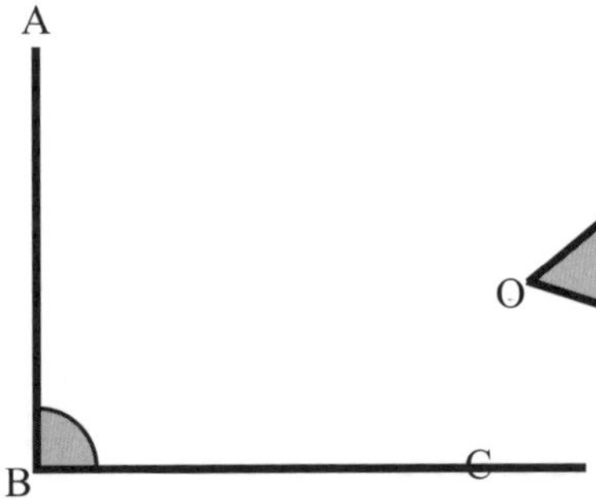

2

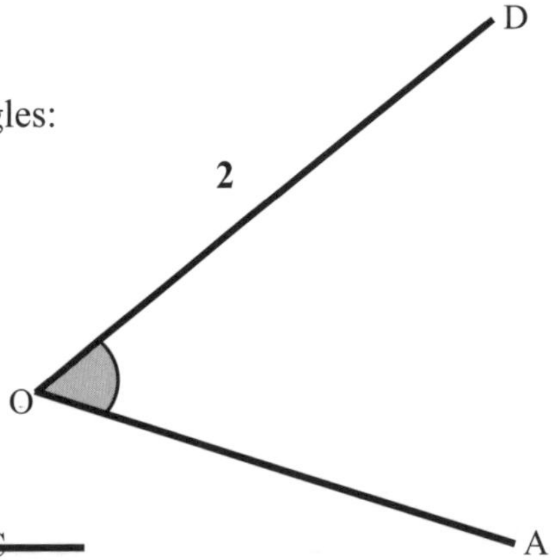

3

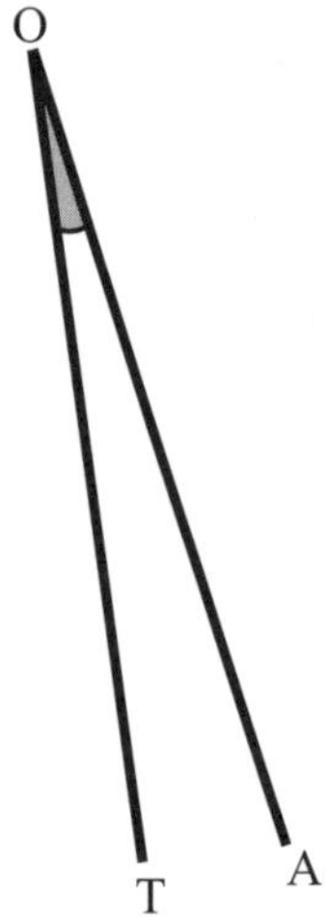

4

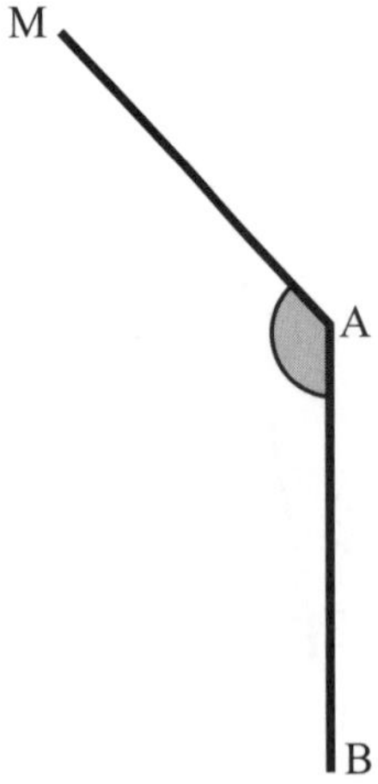

5

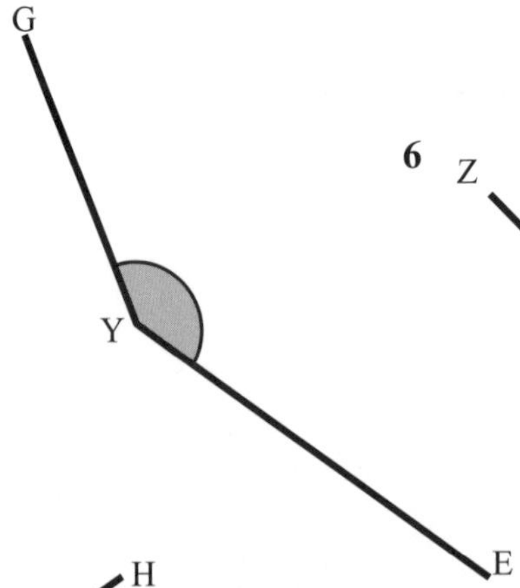

6

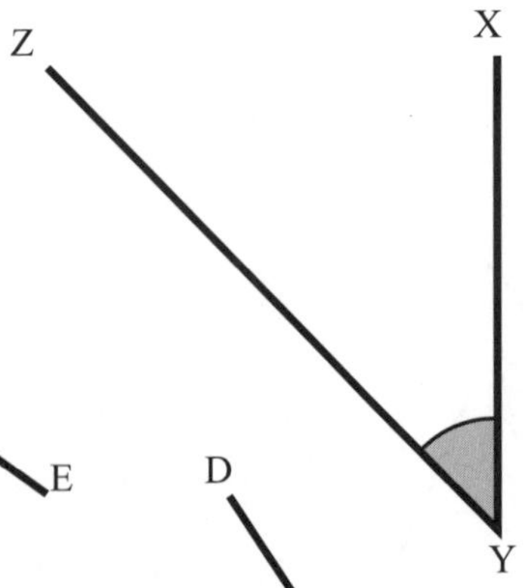

7

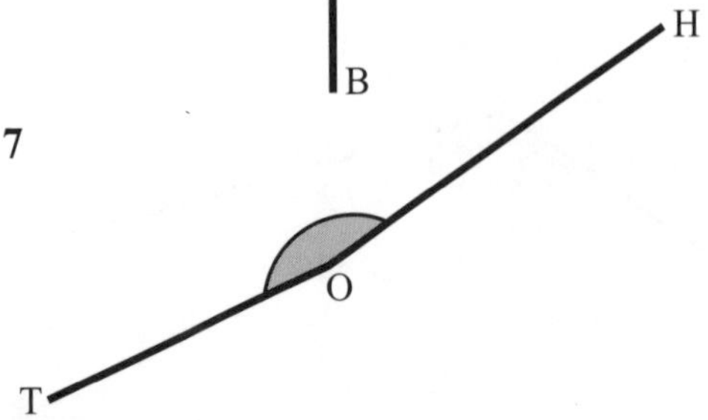

8

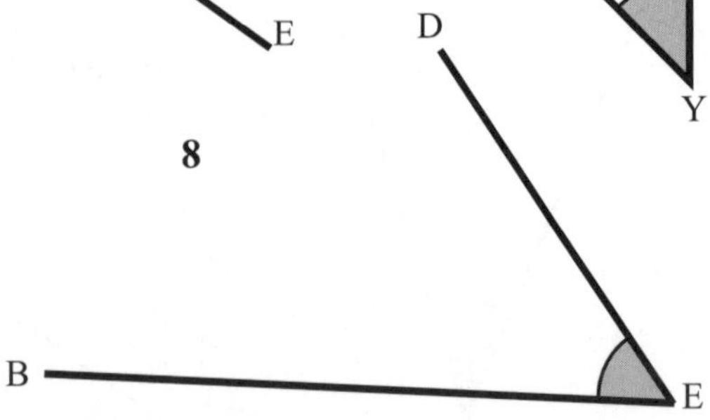

Exercise 3:4

Read the measurements off the protractor below.

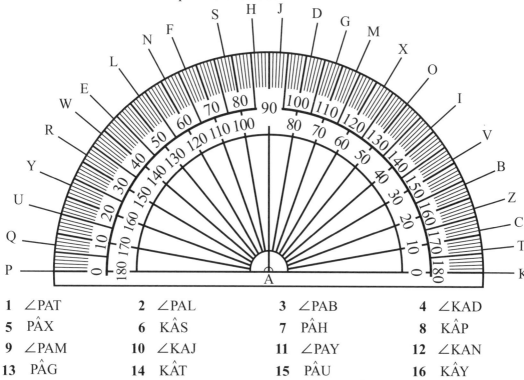

1 ∠PAT	2 ∠PAL	3 ∠PAB	4 ∠KAD
5 PÂX	6 KÂS	7 PÂH	8 KÂP
9 ∠PAM	10 ∠KAJ	11 ∠PAY	12 ∠KAN
13 PÂG	14 KÂT	15 PÂU	16 KÂY

In the exercise below to find the required angle, take two readings from the same scale on the protractor and then take the smaller number from the larger number.

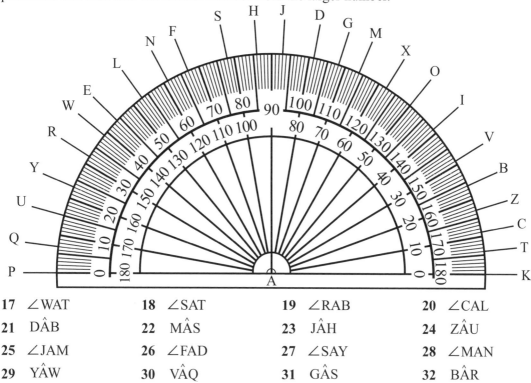

17 ∠WAT	18 ∠SAT	19 ∠RAB	20 ∠CAL
21 DÂB	22 MÂS	23 JÂH	24 ZÂU
25 ∠JAM	26 ∠FAD	27 ∠SAY	28 ∠MAN
29 YÂW	30 VÂQ	31 GÂS	32 BÂR

Letters can be used to name the sides and angles of shapes.

This shape is named **ABCD**

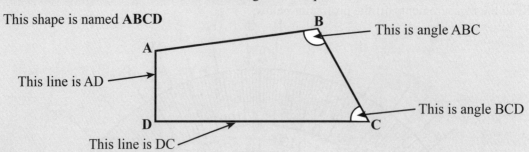

This is angle ABC

This line is AD

This is angle BCD

This line is DC

Exercise 3:5

Measure and name the angles indicated in each shape.

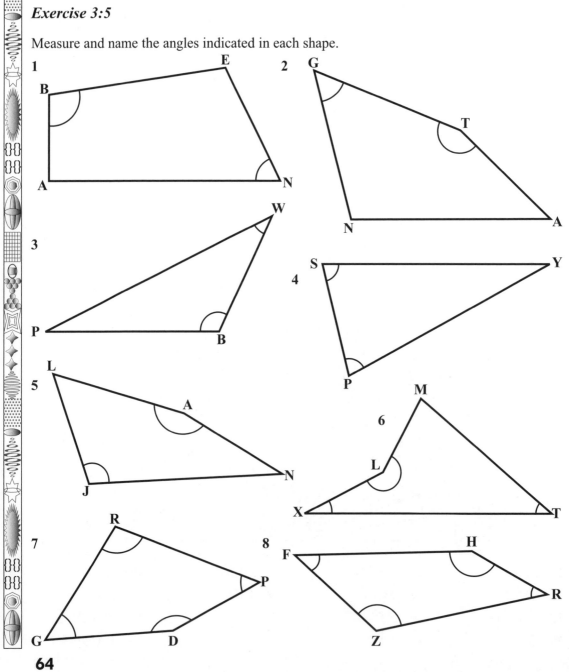

1

2

3

4

5

6

7

8

3　Drawing angles and shapes

Draw angle ABU = 78° on line AB which is 4 cm.

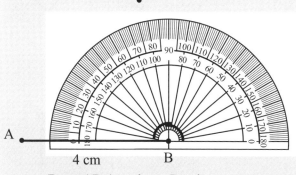

Draw AB 4 cm long. Put the protractor
cross at B and mark a point.

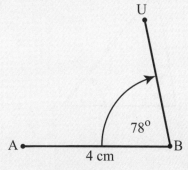

Join points B and U
to give angle ABU.

Draw accurately the triangle ESI with line ES = 5 cm,
∠SEI = 65°, and ∠ESI = 52°.

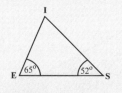

Sketch the
triangle first.

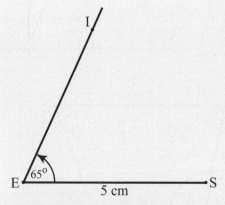

Draw the line ES and measure
angle SEI to be 65°. Stretch
the line EI a little bit longer.

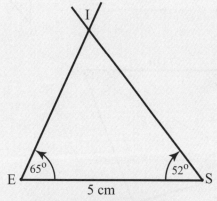

Draw the angle ESI (52°).
Draw the line SI until it
crosses line EI.

Exercise 3:6

Use your ruler and protractor to draw these angles in the direction shown in the diagram.
Make both your lines 5 cm long.

1 a KAN = 48° ↻   b EDU = 92° ↻   c ATE = 106° ↻

d DAS = 35° ↺   e OLE = 60° ↺   f YAW = 156° ↺

g KEN = 88° ↻   h ADO = 100° ↺   i ABE = 22° ↻

j NET = 173° ↺   k SAM = 112° ↻   l DOE = 59° ↺

3

2 Make accurate drawings of these shapes:

a
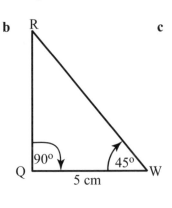

b

c
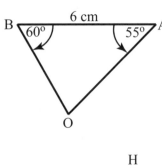

d

e
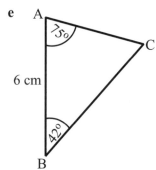

f
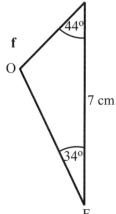

g
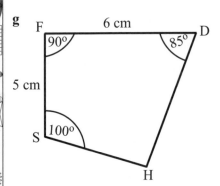

h
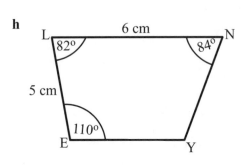

i
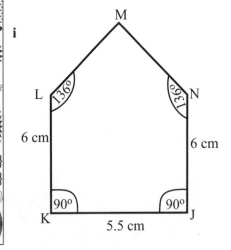

j
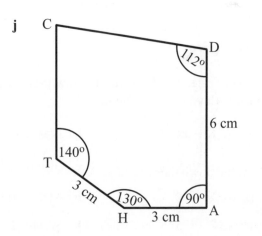

4   Types of angles

Acute angle	An angle less than 90°.	
Right angle	A 90° angle or a quarter turn.	
Obtuse angle	Angle between 90° and 180°	
Straight angle	A 180° angle	
Reflex angle	An angle between 180° and 360°	
Revolution	A complete turn or an angle of 360°	
Complementary angles	Angles whose sum is 90° (e.g. 26° and 64°)	
Supplementary angles	Angles whose sum is 180° (e.g. 67° and 113°)	

Exercise 3:7

1 Write the type of each of these angles. Choose from acute, right, obtuse, straight, reflex.

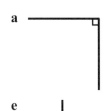

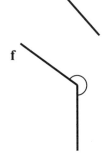

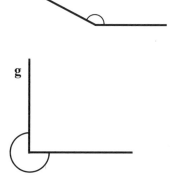

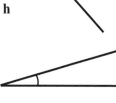

2 Write down the type of each of these angles.

a	265°	**b**	124°	**c**	89°	**d**	300°	**e**	7°
f	159°	**g**	359°	**h**	270°	**i**	45°	**j**	93°

3 Write down the type of each of the angles marked with letters.

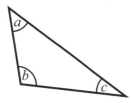 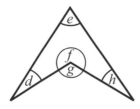 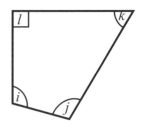

4 How many degrees are there in:

a $1\frac{3}{4}$ right angles   b 0.9 of a right angle   c $2\frac{1}{3}$ right angles

d $1\frac{1}{2}$ straight angles   e 0.45 revolution   f $\frac{1}{8}$ revolution

g 1.7 right angles   h 0.95 revolution   i 1.55 straight angles?

5 a Two angles are complementary. One is 58°. What is the size of the other?

b Two angles are supplementary. One is 103°. What is the size of the other?

c Angle X and Y are supplementary. If X is 58°, what is the size of Y?

6 This is Ama's use of shades of black in his art lesson. The angles are marked with the **Russian Cyrillic** alphabet. Measure all the marked angles.

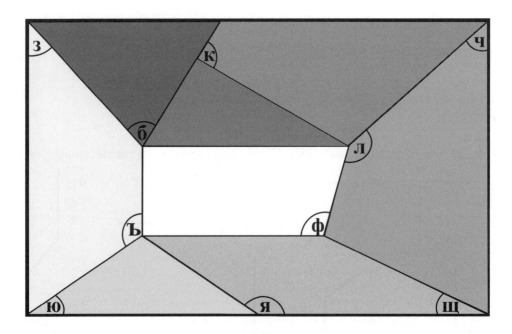

5   Angles on a straight line

Here are two angles ABC and CBD

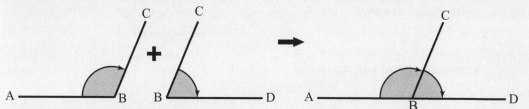

These two angles add up to a straight angle (180°) $\angle ABD + \angle CBD = 180°$

The two angles are joined together to make $\angle ABD$ which is on a straight line.

> **Angles on a straight line add up to 180°**

Examples   **a** What size is angle CBD?

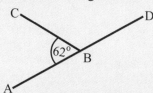

The angles make a straight line ABD
so: $62° + \angle CBD = 180°$
$\angle CBD = \angle 180° - 62°$
$= 118°$

b What size is the angle d?

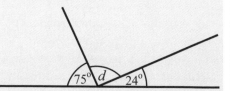

The three angles make a straight line
so: $75° + d + 24° = 180°$
$d = 180° - 75° - 24°$
$d = 81°$

Exercise 3:8

Find the size of angle ABC in each of the following:

1

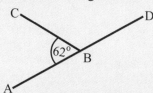

2

3

Find the value of the letter in each of these:

4

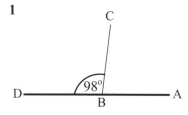

5

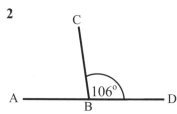

6

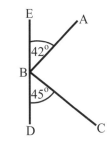

7

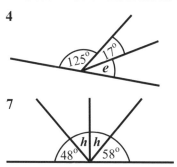

8

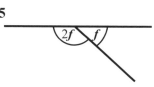

9

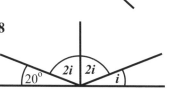

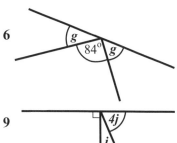

6 Angles at a point

When several angles make a complete revolution they are called angles at a point.

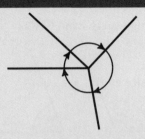

> **Angles at a point add up to 360°**

Examples

a Find the size of angle *d*.

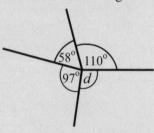

$$d = 360° - (97° + 58° + 110°)$$
$$= 360° - 265°$$
$$= 95°$$

b Find the size of angle *x*.

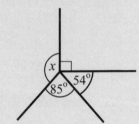

$$x = 360° - (90° + 54° + 85°)$$
$$= 360° - 229°$$
$$= 131°$$

Exercise 3:9

Find the size of each angle marked with a letter. Show your working and give reasons.

1

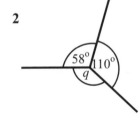

2

3

4

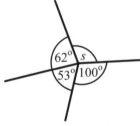

5

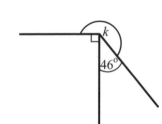

6

7

8

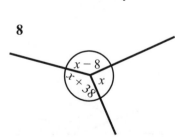

9

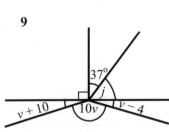

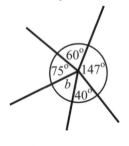

7 Opposite angles

When two straight lines cross, four angles are formed. The angles opposite each other where the lines cross are called **opposite angles**.

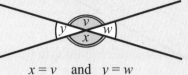

> **Opposite angles are equal**

$x = v$ and $y = w$

Examples   Find the angles marked with letters.

a

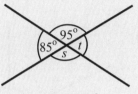

b

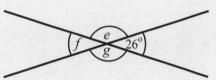

t is opposite $85°$
$\therefore t = 85$

s is opposite $95°$
$\therefore s = 95°$

e and $26°$ make a straight line
$\therefore e = 180° - 26°$
$\quad e = 154°$

f is opposite $26°$
$\therefore f = 26°$

g is opposite e
$\therefore g = 154°$

Exercise 3:10

Use the angle properties above to work out the angles marked with letters:

1

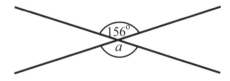

2

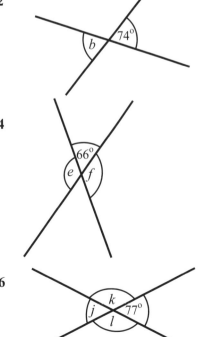

3

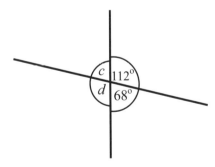

4

5

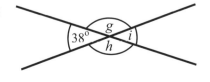

6

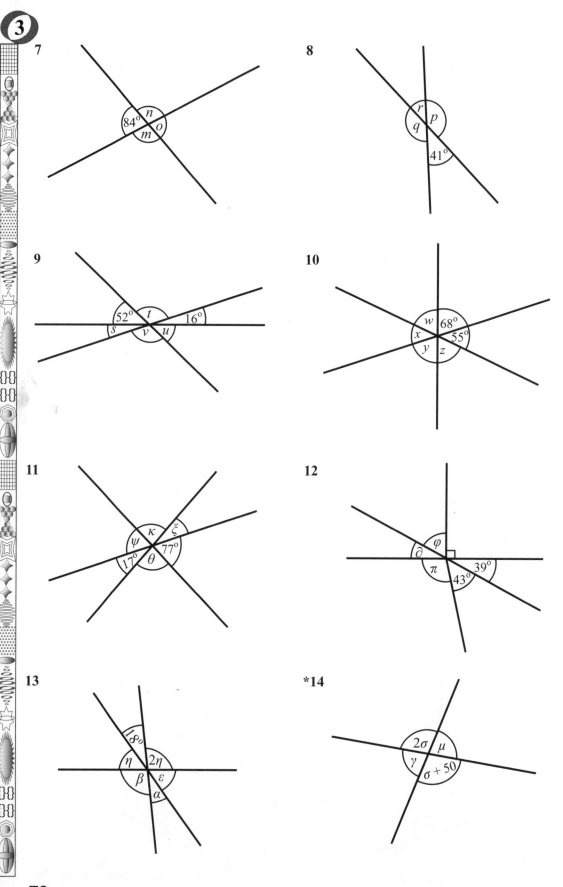

3

7

8

9

10

11

12

13

*14

72

8   Angles in triangles

Draw and cut out a triangle on a piece of paper.   Tear off the corners.   Put the angles together.

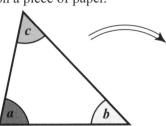 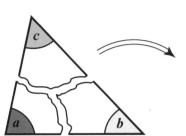 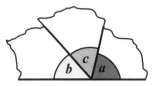

They make a straight line which is an angle of 180°.

The exercise concludes that: **The three angles of a triangle add up to 180°**

Example   Work out angle x in the triangle shown.

$x = 180° - (67° + 30°)$
$\quad = 180° - 97°$
$\quad = 83°$

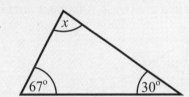

Exercise 3:11

i Copy this table.

ii Carefully measure all the angles in each of these triangles.

iii Complete the table.

iv Write the sum of the three angles in the last column.

	Triangle	Angle α	Angle β	Angle γ	
1	A				
2	B				
3	C				
4	D				
5	E				
6	F				

1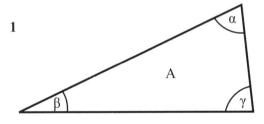

2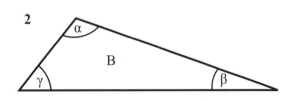

3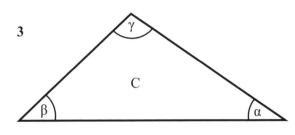

4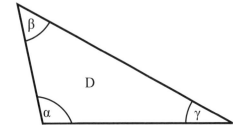

73

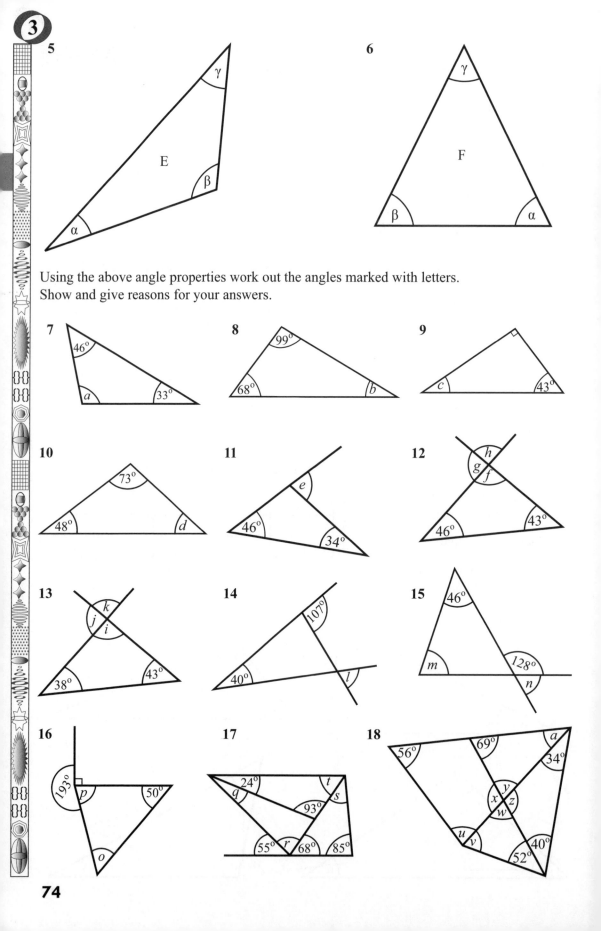

5

E

γ

β

α

6

F

γ

β

α

Using the above angle properties work out the angles marked with letters.
Show and give reasons for your answers.

7

46°

a

33°

8

99°

68°

b

9

c

43°

10

73°

48°

d

11

e

46°

34°

12

h

g

f

46°

43°

13

k

j

i

38°

43°

14

107°

40°

l

15

46°

m

128°

n

16

193°

p

50°

o

17

24°

q

t

s

93°

55°

r

68°

85°

18

56°

69°

a

34°

y

x

z

w

u

v

40°

52°

74

9   Exterior angles of triangles

Prove that *"the exterior angle of a triangle is equal to the sum of the two opposite interior angles"*

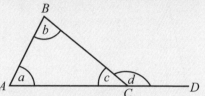

The exterior angle is $\hat{d}$.

The opposite interior angles are $\hat{a}$ and $\hat{b}$.

Proof   Consider $\triangle ABC$: $\hat{a} + \hat{b} + \hat{c} = 180°$ i   (sum of angles in a triangle)

$$\hat{c} + \hat{d} = 180° \qquad \text{ii} \quad \text{(sum of angles on a straight line)}$$

$$\hat{c} + \hat{d} = \hat{a} + \hat{b} + \hat{c} \qquad \text{(from i and ii)}$$

$$\cancel{\hat{c}} + \hat{d} = \hat{a} + \hat{b} + \cancel{\hat{c}}$$

$$\hat{d} = \hat{a} + \hat{b}$$

$$\therefore \; B\hat{C}D = B\hat{A}C + A\hat{B}C \qquad \text{QED}$$

> The exterior angle of a triangle is equal to the sum of the two opposite interior angles.

Example   In the shape shown: $p + 64° + 72° = 180°$

$$p = 180° - 64° - 72°$$

$$p = 44°$$

$p + q = 180°$ (angles on a straight line)

$$q = 180° - p$$

$$q = 180° - 44° = 136°$$

Also $q = 72° + 64°$

$$q = 136°$$

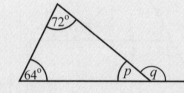

> **QED** stands for:
> *Quod erat demonstrandum*; Latin meaning *'which was to be proved or demonstrated'*.

Exercise 3:12

Find the angles p and q shown in these diagrams:

1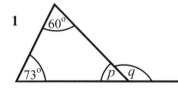

2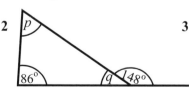

3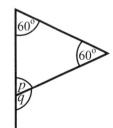

4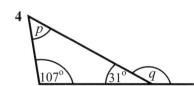

5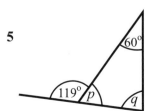

6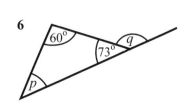

3

Use the properties of angles to work out each of these angles:

7

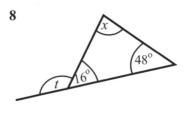

8

9

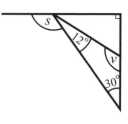

10

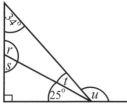

11

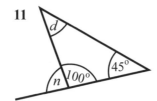

12

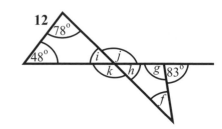

13

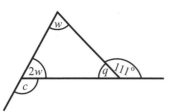

14

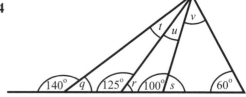

15

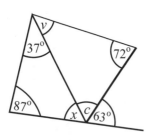

16

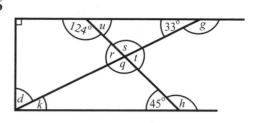

17

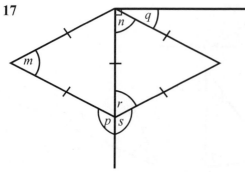

18

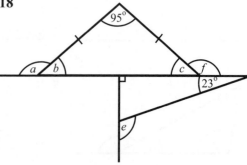

10   Angles and parallel lines

Transversal   A straight line which crosses two or more lines is called **transversal**.

Parallel lines   Lines which never meet and which are always the same distance apart are called **parallel lines**. They are often shown with arrows on them.

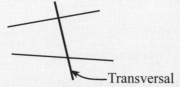 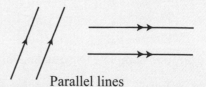

Transversal   Parallel lines

Corresponding angles   Angles in similar positions on the same side of a transversal which crosses parallel lines are called **corresponding angles**.
Look for the letter **F**.
Corresponding angles are also known as **F-angles**.

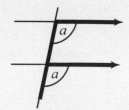

Corresponding angles are equal

Alternate angles   When a transversal crosses two parallel lines the pairs of angles on either side of the transversal are called **alternate angles**.
Look for the letter **Z**.
Alternate angles are also known as **Z-angles.**

Alternate angles are equal

Interior angles   When a transversal crosses two parallel lines, the pairs of angles on the same side of the transversal and between the parallel lines are called **interior angles**.
Look for the letter **U**.
Interior angles are also known as **allied** or **conjoined** angles.

Interior angles add up to 180° $c + d = 180°$

Example   Find the angles shown by letters below.

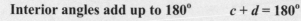

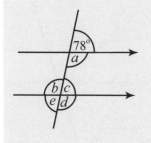

$a = 180° - 78° = 102°$ (*a* and 78° are on a straight line)

$b = 102°$ (*a* and *b* are alternate angles)

$c = 180° - 102° = 78°$ (*a* and *c* are interior angles)

$d = 102°$ (*a* and *d* are corresponding angles)

$e = 78°$ (*e* and c are opposite)

Exercise 3:13

1 Draw two parallel lines about 5 cm apart and a transversal line as shown.
Label these *a*, *b*, c, *d*, *e*, *f*, *g* and *h*.
Measure angle *a* and *b*.

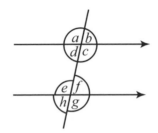

2 Copy and complete these statements about **question 1** to make true:

   i *a* and .... are corresponding angles

   iii *b* and .... are vertically opposite angles

   v *h* and .... are corresponding angles

   vii *e* and .... are vertically opposite angles

   ix *g* and .... are corresponding angles

   ii *e* and .... are alternate angles

   iv *c* and .... are interior angles

   vi *d* and .... are alternate angles

   viii *d* and .... are interior angles

   x *h* and *g* are .... angles

3 a Write down the letters of all the angles that are 74°.

  b Write down the letters of all the angles that are 106°.

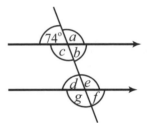

Find the size of each marked angle below:

4

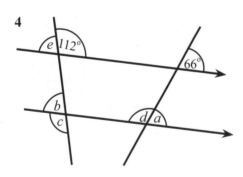

5

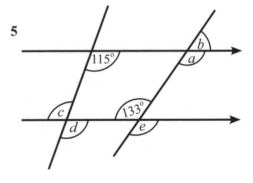

6

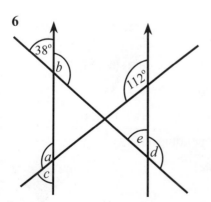

7

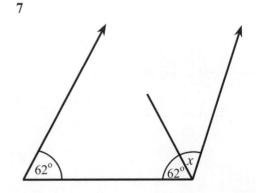

8

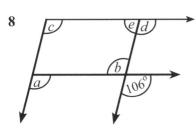

9

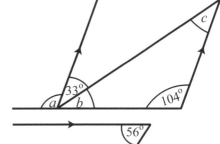

10

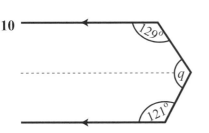

11

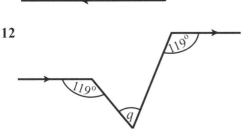

12

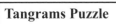

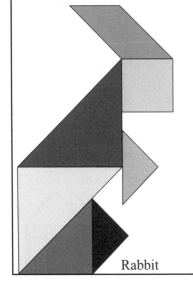

13

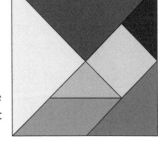

Tangrams Puzzle

A **tangram** uses seven geometric shapes cut from a square: five right angled triangles of different sizes, one square and one parallelogram to make various figures.

a Copy the two figures ('rabbit' and 'running person'), measure and show all obtuse angles on each figure.

b Draw the square twice the size as shown. Cut out each shape in the square and make your own figures. Make these figures: a dog, a cat, a duck, a man bowing, a house.

Rabbit

Man running

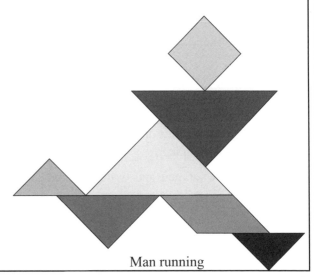

11   Turtle geometry

Logo is a computer program in which instructions in the form of commands are written to control the movement of a floor or computer screen turtle. This program is sometimes referred to as **turtle geometry** as it produces geometrical shapes. The unit used in this exercise is millimetres.

Logo commands: **FD** - Forwar**D**   **BK** - Bac**K**   **LT** - **L**eft **T**urn   **RT** - **R**ight **T**urn
              PU - **P**en **U**p   **PD** - **P**en **D**own   **The turtle always starts facing up**.

Examples   **a**   FD 40   Draws a straight line 40 mm turtle steps up

             40 mm

        b   Forward 40 mm, right turn 90° and forward 60 mm is written as:
            FD 40 RT 90 FD 60

                  60 mm
         40 mm

In Logo the turtle always turns the exterior angle.

Exercise 3:14

Copy these commands. Draw the shape that the turtle traces on 5 mm squared paper and show the direction the turtle is facing.

1   FD 40   LT 90   FD 60   **2**   FD 50   RT 90   FD 70   RT 90   **3**   RT 90   FD 70
                              FD 50   RT 90   FD 70   RT 180 FD 70

4   FD 50   PU   FD 50   PD   **5**   FD 60   RT 90   FD 40   LT 90 FD 50   **6**   FD 35   RT 90   FD
    FD 50   LT 90   FD 60   LT 90   FD 80   LT 90   FD 110   45   LT 45 FD 55

Write instructions using Logo commands to draw these shapes on a 5 mm squared paper.

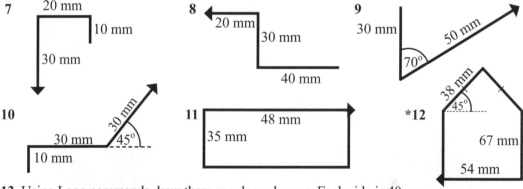

7   20 mm   **8**   **9**
            10 mm   20 mm   30 mm   50 mm
    30 mm   30 mm   70°
                          40 mm

10   30 mm   **11**   48 mm   *12   38 mm 45°
     30 mm   45°   35 mm   67 mm
    10 mm   54 mm

13 Using Logo commands draw these regular polygons. Each side is 40 mm.
    a Equilateral triangle   **b** Square   **c** Pentagon   **d** Hexagon

14 Using your own dimensions write the Logo commands to produce these shapes:

EXTENSION

1 What angle in degrees corresponds to:

   a $\frac{2}{3}$ of a right angle   **b** 1.9 of a right angle   **c** 0.75 of a right angle

   d 2.07 of a right angle   **e** $3\frac{3}{5}$ of a right angle   **f** 5.45 of a right angle?

2 How many right angles do you turn through if you face:

   a north and turn anticlockwise to face east

   b face south-east and turn anticlockwise to face north-west

   c face west and turn clockwise to face north-west?

3 The Earth turns once on its axis in 24 hours.

   a How many degrees has the Earth turned through after one hour?

   b How many hours does it take to turn through: **i** 135°   **ii** 315°?

4 Measure each of these angles:

   a   **b**   **c**

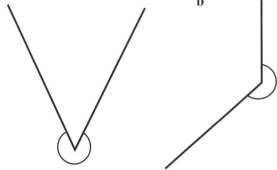 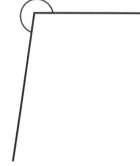

5 Construct triangle ABC: $AB = 5.8$ cm $\angle CAB = 72°$ $\angle ABC = 56°$
   Measure lines AC and BC.

6 In triangle ABC line AB is c, line AC is b, line BC is a,
   $\angle BAC = \angle A$, $\angle ABC = \angle B$ and $\angle ACB = \angle C$.
   Construct each of the triangles listed in the table below.
   a, b and c are stated in centimetres.
   (Hint: Sketch each triangle first.)
   Complete the table.

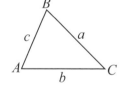

Triangle	A	B	C	a	b	c
i	74°	36°		8		
ii	100°	42°				6
iii		65°	67°	8		
iv			85°	7		9
v	73°			8		7
vi			112°	6.5	6.5	
vii		44°		5		8
viii	105°	50°				7

7 Work out the value of x and the value of the angles in each triangle.

a

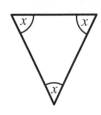

b

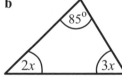

c

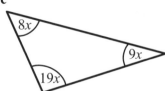

8 Angle t is twice angle p.
Find angles p, q, r, s and t.

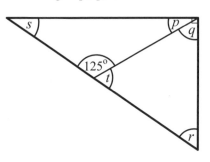

9 Work out the value of x and the value of the angles in each sector.

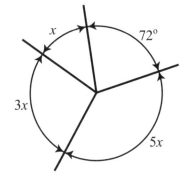

10 Work out the value of x and y.

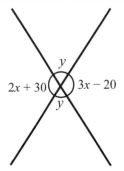

11 Work out the value of t and x.

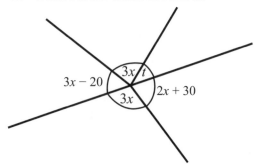

12 Work out the angles marked with the letters in the square. The angles are not in any order.

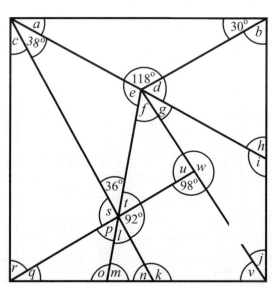

SUMMARY

Angle An angle is a measure of change of direction or turning about a point.
An object can turn around clockwise.
This is the same direction as the hands of a clock.

Symbol: ↻

An object can turn anticlockwise. This is the opposite direction to clockwise.
Anticlockwise is also known as counter-clockwise.

Symbol: ↺

The size of an angle is usually measured in degrees ($^{\circ}$). A protractor is used to measure and draw angles accurately.

Protractor

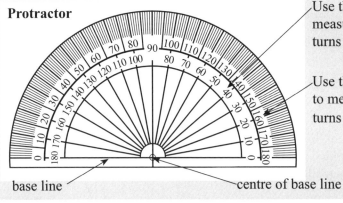

Use the inside scale to measure anti-clockwise turns ↻.

Use the outside scale to measure clockwise turns ↺.

base line   centre of base line

Types of angles

Acute angle   An angle less than 90°.

Right angle   A 90° angle or a quarter turn.

Obtuse angle   Angle between 90° and 180°

Straight angle   A 180° angle

Reflex angle   An angle between 180° and 360°

Revolution A complete turn or an angle of 360°

Complementary angles   Angles whose sum is 90° (e.g. 26° and 64°)

Supplementary angles   Angles whose sum is 180° (e.g. 67° and 113°)

Angles on a straight line add up to 180°

Example   What size is angle CBD?

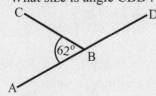

The angles make a straight line ABD
so: $62^{\circ} + \angle CBD = 180^{\circ}$
$\angle CBD = \angle 180^{\circ} - 62^{\circ}$
$= 118^{\circ}$

Angles at a point add up to 360°

Example   Find the size of angle d.

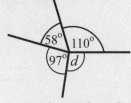

$d = 360^{\circ} - (97^{\circ} + 58^{\circ} + 110^{\circ})$
$= 360^{\circ} - 265^{\circ}$
$= 95^{\circ}$

Opposite angles are equal

Example Find the angles marked with letters.

t is opposite $85°$

$\therefore t = 85$

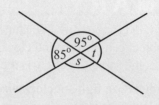

s is opposite $95°$

$\therefore s = 95°$

The exterior angle of a triangle is equal to the sum of the two opposite interior angles.

Example In the shape shown: $p + 64° + 72° = 180°$

$$p = 180° - 64° - 72°$$

$$p = 44°$$

$p + q = 180°$ (angles on a straight line)

$$q = 180° - p$$

$$q = 180° - 44° = 136°$$

Also $q = 72° + 64° = 136°$

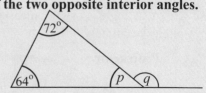

Transversal
Parallel lines

A straight line which crosses two or more lines is called **transversal**. Lines which never meet and which are always the same distance apart are called **parallel lines**. They are often shown with arrows on them.

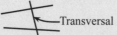

Transversal   Parallel lines

Corresponding angles

Angles in similar positions on the same side of a transversal which crosses parallel lines are called **corresponding angles**.
Corresponding angles are also known as **F-angles**.
Corresponding angles are equal

Alternate angles

When a transversal crosses two parallel lines the pairs of angles on either side of the transversal are called **alternate angles**.
Alternate angles are also known as **Z-angles**.
Alternate angles are equal

Interior angles

When a transversal crosses two parallel lines, the pairs of angles on the same side of the transversal and between the parallel lines are called **interior angles**.
Interior angles are also known an **allied** or **conjoined** angles.
Interior angles add up to 180° $c + d = 180°$

Example   Find the angles shown by letters.

$a = 180° - 78° = 102°$ (a and $78°$ are on a straight line)

$b = 102°$ (a and b are alternate angles)

$c = 180° - 102° = 78°$ (a and c are interior angles)

$d = 102°$ (a and d are corresponding angles)

$e = 78°$ (e and c are opposite)

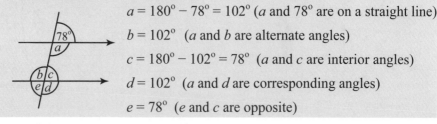

Statistics

Statistics began in Germany in the 1700s and 1800s.

A statistician collects facts called data, sorts them out, shows a diagram of them and makes a conclusion from them. Statistical methods help to organise business and industrial facts, and uncover the principles and trends at work behind the facts.

Country	Capital	Population	Area km²	Birth rate per 1000	Adult literacy %	Roadways km	GDP per capita $	Time zones ± GMT
Benin	Cotonou	8 935 000	112 622	39	35	16 000	1500	+1
Burkina Faso	Uagadougou	15 746 232	274 200	44	23	92 495	457	0
Cameroun	Yaunde	18 879 301	475 440	34	68	50 000	2300	+1
Chad	Ndjamena	10 329 208	1 284 000	41	26	33 400	863	+1
Equatorial Guinea	Malabo	676 000	28 051	37	87	2880	14931	+1
Gambia	Banjul	1 782 000	11 295	39	40	3074	810	−1
Ghana	Accra	23 837 000	238 535	29	58	62 221	900	0
Guinea	Conakry	10 057 975	245 857	38	30	44 348	439	−1
Guinea Bissau	Bissau	1 533 964	36 125	36	42	3455	264	−1
Ivory Coast	Yamoussoukro	20 179 602	322 463	32	49	80 000	1132	0
Liberia	Monrovia	3 955 000	111 369	42	58	10 600	215	0
Mali	Bamako	12 666 987	1 240 192	49	46	18 709	656	0
Mauritania	Nouakchott	3 291 000	1 030 700	34	51	11 066	1042	0
Niger	Niamey	15 290 000	15 200 000	52	28	18 550	391	+1
Nigeria	Abuja	154 729 000	923 768	37	68	193 200	1401	+1
Sierra Leone	Freetown	6 440 053	71 740	45	35	11 300	725	0
Senegal	Dakar	13 711 597	196 723	37	51	13 576	1066	0
Togo	Lome	6 019 877	56 785	36	61	7520	436	0

The governments in countries in West Africa want to improve the living standard of their citizens. What part of the data will they use?

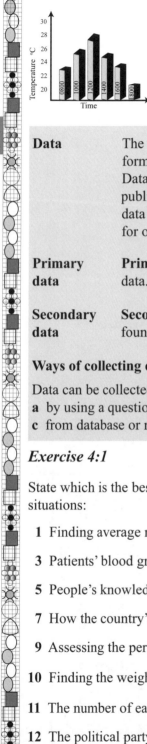

Countries	Life Expectancy 2007
Algeria	75.21 yrs
Djibouti	44.65 yrs
Ghana	59.95 yrs
Japan	85.56 yrs
Norway	82.46 yrs
Sierra Leone	42.87 yrs
United Kingdom	81.3 yrs

Charts and tables like these are often seen in newspapers, books and on the television. They give information to make forecasts and plans for the future. For example forecasting the temperature for tomorrow or predicting life expectancy over the next five years.

Data	The word **data** means information or facts about something, usually in the form of number. Singular for the word data is *datum* - it is not often used. Data is required in almost all academic, scientific, medical and business publications in newspapers and government reports. The purpose of collecting data could be for assessing the opinion polls, finding a new drug, budgeting for or pricing a product.
Primary data	**Primary data** is data that is collected by the person who is going to use the data. The data is obtained directly for the purpose of the survey.
Secondary data	**Secondary data** is data that is already collected or processed. This can be found in books or on the internet.

Ways of collecting data

Data can be collected by using these methods:
a by using a questionnaire   b carrying out tests and experiments
c from database or records   d observation and recording results

Exercise 4:1

State which is the best method (**a**, **b**, **c**, or **d** above) for collecting data for each of these situations:

1 Finding average monthly temperatures.   2 People's favourite type of music.

3 Patients' blood groups in a clinic.   .   4 The number of people entering a shop.

5 People's knowledge on lawn tennis.   6 The height of trees in the Volta region.

7 How the country's wealth is measured.   8 The height of past Heads of State in Ghana.

9 Assessing the performance of boys doing mathematics in a class.

10 Finding the weights of babies born in a hospital.

11 The number of earthquakes that have occurred in West Africa.

12 The political party that people will vote for.

13 The number of cars passing on a road within a certain time.

14 The amount of body fat in Ghanaian men and women.

2   Types of data

100, 200, 300, 400, 500, ...

Yes, No, Yes, Yes, No, Yes, No,

24.37, 24.375, 24.3758, 24.37586

Statistical data can be about things or people or what people do and say. Most of this data is first hand or second hand.

Data can take any form or it can be given a numerical value.

Statistics	The collection and arrangement of data is called **statistics**.
	There are two types of data: qualitative and quantitative data.
Qualitative data	Data which is described in words is called **qualitative data**. Values are not numerical. *Examples* are: type of cars or houses.
Quantitative data	Data that can be measured or counted is called **quantitative data**. It is given a numerical value. Examples of quantitative data are temperatures, masses, number of pupils and test marks. There are two types of quantitative data: discrete data and continuous data.
Discrete data	When data can only take certain individual values they are called **discrete data**. Discrete data can be counted and have exact value.
Examples	**a** The number of passengers in a minibus can only be a whole number.
	b The number of taxis in a town can only be 0, 1, 2, 3, 4, 5, 6, etc.

c These shoe sizes are separate. There are no values between them.

Continuous data	**Continuous data** is data which is measured or weighed and can have any value within a certain range. The accuracy of measurement depends on the accuracy of the measuring device. The significant point about continuous data is that it cannot assume exact values and the best we can do is to allocate a range within which an item lies. The value 2.40, measured can be allocated the range from 2.395 and up to 2.405.
Examples	The height of a boy can be 163 cm, 162.8 cm, or 162.8459 cm depending on the accuracy of measurement. The mass of a new born baby could be 3.6 kg, 3.846 kg or 4.0134 kg. Your waist could be 60 cm.

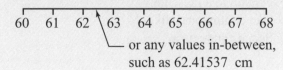

or any values in-between, such as 62.41537 cm

> Continuous data cannot be measured exactly.

Exercise 4:2

1 For each of these sets of data write down whether it is qualitative or quantitative data.

   a The masses of parcels sent by post   b Pupils favourite sport

   c The colours of shirts sold in a shop   d The ages of pupils at Boley High School

   e Types of employment in Navrongo   f Amount of monthly rainfall in Mole Park.

2 For each of these sets of data write down whether it is continuous or discrete data:

   a Favourite radio programmes   b The number of votes in an election

   c The temperature of Lake Bosomtwi   d The number of cars sold in a car shop

   e The area of a school sports field   f The speed at which a car is travelling.

3 Appiah is decorating his lounge. He wants answers to these questions.

   For each question write whether the data is continuous or discrete.

   a How long is his sofa?
   b How many CDs can fit the top shelf?
   c What is the length of the centre table?
   d How tall is the book shelf?
   e What is the reading on the thermometer?
   f How many electrical switches will be needed?
   g What is the area of the carpet?
   h What is the colour of the cushions?

4 State which of these are discrete data and which are continuous data:

a The amount of water in a bottle   b The areas of school football pitches

c The length of cows' tails   d The diameters of drinking cups

e The number of windows in a room   f The number of pupils who wear glasses

g The speed at which a car is travelling   h The number of skirts sold per day

i Daily temperatures   j The length (in mm) of shoes

5 You are planning a school excursion to a museum.
   a Write five questions to collect continuous data.
   b Write five questions to collect discrete data.

3   Frequency tables

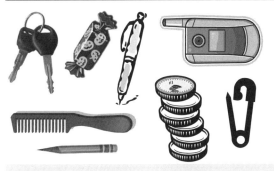

Suppose you want to know what people are carrying in their pockets, you will need to ask people to empty their pockets out, sort the things out into piles and then make a list.

Can you easily tell from these items what people mostly carry in their pockets?

Your answer to the above question was probably no. All the items are too jumbled up to be easy to read. It needs sorting! To sort out information like this we often use a **data collection sheet**, also called a **tally table**. After collecting the data on a tally table we use a **frequency table** to arrange it. A tally table is also called a **tally chart**.

Tally   A method of counting in fives using strokes, e.g. ⌁ or ⌁.

Tally table   A table used to help record numbers of items.

Frequency   The number of times something occurs.

Frequency table is a table showing the number of times something has occurred.

Three methods are used to collect data:

Sampling   - Taking a few out of the whole population.

Observation   - Noticing what is happening and recording the information.

Experiment   - Trying and testing something unknown in order to collect data.

Example   Kuffour kept a record of the number of goals scored by Kotoko football club in the last 30 matches:

1	2	1	0	0	3	2	1	4	1
5	1	0	3	2	1	4	2	2	0
3	2	1	4	1	2	5	3	1	3

This frequency table illustrates the data.

Number of goals	Tally	Frequency
0	IIII	4
1	⌁ IIII	9
2	⌁ II	7
3	⌁	5
4	III	3
5	II	2
	Total	30

The frequency table shows in an orderly manner how the goals have been recorded. We can easily read the table and draw conclusions.

Exercise 4:3

1 For these surveys, decide whether the data should be collected by:
   i Sampling   **ii** Observation   **iii** Experiment

   a The examination results of 50 pupils   **b** The number of people using a store
   c Where people go to eat   **d** The number of letters received by pupils
   e The volume of bottled water   **f** How people vote in an election
   g The number of eggs laid by hens   **h** The frequency of bus services on a route.

2 Kobi carried out a survey to find how pupils to travelled to school. His frequency table looked like this:

Method of travel	Tally	Frequency
Bus	ЖҜ ЖҜ ЖҜ ЖҜ |||	23
Taxi	ЖҜ	8
Walk	ЖҜ ЖҜ ЖҜ ЖҜ ЖҜ ЖҜ ||	
Car	ЖҜ	11
Bicycle	ЖҜ		

   a Copy and complete his frequency table.
   b How many pupils took part in the survey?
   c What are your conclusions?

3 Draw up a frequency table for this data on the number of books carried by pupils to school.

1	4	2	2	1	6	6	4	3	1
2	1	2	5	3	2	2	1	4	3
5	2	3	4	2	5	1	1	6	3

4 Draw up a frequency table for this data on the number of people passing in front of a school between 9:00 and 9: 20 am.

4	3	3	4	4	5	2	1	2	4
3	2	1	5	3	1	2	3	3	3
4	3	1	5	4	3	5	5	2	1
5	4	3	3	4	5	3	1	3	2
2	2	4	2	3	2	3	3	3	5

5 **a** Draw up a frequency table for this data on the volumes in millilitres of 60 bottles of drink on a production line.

302	300	301	304	306	298	300	301	302	301
306	299	298	298	300	299	301	304	303	299
301	301	305	303	300	304	300	305	301	298
301	300	304	300	298	298	301	300	304	305
300	301	300	299	300	302	305	308	300	301
303	302	303	303	302	299	302	299	302	299

   b What conclusions can you draw?

4 Grouped data

When there is a large amount of data it is often easier to put it into groups. This makes it easier to record the data and to spot any pattern or trends before attempting to compile a frequency table. These groups of data are called classes.

Class interval is the difference between the class boundaries.

Types of classes

21 – 30	This means from 21 up to and including 30.
5 –	This means from 5 up to but not including 10.
40 –	This means from 40 up to but not including 50.
100 –	This means from 100 up to but not including 200.
$20 < x \leq 30$	This means 20 is not included, up to and including 30.
$20 \leq x < 30$	This means 20 is included, up to but not including 30.

There should not be any gaps between the class intervals in the group and groups *must not* overlap. All the numbers in the data must be included.

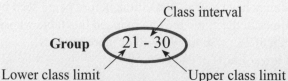

Class interval

Group 21 - 30

Lower class limit   Upper class limit

Example   This data shows the number of eggs laid by each of the 40 hens in two weeks.

```
16  18  13  15  12  15  25  30  28  12
24  28  19  27  25  22  23  22  19  17
22  13  16  29  30  16  15  20  21  25
30  25  23  17  18  14  29  22  17  20
```

This is the grouped frequency table for the data with a suitable class interval.

Number of eggs	Tally	Frequency
11 – 15	JHT III	8
16 – 20	JHT JHT II	12
21 – 25	JHT JHT II	12
26 – 30	JHT III	8

Open-ended classes   Sometimes the last group does not have an upper limit. It is left **open-ended**. This class is called an **open-ended class**.

Open ended classes are used when there are few items at the end of the data. These are spread over a range that could represent several classes, some of which could be empty.

Examples   **a** > 25 **b** above 40   **c** greater than 10   **d** ≥ 29.5

Exercise 4:4

1 Amponsah asks the boys in his year group how many marks they each got in their Mathematics test. He is going to use these groups for his data:

1 – 10   10 – 20   20 – 30   30 – 40   40 – 50   above 50

Explain what is wrong with his group.

2 Akosua asks the girls in her class the same question.
These are the groups that she uses:

1 ≤ marks < 10   11 ≤ marks ≤ 20   21 ≤ marks ≤ 30

31 ≤ marks ≤ 40   41 ≤ marks ≤ 50   > 51

She has made two mistakes. Write down what they are.

3 People's weights are recorded to the nearest kilogram and presented in a table. The classes in this table are labelled 40 – 44, 45 – 49, 50 – 54, 55 –59.
What are the exact upper and lower limits in each class?

4 People attending a clinic may have to wait some time before being seen by a doctor.
The records of waiting times in the clinic are summarised in a table whose classes are:
'less than 20 minutes', '20 to 29', '30 to 39', '40 or more minutes'
What are the upper and lower limits of each class?

5 In question 4 the numbers in the classes are 7, 11, 11, 4 respectively.
Show this on a frequency diagram.

6 Draw up a grouped frequency table for the the number of phone calls per day in a company.
Use the following equal groups:

8	4	7	20	15	21	33	6	47	5
14	2	9	10	19	29	38	14	1	42
33	21	8	38	34	23	15	17	5	3
40	44	11	31	22	24	41	34	18	28
45	36	9	25	8	16	36	10	20	17

   i 1 ≤ calls ≤ 5,   6 ≤ calls ≤ 10, ...,
       46 ≤ calls ≤ 50

   ii 1 ≤ calls ≤ 10, 11 ≤ calls ≤ 20, 21 ≤ calls ≤ 30, 31 ≤ calls ≤ 40, 41 ≤ calls ≤ 50

   iii Which is the most suitable of these tally-tables?

7 Using a suitable class interval draw up a grouped frequency table for the diameter (to the nearest mm) of 30 oranges sold in a shop within 20 minutes.

68	70	78	59	75	66	82	86	90	92
77	69	87	93	58	64	77	86	89	64
88	74	81	72	61	90	83	88	67	79

8 Using a suitable class interval draw up a grouped frequency table for electrical units in kWh used by 30 households in Cape Coast.

16.87	31.22	15.6	45.80	7.56	33.06	25.5	9.67	33.67	0.56
32.50	36.75	10.04	4.42	2.53	45.2	15.70	10.09	31.79	25.79
18.25	25.79	9.86	31.79	17.20	0.45	0.95	4.44	24.70	15.45

5   Bar charts

Axis A fixed reference line used to mark the scale for the measurement of coordinates of a graph is called an **axis**.

Bar chart A diagram made up of bars of equal width drawn either vertically (upright) or horizontally (sideways) from an axis. A bar chart is sometimes called a **bar graph**.
Properties of bar charts
The length of the bar is proportional to the size of the item to be considered. Bars can be separate. A bar chart must have a title.
Advantages of bar charts
They are easy for the eye to gauge, very versatile and easy to compare data.

Bar line It is very similar to a bar chart except that it uses lines instead of bars.

Example Dansowaah kept a record of the weather in April. She wrote **S** for sunny, **C** for cloudy and **R** for rainy. These are her results:

R R C C C R C C S C C S S C S S S C S S S C C S R C C R R C

a Make a tally table of her data.
b Use the table and a *scale of 1 cm = 2 units* to draw a bar chart and a bar line.

Weather	Tally	Frequency
Sunny	ЖЖ ЖЖ	10
Cloudy	ЖЖ ЖЖ IIII	14
Rainy	ЖЖ I	6
	Total	30

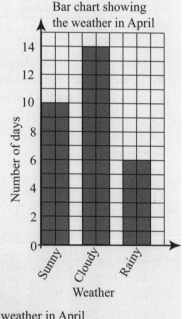

Bar chart showing the weather in April

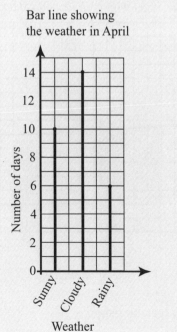

Bar line showing the weather in April

A bar chart can be drawn sideways.

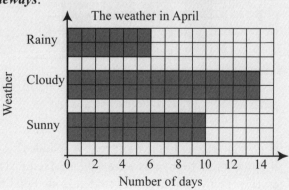

The weather in April

4

Exercise 4:5

1 a Find the number of votes for each
   of these four girls competing for the
   school prefectship.

   b Who won the election and by how
   many votes?

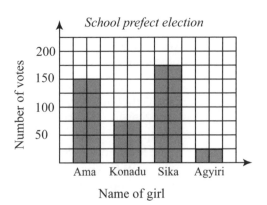

School prefect election

2 Draw a bar chart for the information which relates to the number of weekly letters
   collected in six village post offices.

Atuobo	Esiama	Ahobre	Beku	Edabu	Beyin
45	28	80	64	75	98

3 The table shows a survey of people's employment in a town.

Drivers	Nurses	Labourers	Farmers	Shop workers	Carpenters
19	14	25	36	28	20

   a Draw a vertical bar chart to represent the information.
   b Draw a horizontal bar chart to represent the information.
   c How many people took part in the survey?

4 These bar charts are for two market stalls. They show how many root vegetables are sold
   in a day.

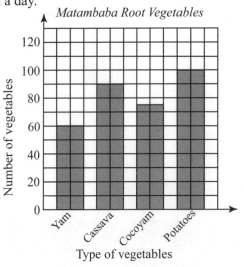

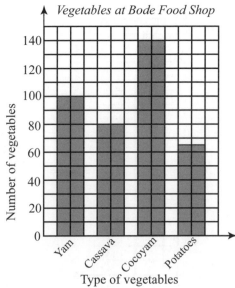

   a Which shop sold the most root vegetables?
   b How many cocoyams were sold at Matambaba Root Vegetables shop?
   c How many potatoes were sold at Bode Food Shop?

94

5 Here are the results of a survey made of 72 spectators leaving a football stadium to find out how they are travelling home.

Car	Walk	Walk	Bicycle	Car	Walk	Bus	Walk	Car
Bicycle	Walk	Bus	Bus	Bus	Walk	Car	Bus	Walk
Car	Bus	Car	Car	Bus	Car	Walk	Walk	Bicycle
Walk	Walk	Walk	Car	Walk	Bus	Walk	Walk	Car
Walk	Walk	Bicycle	Walk	Car	Bicycle	Bus	Walk	Walk
Bus	Car	Bus	Car	Walk	Walk	Car	Walk	Walk
Walk	Bus	Bus	Walk	Walk	Car	Bus	Car	Bus
Walk	Walk	Car	Car	Bus	Walk	Car	Bicycle	Car

a Using a suitable class interval construct a tally chart.
b Draw a bar chart.
c About what percentage of people travelled by car?

6 The table shows the times (in minutes) that Tahiru spent on different daily activities.

Travelling	Working	Eating	Shopping	Sleeping	Doing sports
130	510	80	110	490	120

Draw a bar line using Tahiru's data.

Multiple bar chart

Multiple bar charts are often useful if we want to compare two or more sets of data. This diagram shows the sale of three electrical appliances over three months in a shop.

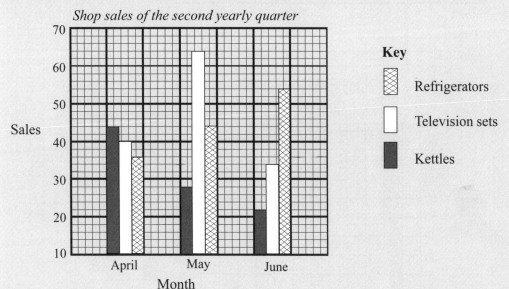

You can see the changes in sales over the three month period. It is easy to note that the sale of kettles has decreased over the three months. There has been a gradual increase in the sale of refrigerators. Sales of television sets peaked in May and dropped sharply in June.

7 The table shows the number of bikes sold per month at Hassan Bike Shop from January to July.

Month	January	February	March	April	May	June	July
No. of Racer bikes sold	40	50	55	60	42	50	68
No. of Mountain bikes sold	28	32	25	48	50	45	30

Copy and complete this multiple bar chart using the table above.

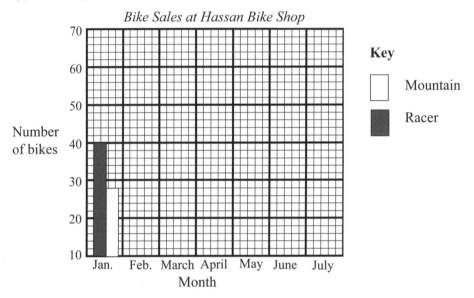

8 The table shows the percentage of her income that Mrs Baidoo spends on food, travel, and clothes for her family.

Year	2008	2009	2010
Food	52%	55%	50%
Travel	20%	25%	24%
Clothes	28%	20%	26%

Copy and complete the multiple bar chart to show the data.

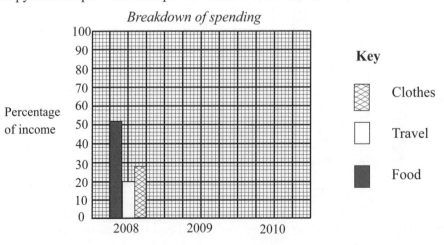

6   Block graphs

Block graph   A **block graph** is similar to a bar chart but with blocks or rectangles touching each other. The data can be discrete as well as continuous. Block graphs are also known as **block diagrams**.

Example   The numbers of match appearances of 24 members in a football club during a season were as follows.

18	37	33	21	34	6	45	2
39	45	43	16	30	19	43	48
27	4	35	2	34	7	32	40

These are the frequency table and the block diagram for the data.

Matches	Tally	Frequency
1 – 10	JHT	5
11 – 20	|||	3
21 – 30	|||	3
31 – 40	JHT |||	8
41 – 50	JHT	5
	Total	24

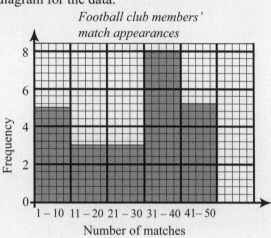

Football club members' match appearances

Exercise 4:6

1 Here is a frequency table showing the number of minutes pupils spent on their homework.
   a Copy and complete the frequency table and the block diagram.
   b What percentage of pupils spent less than 20 minutes on their homework?
   c How many pupils spent no time on their homework? Explain.
   d What was the longest time spent by a pupil doing the homework? Explain.

Time, t (minutes)	Tally	Frequency
$0 \leq t < 10$	JHT	5
$10 \leq t < 20$	JHT JHT	10
$20 \leq t < 30$		11
$30 \leq t < 40$	JHT JHT JHT	
$40 \leq t < 50$	JHT	18
$50 \leq t < 60$	JHT JHT JHT JHT |||	
$60 \leq t < 70$	JHT JHT ||	12
$70 \leq t < 80$		6

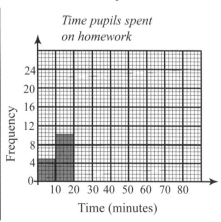

Time pupils spent on homework

2 In a mathematics test the percentage of 100 pupils were recorded in the table.

The lowest mark is 32 and the highest mark is 96 therefore the class interval could be 31 – 40, ..., ..., to 91 – 100 to include all the marks.

a Draw up a group frequency table for this data.

b Show the data on a block chart.

72	56	91	38	75	33	56	46	61	70
53	63	49	35	43	65	47	74	62	81
62	65	86	82	46	78	98	86	54	62
40	81	58	75	44	51	49	80	69	66
60	31	47	69	81	62	74	46	72	52
58	74	63	68	81	55	52	32	41	35
64	89	96	65	50	63	75	53	40	79
64	76	58	54	42	66	77	74	39	72
50	52	64	75	70	62	43	73	77	66
86	73	47	59	67	49	38	52	52	93

3 Sixty 15-year-old girls were tested to find their pulse-rate when they were resting. This data of the number of beats per minute was obtained.

62	70	56	72	69	77	86	71	79	82
64	89	73	75	70	73	63	86	56	76
76	74	65	84	79	80	76	72	68	65
70	69	72	72	61	83	80	75	67	78
58	92	74	67	62	91	73	64	65	80
62	57	53	74	70	81	66	70	72	74

a Draw a frequency table using the groups: 51 – 55, 56 – 60, etc.;
b Show the data in a block graph.

4 A work and time study for one month records the length of a salesman's 70 phone calls in minutes.

a Using a suitable class interval draw a frequency table for the data.

b Illustrate the data in a block diagram.

c Work out the percentage of the group with the highest frequency.

23	16	56	17	37	12	2	10	30	9
55	30	52	6	8	8	13	11	15	13
21	43	37	19	14	24	41	9	32	16
2	38	24	1	11	29	44	7	14	11
37	2	24	20	49	32	29	36	13	5
16	45	6	38	14	28	32	35	58	40
23	35	13	27	10	51	17	21	38	28

5 The playing times for CDs are given to the nearest minute.

a Draw a frequency table for the data.

b Illustrate your data in a block graph.

c In which class interval would a time of 38 min. 32 s be put?

d What percentage of the CDs play less than 40 minutes?

35	52	60	31	38	65	38	53	68	56
39	62	42	48	55	37	49	57	67	62
49	38	71	44	68	34	66	38	50	48
53	67	39	63	57	48	43	30	54	48
43	47	72	70	45	51	48	56	40	49

7 Stem and leaf diagrams

Up to 25 cm

Length of leaves (cm)

Up to 20 cm

Up to 15 cm

Up to 10 cm

Number of leaves

Farmer Amoah wants to find out the health of his cocoa plants. He has collected some cocoa leaves and measured the lengths of the leaves.

The diagram shows the distribution of lengths.

Stem and leaf diagram   A **stem and leaf** diagram organises data to show its shape and distribution. Each item is split into "***stem***" and "***leaf***". The leaf is usually the last digit of the number and the digit or digits to the left of the leaf form the stem.

Examples   **1 a**   The number 64 would be split as: stem 6   leaf 4

  b   The number 289 would be split as: stem 28   leaf 9

  c   The number 14.6 would be split as: stem 14.   leaf 6

2   These are marks gained by 28 pupils in an examination:

| 50 | 85 | 80 | 75 | 64 | 84 | 79 | 69 | 78 | 75 | 78 | 91 | 69 | 54 |
| 80 | 62 | 91 | 43 | 71 | 86 | 57 | 48 | 77 | 54 | 67 | 90 | 41 | 73 |

The marks can be shown in a stem and leaf diagram.

Step 1   Separate each number into a stem and leaf.
The tens digits form the stem and the unit digits form the leaf.

Step 2   Write a title for the diagram.
Go through the marks one by one and group the numbers with the stems.

Step 3   Rewrite the table so that the numbers are in order of size from smallest to highest.

Marks in examination

Stem	Leaf
4	3 8 1
5	0 4 7 4
6	4 9 9 2 7
7	5 9 8 5 8 1 7 3
8	5 0 4 0 6
9	1 1 0

Marks in examination

Stem	Leaf
4	1 3 8
5	0 4 4 7
6	2 4 7 9 9
7	1 3 5 5 7 8 8 9
8	0 0 4 5 6
9	0 1 1

Step 4   Add a key to the diagram i.e. Key: 4 │ 3   **means 43**
The different rows of the stem and leaf, 4, 5, 6, ..., ..., 9, are called **levels**.

If the stem and leaf plot is turned anti clockwise through 90° the shape looks similar to a bar chart.

Advantages of stem and leaf diagram include these:
  i   All the raw data can be seen; **ii**   It is used when there is a large amount of numbers to analyse;
iii   It can be used to find the mode, median, range and the total of the data;
iv   It displays the frequency for each interval and all the individual values within that interval.

Exercise 4:7

1 Split each of these numbers into a stem and leaf diagram:

    a 128   **b** 3.4   **c** 14.3   **d** 0.038   **e** 3.014

    f 0.09   **g** 7.80   **h** 843.25   **i** $7\frac{1}{2}$ **j** 1653

2 Here are the lengths in millimetres of 27 cuckoo eggs being hatched in a sanctuary. Draw a stem and leaf diagram for this data.

22.3	19.6	23.8	24.0	22.1	21.0	24.4	20.1	21.3
22.4	23.1	20.9	24.1	25.0	20.4	23.4	24.2	23.0
22.6	22.7	22.5	24.0	22.3	23.6	23.8	22.0	22.4

3 Here are the arm span in centimetres of 30 pupils. Draw a stem and leaf diagram for this data.

168	180	146	159	182	160	155	171	168	160
147	156	175	170	157	165	170	164	173	154
169	158	164	161	163	166	175	149	178	173

4 Here are the weights in grams of 24 letters and parcels at the post office. Draw a stem and leaf diagram for this data.

72	84	79	60	87	92	65	62
80	75	98	84	75	62	90	74
76	90	77	61	87	64	93	81

5 The volume in centilitres of 50 bottles of fizzy drink. Draw a stem and leaf diagram for this data.

29.91	29.63	29.95	30.22	30.08	30.39	29.97	30.27	29.47	29.77
30.48	29.73	29.82	29.51	30.17	29.79	30.05	29.89	29.85	29.96
30.36	29.93	30.02	30.06	29.81	30.32	29.93	30.33	30.04	29.84
30.29	29.67	29.55	29.90	30.16	29.78	29.66	30.22	29.90	30.14
30.45	29.52	29.74	29.83	30.11	30.34	29.98	30.24	29.99	30.01

6 The circumference (in centimetres) of 60 girls' heads. Draw a stem and leaf diagram for this data.

54.8	51.9	55.5	52.6	57.5	54.5	55.9	53.4	52.7	49.6
53.8	53.4	55.1	55.4	57.0	54.2	51.4	56.1	53.9	53.5
51.6	57.3	51.8	52.3	50.3	55.8	52.5	56.3	53.7	54.6
55.2	52.1	50.2	54.0	49.9	54.6	56.6	54.3	56.7	56.3
51.2	54.4	57.1	58.2	55.3	54.1	56.7	53.2	55.7	54.9
55.8	54.5	50.7	49.8	55.6	52.9	54.2	50.0	53.0	52.6

A stem and leaf diagram is a kind of frequency chart. The diagram shows the data in order of size. It can be used to find the mode, the median and the range.

Example   This stem and leaf diagram shows the heart rate (beats per minute) of 23 boys.

Stem	Leaf
4	9
5	3 8 8
6	0 1 7 9
7	2 2 2 4 5 6 6 7
8	3 5 6 8 9
9	0 4

Key

4 | 9   means 49 beats per minute

72 appears the most. Therefore the **mode** is 72. The modal group is 70 – 79.

To find the median heart rate we need to find the pupil who lies in the middle. The 12th number in this data is the middle value. Therefore the median heart beats per minute is 74.

The **range** is the highest number minus the lowest number. The range in this data is $94 - 49 = 45$

Exercise 4:8

1 Miss Fremah wanted to find out how long her pupils take to solve an algebra problem. The stem and leaf diagram shows these times in seconds.

Stem	Leaf
3	7 8
4	0 1 1 4 5
5	3 4 4 5 5 5 8
6	1 3 4 5 6
7	2 2 4 6

Key

3 | 7   means 37 seconds

Use this diagram to find:
a the mode   **b** the median time   **c** the range

2 An obstetrician in a hospital recorded the weights of 22 babies. The stem and leaf diagram shows the weights in kilograms.

Stem	Leaf
1.	6 7 8 8
2.	2 4 6 8 9
3.	0 3 5 6 6 6 8 9
4.	0 1 3 5 7

Key

1. | 6   means 1.6 kg

Use this diagram to find:
a the mode   **b** the median weight   **c** the range

101

3 Mr Bonsu is a tailor.
He measures the heights of 31 boys
in centimetres to make school uniforms.

Rearrange the table and find:

a the modal interval

b the median height

c the modal height

d the range.

Stem	Leaf
13	8
14	5 2 2 3
14	9 6 8 4 5
15	4 1 4 3 0 3 2
15	6 9 6 8 6
16	2 4 1 1 3
16	9 7
17	3 0

Key

13 | 8 means 138 cm

4 At the end of a term Class 2B did a mathematics
test and were given a percentage. These are
their results. Use the data to:

a produce a stem and leaf diagram with a key.

b find: **i** the mode

  ii the median mark

  iii the range of the marks

81	57	52	91	74	70
68	56	68	24	45	35
65	49	54	48	69	96
58	83	58	73	51	29
63	89	66	57	68	77

**Back to back
stem and leaf
diagrams**

Two stem and leaf diagrams can be drawn on the same stem.
This is called a **back to back stem and leaf diagram**.
It is used to compare two sets of data.
The leaves of one set of data are put on the right stem.
The leaves of the other sets of data are put on the left stem.

Example

a Make a back to back stem and leaf diagram of the results of these
two science tests taken by 19 pupils.

b Find the mode, median and the range of each paper.

Paper 1

98	82	36	50	67	43	39
64	73	83	51	70	74	71
81	87	64	83	48		

Paper 2

70	64	39	44	46	90	53
72	71	48	57	82	65	63
84	55	78	65	69		

a

Leaf	Stem	Leaf
Paper 1		Paper 2
9 6	3	9
8 3	4	4 6 8
1 0	5	3 5 7
7 4 4	6	3 4 5 5 9
4 3 1 0	7	0 1 2 8
7 5 3 2 1	8	2 4
8	9	0

Key

6 | 3 | 9 means 36 marks on paper 1
  and 39 marks on paper 2

b For paper 1: the mode is 64
  the median is 70
  the range is 98 − 36 = 62
  modal class is 80 − 89

For paper 2: the mode is 65
  the median is 65
  the range is 90 − 39 = 51
  modal class is 60 − 69

Exercise 4:9

1 Use a back to back stem and leaf
   diagram to find:
   a the median
   b the mode and
   c the range of these two test results.
   Key

   0 | 1 | 1   means 10 marks on history
           and   11 marks on physics

History		Physics
6 3 0	1	1 4
7 6 5 4	2	3 4 6 7
9 8 4 2 2	3	0 1 2 4 5 6 7
8 7 6 5 3 1 0	4	4 5 6 7 8 9
6 3 2 1 0	5	0 2 3 4 4
9 8 5	6	0 1 2

2 Adama and Yeboah visited a zoo with their parents who wanted to compare the time (to
   the nearest tenth of a minute) each spent watching an animal.
   Draw a back to back stem and leaf diagram to compare the data. Find the mode and median.

   Adama   5.3   5.7   2.4   5.8   4.5   3.2   2.3   2.5   5.5   4.3
   Yeboah   4.5   5.4   4.6   5.2   5.5   3.8   3.6   4.3   4.1   3.8

3 Akua wanted to find out the height of pupils in her class. She measured the height in
   centimetres.

   Girls   Boys

   155   149   181   175   170   166   182   170   158   148   169   157
   166   156   177   154   166   160   176   174   183   167   175   179
   173   167   168   166   159   156   165   178   166   170

   a Draw a back to back stem and leaf diagram to compare the heights of the girls and the
      boys. Use 14, 15, 16, ...,..., as the stems.
   b Find the median and the modal height of the girls.
   c Find the median and the modal height of the boys.
   d Find the range of heights for the girls and the boys.

4 The diameter (mm) of steel components drilled by two machine operators, Musah and
   Azumah was checked by an inspector in an engineering company.

   Musah's drilled components   Azumah's drilled components

   20.27   20.47   20.64   20.08   20.30   20.10   20.25   20.63   20.48   20.04
   20.01   20.16   20.52   19.89   19.93   19.72   20.57   20.43   20.43   20.02
   19.98   20.39   20.04   19.94   19.71   19.91   20.51   20.32   20.17   20.34
   20.13   20.37   20.13   20.05   19.84   19.98   19.84   19.89   20.14   20.41
   20.28   20.07   20.14   20.60   20.85   20.37   20.52   20.21   19.82   20.44
   20.25   19.87   20.02   20.12   19.90   20.15   20.22   20.24   20.02   20.31

   a Draw a back to back stem and leaf diagram to compare the work done by the two
      machine operators.
   b Find the modal group for each operator's work.
   c Find the mode, median and the range of the diameter of Musah's components.
   d Find the mode, median and the range of the diameter of Azumah's components.
   e Does the mode or median give the better value for the average? Explain.

8 Pie charts

Pie Chart A **pie chart** is a circle which is divided into slices. Each slice is called a **sector** which represents one group of data. The size of each sector depends upon what fraction of the total each group is. The size of the sector corresponds to the frequency of the set of data. The total angle of the pie is 360°. The angle of each sector is a fraction of 360°.
A pie chart is also known as **circular diagram**.

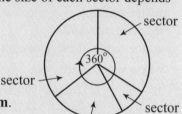

Examples **a**

This shows how pupils travel to school.

This shows pupils' favourite type of music.

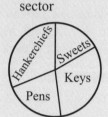

This shows the type of articles in peoples' pockets.

b In a survey 30 people were asked to name their favourite colour.
The table shows the results of the survey in a frequency table.

Colour	Frequency
Green	8
Red	12
Blue	6
Yellow	4

Step 1 Find the fraction of 360° which represents each primary colour:

8 out of 30 or $\frac{8}{30}$ named green.

$\frac{8}{30}$ of 360° = $\frac{8}{30} \times 360 = 96°$ ∴ the angle of the green sector is 96°.

We can work out the other angles in the same way:

red: $\frac{12}{30} \times 360 = 144°$ blue: $\frac{6}{30} \times 360 = 72°$ yellow: $\frac{4}{30} \times 360 = 48°$

Step 2 Using a protractor draw a pie chart with these angles at the centres of the sectors.

Draw a radius on the circle.

Use a protractor to measure a 96° angle from the radius. Draw a sector and label it Green.

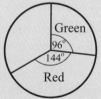

Use a protractor to measure a 144° angle from the last line. Draw a sector and label it Red.

Use a protractor to measure a 72° angle from the last line. Draw a sector and label it Blue. Check that the last sector is 48° and label it Yellow. Make sure the total is 360°.

Exercise 4:10

1 40 students in a university campus were asked in which region of Ghana they were born:
Northern, Volta, Ashanti or Central region.
Work out how many students were born in each region.

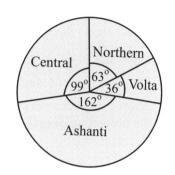

2

This pie chart shows the favourite lessons of 72 Form 2 pupils in a Junior high school in Sunyani.
Work out how many pupils liked each subject.

3 A farmer's yield of each crops per hectare in 2008 was:

Crop yield	Corn	Rice	Beans	Maize	Onions
Weight (tonnes)	2.5	1.5	1.8	1	2.2

a Work out the angles for a pie chart.
b Draw a circle of radius 4 cm.
c Draw the pie chart to show the information. Label it carefully.

Sometimes it is easier to show the calculations on a table.

Example Ekow collected data on the colour of 40 cars being sold in a car showroom.
The table shows the results of his survey.

Colour of car	White	Green	Blue	Black	Red
Frequency	13	10	6	5	11

Draw a circle of radius 5 cm and draw a pie chart to show the information

Work out the fraction of 360° which represents the colour of cars in a table shown. Check that all the angles add up to 360°

Colour of car	Frequency	Calculation	Angle
White	13	$\frac{13}{45} \times 360° = 104°$	104°
Green	10	$\frac{10}{45} \times 360° = 80°$	80°
Blue	6	$\frac{6}{45} \times 360° = 48°$	48°
Black	5	$\frac{5}{45} \times 360° = 40°$	40°
Red	11	$\frac{11}{45} \times 360° = 88°$	88°

Total angles = 104° + 80° + 48° + 40° + 88° = 360°

4

4 A survey was carried out about the type of soup that 160 people liked best. The table shows the results of the survey.

a Copy and complete the table.

b Draw a circle of radius 3.5 cm.

c Draw and label a pie chart to show the proportion of each soup.

Soup	Frequency	Calculation	Angle
Palm nut	28		
Spinach	20		
Peanut		$\frac{\ \ \ }{160} \times 360° =$	
Fish	36		
Meat	32		

5 Data supplied by a survey of 120 people will be used in various pie charts.

Copy and complete the table for some of the sectors.

Number of people	Angle
120	360°
50	
100	
76	
	321°
11	
	207°
98	
	195°
119	

Using a circle of radius 3 cm draw and label pie charts to represent each of these sets of data.

6 The favourite sports of 90 pupils

Sport	Athletics	Football	Table tennis	Draughts
Frequency	14	34	25	17

7 Type of newspapers read by 96 women

Newspaper	Daily Graphic	The Times	Pioneer	The Mirror	Daily Guide
Frequency	14	34	25	17	6

8 Shoe sizes of 144 boys in a school

Shoe sizes	6 & 6½	7 & 7½	8 & 8½	9 & 9½	10 & 10½
Frequency	31	44	32	20	17

EXTENSION

1 The data gives the diameter of machine parts produced in Precision Engineering Company.

 a Write down the class interval for the first class.

 b Illustrate the data on a bar chart.

Diameter (mm)	Frequency
24.90 – 24.92	13
24.93 – 24.95	17
24.96 – 24.98	22
24.99 – 25.01	28
25.02 – 25.04	21
25.05 – 25.07	9

2 The passage shown was taken from a chapter from page 4 of the book "Topics in West African History" by Prof Adu Boahen.

> ... Ghana was the first of these kingdoms to emerge and to attain the greatest fame and glory. It was probably in existence by A.D. 500 and had attained the peak of its power by the middle of the eleventh century. By then it extended over an area now occupied by the three independent states of Senegal, Mauritania, and Mali. Many Arabic scholars and merchants collected and wrote up accounts from traders who had visited Ghana as well as from Ghanaians visiting the coast. The best known of these scholars were Al-Bakri and Al-Idrisu who wrote their description of Ghana in 1067 just when the empire was at the height of its power and in 1154, respectively....

 a Count the number of letters in each word in the excerpt using the groups: 1 and 2, 3 and 4, 5 and 6, ..., ..., 11 and 12 and draw up a frequency table for the data.

 b Draw a bar chart to illustrate the data.

3 The areas of the seven continents of the world are given in the table.

Continent	Area (1 000 000 km²)
Europe	10
Asia	44
Africa	30
North America	24
South America	18
Australia	8
Antarctica	14

Display this data by means of a pie chart.

4 Give the inclusive class interval for each of these (round to 1 d.p.).
(*Example*: The class interval for: 38.45 – 48.44 is 9.99.)

 a $2.5 \leq x < 5.5$
  $5.5 \leq x < 8.5$

 b from 201.5 up to 201.9
  from 210.0 up to 210.4

 c 0.545 – 0.644
  0.645 – 0.744

 d 5 –
  11 –

 e 100 –
  200 –

 f 1 – 500
  501 – 1000

5 The following data show the age distribution of an area in Accra.

Age in (years)	Frequency
15 up to 20	62
21 up to 25	97
26 up to 30	210
31 up to 35	247
36 up to 40	196

Age in (years)	Frequency
41 up to 45	70
46 up to 50	83
51 up to 55	65
56 up to 60	18
61 up to 65	19

Display the data by means of a block diagram.

6 Use the data of Nimoh's survey about peoples' favourite football clubs to draw a pie chart.

Football Club	Olympics	Hearts	Kotoko	Arsenal	BA United
Number of pupils	14	34	25	17	2

7 Bole junior high school organised a sports day at the end of the school term.
These are the results of the shot putt competition. The distances are measured in metres.

Girls' results

11.2	6.3	7.9	10.0	9.4
6.2	8.8	9.0	10.5	8.7
9.5	10.4	9.6	7.4	8.2
9.6	8.2	8.8	6.7	6.9
8.5	7.8	9.0	8.0	9.9
9.6	8.3	8.9	7.0	7.7
7.2	8.1	11.7	7.5	10.6

Boys' results

10.7	6.8	12.7	12.2	11.0
10.2	8.9	10.3	9.7	12.5
7.9	9.2	9.8	7.3	9.4
7.6	8.4	11.1	10.9	10.9
8.3	11.9	9.6	10.8	10.7
11.5	12.8	9.5	8.2	12.4
10.9	10.5	11.3	11.7	11.0

a Draw a back to back stem and leaf diagram to compare the distances of girls and boys. Write down the key to the diagram.

b Find the median, mode and the range of the time for: **i** the girls   **ii** the boys

c Does the median or the mode give the better value to represent the data for the girls and the boys. Explain your answer.

8 The table shows the marital status of adult males in a certain area of Ghana at a particular time. Display the data on a pie chart.

Marital status	Male
Single	27%
Married	36%
Widowed	18%
Divorced	12%
Other	7%

9 These are the main chemical elements that make up the Earth's crust:

Oxygen - 47%   Silicon - 28%   Aluminium - 8%   Iron - 5%

Potassium - 2.5%   Calcium - 3.5%   Others - 6%

Illustrate the data on a pie chart.

10 The percentage of weights in kilograms of 154 patients in a hospital are shown in the table.

Weight (kg)	Percentage of patients
$30 \leq w < 40$	10%
$40 \leq w < 50$	14%
$50 \leq w < 60$	33%
$60 \leq w < 70$	28%
$70 \leq w < 80$	15%

a Work out the number of people (to the nearest whole number) in each group.

b Find the angle of each sector needed to draw a pie chart.

c Draw the pie chart to illustrate the data.

11 The table gives the average hours in a certain week that male and female farmers in different towns in Ghana spent working.

a Draw a back to back stem and leaf diagram to compare the hours of male and female farmers.

b Find the modal group for both males and females.

c Find the mode median and the range of the hours that males worked.

d Find the mode, median and the range of the hours that females worked.

	Hours	
Towns	**Males**	**Females**
Mankranso	47.5	47.0
Yendi	45.2	42.8
Kunkwa	43.8	43.5
Anomabu	42.3	43.8
Ejura	46.9	44.7
Dunkwa	47.8	46.4
Bogoso	45.6	44.1
Bango	42.9	42.0
Dawa	44.6	45.6
Ofoase	45.5	44.3
Yeji	43.9	43.4
Zoggo	43.8	42.6
Kenyasi	46.8	45.4
Ada	46.7	45.8
Paga	44.3	44.9
Asuboa	45.7	45.0
Kumawu	45.0	44.2
Tsito	46.3	46.1
Esaase	47.2	44.8
Wenchi	45.5	43.8
Atebubu	44.8	44.0

12 Use this data to draw a circular diagram showing the angle of the sector of each crop.

Crop yield	Corn	Rice	Beans	Peppers	Okra
tonnes	3	1	2	0.5	0.5

109

SUMMARY

Data	The word **data** means information or facts about something, usually in the form of number. Singular for the word data is *datum* - it is not often used.

Primary data	Data that is collected by the person who is going to use the data.
Secondary data	Data that is already collected or processed.
Statistics	The collection and arrangement of data.
Qualitative data	Data which is described in words. The data values are not numerical.
Quantitative data	Data that can be measured or counted.
Discrete data	Data which can be counted and has exact value.
Continuous data	Data which is measured or weighed and can have values within a certain range.

Tally	A method of counting in fives using strokes, e.g. ⊁⊁ or ⊠.
Tally table	A table used to help record numbers of items.
Frequency	The number of times something occurs.
Frequency table	a table showing the number of times something has occurred.

Three methods are used to collect data.

Sampling	Taking a few out of the whole population.
Observation	- Noticing something happening and recording the information.
Experiment	- Trying and testing something unknown in order to collect data.

Class interval	is a subdivision of the total range of values
Open-ended classes	Sometimes the last group does not have an upper limit. It is left **open-ended**. It is called an **open-ended class**.

Lower class limit **Group**

21 - 30

Upper class limit

Examples	**a** > 25	**b** above 40	**c** greater than 10	**d** ≥ 29.5

Axis	A fixed reference line used to mark the scale for the measurement of coordinates of a graph is called an **axis**.

Title
Vertical axis
Horizontal axis

Bar chart	is a diagram made up of bars of equal width drawn either vertically (upright) or horizontally (sideways) from an axis. A bar chart is sometimes called a **bar graph**.
Bar line	is very similar to a bar chart except that it uses a line instead of a bar.
Block graph	**Block graph** (or block diagram) is similar to a bar chart but with blocks or rectangles touching each other. The data can be discrete as well as continuous.

Stem and leaf diagram	A **stem and leaf** diagram organises data to show its shape and distribution. Each item is split into "*stem*" and "*leaf*".

Pie Chart	A **pie chart** is a circle which is divided into slices. Each slice is called a **sector** and it represents one group of data. The angle of each sector is a fraction of $360°$ proportional to the size of the data.

Rational and irrational numbers

EXTENSION

SUMMARY

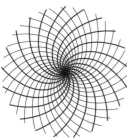

The daisy flower can have 21 clockwise and 34 anticlockwise spirals as shown.

The shell of the chambered nautilus looks similar to the spiral.

The Fibonacci numbers are 1, 1, 2, 3, 5, 8, 13, 21, 34, 55, 89, 144, 233, ..., ...

The ratios $\frac{1}{1}$, $\frac{2}{1}$, $\frac{3}{2}$, $\frac{5}{3}$, $\frac{8}{5}$, $\frac{13}{8}$, $\frac{21}{13}$, $\frac{34}{21}$, $\frac{55}{34}$, $\frac{89}{55}$.

$\frac{144}{89}$, $\frac{233}{144}$, ..., ..., ..., go to phi $\quad \varphi = \frac{1 + \sqrt{5}}{2}$

The ratio approaches 1.61803 39887 49894 84820 45868 34365
63811 77203 09179 80576 28621 354 ...

This value is the **Golden ratio** and it is an **irrational number**.

These are golden rectangles using the fractions above.

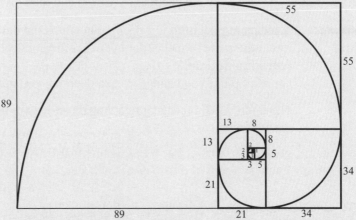

This spiral is based on the Golden ratio. Natural examples occur on the shell of the chambered nautilus mollusc and the daisy flower.

1 Terminating and recurring decimals

A fraction can be written as a decimal by dividing the numerator (top number) by the denominator (bottom number).

Example $\frac{3}{16} = 3 \div 16 = 0.1875$ (The answer is exactly 0.1875).

Terminating decimal   A **terminating decimal** is a decimal which has a fixed number of decimal places. A terminating decimal occurs when the denominator divides exactly into the numerator.

Examples   **a** Change $\frac{1}{4}$ and $\frac{7}{8}$ into decimals.

$$\frac{1}{4} = 1 \div 4 = 4\overline{\smash{)}1.0_20} \quad\quad \frac{0.25}{}$$

$$= 0.25$$

$$\frac{7}{8} = 7 \div 8 = 8\overline{\smash{)}7.0_60_40} \quad\quad \frac{0.875}{}$$

$$= 0.875$$

Every terminating decimal can be converted into a fraction.

Examples   **b** Convert 0.25 into a fraction.

0.25 has two decimal places
∴ we multiply it by 100,
divide the result by 100 and
then simplify the fraction.

$0.25 \times 100 = 25$

$\frac{25}{100} = \frac{1}{4}$ (cancel out by 25)

c Convert 0.875 into a fraction

0.875 has three decimal places
∴ we multiply it by 1000,
divide the result by 1000 and
then simplify the fraction.

$$\frac{0.875 \times 1000}{1000} = \frac{875}{1000} = \frac{7}{8}$$

In general to convert a decimal which terminates after:

1 decimal place: → multiply the decimal by 10 and then divide the result by 10.
2 decimal places: → multiply the decimal by 100 and then divide the result by 100.
3 decimal places: → multiply the decimal by 1000 and then divide the result by 1000.
4 decimal places: → multiply the decimal by 10000 and then divide the result by 10000.

Recurring decimal   A **recurring decimal** is a decimal in which the digits after the decimal point repeat the same sequence for ever. A recurring decimal is also known as a **repeating decimal**.
For example if you change $\frac{7}{11}$ to a decimal, you get: 0.6363636363636363 ...

The figures '63' repeats or occur again and again for ever as shown in this short division.

Simply $\frac{7}{11} = 7 \div 11 = 11\overline{\smash{)}7.0_40_70_40_70_40_70_40_70_40...} \quad\quad 0.6\,3\,6\,3\,6\,3\,6\,3\,6\,3...$

$$= 0.\overset{..}{6}\overset{}{3}$$

The recurring decimal is written in short with dots at the top of the repeating decimal digits.

Examples $0.555555... = 0.\dot{5}$ $2.090909... = 2.\dot{0}\dot{9}$ $7.08162162.... = 7.08\dot{1}6\dot{2}$

Exercise 5:1

Convert these fractions into decimals;

1 $\frac{1}{4}$ **2** $\frac{3}{5}$ **3** $\frac{1}{5}$ **4** $\frac{3}{8}$

5 $\frac{5}{8}$ **6** $\frac{5}{16}$ **7** $\frac{1}{32}$ **8** $1\frac{13}{20}$

Convert these decimals into fractions and simplify the results:

9   0.6   **10**   0.14   **11**   0.23   **12**   0.123

13   0.125   **14**   0.85   **15**   2.12   **16**   4.275

17   Write out these recurring decimals in short:

    a   0.222222...   **b**   1.13513513...   **c**   6.01474747...   **d**   9.1487148714...

    e   3.017471471...   **f**   8.093325325...   **g**   8.11457145714...   **h**   10.892189218...

18   Write out the recurring decimals which are equivalent to the following:

    a $\frac{1}{3}, \frac{2}{3}$ **b** $\frac{2}{11}, \frac{3}{11}, \frac{4}{11}$ **c** $\frac{2}{9}, \frac{4}{9}, \frac{2}{3}, \frac{8}{9}$ **d** $\frac{1}{7}, \frac{2}{7}, \frac{3}{7}, \frac{4}{7}$

    Explain the relationship between the pattern of the recurring decimals.

Finding a fraction equivalent to a recurring decimal

Every recurring decimal can be converted into a fraction.

Examples   **a**   Change 0.63636363... into a fraction   **b**   Change 0.425425... into a fraction.

       Let $x = 0.63636363$ i   Let $x = 0.425425$ i

       Multiply by 100   Multiply by 100

       $100x = 63.636363$ ......   ii $100x = 425.425425$ ii

       Subtract (i) from (ii)   Subtract (i) from (ii)

       $100x - x = 63.636363 - 0.63636363$ $100x - x = 425.425425 - 0.425425$

           $99x = 63$ $999x = 425$

         $\therefore \ x = \frac{63}{99}$ $\therefore \ x = \frac{425}{999}$

            $= \frac{7}{11}$

Generally to find the equivalent fraction of a recurring decimal:

If the recurring part is a tenth, divide the digits by 9,
If the recurring part is a hundredth, divide the digits by 99,
If the recurring part is a thousandth, divide the digits by 999,
If the recurring part is a ten thousandth, divide the digits by 9999,
If the recurring part is a hundred thousandth, divide the digits by 99 999.

Always simplify your fraction where possible.

Exercise 5:2

Find the fractions which are equivalent to these recurring decimals:
Write each fraction in its simplest form.

1 0.333333...　　　　**2** 0.666666 ...　　　　**3** 0.212121 ...　　　　**4** 0.87878787 ...

5 0.75757575 ...　　　**6** 0.909090 ...　　　　**7** 0.18181818 ...　　　**8** 0.129129129 ...

9 0.153153153 ...　　**10** 0.089108910891...　**11** 2.125125125 ...　**12** 4.1279112791....

Sometimes only part of a decimal recurs. A recurring decimal can be changed into a fraction.

Example　　　　Write 0.678787878 ... as a fraction

The first digit does not recur but the next two digits do.
We have to split the decimal into two parts

$$0.6\dot{7}\dot{8} = 0.6 + 0.0\dot{7}\dot{8}$$

$$= 0.6 + 0.\dot{7}\dot{8} \div 10 \qquad \text{dividing by 10 moves the digit one decimal place to the right}$$

$$= \frac{6}{10} + \frac{78}{99} \div 10 \qquad \left(\frac{78}{99} \div 10 = \frac{78}{990}\right)$$

$$= \frac{6}{10} + \frac{78}{990}$$

$$= \frac{6 \times 99 + 78}{990} \qquad \text{add the fractions using 990 as the lowest common multiple}$$

$$= \frac{672}{990}$$

$$= \frac{112}{165}$$

13 Write these recurring decimals as fractions:

　　a 0.7$\dot{8}$　　　　**b** 0.3$\dot{2}$　　　　**c** 0.5$\dot{3}$　　　　**d** 0.1$\dot{6}\dot{4}$

　　e 0.7$\dot{5}\dot{1}$　　　**f** 0.5$\dot{7}\dot{8}$　　　**g** 0.5$\dot{2}6\dot{1}$　　**h** 5.7$\dot{2}\dot{1}$

　　i 2.4$\dot{1}\dot{3}$　　　**j** 0.8$\dot{1}9\dot{5}$　　**k** 0.3$\dot{1}2\dot{6}$　　**l** 22.8$\dot{4}7\dot{5}$

*14 Write each of these in the form $\dfrac{m}{n}$ where m and n are integers with no common factors:

　　a 0.$\dot{3}$　　　　**b** 0.$\dot{1}42\dot{6}$　　　**c** 0.0$\dot{9}$　　　　**d** $\dfrac{\sqrt{36}}{\sqrt{121}}$

2   Rational numbers

Georg Cantor 1845 - 1918
Born in St Petersburg Russia

Georg Cantor, a Russian-born German, introduced new modes of thinking concerning the nature of number. He demonstrated that rational numbers though infinite are countable. He argued that infinite numbers have actual existence. He based his ideas on ancient and medieval philosophy and his religious training given him by his parents.

Cantor wrote in 1867 that "in mathematics the art of asking is more valuable than solving problems".

Real number   A **real number** is a number which can be written as a decimal (including a non-terminating decimal) whether positive or negative. This includes the roots of all positive numbers.
The symbol for a set of real numbers is **R**.   **R** = {real numbers}.

Infinite series   A series which continues infinitely without stopping is called an **infinite series**, e.g. $\sqrt{2} = 1.414213562...$

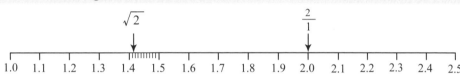

Rational number   A **rational number** is a number which can be written as a fraction in the the form $\frac{a}{b}$ where a and b are whole numbers and $b \neq 0$.

For example $\frac{3}{5}$ is a rational number. A rational number is cancelled into its simplest form if a and b have no common factor.
The symbol for a set of rational numbers is **Q**.   **Q** = {rational numbers}

Example   Explain why each of these numbers is a rational number:

$$\frac{2}{3} \qquad \sqrt{16} \qquad 0.55 \qquad 2\tfrac{1}{2} \qquad 4.\dot{7}$$

$\frac{2}{3}$ is rational since it is in the form $\frac{a}{b}$ where a and b are whole numbers.

$\sqrt{16}$ can be simplified to $\frac{4}{1}$ therefore it is rational.

0.55 is rational since it is a terminating decimal which can be written as $\frac{11}{20}$.

$2\tfrac{1}{2}$ is a rational number which can be written as $\frac{5}{2}$.

$4.\dot{7}$ is rational since it is a recurring decimal which can be written as $4\tfrac{7}{9}$

or $\frac{43}{9}$.

Properties of rational numbers

1   Given two rational numbers a and b, there are three possibilities: $a = b$ or $a < b$ or $a > b$.

2   The sum of two rational numbers is another rational number.

3   The product of two rational numbers is another rational number.

4   With the exception of zero, the reciprocal of every rational number is also a rational number.

Exercise 5:3

1 Express these rational numbers in the form $\frac{a}{b}$:

    a 0.6   **b** 0.5   **c** $2\frac{1}{3}$ **d** 1.05   **e** 2.7   **f** $1\frac{11}{12}$

2 Write four rational numbers which lie between 4 and 5.

3 Express these as rational numbers, in the form $\frac{a}{b}$:

    a 0.24   **b** 0.3   **c** 0.125   **d** 0.805   **e** 2.06   **f** 0.057

4 Write two rational numbers between these pairs of numbers:

    a 7.84 and 7.85   **b** $\frac{2}{5}$ and $\frac{3}{4}$ **c** 8.2 and $\frac{37}{4}$ **d** 11% and 11.2%

5 Write down the rational numbers which represent each of these sets of equivalent fractions:

    a $\left\{ ...., \frac{-2}{-8}, \frac{-3}{-12}, \frac{-5}{-20}, \frac{-8}{-24}, ... \right\}$ **b** $\left\{ ...., \frac{-1}{-5}, \frac{1}{5}, \frac{2}{10}, \frac{4}{20}, ... \right\}$

    c $\left\{ ...., \frac{-6}{-14}, \frac{30}{70}, \frac{15}{35}, \frac{12}{28}, ... \right\}$ **d** $\left\{ ...., \frac{10}{30}, \frac{30}{90}, \frac{50}{150}, \frac{70}{210}, ... \right\}$

    e $\left\{ ...., \frac{-12}{-30}, 0.4, \frac{18}{45}, \sqrt{0.16} .... \right\}$ **f** $\left\{ ...., \frac{-6}{-24}, 25\%, \sqrt{\frac{25}{400}}, \frac{11}{44}, ... \right\}$

6 Which of these are rational numbers?

    a 5   **b** 1.312861....   **c** $\frac{3}{8}$ **d** $\sqrt{36}$ **e** 0.75   **f** $-\frac{13}{52}$ **h** $\sqrt[3]{36}$

Comparing the sizes of rational numbers

One way to compare rational numbers is to change them into a decimal form.
The sizes of 0.33 and $\frac{1}{4}$ can be compared easily if they are all expressed in decimals.
    $\frac{1}{4} = 0.25$ therefore we can say that 0.33 is bigger than 0.25.

Exercise 5:4

1 Copy and complete these by replacing ? with < (less than) or > (more than) or = (equal to):

    a 2.405 ? 2.45   **b** $\frac{1}{2}$? $\frac{1}{3}$ **c** $\sqrt{36}$? 5.98

    d $\sqrt{1}$? $\sqrt{1.21}$ **e** 0.0025 ? $\sqrt{0.25}$ **f** 0.809 ? 0.89

    g 0.3233 ? $\frac{34}{51}$ **h** $\frac{\sqrt{4}}{5}$? $\frac{1}{\sqrt{4}}$ **i** $\frac{7}{\sqrt{100}}$? $\frac{\sqrt{36}}{24}$

2 Put these rational numbers in order, the smallest first:

a 0.75, 0.802, 0.507, 0.299, 0.087

b $\dfrac{3}{4}$, $\dfrac{11}{110}$, $\dfrac{1}{3}$, $\dfrac{15}{60}$, $\dfrac{4}{5}$

c 1.108, 1.08, 1.084, 1.18, 1.008

d $\dfrac{8}{20}$, $\dfrac{1}{3}$, $\dfrac{10}{50}$, $\dfrac{3}{4}$, $\dfrac{6}{100}$

e 2.5, $3\frac{3}{10}$, $1\frac{3}{5}$, 3.31, 0.9

f $\dfrac{1}{2}$, 0.33, 0.1, $\dfrac{1}{8}$, $\dfrac{2}{3}$

3 Put these rational numbers in order, the biggest first:

a $\sqrt{16}$, $\sqrt{0.16}$, $\sqrt{0.0016}$, $\sqrt{1600}$, $\sqrt{100}$

b 0.44, 0.404, 0.444, 0.04, 0.4

c $\dfrac{3}{5}$, $\dfrac{5}{3}$, $\dfrac{9}{10}$, $\dfrac{4}{5}$, $\dfrac{10}{9}$

d 0.77, $\dfrac{1}{5}$, 0.616, $\dfrac{2}{3}$, 0.166

e 1.2, 3.5, $\frac{1}{10}$, $2\frac{1}{10}$, $2\frac{3}{5}$

f $\sqrt{81}$, $\dfrac{\sqrt{4}}{\sqrt{9}}$, $\dfrac{\sqrt{49}}{\sqrt{100}}$, $\dfrac{50}{\sqrt{25}}$, $\left(\sqrt{8}\right)^2$

Operations on rational numbers

Work out these: **a** $\dfrac{5}{8} + \sqrt{16}$ **b** $0.944 - \dfrac{1}{\sqrt{4}}$ **c** $\sqrt{\dfrac{25}{100}} \div \dfrac{1}{4}$

a $\dfrac{5}{8} + \sqrt{16} = 0.625 + 4$

$= 4.625$

b $0.944 - \dfrac{1}{\sqrt{4}} = 0.944 - \dfrac{1}{2}$

$= 0.944 - 0.5$

$= 0.444$

c $\sqrt{\dfrac{25}{100}} \div \dfrac{1}{4} = \dfrac{5}{10} \div \dfrac{1}{4}$

$= \dfrac{1}{2} \times \dfrac{4}{1}$

$= 2$

Note: $\sqrt{a \times b} = \sqrt{a} \times \sqrt{b}$ $\sqrt{\dfrac{a}{b}} = \dfrac{\sqrt{a}}{\sqrt{b}}$ $a\sqrt{b} = a \times \sqrt{b}$

Exercise 5:5

Work out the following:

1 $\sqrt{9} + \sqrt{4}$

2 $4.3 + \sqrt{1}$

3 $5.07 - \sqrt{25}$

4 $\dfrac{3}{8} - \dfrac{\sqrt{4}}{5}$

5 $0.\dot{7} + \sqrt{4} + 0.5$

6 $5\sqrt{4} \times \sqrt{25}$

7 $\left(\sqrt{13}\right)^2 \times \sqrt{4}$

8 $4.414 - \sqrt{0.04}$

9 $\dfrac{3 \times \sqrt{81}}{\sqrt{36}}$

10 $\dfrac{-10}{4} \times \dfrac{10}{\sqrt{4}}$

11 $\sqrt{\dfrac{100}{625}} \div \sqrt{\dfrac{100}{25}}$

12 $\left(\sqrt{4} \times \sqrt{4}\right) - \left(\sqrt{4} \times \sqrt{4}\right)$

13 $(17 - \sqrt{36}) - (15 + \sqrt{49})$

14 $\sqrt{\dfrac{1}{64}} + \sqrt{\dfrac{1}{16}} + \sqrt{\dfrac{100}{625}}$

15 $\left(\dfrac{3}{8}\right)^2 \times \sqrt{\dfrac{36}{81}} \div \dfrac{\sqrt{16}}{27}$

3 Properties of operation on rational numbers

Operation   A rule by which the elements of one or more sets can produce a new set of elements is called an **operation**.

Binary operation   An operation on the elements of two sets at a time is a **binary operation**.

Commutative law   In a binary operation $*$ on two elements a and b if $a * b = a * b$ the operation is said to be **commutative**.

Examples   **i** $a + b = b + a$ **ii** $7 + 5 = 5 + 7 = 12$

           $\therefore$ addition is commutative

Exercise 5:6

1   Work out the following and state whether the operation is commutative.

a $7 + 8$	**b** $15 - 5$	**c** $13 + 4$	**d** $11 - 6$
e $12 - 19$	**f** $18 \div 3$	**g** 17×3	**h** $12 \div 4$
i 3×12	**j** $51 \div 17$	**k** $4 - 9$	**l** -3×6

Associative law   When we are able to pair (or associate) numbers under an operation and get the same answer, we say that the operation is associative or that the operation obeys the **associative law**.
If the answers in the operation are different the operation does not obey the associative law. Brackets are used to show the order of arithmetic operation on each pair of numbers.

Example $5 \times 4 \times 2 = 5 \times (4 \times 2)$ $\left\{ \begin{array}{l} \text{Multiply 4 by 2 to get 8 and then multiply} \\ \text{this answer by 5.} \end{array} \right\}$
                   $= 5 \times 8$
                   $= 40$
      Also $5 \times 4 \times 2 = (5 \times 4) \times 2$ $\left\{ \begin{array}{l} \text{Multiply 5 by 4 to get 20 and then multiply} \\ \text{this answer by 2.} \end{array} \right\}$
                        $= 20 \times 2$
                        $= 40$

2   Work out the following and state whether the operation obeys the associative law.

a $8 \times 2 \times 5$	**b** $20 \times 8 \times 15$	**c** $7 + 8 + 10$	**d** $17 + 10 + 23$
e $7 - 5 - 3$	**f** $16 - 19 - 5$	**g** $23 - 20 - 4$	**h** $36 - 20 - 11$
i $40 \div 2 \div 8$	**j** $40 \div 5 \div 2$	**k** $48 \div 3 \div 9$	**l** $20 \times (-1) \times 4$

Distributive law A binary operation ᴏ is **distributive** over another binary operation ∗ if for any three elements a, b, c. $a \, ᴏ \, (b ∗ c) = (a \, ᴏ \, b) ∗ (a \, ᴏ \, c)$

Examples $4 × (5 + 9) \leftrightarrow (4 × 5) + (4 × 9)$
$4 × 14 \leftrightarrow 20 + 36$
$56 = 56$ **∴ *multiplication is distributive over addition*.**

3 Work out each of these and state which operation is distributive over the the other.

a $4 + (3 × 6)$	**b** $10 + (7 × 3)$	**c** $5 + (32 ÷ 8)$	**d** $35 + (20 ÷ 4)$
e $9 - (14 × 4)$	**f** $24 - (8 × 2)$	**g** $18 - (30 ÷ 3)$	**h** $27 - (2 ÷ 6)$
i $6 × (5 - 16)$	**j** $19 × (1 - 11)$	**k** $6 × (5 ÷ 35)$	**l** $14 × (22 ÷ 11)$
m $7 ÷ (25 × 2)$	**n** $5 ÷ (\frac{1}{8} × 25)$	**o** $3 ÷ (26 - 19)$	**p** $60 ÷ (8 - 3)$
q $4 + (13 - 6)$	**r** $60 + (22 - 17)$	**s** $28 - (5 + 16)$	**t** $100 - (34 + 7)$
u $7 × (9 + 16)$	**v** $45 × (3 + 2.1)$	**w** $63 ÷ (4 + 50)$	**x** $7 ÷ (8 + 48)$

Closure If we put all our numbers within a wall, and the gate is closed we can find the answers to our operations within the walls, we have no need to go outside.

A set is closed under an operation when the result of the operation is itself an element of the set.

If **N** = {natural numbers} = {1, 2, 3, 4, 5, 6, 7, ...}
$2 × 3 = 6, \ 8 × 1 = 8, \ 6 × 4 = 24, \ 5 × 19 = 95, \ 12 × 0 = 0$

No matter which elements of **N** we choose, the result of the operation of multiplication (the numbers 6, 8, 24, 95, 0) are always elements of **N**. We say that the set N is closed under the operation of multiplication.

4 Copy and complete each of these statements, giving two examples in each case:

a If we multiply an odd number by an odd number the answer is an ....

b An even number + an even number is always .... number.

c D = {1, 3, 5, 7. 9, ... } Multiplying odd numbers together in the set D will give answers which are also .... numbers.

d Adding any even numbers in the set A will give answers which are also .... numbers.

e To get the results of the addition operation we do not need to go out of the set A. So the set of even numbers is .... under the .... of ....

f The gate of the set J can be closed since all multiplications can be done within this set. The set of odd numbers is ...... under the operation of .... .

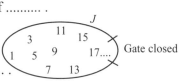

119

4 Irrational numbers

Irrational number An **irrational number** is a number with a decimal part that goes on for ever but does not have any recurring pattern.
It cannot be written as a fraction in the form $\frac{a}{b}$, where a and b are whole numbers. An irrational number is not a rational number.

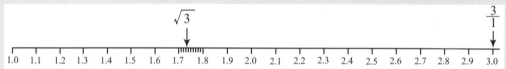

$\sqrt{3}$ lies somewhere on the real number line between 1.7 and 1.8.
The value of $\sqrt{3}$ goes on forever, that is:
1.7320508075688772935274463415058... is called an **irrational number**.
Here are possibilities of never ending decimals:
   0.1211221112222111112222.....
   0.12345678910111213141516171.....
   5.7412331122111224443308.....
These numbers are called irrational numbers.

Examples of irrational numbers:

a $\sqrt{2}$ or 1.4142135623730950488016887242097....,

b $\sqrt{10}$ or 3.16227766016837933199889354444327....

The square root of any number, other than a square number, is irrational.

Exercise 5:7

A calculator will help these exercises.

1 Which of these square roots are irrational numbers:

   a $\sqrt{1}$ **b** $\sqrt{2}$ **c** $\sqrt{4}$ **d** $\sqrt{5}$ **e** $\sqrt{6}$

2 Which of these square roots are irrational numbers:

   a $\sqrt{100}$ **b** $\sqrt{1000}$ **c** $\sqrt{10\,000}$ **d** $\sqrt{100\,000}$ **e** $\sqrt{1\,000\,000}$

3 Which of these square roots are irrational numbers:

   a $\sqrt{25}$ **b** $\sqrt{250}$ **c** $\sqrt{2500}$ **d** $\sqrt{490}$ **e** $\sqrt{4900}$

4 Which of these are irrational numbers:

   a $\frac{3}{8}$ **b** 0.262626...   **c** $\sqrt{20}$ **d** $\frac{1}{0.3}$ **e** $\frac{1}{\sqrt{2}}$

5 Find the square root of these to 2 d.p.

   a $\sqrt{2}$ **b** $\sqrt{5}$ **c** $\sqrt{7}$ **d** $\sqrt{11}$ **e** $\sqrt{13}$

6 Simplify each of the following expressions and explain whether your answer is irrational.

   a $\sqrt{3} \times \sqrt{3}$ **b** $\sqrt{2} \div \sqrt{81}$ **c** $\sqrt{7} \times \sqrt{49}$ **d** $\sqrt{20} \div \sqrt{2}$ **e** $\sqrt{32} \div \sqrt{2}$

INVESTIGATION   *Historical estimates for* π

Historically mathematicians from varying civilisations have proposed estimates for π (pi).

$$\pi \text{ is the value of } = \frac{\text{circumference}}{\text{diameter of the circle}}$$

The ancient Egyptians used $\frac{256}{81} = 3.1604938272$ to 7 d.p. This is recorded in the Rhind Papyrus in 2000 B.C.

a   The Jews of Old Testament Bible 1 Kings, chapter 7 verse 23 used π as 3.
Find and read this verse in the Bible.

b   Work out the value of π to 10 d.p. (where possible) used by these mathematicians:

Archimedes of Syracuse   (250) B.C. $3\frac{1}{7}$
(Greek 287 - 212 BC)

Claudius Ptolemy   (150 AD) $3 + \frac{8}{60} + \frac{30}{3600}$
(Greek 90 - 168)

Nicholas of Cusa   (1464 AD) $\frac{3}{4}(\sqrt{3} + \sqrt{6})$
(German 1401 - 1464)

Asian mathematicians:

Zu Chonghzi   (480 BC) $\frac{355}{113}$
(Chinese 429 - 500)

Arya-Bhata   (499 BC) $\frac{62832}{20000}$
(Indian 476 - 550 BC)

Brahmagupta   (640 AD) $\sqrt{10}$
(Indian 598 - 665)

Baudhayana   (800 BC) $\frac{49}{16}$
(Indian)

> Here is a sentence which will help you to remember the value of π to six decimal places :
> **'How I wish I could calculate pi'**
> 3.   1   4   1   5   9   2

c   π is an irrational number which can never be expressed exactly as a decimal fraction although using modern computers it has been calculated to an accuracy of more than a million decimal places.

The first 100 digits of π = 3.1415926535 8979323846 2643383279 5028841971
6939937510 5820974944 5923078164 0628620899
8628034825 3421170679.... and it goes on forever.

d   Can you tell what the next digit is?

e   Put the historical estimates (in **b**) in order of increasing accuracy.

f   What is the point of calculating a lot of digits of pi?

> **Transcendental number** is a real number which is not a a root of an algebraic equation with rational coefficients.

Features of pi

* It is an irrational number.
* It is one of the mathematical constants.
* It is one of the few transcendental numbers.
* Some computer manufacturing companies calculate the value of pi to show the quality of their machines because computer programs that are able to calculate millions of pi digits show speed, reliability and high performance.

g   Using the formula for finding the value of pi, measure the circumference and diameter of a circular object and work out the value of π to ten or more decimal places.

5 Subsets of rational numbers

Subset If all the members of a set A are also members of a set B, then A is said to be a subset. We write $A \subset B$, which is read '***A is a subset of B***' or '***A is contained in B***'. $B \not\subset A$ means 'B is not a subset of of A'

Let **N** denote the set of natural numbers.
$N = \{$ natural numbers $\} = \{1, 2, 3, 4, 5, \ldots\}$
Natural numbers are a subset of real numbers, denoted by: $N \subset R$

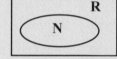

Let **Z** denote the set of integers.
$Z = \{integers\} = \{\ldots, -3, -2, -1, 0, 1, 2, 3, \ldots\}$

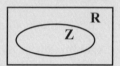

Integers are a subset of real numbers, denoted by: $Z \subset R$

Example If a and b are natural numbers show that $a + b$ is always a natural number

    i Let $a = {}^+5$ and $b = {}^+7$
        $a + b = +5 + {}^+7 = {}^+12$ (natural number, **N**)

    ii Let $a = 9$ and $b = 4$
        $a + b = 9 + 4 = 13$ (natural number, **N**)

Exercise 5:8

1 Draw a diagram to represent the relationship between **N**, **R** and **Z**.

2 Let $a = 4$ and $b = 6$ and answer the following:
State whether the answer is a natural number **N**, an integer **Z**, both or neither.
  i $a + b$ **ii** $a - b$ **iii** $a \times b$ **iv** $a \div b$

3 Let $a = 7$ and $b = 2$ and answer the following:
State whether the answer is a natural number **N**, an integer **Z**, both or neither.

  i $a + b$ **ii** $b \times a$ **iii** $a \times b$ **iv** $a \div b$

Closed operation For a pair of natural numbers a and b
$a + b$ is always a natural number, **N**.
$2a + 2b$ is always a natural number.
We say that **N** is closed under addition.

> Arithmetic operations are addition, subtraction, multiplication and division.

4 If $a = 8$ and $b = 3$ work out the following:
State whether the answer is always a natural number **N**, an integer **Z**, both or neither.
    i $a + b$ **ii** $b + a$ **iii** $a - b$ **iv** $b - a$
    v $a \times b$ **vi** $b \times a$ **vii** $a \div b$ **viii** $b \div a$

5 Under which arithmetic operation is the set of natural numbers **N** closed?

6 Under which arithmetic operation is the set of integers **Z** closed?

Set symbols $\in$ means '**is a member of**' (or '**belongs to**') the set.

$\notin$ means '**is not a member of**' (or '**does not belong to**') the set.

$A \cap B$ means the intersection of sets A and B, or the elements of A which are also members of B.

$\mathbf{Q} = \{\text{rational numbers}\} = \dfrac{p}{q}$

p and q are integers with no common divisors.
q is not equal to zero.

The diagram shows the relationship between natural numbers **N**, integers **Z**, rational numbers **Q**, and real numbers **R**.

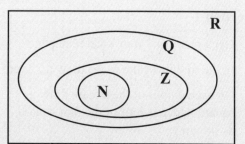

For a pair of rational numbers a and b if the operation of a and b always give another rational number we say that Q is closed under the operation.

Examples   **i** Let $a = \frac{1}{4}$ and $b = \frac{1}{7}$

$$a + b = \tfrac{1}{4} + \tfrac{1}{7}$$

$$= \tfrac{11}{28}$$

$\frac{11}{28}$ belongs to the set of rational numbers, **Q**

ii   Let $a = 0.125$ and $b = 3$

$$a + b = 0.125 + 3$$

$$= \tfrac{1}{8} + \tfrac{3}{1}$$

$$= 3\tfrac{1}{8} = \tfrac{25}{8}$$

$3\frac{1}{8}$ belongs to the set of rational numbers, **Q**

We can conclude that **Q** is closed under addition.

Exercise 5:9

1 Under which operation is the set of rational numbers **Q**, closed?

2 Under which operation is the set of rational numbers **Q**, not closed?

3 Copy and complete the following by inserting $\cap$, $\notin$, $\in$, $\subset$ or $=$ symbols in place of ?.

   a N ? Z   **b** N ? Q   **c** Z ? N   **d** Q ? Z

   e Z ? Q   **f** Q ? N   ***g** N $\cap$ Z ? N   ***h** N ? Z ? Q $\in$ R

4 Let $a = \frac{1}{5}$ and $b = 0.75$ and $c = 2$
Work out these each of these and state whether the answer is a rational number **Q**.

   i $c - a$ **ii** $a + b$ **iii** $b \times c$ **iv** $(a + b) + c$

   v $b(c - a)$ **vi** $a \div c$ **vii** $(a - b)c$ **viii** $2ac^2 - b^2$

   ix $\sqrt{c - b}$ **x** $\sqrt{\dfrac{1}{4a^2}}$ **xi** $c^2 \div b$ **xii** $a \div (b + c)$

6　Fractal geometry

Fractal   A **fractal** is a geometrical shape, each part of which has the same character as the whole. Fractals are useful in modelling structures in which similar patterns recur at progressively smaller scales.

Section 1

1　Get a piece of 1 mm squared paper.

2　In the middle of the paper draw a 32 mm square.

3　On each corner of the square draw a square which is half of the first square, as shown.

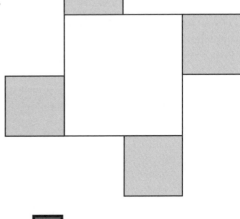

4　On each corner of each 16 mm square draw a 8 mm square as shown.

5　Repeat these steps three more times. (Note that potentially this can go on forever.)

6　Now shade or colour your design. Use a different colour for each size of square.

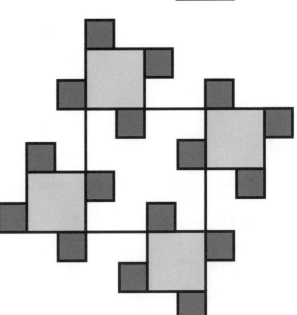

7　On a different piece of paper copy and complete the chart shown here. The first two rows have already been completed.

Size of square	Number of squares	Area of each square	Total area of squares	Total number of squares
32 mm by 32 mm	1	$32 \times 32 = 1024$ mm²	$1 \times 1024 = 1024$ mm²	1
16 mm by 16 mm	4	$16 \times 16 = 256$ mm²	$4 \times 256 = 1024$ mm²	5
⋮	⋮	⋮	.	⋮

8 What is the total number of squares of the fractal?

Note that the smallest square of of this fractal is 2 mm by 2 mm

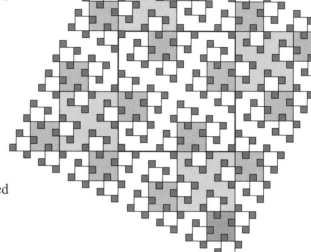

9 Take each size square and express as a fraction of the original square.

10 What is the total area occupied by the entire shape drawn?

11 **i** What is the ratio of the areas of the smallest square compared to the original square?
 ii What is the ratio of the areas of the original square compared to the area of the total area?

12 Investigate with initial squares of: **i** side 64 mm **ii** 128 mm.

Section 2

Draw these fractals:

1 Starting with the first square whose side is 8 cm.

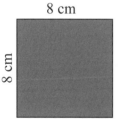

Keep joining the midpoints of the sides.

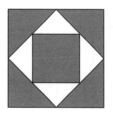

2 Use your own dimensions for this triangle. On each side of a triangle draw a triangle. And on each side of these triangles draw a triangle. And on each side . . .

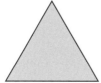
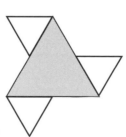
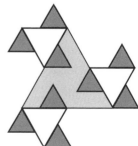

3 Continue as far as you can.

4 Investigate with different size triangles.

Natural resources are not infinite.

Charcoal production

Forest

Timber

Charcoal

Charcoal packed in sacks

Charcoal production:
- Trees are felled in the forest,
- They are chopped into timber and small branches,
- They are then burnt at a temperature above 300 °C in a kiln made of earth.
  This burning process limits the air supply so the absence of oxygen produces charcoal.

Charcoal is produced mainly in the form of lumps and briquettes (compressed charcoal).
Ghana consumes about 16 million m³ of charcoal per year.
About 80-90% of urban population depend on wood fuel.

1 How can this production process be continued indefinitely?
2 Explain why the wood must not be allowed to run out.
3 What are the effects of charcoal production on:
   i local farming, afforestation and deforestation;
   ii human activities;
   iii the environment;
   iv land use?
4 Write down six uses of charcoal and six ways to restrict charcoal production.

Consider other **local resources** such as energy, fishing, animal husbandry or transportation.

Railway train

Dam

1 Describe how these resources are used up.

2 Explain the impact of these on the environment, employment, human activities and the labour market.

3 What are the effects on local:
   a economy   **b** standards of living   **c** employment/unemployment?

4 Give reasons why these resources could terminate, or continue to be exploited.

5 Propose three policies to promote these resources.

EXTENSION

1 Convert each of these fractions into a decimal and state whether it is terminating or recurring.

   a $\frac{3}{11}$ **b** $\frac{3}{10}$ **c** $\frac{3}{8}$ **d** $\frac{3}{7}$ **e** $\frac{3}{5}$

2 How many digits are there in the recurring pattern of decimals of the fraction $\frac{3}{17}$?

3 Find the fractions which are equivalent to the recurring decimals:

   a 0.100110011001....   **b** 0. 1919191919....

   c 5.721721721721....   **d** 13.7474747474....

4 Write these recurring decimals in the form $\frac{a}{b}$ where a and b are integers.

   a $0.05\dot{3}$ **b** $0.5\dot{1}\dot{2}$ **c** $0.3\dot{4}$ **d** $2.308\dot{4}$ **e** $10.66\dot{5}\dot{1}$

5 Find a rational number which lies between:

   a $\sqrt{2}$ and $\sqrt{3}$ **b** $\sqrt{12}$ and $\sqrt{15}$ **c** $\frac{3}{5}$ and $\frac{3}{4}$ **d** $\frac{7}{10}$ and $\frac{71}{100}$

6 Work out the following:

   a $\sqrt{\dfrac{2}{50}}$ **b** $\sqrt{\dfrac{7}{63}}$ **c** $\sqrt{\dfrac{5}{50\,000}}$ **d** $\sqrt[3]{\dfrac{64}{125}}$ **e** $\sqrt[3]{\dfrac{343}{2744}}$

7 Write down an irrational number between: **a** 6 and 7   **b** 3.1 and 3.2

8 State whether **N** and **Z** are closed or not closed under the operations.

   i $a \blacklozenge b = a \times 2b$ **ii** $a \bullet b = 2a + 3b$

   iii $a \blacksquare b = 2a - 3b$ **iv** $a \blacktriangle b = \pm\sqrt{ab}$

9 Are the following statements true or false? If they are true give examples.

   a rational number + rational number = rational

   b rational number × rational number = rational

   c rational number − irrational number = rational

10 Here is a set of numbers:

   $\{\,9,\ -3.3,\ \sqrt{4.9},\ \frac{1}{3},\ 2\frac{1}{2},\ \sqrt{3},\ -7.5,\ 0,\ \sqrt{21},\ 7.8,\ -2,\ -\sqrt{7},\ 5.05,\ \sqrt{0.9}\,\}$

   a Show the numbers on a number line.

   b From the set of numbers list the set of:

      i natural numbers   **ii** integers   **iii** positive integers

      iv irrational numbers   **v** non-negative numbers   **vi** whole numbers

      vii negative integers   **viii** rational numbers

11 Copy this statement and give four examples:

   'the set of odd numbers is closed under the operation of multiplication'

12 Simplify these: **a** $\sqrt[3]{3\frac{3}{8}}$ **b** $\sqrt{180} \div \sqrt{8}$ **c** $\sqrt{42} \div \sqrt{2}$ **d** $\sqrt{10} \times \sqrt{8} \times \sqrt{6}$

13 An irrational number is multiplied by another irrational number.
   Give an example to show that the answer could be a rational number.

SUMMARY

Terminating decimal	A **terminating decimal** is a decimal which has a fixed number of decimal places. A terminating decimal occurs when the denominator divides exactly into the numerator.
Recurring decimal	A **recurring decimal** is a decimal in which the digits after the decimal point repeat the same sequence for ever. A recurring decimal is also known as a **repeating decimal**. For example if you change $\frac{7}{11}$ to a decimal, you get: 0.6363636363636363 ...
Real number	A **real number** is a number which can be written as a decimal (including a non-terminating decimal) whether positive or negative. This includes the roots of all positive numbers. The symbol for a set of real numbers is **R**. **R** = {real numbers}.
Infinite series	A series which continues infinitely without stopping is called an **infinite series**. e.g. $\sqrt{2} = 1.414213562...$
Rational number	A **rational number** is a number which can be written as a fraction in the form $\frac{a}{b}$ where a and b are whole numbers and $b \neq 0$. For example $\frac{3}{5}$ is a rational number. A rational number cancels into its simplest form if a and b have no common factor. The symbol for a set of rational numbers is **Q**. **Q** = {rational numbers}.
Irrational number	An **irrational number** is a number with a decimal part that goes on for ever but does not have any recurring pattern. It cannot be written as a fraction in the form $\frac{a}{b}$, where a and b are whole numbers. An irrational number is not a rational number.
Subset	If all the members of set A are also members of set B, then A is said to be a subset. We write $A \subset B$, which is read '*A is a subset of B*' or '*A is contained in B*'. $B \not\subset A$ means '*B is not a subset of of A*'

Let **N** denote the set of natural numbers.
N = { natural numbers } = {1, 2, 3, 4, 5, ...}
Natural numbers are a subset of real numbers denoted by: **N** $\subset$ **R**

Q = {rational numbers} = $\frac{p}{q}$

p and q are integers with no common divisors.
q is not equal to zero.

The diagram shows the relationship between natural numbers, **N**, integers, **Z**, rational numbers, **Q** and real numbers, **R**.

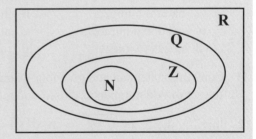

Fractal	A **fractal** is a geometrical shape, each part of which has the same character as the whole.

Shape and space

EXTENSION

SUMMARY

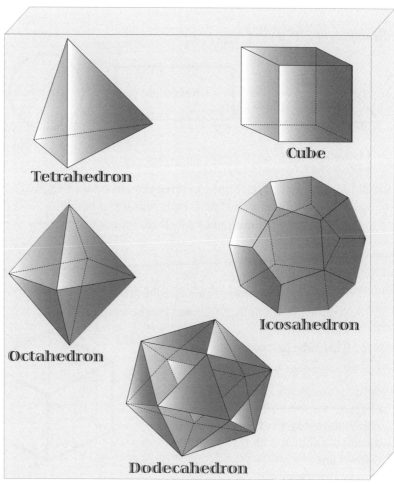

Tetrahedron

Cube

Octahedron

Icosahedron

Dodecahedron

1   Identifying solids

A point has no dimension.   •
A line has one dimension.   ——————
A line is the track of a moving point.

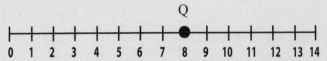

Q is in one dimension at the point 8.
A straight line is one-dimensional, expressed as 1-D. It has a length.

On the graph the position of *P* is given in
two-dimensions (2-D) in the X and Y axes (4, 3).
All 2-D shapes are flat and they have no thickness.
They have area.

A flat surface is called a **plane**.

A page of this book is a plane when it is lying flat.

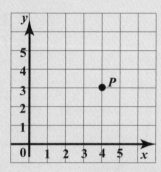

Examples of 2-D shapes

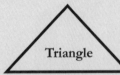

Triangle   Rectangle   Circle

3-D (solid) shapes

Solid   A **solid** is a shape formed in three-dimensional (3-D) space.
The three dimensions are: length, width and height.
A 3-D shape is described by its faces, edges and vertices (vertices is the plural of vertex).
A **vertex** is a corner.
A **face** is a flat surface.
An **edge** is a line where two faces meet.
A **cube** has a length, width and height which are equal.

This cube has: 6 faces,
              12 edges and
              8 vertices

The 'hidden edges' of
a solid are shown with
dashed lines.

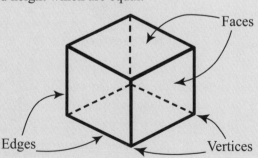

Faces

Edges   Vertices

Exercise 6:1

You need squared paper, pencil and eraser for these exercises.

1 Follow this method below to draw a cube.

   a Draw a square of side 2 cm.

   b Draw a second square of the same side overlapping.

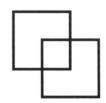

   c Join the corners of the squares.

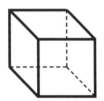

   d Rub the 3 inside lines and make them dotted to show that they are hidden.

You have just drawn a cube of length 2 cm, breadth 2 cm and width 2 cm or a cube of side 2 cm.

2 Draw two different cubes of side 3 cm and 4 cm.

A **cuboid** has six rectangular faces. Opposite faces are the same, and all the angles between its faces are 90°.

3 Follow this method to draw a cuboid:

   a Draw a 4 cm by 2 cm rectangle

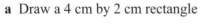
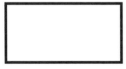

   b Draw a second rectangle of the same dimensions overlapping.

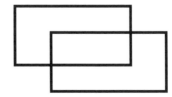

   c Join the corners of the rectangles and rub the 3 inside lines and make them dotted to show that they are hidden.

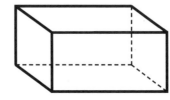

Plato	Plato (*c*429 - *c*347 BC) was a Greek mathematician and philosopher. He insisted that ordinary things change but their forms do not. For example a particular triangle may be altered in size or shape but the form of triangularity can never change. He also concluded that unchanging and perfect forms can not be part of an everyday world which is changing and imperfect. He proposed that numbers and other mathematical objects have an independent existence and are not simply inventions of the mind.
Platonic solids	Regular polyhedra with faces which are regular polygons are called **platonic solids.** They were proved to be the only possible regular polyhedra and named after Plato. The same number of these polygons meet at each vertex. All the face-angles at every vertex and all the **dihedral** angles are equal.

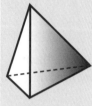 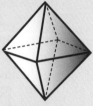  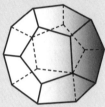

Tetrahedron	Cube	Octahedron	Dodecahedron	Icosahedron

There are other solids which have straight edges and curved edges.

Pyramid	A **pyramid** is a polyhedron whose base is a polygon. Each vertex of the base is joined to a common vertex called an **apex**. A pyramid takes its name from the shape of its base.

Cone	A **cone** is a solid figure with one circular base. A cone is a type of pyramid which has a circular base.

Cylinder	A **cylinder** is a solid figure which has two equal ends and parallel circles.

Sphere	A **sphere** is a round figure with every point on its surface equidistant from its centre. A sphere is a perfect ball or globe.

Prism	A **prism** is a solid whose base lies in parallel planes and whose faces are parallelograms.

Polyhedron	A **polyhedron** is a solid with many faces. **Polyhedra** is the plural of polyhedron.

Dihedral	A shape that has two plane faces.

Dihedral angle The angle θ between two plane faces.

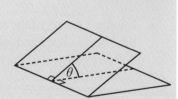

Exercise 6:2

1 Sketch and label these solids:

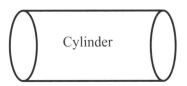
Cylinder

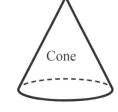
Cone

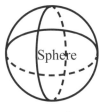
Sphere

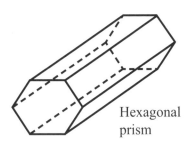
Hexagonal prism

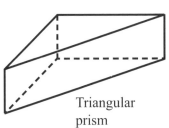
Triangular prism

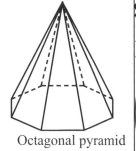
Octagonal pyramid

2 For each of these objects name the solid that closely matches its shape.

a

b

c

d

e

f

3 Sketch and write down the number of faces, edges and vertices of the following:

a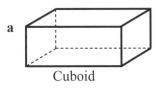
Cuboid

b
Tetrahedron

c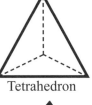
Parallelepiped

d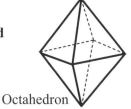
Octahedron
(*Octa: eight; Hedron: face*)

e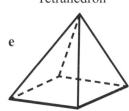
Square based pyramid

f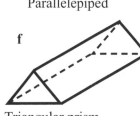
Triangular prism

133

4 a How many edges has this shape?

b How many vertices has this shape?

c How many faces has this shape?

d Find two edges that are parallel to BC.

e This shape is a cube. What shape is each face?

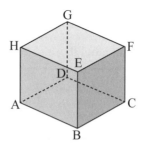

5 a How many edges has this shape?

b How many vertices has this shape?

c How many faces has this shape?

d Which edge is parallel to DE?

e Which edges are parallel to BC?

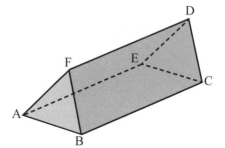

6 a How many edges has this shape?

b How many vertices has this shape?

c How many faces has this shape?

d What shape is the base of this shape?

e How many triangles meet at the apex of this shape?

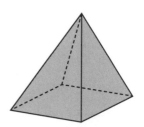

7 Describe the 2-D shapes needed to make these solids:

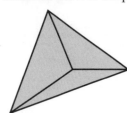 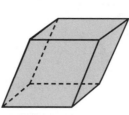 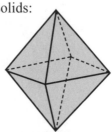 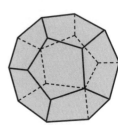

Tetrahedron   Parallelepiped   Octahedron   Icosahedron

8 Copy and complete this table:

Name of solid	Number of faces F	Number of vertices V	Number of edges E
Cone	2		
Cuboid			
Cylinder			
Sphere			
Parallelepiped			
Hexagonal prism	8		

9 What is the relationship between F, V and E?

2 Nets of solids

Net A **net** is a flat shape that folds up into a 3-D solid shape.

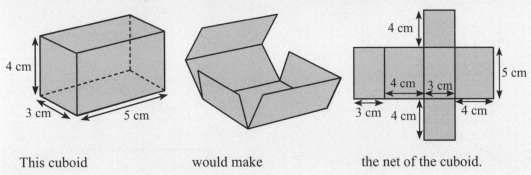

This cuboid   would make   the net of the cuboid.

Exercise 6:3

Copy, cut out these nets and make the shapes. You must include the flaps to attach or glue the edges. The flaps are not part of the net.

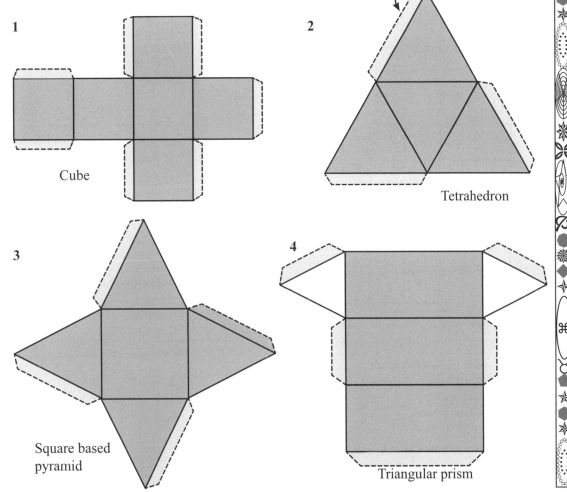

1   Cube

2   Tetrahedron

3   Square based pyramid

4   Triangular prism

6

Draw the nets of these solids.

5
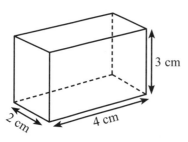
3 cm
2 cm
4 cm

6
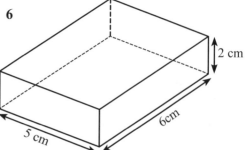
2 cm
5 cm
6cm

7
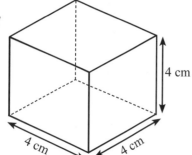
4 cm
4 cm
4 cm

8
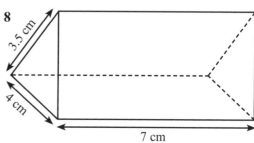
3.5 cm
4 cm
7 cm

9 Draw these nets on a squared paper, cut them out and fold them to see which ones do make cubes.

a

A			
B	C	D	E
F			

b

A			
B	C		
	D	E	F

c

	A		
B	C	D	
		E	F

d

A	B	C	
		D	E	F

e

	A	
B	C	D
E	F	

f

A	B		
	C	D	
		E	F

g

	A	
	B	C
D	E	F

h

A	B	C	
	D	E	F

10 For the nets which *did* make cubes in **question 3**, state which of the faces *B*, *C*, *D*, *E* or *F* was opposite to face *A* on the cube.

11 Here is a net of a solid.

    a Write the name of the solid.

    b How many faces will the solid have?

    c How many edges will the solid have?

    d How many vertices will the solid have?

12 The net given can be folded to form a solid.

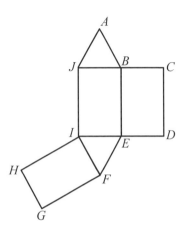

    a Name the solid.

    b Which letter will point *J* meet?

    c Which letters will point *A* meet?

    d Which edge will meet edge *FG*?

13 Name the 3-D shape that you can make by folding each of these nets.

a

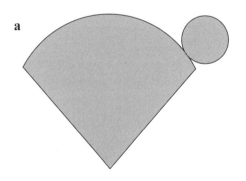

b

14 Draw the net of this pyramid.

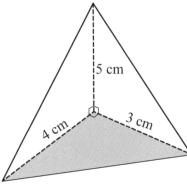

11 Draw the solid of this net.

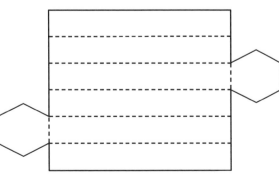

Cross-section of solids

If a solid is cut through parallel to the ends, the section produced is called a **cross-section** of the solid.

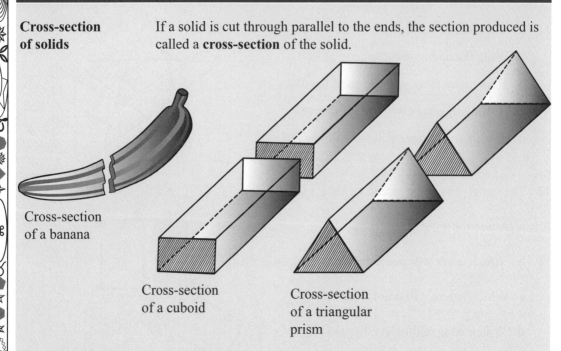

Cross-section of a banana

Cross-section of a cuboid

Cross-section of a triangular prism

When a cross-section of a solid has the same shape and size as the ends, the cross-section is said to be **uniform**. Solids with this property are called **prisms**.

Exercise 6:4

Draw a cross-section of each of these solids:

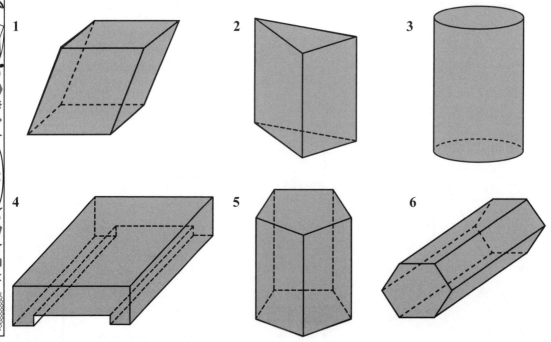

1　　　　**2**　　　　**3**

4　　　　**5**　　　　**6**

4   Drawing solids

The 3 by 3 by 3 cube shown on the isometric paper
has been made from small cubes. There are 27 cubes.

The whole of the outside of the large cube has been
painted in shades of grey.

There are 54 faces shaded grey altogether.

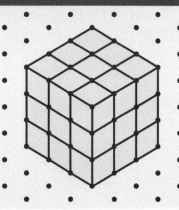

Exercise 6:5

1   The whole of the outside of these solids has been painted grey.
   Draw these solids on triangular dotted paper.

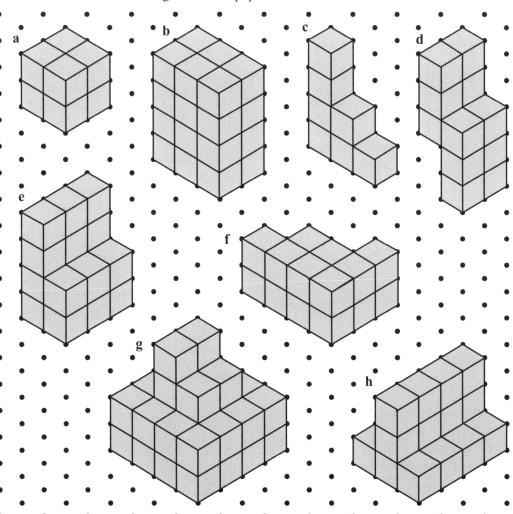

a   b   c   d   e   f   g   h

6

2 Using the information on the solids in **question 1** copy and complete this table.

Solid	Number of cubes	Number of faces painted
a	8	24
b		
c		
d		
e		
f		
g		
h		

3 Which of the solids in question 1 can be classified as a prism?

4 Draw sketches of these solids on triangular dotted paper. Add two extra cubes to the faces shown to complete the solid.

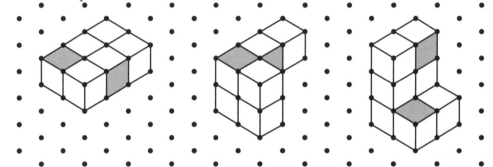

5 Draw a copy of this shape accurately on isometric paper. The line PQ has been drawn for you.

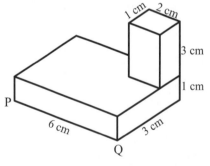

6 Using the shape in **question 5**, turn the top block on its side to make a prism. Draw the 3-D prism that you have created on isometric paper.

7 Each of these shapes show one end of a prism. All measurements are in centimetres. The prisms are 3 cm long. Draw the shapes on isometric paper.

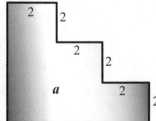

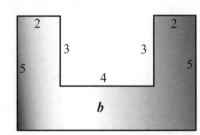

140

5 Elevation of solids

Elevation

A carefully drawn figure showing a view from above, the front or the side of an object is called the **elevation** of the object. Elevations can be used to draw accurate 2-D pictures of 3-D shapes.

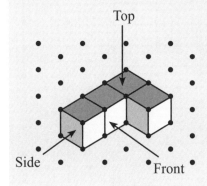

Top

Side

Front

The view from the front is a front elevation.

The view from above is a plan.

The view from the side is a side elevation.

Exercise 6:6

Draw the plan, the front elevation and the side elevation of each of these solids.

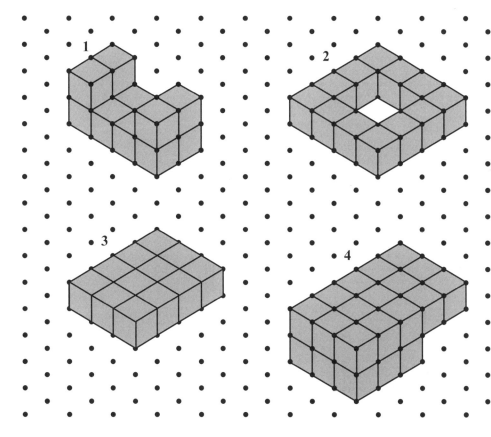

1

2

3

4

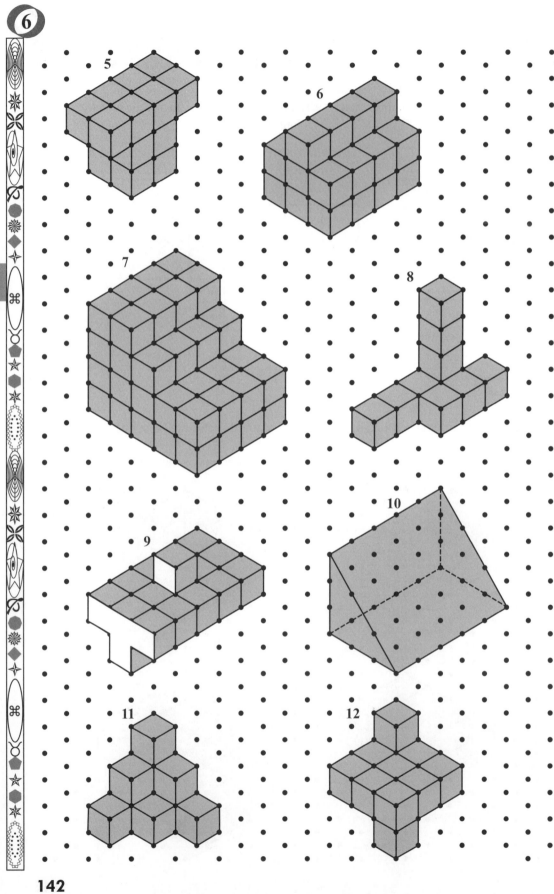

6   Orthographic projections

Projection   The presentation of an image on a surface is called a **projection**.

Orthographic projection   A method of projection in which an object is depicted using parallel lines to project its outlines onto a plane is called an **orthographic projection**.

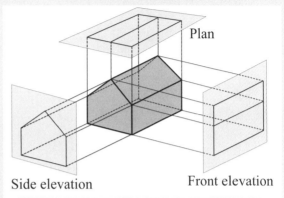

Usually three orthographic projections of an object are drawn to give a 'total picture' of it. These are:
the plan (view from above),
the front elevation (view from front) and
the side elevation (view from side).

Orthographic projections are greatly used by designers, architects and engineers so that accurate measurements can be taken from drawings .

Exercise 6:7

Copy and draw roughly a plan and two orthographic projections of each of the following. Show all the hidden features with dotted lines.

1
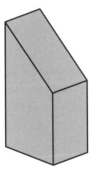

2
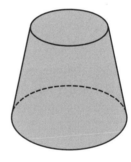

3
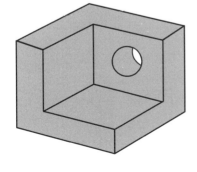

4
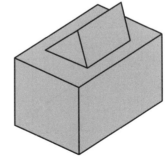

5

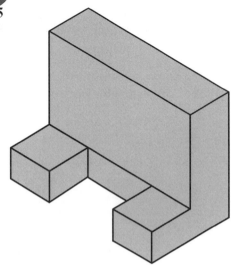

6

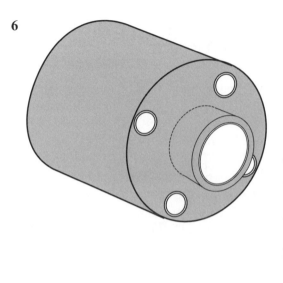

Draw the plan, front elevation and the side elevation of these two shapes.

7

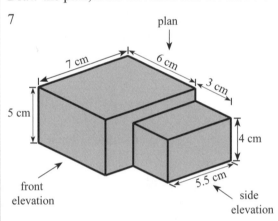

plan

7 cm   6 cm   3 cm

5 cm

4 cm

front
elevation

5.5 cm

side
elevation

8

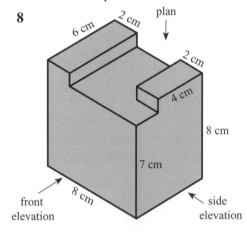

plan

6 cm   2 cm

2 cm

4 cm

8 cm

7 cm

front
elevation

8 cm

side
elevation

9 This is the technical drawing of a metal block. It shows three orthographic projections of the component full size. Copy the shapes and draw the 3-D version of the block on isometric paper. All measurements are in centimetres and are drawn accurately.

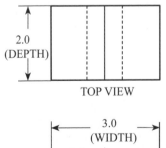

2.0
(DEPTH)

TOP VIEW

Ø means the diameter of a hole

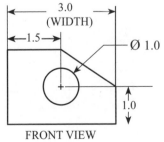

3.0
(WIDTH)

1.5

Ø 1.0

1.0

FRONT VIEW

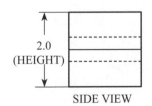

2.0
(HEIGHT)

SIDE VIEW

7 Networks and polyhedra

Network	A **network** is a set of points joined by lines called arcs.
Node	A **node** is one of the set of points in a network.
Arc	An **arc** is the line joining two nodes in a network.
Region	A **region** is the space between enclosed arcs in a network.

This is the shape obtained when the front face of a cube is removed and the other faces are stretched outwards and backwards until it lies flat.
The shape obtained becomes a network with nodes (8), regions (5) and arcs (12).

Exercise 6:8

These are the networks of the polyhedra with one face removed and stretched outwards and backwards until they lie flat.

  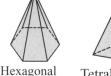

Cube   Triangular prism   Hexagonal pyramid   Tetrahedron   Octahedron   Pentagonal pyramid

 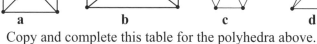 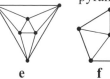

   a   **b**   **c**   **d**   **e**   **f**

1 Copy and complete this table for the polyhedra above.

Polyhedra	Number of faces F	Number of vertices V	$F + V$	Number of edges E
Cube				
Triangular prism				
Hexagonal pyramid				
Tetrahedron				
Octahedron				
Pentagonal pyramid				

2 Copy and complete this table for the networks above.
Do not forget to include the outside region represented by the stretched face.

Network	Number of regions R	Number of nodes N	$N + R$	Number of arcs A
a				
b				
c				
d				
e				
f				

3 What is the relationship between N, R and A?

4 Compare the two tables. What do you notice?

EXTENSION

1 For the eight objects given, sort out the objects into four groups: prisms and non-prisms and two other groups. Write down your two other groups and how you chose your groups.

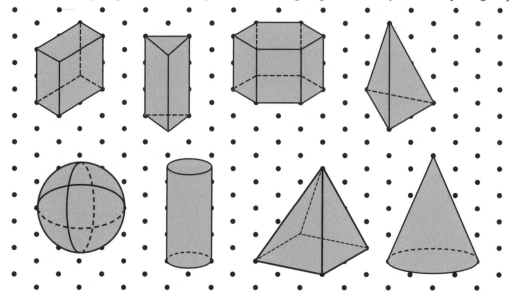

2 This cube is made of wire. Each edge is 7 cm long. What is the total length of wire needed?

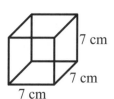

7 cm
7 cm
7 cm

3 Write down the names of the solids that can be made from these nets.

a

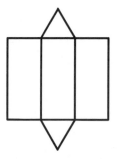

b

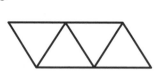

c

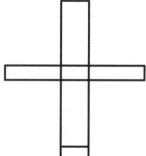

4 Here is a net of a triangular-based prism:

a What sort of triangle forms the base?

b How many edges does the solid have?

c Which points will meet edge *IJ*?

d Which points will meet at *C*?

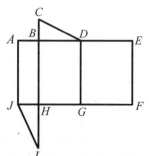

5 Draw the net of a cone without a base.

6 Draw the net of a closed cuboid measuring 5 cm × 3 cm × 2 cm.

7 Describe two different ways in which you could cut a cylinder into two identical pieces. describe and sketch the solids that you would obtain in each case.

8 Sketch the net to make this prism. Label the lengths for each side.

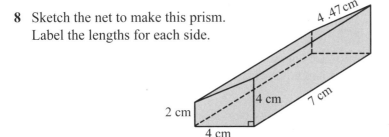

9 Make an isometric sketch of the solid shown by the plan, showing the front elevation and the side elevation.

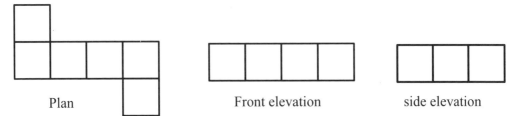

Plan   Front elevation   side elevation

10 Measure these 2-D shapes and draw the 3-D projection of the solid.

Plan   Front elevation   Side elevation

11 The given shape has been made from cubes. The whole of the outside of the shape has been painted white.

  i How many small cubes are there?

  ii How many faces were painted altogether?

  iii If the edge of each small cube measures 20 cm, what is the area of each face of a small cube?

  iv What is the total area that has been painted? Give your answer in centimetres squared.

  v How many cubes have:
    a one face   **b** two faces
    c three faces   **d** four faces painted white?

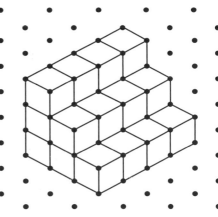

SUMMARY

Solid   A **solid** is a shape formed in three-dimensional (3-D) space.
The three dimensions are: length, width and height.
A 3-D shape is described by its faces, edges and
vertices. Vertices is the plural of vertex.
A **vertex** is a corner.
A **face** is a flat surface.
An **edge** is a line where two faces meet.
A **cube** has length, width and height which are equal.

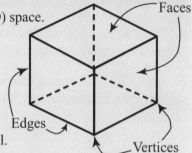

Faces

Edges

Vertices

Pyramid   A **pyramid** is a polyhedron whose base is a polygon.
Each vertex of the base is joined to a common vertex
called **apex**. A pyramid takes its name from the shape
of its base.

Cone   A **cone** is a solid figure with one circular base.
A cone is a type of pyramid which has a circular base.

Cylinder   A **cylinder** is a solid figure which has two equal
ends and parallel circles.

Sphere   A **sphere** is a round figure with every point on its
surface equidistant from its centre.
A sphere is a perfect ball or globe.

Prism   A **prism** is a solid whose base lies in parallel
planes and whose faces are parallelograms.

Polyhedron   A **polyhedron** is a solid with many faces.

Net   A **net** is a flat shape that folds up into a 3-D solid shape.

Cross-section   If a solid is cut through parallel to the ends, the section produced is called a
of solids   **cross-section** of the solid.

Elevation   A carefully drawn figure showing a view from above, the front and the side
of an object is called the **elevation** of the object.
Elevations can be used to draw accurate 2-D pictures of 3-D shapes.

Orthographic   The method of projection in which an object is depicted using parallel lines
projection   to project its outlines on to a plane is called a **orthographic projection**.

Network   A **network** is a set of points joined by lines called arcs.
Node   A **node** is one of the set of points in a network.
Arc   An **arc** is the line joining two nodes in a network.
Region   A **region** is the space between enclosed arcs in a network.

7 Geometric construction

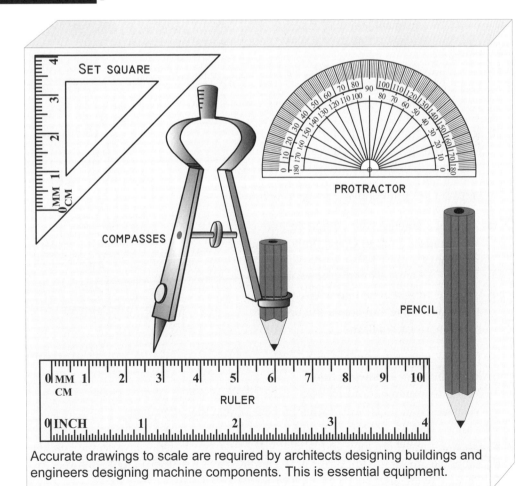

Accurate drawings to scale are required by architects designing buildings and engineers designing machine components. This is essential equipment.

1 Constructing perpendicular lines

Perpendicular lines If two lines meet at right angles (90°) then the two lines are said to be **perpendicular** to each other. The symbol ⊥ means "is perpendicular to".

Bisecting a line **Bisecting a line** means cutting it in two equal parts.

Perpendicular bisector On this diagram: CD is perpendicular to AB
CD bisects AB
CD is called the **perpendicular bisector** of AB.

Construction equipment The equipment needed for construction are:
a pair of compasses, protractor (angle measure), a set square, pencil, eraser.

Example Draw the perpendicular bisector of line XY.

With the compass point first at X then Y
and a distance just over half the length
of the line XY draw two arcs.

The perpendicular bisector is shown as a broken line.

Exercise 7:1

1 a Draw a line 6 cm long.
Label the ends P and Q.

   b Put your compass point on P
Move your pencil until you can tell
it is more than halfway along line PQ.

   c Draw an arc from above the line to below it.

   d Without changing your compasses move
the compass point to Q and draw another
arc from Q.

   e Using a straight edge join where your
arcs cross above and below the line.
Label these points R and S.

   f Line RS bisects line PQ at right angles.
Mark the point of intersection T.
This is the midpoint of line PQ.
Measure PT and QT with a ruler and check that they are equal.

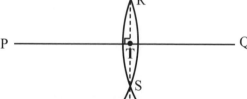

2 a Draw a line 8.4 cm long and label it GH.
   c Label the crossing point of the arcs J and K.
   e Check that JK bisects GH by measuring.

   b Draw arcs from G and H.
   d Join J and K to bisect the line.

3 Draw a horizontal line AS 7.4 cm long. Bisect the line using a ruler and compasses.

4 Draw a vertical line UE 6.9 cm long. Bisect the line using a ruler and compasses.

5 Draw a horizontal line VR of length 9.7 cm. Construct the perpendicular bisector of VR.

6 Draw a vertical line BA 7.1 cm long. Construct the perpendicular bisector of BA.

Perpendicular bisectors can be constructed through the midpoint of any straight line.

Example   Draw the line KG of length 7 cm tilted vertically about 15°.

Put your compass at K and draw an arc below K.

Put your compass at G and draw an arc above G.

Label the crossing points of the arcs J and H.

Join J and H to bisect the line.

JH is the perpendicular bisector
of KG because NG is equal to NK.

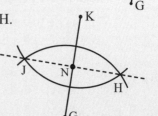

---

7 Draw the line PK of length 5 cm tilted vertically about 10°W.
Put your compass at P and draw an arc below P.
Put your compass at K and draw an arc above K.
Label the crossing points of the arcs C and D
Join C and D to bisect the line.
Check that CD bisects PK by measuring.

8 Draw a perpendicular bisector XY, 6.5 cm tilted 5° anticlockwise.

9 **a** Using a set square draw the right-angle shown.

  b Construct the perpendicular bisector of TN.

  c Construct the perpendicular bisector of TU.

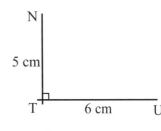

10 a Using a set square draw the right-angled triangle BOA.

  b Construct the perpendicular bisector of OB.

  c Construct the perpendicular bisector of OA.

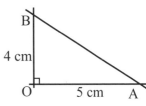

2 Bisecting angles

This pie is to be shared among two people.
It needs to be divided so that each person
can have exactly half.

Bisecting an angle

Bisecting an angle means splitting it exactly in half. It is more accurate to use a ruler, pencil and a pair of compasses.

Example Bisect angle GBC.

With the compass point at B draw
an arc GC.
With compasses at G and then C
draw two more arcs as shown.

The angle bisector is then drawn
as shown with a dotted line.

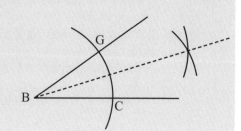

Exercise 7:2

1   Follow these instructions to draw
    the bisector of the angle shown:

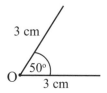

a   Draw a 50° angle and make the two sides 3 cm each.

b   Open your compasses a small distance and fix the point at O.

c   Draw a small arc which crosses both arms of the angle.
    Label the points P and Q.

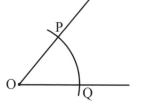

d   Place the compass point at P and draw
    another arc in the middle of the angle.

e   Place the compass point at Q and draw
    another arc in the middle of the angle
    so that it crosses the first arc.

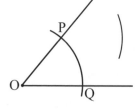

f   Draw a line where the two arcs cross
    through to point O.
    This line bisects the angle.
    This line is called the **angle bisector**.

g   Measure the two angles to make sure they are both equal.

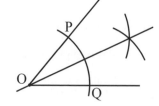

2 a Draw a 53° angle.
  b Draw a small arc which crosses both arms of the angle. Label L and M.
  c Draw arcs from L and M making sure that these two arcs cross.
  d Draw the line which bisects the angle.
  e Check that the two angles are equal by measuring.

3 a Draw a 38° angle.
  b Draw a small arc which crosses both arms of the angle. Label R and S.
  c Draw arcs from R and S making sure that these two arcs cross.
  d Draw the line which bisects the angle.
  e Check that the two angles are equal by measuring.

4 a Draw an angle of 95°
  b Bisect the angle
  c Measure the two parts of the angle to check that the two angles are equal.

5 Draw and bisect each of these angles. Make each side 4 cm.
  a 48°   **b** 54°   **c** 75°   **d** 110°   **e** 124°

6 a Copy the given angle:

  b Using only a ruler, a pencil and a pair
    of compasses bisect angle YAW.

  c Measure the two parts of the angle to check
    that the two angles are equal.

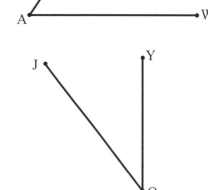

7 a Copy the given angle:

  b Bisect the angle JOY.

  c Measure the two parts of the angle.
    Check that the two angles are equal.

8 a Copy the given angle:

  b Bisect the angle TWI.

  c Measure the two parts of the angle.
    Check that the two angles are equal.

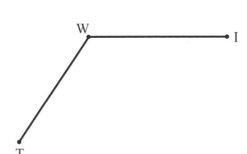

9 **a** Copy the given angle:

b Bisect the angle PEN.

c Bisect one of the resulting angles.
Check that each of the new angles is 25°.

10 **a** Draw and bisect angle 168°.
b Bisect one of the resulting angles and check that each of the new angles is 42°.

11 **a** Copy the given angle:

b Bisect the angle RAM.

c Bisect one of the resulting angles.
Check that each of the new angles is 54°.

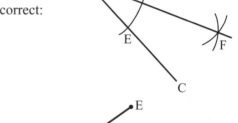

12 The figure shows the construction
of the bisector of angle CAB.
Which of these is true if the construction is correct:
  i AD = AE
  ii AE = EF
  iii DF = EF
  iv AB = AF ?

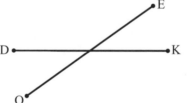

13 **a** Draw any pair of intersecting lines.
b Bisect the acute angles.
c Bisect the obtuse angles.
d What do you notice?

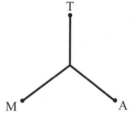

14 **a** Draw the shape shown. Each arm is 2 cm.
b Bisect all the three angles. Make each bisector 3 cm.
c Label the new lines EJ, EK and EL.
d Join the ends of all six lines.
e What is the mathematical name of the new shape?

15 The diagram shows a house garden with a fence
on two sides and trees at two corners.

A water butt is to be placed so that it is:
  i equidistant from the two fences and
  ii equidistant from the 2 trees.

  Make a scale drawing (1 cm = 1 m) and
  mark where the water butt goes.

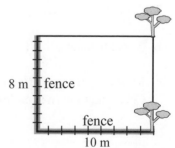

154

Constructing a perpendicular from a point to a line

To construct a perpendicular from a point means to draw a line through the point which is at a right angle to the line.

Example Construct a perpendicular from point C, 4 cm to the line AB which is 6 cm.

Draw line AB of length 6 cm.

Draw the point C, 4 cm above AB.

Open the compass to a radius which is about $1\frac{1}{8}$ times the distance of C from AB.

With the point at C, draw arcs to cut the line AB at P and Q as shown.

With the point at P draw an arc below line AB.

Move the point to Q and draw an arc to cut the last arc at D.
Join CD.
CD is now perpendicular to AB.

Exercise 7:3

1 Construct a perpendicular from the point C to the line AB.
   C is 3 cm from AB.

• C

A ⊢————————————⊣ B
        4 cm

2 Construct a perpendicular from the point D to the line PQ.
   D is 4.5 cm from PQ

• D

P ⊢————————————⊣ Q
        6 cm

3 Construct a perpendicular from the point X to the line ST.
   X is 4 cm from ST.

S ⊤

X •   5 cm

T ⊥

4 Construct a perpendicular from the point O to the line LN.
   O is 3.8 cm from LN.

• O

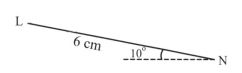

155

3   Constructing angles

Some angles can be constructed without using a protractor. Four of these angles are 90°, 60°, 30° and 45°. Other angles can be constructed by combining these angles.

Exercise 7:4

1 Follow these instructions to construct a 90° angle.

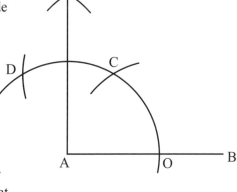

   a Draw line AB about 5 cm.

   b Place the compass point a at A and draw wide arc that cuts the line. Label this point O.

   c Place the compass point at O and draw an arc of radius AO. Label this point C.

   d Keeping the same radius place the compass point at C and draw an arc that cuts the first arc. Label this point D.

   e Keeping the same radius place the compass point at C draw another arc at a point near E.

   f Keeping the same radius place the compass at D and draw an arc to cut the arc drawn in step **e**.

   g Join E to A. The angle BAE is 90°.

2 Follow these instructions to construct a 60° angle.

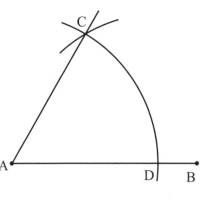

   a Draw a line AB about 5 cm long.

   b Open your compasses to a radius of 4 cm or more.

   c With the compass point on A draw a wide arc to cut the line at D.

   d With the same radius move the point to D and draw an arc above the line to cut the first arc at C.

   e Draw a line through A and C. Angle A is now 60°.

3 Follow these instructions to construct a 30° angle.

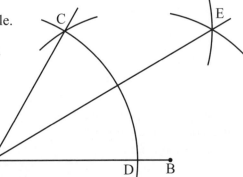

   a Draw a 60° angle as described in **question 2**.

   b Place your compass point at D and draw an arc.

   c Move the point to C and draw another arc to cut the third arc at E. Angle EAB is now 30°.

We know that $\frac{1}{2}$ of 60° = 30°, so to construct 30°, first construct a 60° angle and then bisect it applying the same instructions as shown in **question 3**.

The table shows the combination of angles. Use the table to draw and bisect various angles.

To make	Combine
75°	30° + 45°
105°	45° + 60°
120°	30° + 90° or 60° + 60°
135°	90° + 45°
150°	60° + 90°

4 Follow the instructions in **question 3** and construct a 15° angle.

5 Follow these instructions to construct a 45° angle.

    a Draw the line XY of length 6 cm.

    b Bisect the line to make a 90° angle.

    c Bisect the angle 90° to construct a 45° angle.

6 Draw the line PQ of length 5 cm. Construct a 90° angle and then construct a 45° angle.

7 Follow the instructions on **question 1** and construct a $22\frac{1}{2}°$ angle.

8 Construct the following angles using a ruler and a pair of compasses.

    a 75°   **b** 105°   **c** 120°   **d** 135°   **e** 150°

    f 210°   **g** 245°   **h** 15°   **i** $82\frac{1}{2}$ **j** $112\frac{1}{2}°$

An alternative method of constructing a right angle, 90°

a Draw a 8 cm horizontal line AB and place a point at A.

b Put a point about 6 cm from point A. Label it P.

c Using your compasses measure a radius of distance AP.

d With the compass point at P draw an arc that crosses the line and extends below and above point P.

e Draw a line through P from the point where the arc crosses the line. Label the point Q.

f Draw a line from Q through P to cut across the arc. Label this new point C. Note that CQ is the diameter of the circle.

g Joint C and A. The line drawn is perpendicular to the line AB. Therefore angle CAB is 90°.

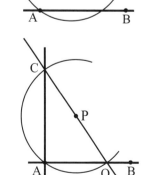

9 Follow the steps above using a radius of: **a** 5.5 cm   **b** 7 cm to draw 90° angles.

4   Constructing parallel lines

Parallel lines Lines which remain the same distance apart are called **parallel lines**.
Parallel lines never meet. They are usually marked with arrows.
Lines with the same number of arrows are parallel to each other.

Examples of parallel lines:

The symbol for parallel lines is $\parallel$

For example AB $\parallel$ CD indicates
line AB "is parallel to" line CD

Exercise 7:5

1 Using the symbol of parallel lines, find and name all the pairs of parallel lines.

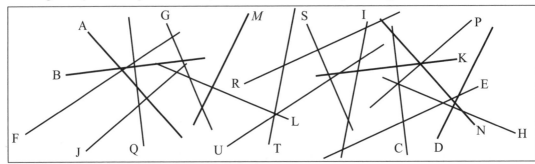

2 Construct a line parallel to AB through the point C.

C•

   a Draw the line AB 6 cm.
      Mark a point P on the line.

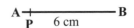

C•

   b Open out the compass to the length CP.
      Keep this length on the compass throughout.

   c Place the compass point at P and draw an arc
      to meet AB. Call this point Q.

   d Place the compass at Q and draw an arc above line AB.
      Place the compass at C and draw another arc to cross at R.

   e Join C and R
      The line CR should be parallel to line AB.
      Check by measuring the distance apart.

3 **a** Draw line JK 7 cm long.
    b Construct a line parallel to JK at B.

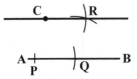

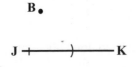

4 **a** Draw line ST 6 cm long.
    b Construct a line parallel to ST at O.

Set square   A **set square** is a right-angled triangular plate used to draw lines.
There are two types of set squares. They are named according to the angles present on each.

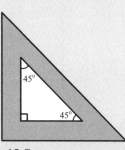

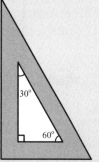

45 Set square   60 - 30 Set square

Parallel lines can be constructed using a set square and a ruler. Some set squares have millimetre and or inch graduations along the edges. This makes lines easy to draw and measure.

Ways of measuring angles: $30°$ to the horizontal $30°$ to the vertical

Exercise 7:6

1   Follow these steps to construct a pair of parallel lines which are 5 cm apart.

a   Draw a 5 cm horizontal line. Leave the ruler there.

b   Place an edge of the set square against the ruler and draw a line.

c   Slide the set square into a new position keeping the ruler fixed at the same position.

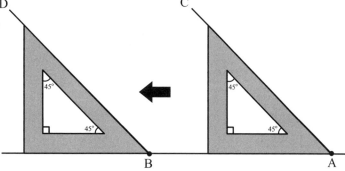

d   Draw a line along the same edge that was used in step **b**.

e   Carefully measure the distance between line AC and line BD.

f   We can now conclude that AC $\parallel$ BD.

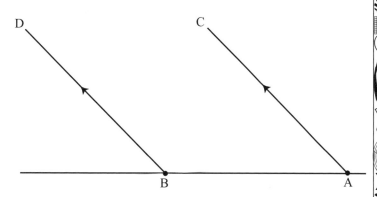

2   Follow the instructions in **question 1** and draw the line PQ parallel to line RT 6.5 cm apart.

159

3 Using the steps in **question 1** draw these vertical parallel lines along the same edge.

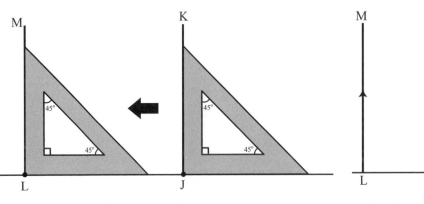

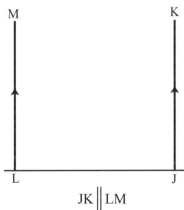

JK ‖ LM

4 Using the steps in **question 1** draw these parallel lines along the same edge.
The lines are 15° to the horizontal.

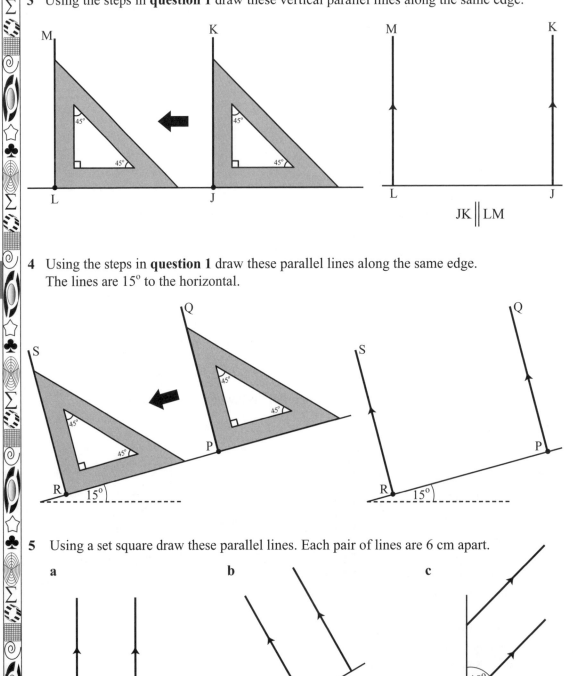

5 Using a set square draw these parallel lines. Each pair of lines are 6 cm apart.

   a   **b**   **c**

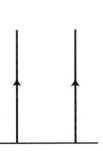
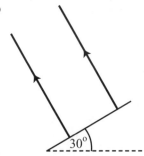
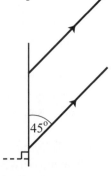

6 Using a set square draw these parallel lines. Each pair of lines are 5 cm apart.

   a YZ ‖ WX 15° to the horizontal   **b** CD ‖ AB 45° to the horizontal

   c OP ‖ MN 105° to the vertical   **d** IJ ‖ GH 30° to the vertical

5 Constructing triangles

The triangle ABC has three sides AB, BC, AC and three angles $\hat{A}$, $\hat{B}$ and $\hat{C}$.
Sometimes an angle is written using the two sides
that form the angle, so that

$\hat{A}$ can be written as $B\hat{A}C$ or $C\hat{A}B$

$\hat{B}$ can be written as $A\hat{B}C$ or $C\hat{B}A$

$\hat{C}$ can be written as $B\hat{C}A$ or $A\hat{C}B$

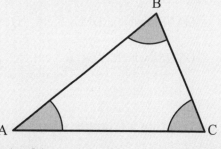

There are three ways of constructing a triangle:

 i Given one side and two angles, **ASA (Angle Side Angle)**.

 ii Given two sides and the angle between them, **SAS (Side Angle Side)**.

 iii Given the lengths of three sides, **SSS (Side Side Side)**.

You can also measure $\hat{C}$ to check the construction.

> The sign △ usually represents
> a triangle e.g. △ABC

Constructing a triangle where one side and two angles are given

Exercise 7:7

1 Construct △ABC in which AC = 6 cm,
  $\hat{A}$ = 35°. and $\hat{C}$ = 40°.

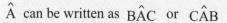

  Follow these steps to construct the triangle:

  a Make a rough sketch △ABC and mark
   all the measurements on it

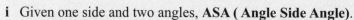

  b Draw the line AC, making it 6 cm long.
   Label both ends AC.

  c At A use your protractor
   to make a 35° angle.

  d At C use your protractor
   to make a 40° angle.

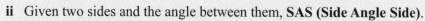

  e Draw both angle arms until they meet. Label this point B.

  f Since $\hat{A} + \hat{B} + \hat{C}$ = 180° $\hat{B}$ = 180° − 35° − 40° = 105°. Measure to check.

Construct these triangles and check that all your angles add up to 180°.

2 △ABC in which AC = 7 cm, $\hat{A}$ = 45°, $\hat{C}$ = 55°. Measure AB, BC and $\hat{B}$.

3 △GAP in which GP = 8 cm, $\hat{G}$ = 53°, $\hat{P}$ = 64°. Measure GA, AP and $\hat{A}$.

4 △BRO in which BR = 6.5 cm, $\hat{B}$ = 38°, $\hat{O}$ = 70°. Measure RO, BO and $\hat{O}$.

5 △DAM in which DM = 5 cm, $\hat{D}$ = 65°, $\hat{M}$ = 48°. Measure AD, AM and $\hat{A}$.

6 △GYE in which YE = 6.5 cm, $\hat{G}$ = 125°, $\hat{E}$ = 30°. Measure GY, GE and $\hat{Y}$.

Constructing a triangle where two sides and the angle between them are given

Exercise 7:8

1 Construct △XYZ in which XY = 5 cm,
XZ = 6 cm and $\hat{X}$ = 64°

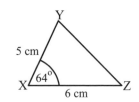

Follow these steps to construct the triangle:

a Sketch △XYZ and mark all the measurements on it.

X ————————————————————— Z

b Draw the line XZ, making it 6 cm long.

c Use the protractor to make angle 64° at X. Draw the arm quite long.

d Use a ruler to set your compasses to length of XY, 5 cm.

e With the compass point at X draw an arc to cut the arm of the angle.

Label this point Y.
Join Z and Y.

△XYZ is the required triangle.

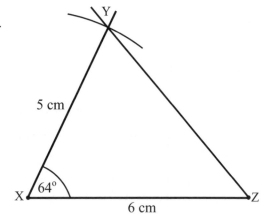

Construct these triangles. In each case draw a rough sketch first.
Check that all your angles add up to 180°.

2 △CAR where $\hat{C}$ = 55°, CA = 6 cm, CR = 5.5 cm. Measure AR, $\hat{A}$ and $\hat{R}$.

3 △PEN in which $\hat{P}$ = 35°, PN = 4 cm, PE = 5.5 cm. Measure EN, $\hat{E}$ and $\hat{N}$.

4 △TOW in which $\hat{T}$ = 30°, TW = 7.2 cm, TO = 7.2 cm. Measure OW, $\hat{W}$ and $\hat{O}$.

5 △YOU in which $\hat{Y}$ = 86°, YU = 7.8 cm, YO = 6 cm. Measure OU, $\hat{U}$ and $\hat{O}$.

6 △ZIP in which $\hat{Z}$ = 74°, ZP = 5.2 cm, ZI = 5.9 cm. Measure PI, $\hat{P}$ and $\hat{I}$.

Constructing a triangle where the lengths of three sides are given

Exercise 7:9

1 Construct △PQR in which PQ = 5 cm,
PR = 4 cm and QR = 6.5 cm.

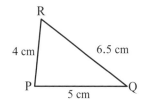

Follow these steps to construct the triangle:

a Sketch △PQR and mark all the measurements on it.

b Draw line PQ, 5 cm.

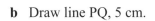

c Set the compasses to the length of PR
for 4 cm.
Put the compass point at P and draw
a wide arc.

d Using a ruler set the compasses to the
length of QR for 6.5 cm.
With the point at Q, draw another arc
to cut the first arc at R.

e Join PR and QR.

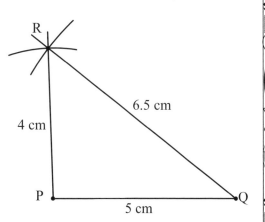

Construct these triangles. In each case draw a rough sketch first.
Check that all your angles add up to 180°.

2 △SAW where SA = 7.3 cm, AW = 6.3 cm, SW = 6.8 cm. Measure Ŝ , Â and Ŵ.

3 △TIP where TI = 9.5 cm, IP = 9.5 cm, TP = 8.8cm. Measure T̂ , Î and P̂ .

4 △JOY where JO = 10 cm, OY = 7.7 cm, JY = 4.4 cm. Measure Ĵ , Ô and Ŷ .

5 △FLY where FL = 4.2 cm, LY = 5.7 cm, FY = 5.7 cm. Measure F̂ , L̂ and Ŷ .

6 △END where EN = 9.6 cm, ND = 4.2 cm, ED = 11.4 cm. Measure Ê , N̂ and D̂ .

7 Construct these triangles
and measure all the three
angles.

a

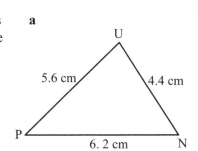

b

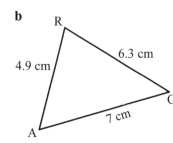

6 Constructing a regular hexagon

Hexagon A **hexagon** is a polygon with six sides. A **regular hexagon** is a polygon with six equal sides. It can be drawn using the method of constructing a 60° angle.

Exercise 7:10

1 Construct a regular hexagon in which one side is 4 cm.
  Follow these steps to construct the hexagon shown:

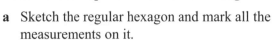

  a Sketch the regular hexagon and mark all the measurements on it.

  b Draw the line HE of length 4 cm and construct a 60° angle.

  c Label the point where the two arcs meet, X.

  d Construct another 60° angle using the points HX and label where the two arcs intersect A.

  e Continue the process until all the six angles have been constructed.

  f Join the points E, X, A, G, O, N and E.

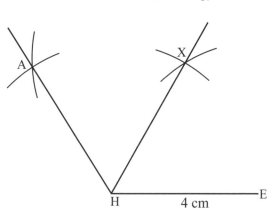

2 Construct each of these regular hexagons with the length of sides shown.

i 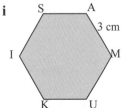 3 cm

ii 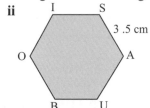 3.5 cm

iii 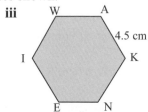 4.5 cm

Circumcircle A circle touching all the vertices of a triangle is called a **circumcircle**.

2 Follow these steps to construct a circumcircle:

  a Draw any triangle XYZ.
  b Construct the perpendicular bisector XZ and XY.
  c The point where the two bisectors meet, W, is the **circumcentre**. This point could be outside.
  d Using the compasses set the radius from W to one of X, Y or Z.
  e Draw a circle that will pass through all the three vertices.

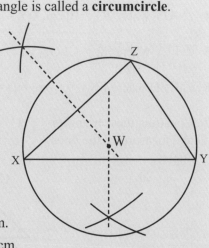

3 Draw a circumcircle of:
  a △JAM in which $\hat{J}$ = 80°, $\hat{M}$ = 35°, JM = 5.8 cm.
  b △POT where PO = 8.2 cm, OT = 7.5 cm, PT = 6 cm.

EXTENSION

1 Draw a horizontal line AB of 10.5 cm. Using the perpendicular bisection divide the line into four equal parts.

2 Draw a line VW = 8.4 cm which is 60° to the horizontal. Using the method of perpendicular bisection divide the line into four equal parts.

3 a Make a rough sketch of this treasure map.

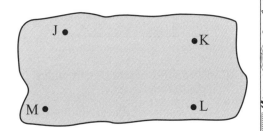

b The treasure is buried at a point which is equidistant from M and K.
It is also equidistant from J and L.
Find where the treasure is buried.

4 a Draw the shape of this rectangular room.
Use the scale of 1 cm = 1 m.

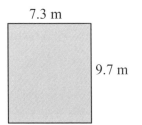

b A table is to be placed in the centre of the room.
Show exactly where the table can be placed.

5 Draw the shape shown.
Bisect the line CO.
Bisect the line PO.
Mark the point of intersection W.
Join W with C, P and O. Measure the angles WOP and COW.

What can you say about the two angles?

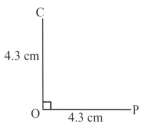

6 a Draw a straight line and mark the mid-point O.

b The angle at O is 180°. Bisect angle O.   c What is the size of each new angle?

d Construct an angle of 60°.   e Construct an angle of 22.5°.

7 Draw an angle of 42°.
Bisect the angle using
a pair of compasses.

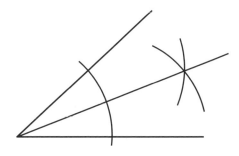

8 Construct these isosceles triangles. Measure each side.

a

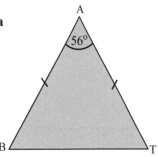

b

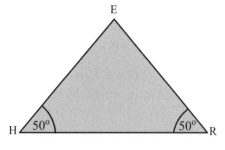

9 Construct these isosceles triangles. Measure each angle.

a

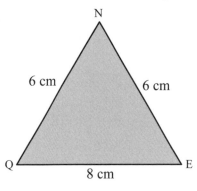

b

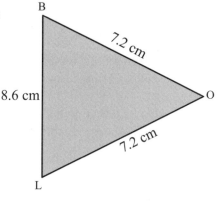

10 Draw line RS 12 cm long. Construct an angle of 60° at R. Construct an angle of 30° at S. Label with T the point where the arms of R̂ and Ŝ cross. What size should T̂ be ? Measure T̂ as a check on your construction.

11 a Draw this triangle accurately.
  b Bisect the angle at vertex Y.
  c Bisect the angle at vertex E.
  d Bisect the angle at vertex S.
  e Draw a point where the three bisectors cross and label this point O.

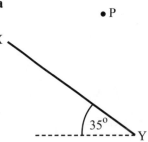

12 Each of these lines is 6 cm from the point, P. Construct a line through P which is parallel to XY.

a

b

c

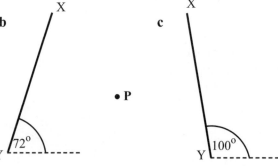

13   Construct an equilateral triangle where each side is 4.9 cm.

14 a   Draw a rectangle 10 cm by 8 cm.

   b   Draw in the diagonals.

   c   Draw the perpendicular bisector of each diagonal.

15 a   Draw a right angle triangle KAE where KA = 40 mm, AE = 30 mm and KE = 50 mm.

   b   Draw the perpendicular bisectors of KA and KE. Let the bisectors meet at M.

16 a   Draw a 70° angle.

   b   With your compass point on the corner, draw an arc crossing both arms of the angle. Label the crossing points A and B.

   c   Draw arcs from points A and B.

   d   Draw the line which bisects the angle.

   e   Measure the two parts of the angle to check that is is correct.

17   Draw and construct circumcircles for each of these triangles. Mark the circumcentre of each triangle.

a 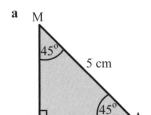   **b** 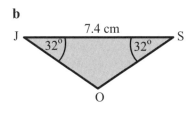   **c**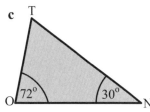

18 a   Construct the isosceles triangle ASH in which AS = 6 cm and SH = AH = 8 cm.

   b   Construct the perpendicular bisector of the side AS. Explain why this line divides △ASH into two.

19   This diagram shows the position of Prempeh, Osei and Tutu.

   a   Copy the diagram.
   They all started at the same point and ran away from each other at the same speed.

   b   Find the point where they started.

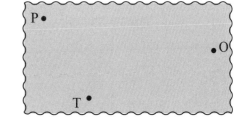

20   Construct these shapes using only a ruler and a pair of compasses. They are not drawn to scale.

a 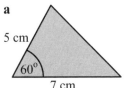   **b** 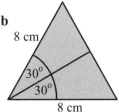   **c**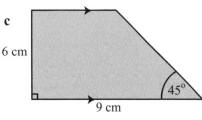

SUMMARY

Perpendicular lines	If two lines meet at right angles (90°) then the two lines are said to be **perpendicular** to each other. The symbol ⊥ means "is perpendicular to".
Bisecting a line	**Bisecting a line** means cutting it into two equal parts.
Perpendicular bisector	On this diagram: CD is perpendicular to AB CD bisects AB CD is called the **perpendicular bisector** of AB.

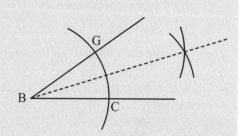

Bisecting an angle **Bisecting an angle** means splitting it exactly in half. To do this accurately use a ruler, pencil and a pair of compasses.

Example Bisect angle GBC.

With the compass point at B draw an arc GC.
With centres at G and C draw two more arcs as shown.

The angle bisector is then drawn as shown with a dotted line.

Parallel lines Lines which remain the same distance apart are called **parallel lines**. Parallel lines never meet. They are usually marked with arrows. Lines with the same number of arrows are parallel to each other.

Examples of parallel lines:

The symbol for parallel lines is ∥

For example AB ∥ CD indicates line AB "is parallel to" line CD

Set square A **set square** is a right-angled triangular plate used to draw lines. There are two types of set squares. They are named according to the angles present on each.

Ways of measuring angles:

30° to the horizontal   30° to the vertical

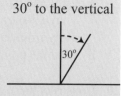

45 Set square   60 - 30 Set square

Hexagon	A **hexagon** is a polygon with six sides. A **regular hexagon** is a polygon with six equal sides. It can be drawn by constructing a series of 60° angles.
Circumcircle	A circle touching all the vertices of a triangle is called a **circumcircle**.
Circumcentre	The centre of a circumcircle is called a **circumcentre**.

Algebraic expressions

EXTENSION

SUMMARY

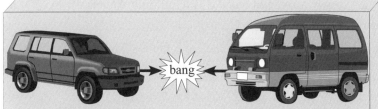

1400 kg @ 8 m/s   1200 kg @ 5 m/s

A Ford car of mass 1400 kg is moving with a speed of 8 m/s when it collides with a second car, a Toyota of mass 1200 kg travelling at a speed of 5 m/s. If the two cars are automatically coupled together at impact, at what speed do they move together?

We use the rule:

Momentum before impact = Momentum after impact

Given that:

$$M_v U_v + M_c U_c = V(M_v + M_c)$$

$$1400 \times 8 + 1200 \times 5 = 2600V$$

Therefore the speed of the coupled cars after impact is,
$V = 6.62$ m/s.

Who is at fault ?

1 Brackets

Delimiter   A pair of symbols used to enclose expressions or as operators.

Brackets   Enclosed pairs of symbols which denote expressions.

Brackets are used to specify the order of operations and to make calculations clear. Terms inside the brackets are evaluated first in any operation.

Types of brackets

( ) Round brackets or parentheses

[ ] Square brackets or box brackets

{ } Curly brackets or braces or chicken lips

< > Angle brackets or diamond brackets

$|x|$ Absolute values of x

$\overline{a+b}$ Grouped, bond, chain or tie brackets

> **'BODMAS'**
> Always perform operations in the following order:
> **B**rackets first
> p**O**wers
> **D**ivide
> **M**ultiply
> **A**dd and Subtract

Nested brackets are strings of brackets. They are used to match the correct pairs of brackets. If there are more than one set of brackets do the inner brackets first.

If a calculation has brackets, work out what is inside the brackets first. It is the first rule of arithmetic operation.

$6 + 2 \times 7$ may mean add 6 and 2 and multiply the answer by 7. It may also mean add 6 to the answer of 2×7

We can use brackets to make it clear what we mean.

Examples   **a** $(6 + 2) \times 7$ means 'do $6 + 2$ first'   **b** $6 + (2 \times 7)$ means 'do 2×7 first'
∴ $(6 + 2) \times 7 = 8 \times 7 = 56$ ∴ $6 + (2 \times 7) = 6 + 14 = 20$

c $(18 + 6) \div (4 + 2) = 24 \div 6 = 4$ **d** $(32 + 5) - (7 \times 4) = 37 - 28 = 9$

Exercise 8:1

Work out the answers to these:

1 $7 + (2 \times 6)$

2 $(18 \div 3) + (20 \div 4)$

3 $6 \times (8 - 5)$

4 $35 \div (16 - 9)$

5 $(15 - 3 \times 2) \div (10 - 7)$

6 $(27 + 25) \div (23 + 7 - 4)$

7 $6 + [2 \times (7 - 2)]$

8 $[8 + 4] \div [(9 - 5) + 2]$

9 $[16 \times (9 \div 3)] - [20 + (44 \div 2)]$

10 $87 \div (12 + 17)$

11 $[9 \div 10] - [\frac{8}{9} \div 10]$

12 $11 - (112 \div 7) - (-2 - 3)$

13 $11 \times (76 \div 4)$

14 $[5 - (18 \div 72)] \times [1 \div 4]$

15 $[14 \div (23 - 17)] + [9 - 2\frac{2}{5}]$

16 $(68 + 12) \div 5$

17 $(20 - 18)(17 - 8) + 6$

18 $[1 - (7 - 11)] \times [2(4 - 9)]$

19 $(18 - 8) \times 5$

20 $13[(16 \div 20)(20 \div 16)]$

21 $51 \div [(102 \div 6)(6.5 \div 1.3)] + 6$

Brackets need to be put in the right place to get the correct answer.

Examples   Rewrite each of these with brackets in the right places and work out the answer:

a $6 + 12 \times 8 = 102$ is correctly written as $6 + (12 \times 8) = 102$

b $51 - 21 \div 3 = 10$ is correctly written as $51 - (21 \div 3) = 10$

c $3 \times 8 - 4 \times 5 = 60$ is correctly written as $3 \times (8 - 4) \times 5 = 3 \times 4 \times 5 = 60$

Exercise 8:2

Rewrite each of these with brackets in the right place and work out the answer:

1 $30 \div 2 + 3 = 6$ **2** $30 \div 2 + 3 = 18$ **3** $2 \times 3 + 4 \times 2 = 28$

4 $15 - 3 \div 2 = 6$ **5** $4 \times 5 - 2 \times 3 = 36$ **6** $15 + 14 - 11 + 13 - 12 = 19$

7 $18 - 8 \times 12 \div 3 = 40$ **8** $6 + 2 \times 3 + 4 = 56$ **9** $52 \div 10 + 3 + 27 - 9 = 22$

10 $8 \div 16 \times 43 - 19 = 12$ **11** $-3 + 56 + 23 - 5 = 71$ **12** $88 - 17 - 91 + 9 - 8 = -19$

13 $7 - 15 \times 8 + 67 = 3$ **14** $3 \times 20 - 14 \div 24 \div 8 = 6$ **15** $-6 \times -43 \div 344 \times 84 = 63$

INVESTIGATION

Biggest wins

This game is for a group of 3 or 4 people.
You will need a pen or pencil and paper.

Instructions

1 Choose a leader.
2 The leader calls out 4 numbers. The numbers must be less than 10.
3 The other players write down the numbers.
4 Each player must use $+, -, \times, \div$ or brackets with the 4 numbers to try to make the biggest answer.
5 Use each number once and use $+, -, \times$ and $\div$ not more than once.

Example   The leader calls these numbers: 9, 7, 4, 1

Mensah writes $1 + 7 \times 9 - 4 = 60$

Oppong writes $(9 + 7) \times 4 - 1 = 63$ Oppong wins!

The player who makes the biggest answer gets 10 points. Others get nothing.

The winner is the player who has the most points after 5 rounds.

Now play the game!

Multiplication of directed numbers

Directed numbers   Positive and negative numbers are collectively known as **directed numbers**. They have one of the signs + or − (superscript: $^+$ or $^-$) to show direction. The + conventionally shows a direction to the right or upwards. The − shows the opposite.

The line 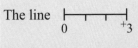 can stand for $^+3$ (or 3).

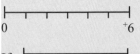 then stands for $2 \times {}^+3$. This new line is twice as long, $2 \times {}^+3 = 6$

If 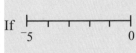 stands for $^-5$ then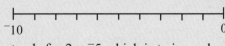

stands for $2 \times {}^-5$ which is twice as long

Exercise 8:3

For each question draw lines to show the given number and the answer to the calculation.

1 Show $^+4$ and $2 \times {}^+4$ 2 Show $^-6$ and $2 \times {}^-6$

3 Show $^+6$ and $3 \times {}^+6$ 4 Show $^-7$ and $2 \times {}^-7$

5 Show $^-3$ and $2 \times {}^-3$ 6 Show $^+5$ and $3 \times {}^+5$

7 Show $^-5$ and $5 \times {}^-5$ 8 Show $^-8$ and $3 \times {}^-8$

Multiplication by $^-1$ causes a rotation through $180°$.

since 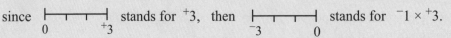 stands for $^+3$, then 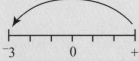 stands for $^-1 \times {}^+3$.

This diagram shows that $^-1 \times {}^+3 = {}^-3$

This diagram shows that $^-1 \times {}^-6 = {}^+6$

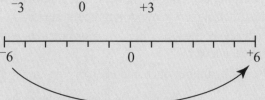

Exercise 8:4

Work out these. You may draw a line to help you.

1 $^-1 \times {}^+4$ 2 $^-1 \times {}^-5$ 3 $^-1 \times {}^-7$ 4 $^-1 \times {}^+7$

5 $^-1 \times {}^-1$ 6 $^-1 \times -12$ 7 $^-1 \times {}^+10$ 8 $^-1 \times {}^-26$

Rules for multiplying and dividing out directed numbers:

$$+ \times + = + \qquad - \times - = + \qquad + \times - = - \qquad - \times + = -$$

$$+ \div + = + \qquad - \div - = + \qquad + \div - = - \qquad - \div + = -$$

Examples
a $^-4 \times 5 = {}^-20$ **b** $^-6 \times {}^-3 = 18$ **c** $^-6 \times -3 \times {}^+5 = 90$

d $^-56 \div {}^-4 = 14$ **e** $^+36 \div {}^-8 = {}^-4\frac{1}{2}$ **f** $^-8a \times -a = 8a^2$

g $^+5 \times {}^-7y = -35y$ **h** $^+7a \times -8 \times {}^+4 = {}^-224a$ **i** $^-78xy \div 13y = \dfrac{\cancel{{}^-78xy}^{6}}{\cancel{13y}_{1}}$

$$= {}^-6x$$

Note: Operations such as: $\times - 2$ can be written as $\times\ {}^-2$;

$\div - 2$ can be written as $\div\ {}^-2$

Exercise 8:5

Work out the following:

1 $6 \times {}^-2$ **2** $^-4 \times 7$ **3** $^-9 \times {}^-11$

4 $^-24 \div {}^+6$ **5** $^-18 \div {}^-3$ **6** $-39 \div {}^-13$

7 $^-6 \times {}^+6$ **8** $^-5 \times {}^-23$ **9** $^-6 \times {}^+2 \times {}^-9$

10 $^-118 \div {}^-4$ **11** $^+95 \div {}^-19$ **12** $^-104 \div {}^-13$

13 $^-2a \times 3$ **14** $^-4 \times {}^-a$ **15** $^-7r \times {}^-10$

16 $^-7a \div {}^-7$ **17** $^+9 \div {}^-3a$ **18** $^-60a \div {}^-15$

19 $-t^2 \times {}^-s$ **20** $^-k \times {}^-8k$ **21** $^-p \times 5p^2$

22 $18p \div {}^-p$ **23** $27xy \div {}^-9y$ **24** $^-75rs \div 15rs$

25 $^-15a \times 7b$ **26** $^-12xy \times 3x$ **27** $y \times {}^-y \times {}^-y$

28 $^-84ab \div {}^-14b$ **29** $121xy \div {}^-22y$ **30** $^-42uv \div 7uv$

31 $2a \times - 16b \times -9$ **32** $^-8ab \times {}^-9b \times {}^-2a$ **33** $^-12x \times {}^-8aw \times 3awx$

34 $^-150p^2 \div {}^-15p$ **35** $189st \div {}^-54t$ **36** $^-49c^2d \div {}^-147cd$

37 $^-10p^2 \div {}^-15p \times 45p$ **38** $\frac{8}{9}xy \div {}^-96y \times 216z$ **39** $-\frac{9}{11}xy^2 \times {}^-132x \div {}^-108y$

173

Removing brackets

In algebra brackets are used for convenience in grouping terms together.

'Expand brackets' in an expression means the same as 'remove the brackets'.

Identity   An **identity** is when the expressions on each side of the equation always give the value whatever numbers are substituted for the letters in the them. The expressions are said to be identically equal.

Example $5(x + 2) = 5x + 10$ is an identity because $5(x + 2)$ and $5x + 10$ always give the same result whatever value x takes.

When removing brackets each term inside the brackets must be multiplied by the quantity outside first, then collect the like terms.

> **Clarity in writing algebraic expressions**
>
> ■ Where possible avoid writing a negative sign in front of an expression. E.g. write:
> $-12x + 6y$ as $6y - 12x$
>
> ■ $-1(2x + y)$ is written as $-(2x + y)$
>
> ■ $--3$ is typed as $-\,^-3$
>
> ■ $\times -3$ is typed as $\times\,^-3$

Examples   **a** $6(x + y) = 6 \times x + 6 \times y = 6x + 6y$

b $8(3x - 2) = 8 \times 3x + 8 \times\,^-2 = 24x - 16$

c $3(4x + 6y) = 3 \times 4x + 3 \times 6y = 12x + 18y$

If a bracket has a minus sign in front of it the signs of all the terms inside the bracket must be changed.
[i.e. $-$ becomes $+$, $+$ becomes $-$]

Examples   **a** $-(s + t) = -s - t$

b $-3(4x - 2y) = {}^-3 \times 4x - {}^-3 \times 2 \times y = -12x + 6y$

c $-2y(5x - b) = -2y \times 5x + {}^-2y \times {}^-b = -10xy + 2by$

Exercise 8:6

Expand the brackets in these expressions:

1 $6(2x + 2y)$

2 $3(x - y)$

3 $5(4 + 6x)$

4 $-2(2x + y)$

5 $4(0.2x - 5y)$

6 $-(3a - 3b)$

7 $-5(6 - 2x)$

8 $2xy(a + 2b)$

9 $-(8m - 6)$

10 $a(x - y - z)$

11 $5(6a + 4b - 2c)$

12 $\frac{1}{2}(x - 1)$

13 $-2m(^-1 - 3m - 4n)$

14 $-\frac{1}{2}(2x + 6y - 10z)$

15 $4(^-6a - 7b + 8c)$

16 $3x^2(x - 2xy + y^2)$

17 $^-0.3(^-4a + 0.4b - 0.04c)$

18 $2.5(^-x - 6y + 10z)$

19 $^-2(^-3p + 4p^2 - 5p^3)$

20 $^-2a(^-a - 2b - 0.25c)$

21 $^-7(3m + {}^-\frac{5}{7}n - 4)$

22 $-(^-6x + {}^-t + {}^-s)$

23 $-\frac{2}{5}(^-a + 7x - {}^-45y)$

24 $-\frac{7}{8}(^-56a - 32b + 72c)$

Multiplying and simplifying brackets

Two or more sets of brackets can be multiplied out before collecting like terms.

Example   Expand and simplify:

a $3(x + 4) + 6(2x + 3)$ **b** $8(2x + 3) - 5(2x - 5)$ **c** $-(x + y) + 3(4 - 6y)$

$$
\begin{aligned}
\textbf{a}\quad 3(x + 4) + 6(2x + 3) &= 3x + 12 + 12x + 18 &&\text{(multiply out brackets)}\\
&= 3x + 12x + 12 + 18 &&\text{(collect like terms)}\\
&= 15x + 30 &&\text{(simplify)}
\end{aligned}
$$

$$
\begin{aligned}
\textbf{b}\quad 8(2x + 3) - 5(2x - 5) &= 16x + 24 - 10x + 25\\
&= 16x - 10x + 24 + 25\\
&= 6x + 49
\end{aligned}
$$

$$
\begin{aligned}
\textbf{c}\quad -(x + y) + 3(4 - 6y) &= -x - y + 12 - 18y\\
&= -x - y - 18y + 12\\
&= -x - 19y + 12 = 12 - x - 19y
\end{aligned}
$$

Exercise 8:7

Expand and simplify these algebraic expressions:

1 $3(x + 2) + 6(3x + 4)$

2 $2(5x + 3b) + 3(a - b)$

3 $3x(4 + y) - y(x + 2)$

4 $5(1 - 2x) - 2(2x - 3)$

5 $-(4a + 3b - 2c) + 3a$

6 $8a + 4(2 + a)$

7 $-(a + b) - 3(2a + 2b)$

8 $3(a + 7) + 4(^{-}7 - 3a)$

9 $-4(4x + 4y) - (3x + 3y)$

10 $5(a + b + c) - 2(a + b + c)$

11 $q(q + 6) - 5(q^2 + z)$

12 $9(l - 4) + l(l - 9)$

13 $g(3 - 7f) - 3(2f - g)$

14 $x(x - 5) - (7x - 2)$

15 $f(f + 8) - (8f - 2)$

16 $z - 4 - z(z + 1)$

17 $2x(7y - 11 - 13x) - 9(x - 5y)$

18 $5a(8 + 21b) - (^{-}3b - 3 - a)$

19 $\frac{1}{4}(6x - 8y) - \frac{1}{2}(14x + 7y)$

20 $0.3(4x + 9y) - 0.4(5x - 10y)$

21 $3(a + b) - 9(^{-}a - b) - ^{-}b$

22 $3 - a - (2a - 8) + (^{-}7b - a)$

23 $\frac{1}{3}(6a - 7b) - \frac{2}{3}(12a - 8b)$

24 $0.2(15 + 6x) + 0.3(10x - 20y - 10)$

Area and multiplication of algebraic expressions

Rectangles can be used to illustrate facts about the multiplication of algebraic expressions.

Area of a rectangle = Base × Height

This rectangle is 2 by 3

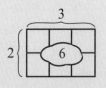

Area = 2 × 3 = 6

This rectangle is 3 by $(4 + x)$

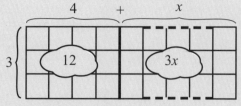

Area is: $3(4 + x) = 12 + 3x$

This rectangle is 6 by t

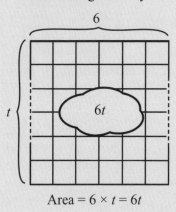

Area = 6 × t = 6t

This rectangle is a by $(5 + b)$

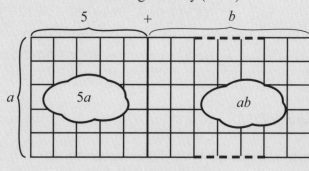

Area is: $a(5 + b) = 5a + ab$

Exercise 8:8

Copy each rectangle. Put the answer of each area in the blob and find the total area.

1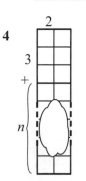

2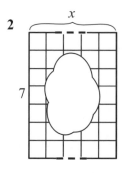

3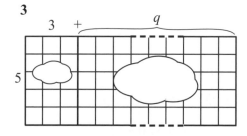

4

5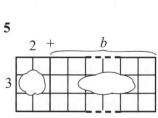

6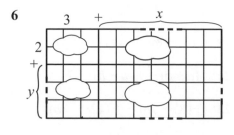

BRACKETS GAME

Copy and make three of each of these cards.

Each card should be measured 6 cm by 4 cm.

$7a$	$-5b$	$8b$	$7b$	$-4a$	$4b$

8	3	-4	$9a$	$5a$	$-6a$

$2(2b-2)$	$5(a-b)$	$3(3a+1)$	$7(a+b)$	$2(4-3a)$	$4(2b-a)$

The Game

▨ The game can be played by a group of 3 or 4 people and a dealer.

▨ The dealer shuffles the cards and gives each player 3 cards face down, then places the next card on the table face up. This card starts the throw-away pile. The rest of the pack is placed face down next to the upturned card.

▨ The winner of the game is the person with a set of 3 cards that make a correct statement.

▨ *Example*

$-5b$		$5(a-b)$		$5a$

This is a winning set of 3 cards since:
$5(a-b) = 5a - 5b$

The Play

▨ The dealer starts, with other players taking their turn in a clockwise direction (or on the dealer's left hand side).

▨ When it is a player's turn they may either:
  i pick a card from the pack and discard one of their cards, or
  ii pick a face up card to complete a set if it could help and then put another card on the throw away pile, or
  iii show their cards as a correct statement: this wins the round.

The Rules

■ If a player chooses to take from the throw-away pile only the top card may be taken.
■ The first player to get a set of 3 cards that makes a correct statement scores a point and then deals for the next round.
■ A player who makes an incorrect statement loses one point.
■ The game is finished after 15 minutes. The person with the highest score wins.

SCORE CARD

Keep the scores as shown:

Name	Point Scored	Point Lost	Final Score
Ama	~~||||~~ |||||	~~||||~~		3
Kwame	~~||||~~ ||	|||	4

(8)

Perimeter The **perimeter** of a shape is the total distance around the edge of the shape. Find all the sides and add them up.

$$Perimeter = 2 \times length + 2 \times width$$
$$P = 2l + 2w$$

Example **a** 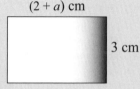 (2 + a) cm

3 cm

The perimeter of this shape is:

$$P = 2(2 + a) + (2 \times 3)$$
$$= 4 + 2a + 6$$
$$= 10 + 2a \text{ cm}$$

b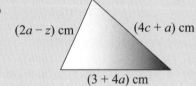

(2a − z) cm   (4c + a) cm

(3 + 4a) cm

The perimeter of this shape is:

$$P = (2a - z) + (4c + a) + (3 + 4a)$$
$$= 2a + a + 4a + 4c - z + 3$$
$$= (7a + 4c - z + 3) \text{ cm}$$

Exercise 8:9

Write and simplify the algebraic expressions for the perimeter of these shapes.

1 *x* cm

y cm

2 (2x + 3) cm

5 cm

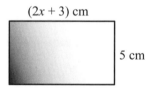

3 (3a + 2) cm

(a + 1) cm

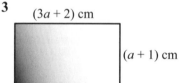

4 (4x + 4) cm

(2x + 6y) cm

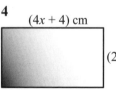

5 (3x + 4) cm   (5 + x) cm

10 cm

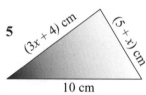

6 (x + 3) cm

(7y − 1) cm

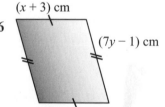

7 (3x − 5) cm

(2x + 4y) cm

(6x + y) cm

(7x + 8y) cm

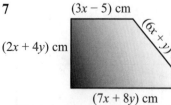

8 (2x + 7) cm

(3z + 6) cm

(x − 4) cm

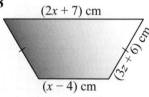

9 (4p − 3) cm

4q cm

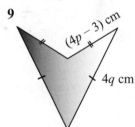

178

2 Substitution

Substitution In **substitution** integers replace the symbols so that the algebraic expression can be solved.

Examples If $x = 2$, $y = 3$ and $z = 4$ work out these:

    a $8x + 2y$ **b** $3x - 4y + 5z$ **c** $\dfrac{4z + 3y}{5}$ **d** $\dfrac{2x + 6y + 8z}{x + y + z}$

    a $8x + 2y = 8 \times 2 + 2 \times 3$ **b** $3x - 4y + 5z = 3 \times 2 - 4 \times 3 + 5 \times 4$

                    $= 16 + 6$ $= 6 - 12 + 20$

                    $= 22$ $= 14$

    c $\dfrac{4z + 3y}{5} = \dfrac{4 \times 4 + 3 \times 3}{5}$ **d** $\dfrac{2x + 6y + 8z}{x + y + z} = \dfrac{2 \times 2 + 6 \times 3 + 8 \times 4}{2 + 3 + 4}$

               $= \dfrac{16 + 9}{5} = \dfrac{25}{5}$ $= \dfrac{4 + 18 + 32}{9} = \dfrac{54}{9}$

               $= 5$ $= 6$

Exercise 8:10

1 If $p = 5$, $q = 7$, $r = 2$ and $s = 4$ work out:

    a $pqr + s$ **b** $pq - rs$ **c** $p(rs - q)$ **d** $pq + qr + rs$

2 If $c = 4$, $d = 7$ and $e = -2$ work out:

    a cde **b** $\frac{1}{2}de + c$ **c** $2e - d + 4$ **d** $\dfrac{d}{c} + e$

3 If $p = -1$, $q = 7$ and $r = 5$ work out:

    a $13p + 5(r - 9)$ **b** $\frac{9}{10}pqr$ **c** $7q - (2p - 4r)$ **d** $p - 21p^2$

4 If $f = 7$, $g = 11$ and $h = 9$ work out:

    a $hf + \frac{1}{11}g^2$ **b** $h^2 + f^2 + g^2$ **c** $(g - h)^2$ **d** $h^2 \times (f^2 + 1) - g^2$

5 If $a = 7$, $b = -12$ and $c = 3$ work out:

    a $6(3a + 2b)$ **b** $2(4a - 12c)$ **c** $\dfrac{a}{b} - 10c$ **d** $14b \div (a \times b)$

6 If $l = -20$, $m = 8$ and $n = -5$ work out:

    a $m(l + n)$ **b** $l + m - n$ **c** $4(l - n)$ **d** $8[(m \div l) + n^2]$

7 If $x = -3$, $y = 34$ and $z = 8$ work out:

    a xyz **b** $y(x \div z)$ **c** $x^2 + z^2 - y$ **d** $(x + z)^2 + y^2$

8 If $x = -4$, $y = 10$ and $z = 11$ work out:

   a $\dfrac{4z + 3y}{5}$ **b** $\dfrac{x + y - z}{10}$ **c** $\dfrac{y^2 + 3x + z}{4}$ **d** $\dfrac{7x + 7y + 7z}{14}$

9 If $x = 11$, $y = -20$ and $z = -28$ work out:

   a $x(y - z)$ **b** $x + y - z$ **c** $\dfrac{x - y - z}{0.5}$ **d** $\dfrac{y + 2(x + z)}{0.2}$

10 If $u = 6$, $v = 9$ and $w = -2$ work out:

   a $2u - 6v + 8w$ **b** $\dfrac{u - v + w}{5}$ **c** $3u^2 + 6v^2 + 7w^3$ **d** $\dfrac{(u - v + w)}{\frac{1}{3}}$

11 If $p = -15$, $y = -6$ and $c = 8$ work out:

   a $4p(y \div c)$ **b** $11y + {}^-5c - {}^-p$ **c** $\dfrac{2p + 6y + 8c}{1 + p + y + c}$ **d** $\dfrac{3p + 4y}{3c - y}$

12 Given that $P = 4q - 2r$ find P when:

   a $q = 0.7$ and $r = -2.5$ **b** $q = -0.44$ and $r = 3.4$ **c** $q = -\frac{5}{8}$ and $r = 43$

13 If $v = u + at$ find v when:

   a $u = 15$, $a = 9.81$ and $t = 5$ **b** $u = -10$, $a = 10$ and $t = 8$ **c** $u = 17$, $a = 7$ and $t = 39$

14 $y = mx + c$ find y when:

   a $m = \frac{1}{2}$, $x = 4$ and $c = 5$ **b** $m = 3$, $x = -2\frac{1}{2}$ and $c = 10$ **c** $m = 8$, $x = 4\frac{3}{10}$ and $c = 3$

15 Given that $r = \dfrac{E + V}{I}$ find r if $E = 1.15$, $V = 1.2$ and $I = 0.03$

16 Given that $y = \dfrac{1 + x}{3 + x}$ find y if $x = -17$

17 If $I = mv - mu$ find I when:

   a $m = 4$, $v = 5$ and $u = 2$ **b** $m = 40$, $v = 5$ and $u = -2$ **c** $m = 25$, $v = -12$ and $u = -10$

18 If $I = \dfrac{P \times R \times T}{100}$ find I when $P = 3506$, $R = 7.5$ and $T = 4$

19 If $A = \dfrac{3y \times 2z}{x + z}$ find A when $x = 66$, $y = 18$ and $z = 6$

20 If $°C = \frac{5}{9}(F - 32)$, change these temperatures from °F into °C.

   a $20.5\,°F$ **b** $-19\,°F$ **c** $-4\,°F$ **d** $85\,°F$ **e** $137\frac{3}{5}\,°F$

3 Factorising

Factorising The process of writing an algebraic expression as a product of factors is called **factorising**.

The expression $4x + 4y$ has the number 2 common to both terms.

4 and $x + y$ are said to be the factors of $4x + 4y$.

Note that $4x + 4y = 2(2x + 2y)$. This is factorised but not completely: it can still be divided by 2, i.e. $4x + 4y = 4(x + y)$.

Examples

a Factorise $3a + 9$

$3a + 9 = 3 \times a + 3 \times 3$

Thus 3 is a factor of each term. We say 3 is a common factor.

Therefore 3 is placed outside the bracket

$3a + 9 = 3(a + 3)$

b Factorise $nx - xy$

x is common to both the terms making up the expression.

$\therefore nx - xy = x(n - y)$

> To factorise completely use the highest common factor to divide.

c Factorise completely $6a + 12ac - 15ab$

$3a$ is a common factor

$\therefore 6a + 12ac - 15ab = 3a(2 + 4c - 5b)$

d Factorise completely $14ax - 42ay$

$14a$ is common factor

$\therefore 14ax - 42ay = 14a(x + 3y)$

Exercise 8:11

Factorise completely the following:

1 $8q + 16$

2 $2a + 4b$

3 $4a - 8$

4 $12a - 9y$

5 $10a - 5$

6 $10x - 30y$

7 $6 - 15x$

8 $x - 6xy$

9 $2xy + xyz$

10 $6xy - 4yz$

11 $xy + 3x$

12 $7a - 49b + 21c$

13 $5d + cd$

14 $5kp - kq$

15 $3jk - 2j$

16 $11ax + 33x - 121xy$

17 $6jk - 9k$

18 $12a + 8b$

19 $17x - 51xy$

20 $0.5x - 1.5ax - 2.5xy$

21 $15ab + 5bc$

22 $\frac{3}{4}ac - 4a$

23 $18g + 72gh$

24 $10a + 5b - 35ab$

25 $72pt - 54t - 9$

26 $xyz + 5wxy$

27 $27efg + 77eg$

28 $0.8nx - 1.6xy + 8x$

29 $27a + 81ab - 108$

30 $75mn - 50mp$

31 $63xyz - 54y$

32 $51p + 17pq - 8\frac{1}{2}$

181

Examples   Factorise   **a** $8x^2 - 10x$ **b** $15ab + 6a^2b$ **c** $18p^2 - 12pq3 + 24pq$

a $8x^2 - 10x = 2x \times 4x - 2x \times 5$ [factor is $2x$]
$= 2x(4x - 5)$

b $15ab + 6a^2b = 3ab \times 5 + 3ab \times 2a$ [factor is $3ab$]
$= 3ab(5 + 2a)$

c $18p^2 - 12pq^3 + 24pq = 6p \times 3p - 6p \times 2q^3 + 6p \times 4q$ (factor is $6p$)
$= 6p(3p - 2q^3 + 4q)$

■ Note that the the first line can be done mentally. It is written here to help explain the thinking involved.
■ Also if the expression has more than one common factor (as in the case of example **b**) the workings might then look like this:

$$15ab + 6a^2b = 3(5ab + 2a^2b) = 3ab(5 + 2a)$$

■ Always take careful steps to factorise completely.

Exercise 8:12

Factorise completely the following:

1 $2x + 3x^2$ **2** $a - a^2$ **3** $ab - ac$ **4** $8c^2 - c$

5 $18p^2 + 12pq$ **6** $9ce^2 + 36e^2$ **7** $3gh^2 + 15g^2h$ **8** $24d^2 + 18yd$

9 $k^2l^2 - 11jk^2$ **10** $a^2 + 5a^2b$ **11** $8y^2 - 32$ **12** $4n^2 - 12m^2$

13 $g^2h^2 - 6gh$ **14** $2p^2q^2 + 6p^2q$ **15** $21k^2l^2 - 14kl$ **16** $16m^2 + 48lm$

17 $30a^2 - 12m^3$ **18** $16x^3y - 15xy$ **19** $6p^2qr - 2pq^2r$ **20** $9s^2 - 6s^3$

21 $7ef^2 + 28f^2$ **22** $18s^2t - 27st^2$ **23** $5a^3b^2 + 10a^3b$ **24** $a^3 - 7a^2 + 5a$

25 $8xyz - 32xyw$ **26** $x^2 + 3x^3 - 5x$ **27** $14x^2y - 21xy^2$ **28** $7a^2x^3 + a^4x$

29 $\pi R^2 - \pi r^2$ **30** $mgh - \tfrac{1}{2}mv^2$ **31** $\tfrac{1}{2}mu^2 - \tfrac{1}{2}mv$ **32** $12a - 20a^2b$

33 $P + \dfrac{PRT}{100}$ **34** $\tfrac{1}{2}ah - \tfrac{1}{2}bh$ **35** $2rh_1 - 2rh_2$ **36** $2p - 4p^2 + 10p^3$

37 $x + 3x^2 - 5x^3$ **38** $\pi r^2 + 4r + r$ **39** $Mn^2 - M^2n$ **40** $2\pi r^2 + 2\pi rh$

41 $3ab + 6a^2b - 9ab^2$ **42** $\tfrac{1}{6}b^2c - \tfrac{1}{3}bc^2$ **43** $\pi r^2h + \pi R^2h$ **44** $\tfrac{4}{3}\pi r^3 - \tfrac{1}{3}\pi r^2h$

EXTENSION

1 Work out the following:

   a -4×3

   b $^-3 \times (^-1)^2$

   c $(^-2)^2 \times (-3)^2$

   d -0.5×0.6

   e $(^-0.2)^2 \times (0.3)^2$

   f $(0.5)^2 + (7.4 \times 0.5)$

2 a $-4p \times 3q$

   b $-13x \times 1.3y$

   c $-6xy \times (-xy)$

   d $3xy \times 2xy \, (^-xy)$

   e $4st \times 0.4st$

   f $-4a \times (-11b) \times (3c)$

3 Expand the brackets in these algebraic expressions and collect the like terms where possible.

   a $\frac{1}{2}(4n + 6d) - d$

   b $\frac{1}{3}(9k - 12c) + 5k$

   c $5(5s + 4t) + 4(h - 2s)$

   d $3(a + 2b - 3c) + 4(6a - b + 4c)$

   e $3(a + 3b - 4c) + 3(5a - 5b + c) - a$

   f $-2y(5x - b) - 3(4x - 2by) + 3(x - by)$

4 Rewrite each of these in the simplest form:

   a $\dfrac{(4x - 6d)}{2}$

   b $\dfrac{(15c + 35d)}{5}$

   c $\dfrac{(18y - 21y)}{3}$

   d $\dfrac{(54x - 117x)}{^-9}$

   e $\dfrac{(4a - 6b)}{^-0.2}$

   f $\dfrac{(^-13a + 6.5k)}{^-1.3}$

5 Find the areas and perimeter of each of these shapes:

a

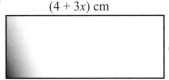

b

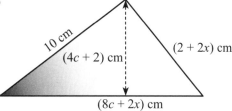

c

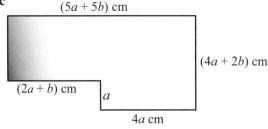

d

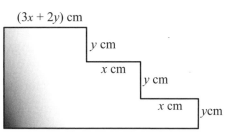

6 If $S = \frac{1}{2}(p + n)$ find S when: **a** $p = 2.5$ and $n = 2.7$ **b** $p = 8$ and $n = 5.9$

7 If $V = \frac{1}{3}Ah$ find V when: **a** $A = 1.7$ and $h = 0.6$ **b** $A = 78$ and $h = 19$

8 If $w = \frac{1}{x} + \frac{1}{y}$ find w when: **a** $x = 4$ and $y = 8$ **b** $x = 2\frac{3}{4}$ and $y = 5\frac{2}{3}$

In this exercise each letter stands for a number and shows a length in metres on each rectangle.

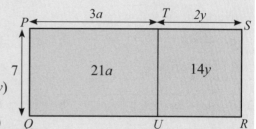

Area of rectangle PQUT = $7 \times 3a$ = $21a$

Area of rectangle TSRU = $7 \times 2y$ = $14y$

Area of rectangle PQRS = $21a + 14y = 7(3a + 2y)$

The rectangle shows that $21a + 14y \equiv 7(3a + 2y)$

The symbol $\equiv$ shows that the two expressions are identical.

Work out the areas of each of these rectangles:

9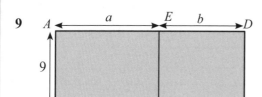

10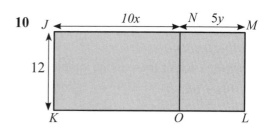

11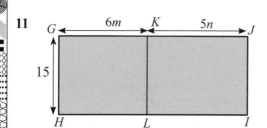

12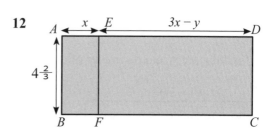

13 Draw rectangles to show that:

a $2x + 8 \equiv 2(x + 4)$ b $12a + 6 \equiv 6(2a + 1)$ c $9m + 9 \equiv 9(m + 1)$

d $6x + 18 \equiv 6(x + 3)$ e $10a + 16 \equiv 2(5a + 8)$ f $15g + 39 \equiv 3(5g + 13)$

g $34f + 51 \equiv 17(2f + 3)$ h $22k + 132l \equiv 22(k + 6l)$ i $253v + 391 \equiv 7\frac{2}{3}(33v + 51)$

14 Find the value of these by factorising:

a $4 \times 13 + 4 \times 20$ b $6 \times 20 + 6 \times 25$ c $15 \times 5 + 15 \times 7$

d $7 \times 5.5 + 7 \times 10$ e $4 \times 72 + 10 \times 72$ f $33 \times 18 + 33 \times 28$

g $49 \times 32 - 49 \times 17$ h $48 \times 74 - 34 \times 48$ i $252 \times 23 - 152 \times 23$

j $71.1 \times 9 - 9 \times 51.1$ k $5.97 \times 3.2 - 13.03 \times 3.2$ l $35.2 \times 4.2 - 25.2 \times 4.2$

m $88.6 \times 5.5 + 88.6 \times 12$ n $7.68 \times 7.9 + 7.68 \times 7.68$ o $97.3 \times 17.9 - 7.9 \times 97.3$

15 Write and simplify algebraic expressions for the perimeter of these shapes:

i

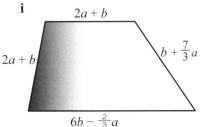

ii

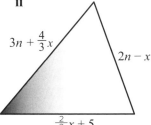

iii

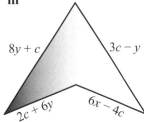

16 Factorise these:

a $9a + 27b + 15c$

b $\frac{1}{4}nx + \frac{3}{4}ny + \frac{1}{2}nz$

c $\frac{2}{5}ab + \frac{2}{5}b - \frac{4}{5}bc$

d $15ab + 18bc + 21bd$

e $x^2y^2 + n^2y + b^2y^2$

f $34abx + 17xy - 51axy$

g $32bxy + 40cxy - 24axy$

h $\frac{1}{5}xy + \frac{2}{5}ny - \frac{3}{5}y$

i $\frac{1}{3}xy + 3x + x^2$

17 Copy and complete the table where $R = 6T - 19$

R	− 5	− 3	− 1	0	2	4	6	n
T								

18 Expand and simplify these algebraic expressions.

a $3(2 - 5a) + 2(3a + 4)$

b $-a(4 - 3a) - 6(2 + 5a)$

c $0.4(x + y) - 0.6(3 - 5y)$

d $\frac{1}{3}(6 - 15a) - \frac{1}{2}(8a - 10)$

e $0.5(2a + 14) - \frac{1}{2}(2 - 8a)$

f $a(12 + b) - b(4a + 2)$

19 Given that $s = t(v - \frac{1}{2}at)$ copy and complete the table to find the corresponding values of s for the given values of a, t and v.

a	4	6	1	9.8	10	5	7	9.81
t	75	10	15	20	38	65	48	3
v	5.5	8.4	7.5	10	18	37	1	17
s								

20 Show that:

i $(x + y)^2 = x^2 + 2xy + y^2$

ii $(x - y)^2 = x^2 - 2xy + y^2$

iii $(x + y)(x - y) = x^2 - y^2$

iv $(x + y)^3 = x^3 + 3x^2y + 3xy^2 + y^3$

PUZZLE

Copy and complete the puzzle by filling in the spaces with $+, -, \times, \div$ to make both horizontal and vertical true.
Use the order of arithmetic operations (BODMAS).
The first row has been done for you.

8	−	6	÷	2	=	5
9		3		2	=	6
5		5		5	=	5
2		7		4	=	10
					=	
14		20		20	=	14

185

SUMMARY

Delimiter	A pair of symbols used to enclose expressions or as operators.
Brackets	Enclosed pairs of symbols which denote expressions.
	Brackets are used to specify the order of operations and to make calculations clear. Terms inside the brackets are evaluated first in any operation.

Examples   **a** $(6+2) \times 7 = 8 \times 7 = 56$ **b** $6 + (2 \times 7) = 6 + 14 = 20$

Rules for multiplying and dividing out directed numbers:

$+ \times + = +$ $- \times - = +$ $+ \times - = -$ $- \times + = -$

$+ \div + = +$ $- \div - = +$ $+ \div - = -$ $- \div + = -$

Examples   **a** $-4 \times 5 = -20$ **b** $-6 \times -3 = 18$ **c** $-6 \times -3 \times {}^+5 = 90$

d ${}^-56 \div {}^-4 = 14$ **e** ${}^+36 \div {}^-8 = {}^-4\frac{1}{2}$ **f** $-8a \times -a = 8a^2$

Removing brackets

In algebra brackets are used for convenience in grouping terms together. The command "expand brackets" means remove the brackets, obeying the rules for doing so.

Example $6(x + y) = 6 \times x + 6 \times y = 6x + 6y$

Identity	An **identity** is when the expressions on each side of the equation always take the value whatever numbers are substituted for the letters in the them. The expressions are said to be identically equal.

Example $5(x +2) = 5x + 10$ is an identity because $5(x +2)$ and $5x +10$ always have the same value whatever value x takes.

Substitution	In **substitution** integers replace the symbols so that the algebraic expression can be solved.

Examples   If $x = 2$, $y = 3$ and $z = 4$ work out these:

a $8x + 2y = 8 \times 2 + 2 \times 3$ **b** $3x - 4y + 5z = 3 \times 2 - 4 \times 3 + 5 \times 4$

$= 16 + 6$ $= 6 - 12 + 20$

$= 22$ $= 14$

Factorising	The process of writing an algebraic expression as a product of factors is called **factorising**.

The expression $4x + 4y$ has the number 2 common to both terms.
4 and $x + y$ are said to be the factors of $4x + 4y$.
Note that $4x + 4y = 2(2x + 2y)$, is factorised but not completely; it can still be divided by 2, i.e; $4x + 4y = 4(x + y)$.

Example   Factorise $3a + 9 = 3 \times a + 3 \times 3$
3 is a factor of each expression; thus we say 3 is a common factor.
Therefore 3 is placed outside the bracket.
$3a + 9 = 3(a + 3)$

Number plane

CORE

1 Maps
2 Coordinates
3 Linear graphs
4 Gradients of lines
5 Contours and profiles
6 Connecting rules

EXTENSION

SUMMARY

The French mathematician and philosopher **René Descartes** (1596 - 1650) created a way of using numbers and lines called axes to locate points in 2D or 3D space.

Descartes' fundamental Cartesian doctrines are:
- the method of systematic doubt;
- the first indubitably true proposition, *Je pense, donc je suis or Cogito ergo sum* (*'I think therefore I am'*);
- the idea of God as the absolutely perfect Being; and
- dualism of mind and matter as separate though interacting.

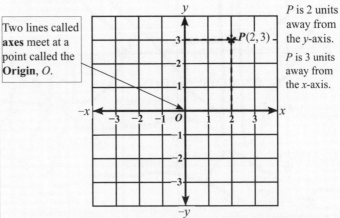

Two lines called **axes** meet at a point called the **Origin**, O.

P is 2 units away from the y-axis.

P is 3 units away from the x-axis.

Coordinates can be used to describe the position of a landmark on a map. They are used in navigation satellite tracking and an essential part of bringing live television by satellite from around the world.

1 Maps

On the map lines show the number of kilometres east and north of a fixed point James Fort (0, 0). The position of the places on the map are described by using two numbers.
(3, 1) means 3 kilometres east and 1 kilometre north and therefore shows the Cathedral.

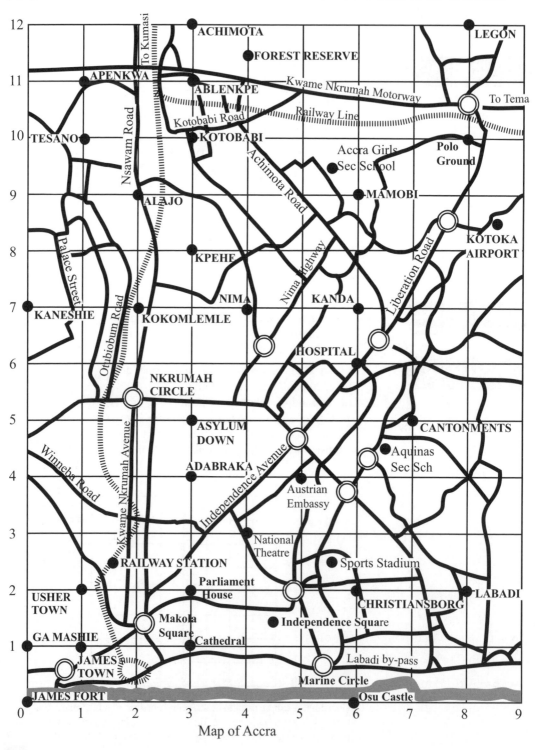

Map of Accra

Exercise 9:1

1. What places on the map are shown by these pair of numbers?

   a $(0, 0)$ **b** $(7, 5)$ **c** $(1, 2)$ **d** $(6, 9)$ **e** $(3, 5)$

2. What pair of numbers give the positions of these places:

   a Austrian Embassy   **b** Polo Ground   **c** Airport

   d Aquinas secondary school   **e** Sports Stadium   **f** National Theatre

3. How many kilometres are there between:

   a Alajo and Kokomlemle   **b** Kaneshie and Kanda

   c Achimota and Kpehe   **d** Forest Reserve and National Theatre

   e Usher Town and Apenkwa   **f** Christiansborg and Mamobi?

4. Work out the pair of numbers that is halfway between:

   a Legon and Achimota   **b** Railway Station and Parliament House

   c Labadi and Legon   **d** Accra Girls School and Sports Stadium

   e Asylum Down and Kotobabi   **f** Usher Town and Labadi

5. The diagonal length of each square is about 1.4 kilometres for example from Kokomlemle to Kpehe is about 1.4 km. Work out the direct distances between these:

   a Ga Mashie and Usher Town   **b** Kotobabi and Alajo

   c Kanda and Kotobabi   **d** Hospital and Apenkwa

   e Railway Station to Kanda   **f** Cathedral to Acquinas Secondary School

6. Work out the perimeter and area bounded by these:

   a Tessano, Kotobabi, Parliament House and Usher Town

   b Achimota, Legon, Labadi and Paliament House.

   c Nima, Mamobi, Achimota and Tesano

The mid-point between Alajo and Mamobi is calculated as:

Alajo is at $(2, 9)$ and Mamobi is at $(6, 9)$.

The mid-point is: $\dfrac{(2 + 6)}{2}, \dfrac{(9 + 9)}{2} = \dfrac{8}{2}, \dfrac{18}{2} = (4, 9)$

---

7. Work out the mid-point of each of these routes:

   a From $(2, 2)$ to $(2, 5)$ **b** From $(0, 8)$ to $(2, 6)$

   c From $(1, 5)$ to $(5, 10)$ **d** From $(5.5, 2.5)$ to $(5.5, 9.5)$

   e From Kotobabi to Polo Ground   **f** From Osu Castle to Kanda

   g From Legon to Labadi   *__h__ From James Fort to Kotoka Airport

2   Coordinates

Number plane	A **number plane** is a flat surface on which every point is related to a pair of numbers called coordinates.
Coordinates	Two numbers or letters used to describe the position of a point in space are the **coordinates** of the point.
Cartesian	The coordinate system is called **Cartesian** because it was developed by the French mathematician René Descartes.
Abscissa	The horizontal ("**x**") value in a pair of coordinates: how far along the point is.
Ordinate	The vertical ("**y**") value in a pair of coordinates: how far up or down the point is.

x and y axis $x \longrightarrow$ The left-right (horizontal) direction is commonly called **x-axis**.

$y \uparrow$ The up-down (vertical) direction is commonly called **y-axis**.

$$(4, 7)$$
x-coordinate   y-coordinate

Writing Coordinates	The coordinates are always written in a certain order: the horizontal direction first, then the vertical direction. This is called an "**ordered pair**" - a pair of numbers in a special order. The coordinates are separated by a comma and parentheses are put around the whole thing; for example **(5, 3)** means 5 units to the right and 3 units up.
The Origin	The point (0, 0) is given the special name **The Origin** and it is sometimes given the letter "*O*".
Quadrants	The *x*-axis and the *y*-axis divide the space into four quadrants. The quadrants are always numbered anti-clockwise.

- In the first quadrant both *x* and *y* are positive.
- In the second *x* is negative but *y* is positive.
- In the third quadrant both *x* and *y* are negative.
- In the fourth quadrant *x* is positive but *y* is negative.

The position of the point *A* in the first quadrant is described as: start from 0 and move 3 squares along O*x* then move 5 squares up, or '*A* is at 3 units along the corridor and 5 units up the stairs'

The coordinates of *B* are:

$$(-3, 2)$$

+3 units in the negative *x* direction   2 units in the positive *y* direction

The intervals between each number line must be equal.

The line **up** the page is called O*y* or the **y-axis**.

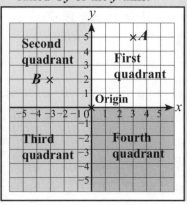

The line **across** the page is called O*x* or the **x-axis**.

Exercise 9:2

1 These are the coordinates
of the points shown on the
diagram:

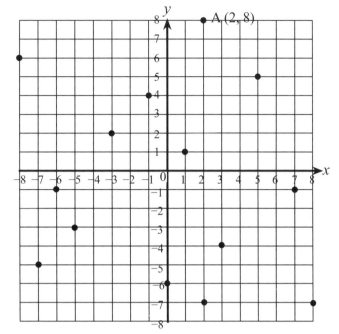

A(2, 8)   B(−3, 2)

C(−1, 4)   D(7, −1)

E(2, −7)   F(−5, −3)

G(1, 1)   H(−8, 6)

I(−7, −5)   J(0, −6)

K(8, −7)   L(5, 5)

M(−6, −1)   N(3, −4)

a Copy the diagram onto squared paper.

b Match the letters to the points and add these: P(−7, −8),   Q(0, 6),   R(−5, 0),   S(8, −4)

d Group the points into four quadrants.

e In which quadrants are: **i** the positive *y* values   **ii** both *x* and *y* values negative?

2 **a** Draw a set of axes from −6 to 6.

b Plot these points and join them up in order: (2, 1),   (2, 6),   (3, 6),   (5, 1),   (2, 1)

c Reflect your drawing into the second quadrant.

d Reflect your original drawing in the *x*-axis.

3 **a** Draw a set of axes from 0 to 10.

b Plot these points, join them in order and name the shape.
   i (1, 4), (4, 4), (4, 1), (1, 1)   **ii** (6, 6), (9, 6), (9, 1), (6, 1)
   iii (5, 7), (5, 10), (8, 10)   **iv** (1, 6), (3, 6), (4, 8), (3, 10), (1, 10), (0, 8), (1, 6)

4 **a** Draw a set of axes from −5 to +5.

b Plot these points on your axes: T(−2, 1), E(2, −3), M(6, 1), A(2, 5).

c Join the points make the figure TEMA.

For each of the following questions you will need to draw your own set of axes.

5 Three corners of a square are at the point (1, 3), (1, −3) and (4, 0).

a Plot these points and draw in the square.

b Write down the coordinates of the fourth corner.

6 Three corners of a square are at the points (3, 4), (−1, 4) and (1, 2).

    a Plot the points and draw in the squares.

    b Write down the coordinates of the fourth corner.

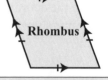

Rhombus

7 Three corners of a rhombus are at the points (−5, 3), (3, 3) and (−1, 1).

    a Plot the points and draw in a rhombus.

    b Write down the coordinates of the fourth corner.

> A **Rhombus** is a parallelogram in which all four sides are equal.
> E.g. diamond and lozenge.

8 Three corners of a rectangle are at the points (−3, 0), (7, 0) and (6, −3).

    a Plot the points and draw in the rectangle.

    b Write down the coordinates of the fourth corner.

9 Write down the letters at each of these coordinates.

(−6, −6), (−2, 2), (−1, −2), (2, 1), (5, 1), (−1, 4), (5, 1)

(−1, −2), (2, 1), (0, 5)

(−4, 6), (3, 6), (0, 5), (0, 5), (4, −6)

(−6, 3), (−5, −1)

(−2, 2), (−6, 0), (−6, 0)

(5, 1), (3, 6), (6, 4), (−3, −4), (0, 5), (2, −2), (−1, −2), (5, 1)

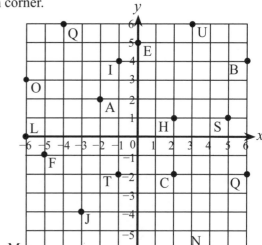

10 Fill in the chart by finding the letter beside each coordinate.
T is filled in for you.

$$\frac{T}{(-4,0)} \quad \frac{}{(-4,-5)} \quad \frac{}{(6,1)} \quad \frac{}{(-6,6)}$$

$$\frac{}{(-7,2)} \quad \frac{}{(-4,-5)} \quad \frac{}{(-3,7)} \quad \frac{}{(-6,6)}$$

$$\frac{}{(0,-7)} \quad \frac{}{(0,0)} \quad \frac{}{(-4,0)} \quad \frac{}{(7,-4)}$$

$$\frac{}{(3,6)}$$

$$\frac{}{(-4,-5)} \quad \frac{}{(-7,-7)} \quad \frac{}{(3,-3)}$$

$$\frac{}{(-6,-2)}$$

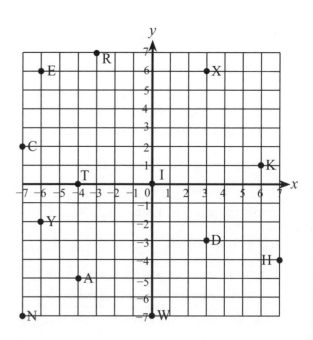

11

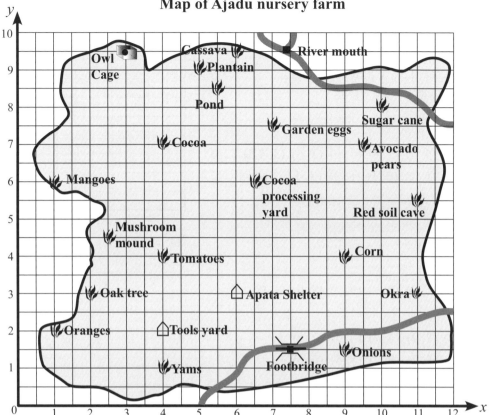

Map of Ajadu nursery farm

Locate these on Ajadu nursery farm:

i a (10, 8)   **b** (4, 4)   **c** (9, 4)   **d** (7, 7.5)   **e** (1, 6)   **f** (5, 9)

ii What are the coordinates of these on Ajadu nursery farm?

   a Tools yard   **b** Apata Shelter   **c** Onions   **d** Cocoa processing yard

   e Owl cage   **f** Pond   **g** Oak tree   **h** Mushroom mound

iii Find the midway point between these:

   a Red soil cave and the Okra patch   **b** Cocoa patch and the Avocado pears

   c Footbridge and River mouth   **d** Oranges and the Tools yard

iv If each unit on the map is 3 metres, work out how long these routes are:

   a From the Pond to (7, 8.5) to Garden egg patch to (7, 2) to Tools yard to (2, 2) and to the Oranges.

   b From Onions to Corn to Tomatoes to (2.5, 4) to (2.5, 6) and to the Mango patch.

   c From Owl Cage to (3, 9) to Plantain to (6.5, 9) to (6.5, 8) to (9.5, 8) to Avocado pears to (9.5, 3) and to the Okra patch.

Exercise 9:3

Picture sets

Draw these set of axes, plot the points
and join them as you go along.

Picture set 1

Join (8, 6) (6, 6) (5, 8) (4, 6) (2, 6) (3, 4.5) (2, 3)
      (4, 3) (5, 1) (6, 3) (8, 3) (7, 4.5) (8, 6)

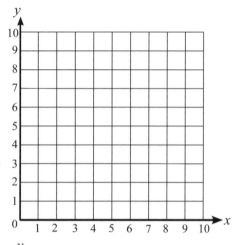

Picture set 2

Join (1, 0) (1, 7) (5, 9) (9, 7) (9, 0) (1, 0)

Start again.

Join (2, 5) (2, 7) (4, 7) (4, 5) (2, 5)
Join (6, 5) (6, 7) (8, 7) (8, 5) (6, 5)
Join (4, 0) (4, 3) (6, 3) (6, 0) (4, 0)

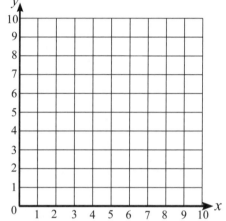

Picture set 3

Join (6, 5) (8, 4) (9, 2) (7, 3) (6, 5)
Join (5, 5) (3, 4) (2, 2) (4, 3) (5, 5)
Join (5, 6) (4, 8) (2, 9) (3, 7) (5, 6)
Join (6, 6) (8, 7) (9, 9) (7, 8) (6, 6)
Join (4, 1) (7, 1) (5.5, 5) (4, 1)
Join (10, 4) (10, 7) (6, 5.5) (10, 4)
Join (4, 10) (7, 10) (5.5, 6) (4, 10)
Join (1, 4) (1, 7) (5, 5.5) (1, 4)

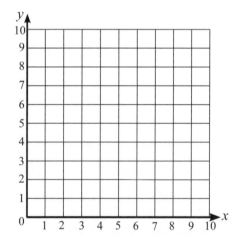

Picture set 4

Join (2, 2) (1, 3) (1, 6) (2, 5) (4, 4)
      (13, 4) (13, 4.5) (13.5, 4.5)
      (13.5, 3.5) (15, 3.5) (15, 2.5)
      (13.5, 2.5) (13.5, 1.5) (13, 1.5)
      (13, 2) (2, 2)

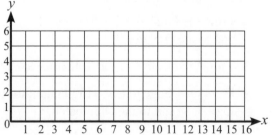

194

3 Linear graphs

Linear graph A graph which is represented by a straight line is called a **linear graph**.

The points marked on the line have the coordinates:

$(3, -5)$, $(3, -4)$, $(3, -1)$, $(3, 2)$, $(3, 4)$.

Any point on the line has an x-coordinate of 3.

The equation of this line is therefore $x = 3$

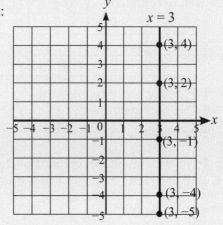

On the line the
x-coordinate is
always 3.

x	y
3	-5
3	-4
3	-1
3	2
3	4

The points lie in a straight line so the relationship is **linear**.

Exercise 9:4

1 a Copy and complete the coordinate table.
  b Draw line A and line B.

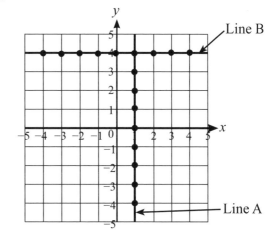

Line A	Line B
(... , −4)	(−4, ...)
(... , −3)	(−3, ...)
(... , −2)	(−2, ...)
(... , −1)	(−1, ...)
(... , 0)	(0, ...)
(... , 1)	(1, ...)
(... , 2)	(2, ...)
(... , 3)	(3, ...)
(... , 4)	(4, ...)

d Write what you notice:
  i about the x-coordinate on line A;
  ii about y-coordinate on line B.

e The equation of line A is $x = 1$
  The equation of line B is $y = 4$
  Label your lines with this rule.

195

2 a Copy the axes shown.

b Complete these coordinates for other rules.

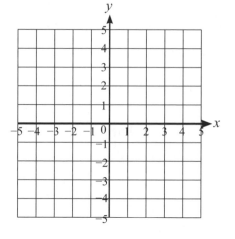

$x = 2$	$x = -3$	$y = 5$	$y = -4$
(..., 5)	(..., 0)	(4, ...)	(3, ...)
(..., 3)	(..., 4)	(2, ...)	(1, −4)
(..., 0)	(..., −1)	(−1, ...)	(0, ...)
(..., −4)	(−3, −5)	(−4, ...)	(−2, ...)

c i Plot each set of coordinates.

ii Join each set to make a line.

iii Label each line with its rule.

3 a Draw the axes shown in **question 2a**.

b Draw and label the lines whose rules are $x = -5$, $x = 3$, $y = 2$, $y = -1$

4 a Copy the diagram.

b Write down the equation of the lines labelled A, B, C, D, E, F, G in the diagram.

c Write down the coordinate of the points where these lines meet.

  i Lines B and C

  ii Lines A and E

  iii Lines D and A

  iv Lines G and $y = 0$

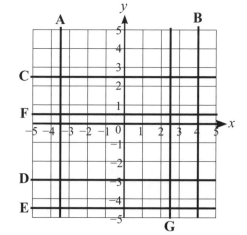

5 a Draw axes from −8 to 8 and plot the points below.

b Draw a straight line through the points and write the equation of the line next to it.

  i (4, −3) (3, −3) (−4, −3)

  ii (−2, −2) (−2, 0) (−2, 7)

  iii (−5, 2) (−5, −3) (−5, −5)

  iv (1, 6.5) (−2, 6.5) (−3.5, 6.5) (6.5, 6.5)

  v (−6, 1) (5, 1) (3, 1)

  vi (−3.5, 0) (−3.5, −1) (−3.5, −6) (−3.5, 7.5)

4 Gradients of lines

Gradient

The **gradient** or *slope* of a line is the measure of how fast the line is rising or falling. The gradient of a line tells you how steep it is.

It is defined as the amount the line rises vertically divided by the distance moved horizontally. Gradient is usually represented by the letter *m*.

$$\text{Gradient} = \frac{\text{difference in } y\text{-coordinates}}{\text{difference in } x\text{-coordinates}}$$

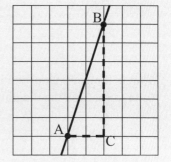

$$\text{Gradient of line AB} = \frac{\text{BC (vertical)}}{\text{AC (horizontal)}}$$

$$= \frac{6}{2}$$

$$m = 3$$

The gradient of a straight line is the same no matter which points on the line are chosen as A and B.

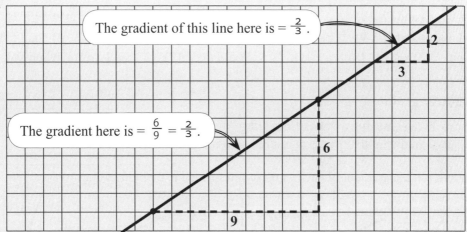

The gradient of this line here is $= \frac{2}{3}$.

The gradient here is $= \frac{6}{9} = \frac{2}{3}$.

Exercise 9:5

1 Write down the gradient of each of these lines as a fraction or a whole number.

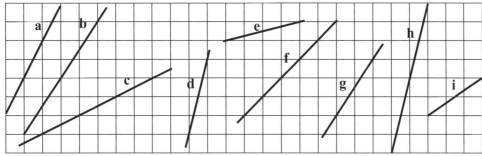

2 a Which lines in **question 1** have the same gradient?

  b What can you say about these lines?

The gradient of the line between the two points (2, 1) and (6, 7) is worked out as:

$$\text{Gradient} = \frac{\text{difference in } y\text{-coordinates}}{\text{difference in } x\text{-coordinates}}$$

$$= \frac{7-1}{6-2} = \frac{6}{4} = \frac{3}{2}$$

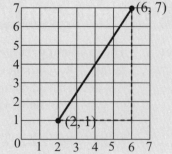

3 What is the gradient of the line from (0, 1) to (6, 5) in the diagram?

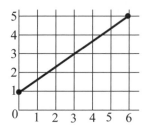

4 Work out the gradient of the line passing through these points.

   a (5, 6) and (7, 18)   **b** (1, 1) and (7, 7)   **c** (3, 1) and (9, 2)

   d (3, 0) and (10, 9)   **e** (5, 5) and (8, 14)   **f** (−6, −8) and (4, 17)

   g (−5, 2) and (1, 18)   **h** (3.5, 7) and (8.5, 17)   **i** (−9, −7) and (−1, −9)

Negative gradient

Lines which slope **downwards** from left to right have negative gradients.
Negative gradients are always measured across **from left to right**.

5 Work out the gradient of each of these lines. Use the method in question 1.

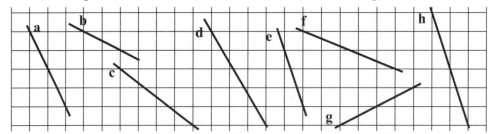

The gradient of the line between the two points (0, 5) and (6, 3) is worked out as:

$$\text{Gradient} = \frac{3-5}{6-0} = \frac{-2}{6} = -\frac{1}{3}$$

The vertical change is negative
Therefore the line has a negative gradient.

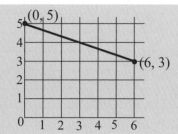

6 Work out the gradient of the line passing through these points.

   a (2, 2) and (7, −17)   **b** (3, 9) and (10, 0)   **c** (−1, −11) and (−10, 10)

   d (−4, 5) and (2, −11)   **e** (−8, 15) and (12, −13)   **f** (0, 12) and (6, −7)

5   Contours and profiles

This is a model of a mountain.
The heights are shown in metres.
0 is at sea level.

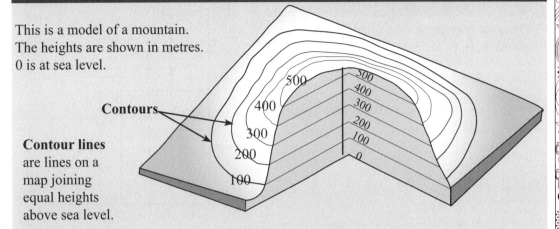

Contours

Contour lines
are lines on a
map joining
equal heights
above sea level.

The 100 m contour goes through all the points whose height is 100 m and similarly for others.

Here is a map of the mountain
with the contours shown on it.

The top of the mountain is marked
with its height 520 m.

The dotted line shows a path up
the mountain side.

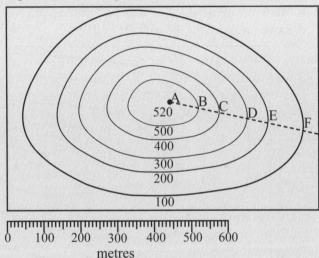

To find the distances between A, B, C, D, E and F we measure the map. The scale of the map
is 1 cm to 100 m. The distances are:
AB = 110 m   BC = 60 m   CD = 75   DE = 57.5   EF = 95

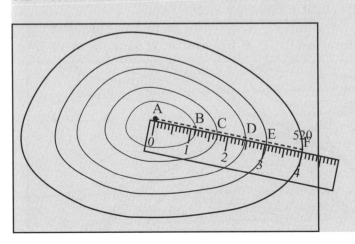

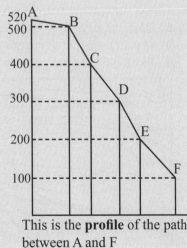

This is the **profile** of the path
between A and F

199

Exercise 9:6

1 Work out the gradient of each part of the path. (Imagine horizontal lines through each of the points A, B, C, D, and E.)

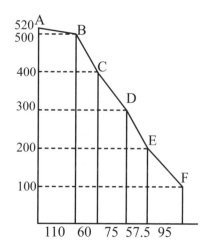

2 **a** Draw the profile of the path JKLMNP on the map below.
   b Work out the gradient of each part of the path.
   c Repeat **a** and **b** for the path DEFGHP.

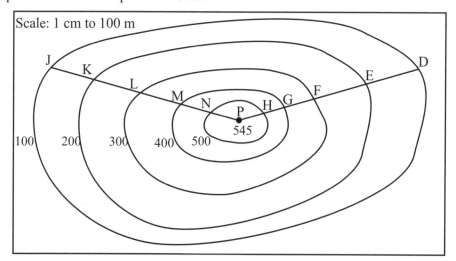

3 This is the contour map of a hilly region. The scale is 1 cm to 50 m.
   a Does the river flow from left to right or from right to left?
   b Is path p steeper than path q? Explain.   **c** Draw the profile along section XY.
   d Work out the gradient between D and E.   **e** Can a person at A see a person at B?

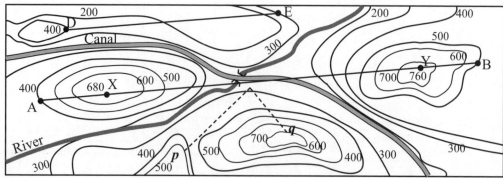

200

6 Connecting rules

y-intercept The *y* value at the point where the line meets the *y*-axis is called a **y-intercept**. It is usually represented by the letter **c**.

Example For points (−1, 1) (0, 2) (1, 3) (2, 4) (3, 5) (4, 6):
- The points are plotted to get a straight line.
- The gradient (*m*) of any two points is 1.
- The connecting rule is:

$$y = 1x + 2 \text{ or written formally as } \mathbf{y = x + 2}$$

Gradient *y*-intercept

The rule for the line graph is: for any value of x add 2 to get the y-value.

> **The general rule of a straight line graph is written as $y = mx + c$**

Exercise 9:7

1 Copy and complete each rule and its set of points.

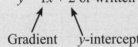

	Rule	Set of points for the rule
a	$y = x$	(0, 0) (1, ...) (2, ...) (3, ...)
b	$y = x + 3$	(1, ...) (3, ...) (4, ...) (7, ...)
c	$y = 2x$	(2, ...) (3, ...) (5, ...) (−2, ...)
d	$y = x - 1$	(3, ...) (5, ...) (8, ...) (12, ...)
e	$y = 3x + 1$	(−2, ...) (0, ...) (4, ...) (7, ...)
***f**	$y = \frac{1}{2}x$	(4, ...) (6, ...) (9, ...) (−14, ...)

> $1x$ means $1 \times x$
> $2x$ means $2 \times x$

2 Plot each set of points on a line and find the connecting rule.
   (Hint: find the gradient and use the general rule to help you.)

	Set of points for the rule	Rule
a	(2, 4) (3, 6) (5, 10) (8, 16) (10, 20)	$y =$
b	(1, 1) (3, 5) (5, 9) (7, 13) (10, 19)	$y =$
c	(0, −2) (3, 1) (4, 2) (6, 4) (9, 7)	$y =$
d	(1, 0) (4, 6) (5, 8) (6, 10) (7, 12)	$y =$
e	(0, 3) (1, 8) (2, 13) (3, 18) (6, 33)	$y =$
***f**	(−4, $9\frac{1}{2}$) (−2, $3\frac{1}{2}$) (0, $-2\frac{1}{2}$) (1, $-5\frac{1}{2}$) (7, $-23\frac{1}{2}$)	$y =$

3 Copy this coordinate table, fill it in and draw the lines. Rule: $y = x$

x	−4	−3	−2	−1	0	$\frac{1}{2}$	1	2	3	4
y				−1						

i Copy and complete the mapping diagram.
ii Write down the rule.
iii Draw the *x* axis from −4 to 4 and find *y*.
iv Plot the points and find the gradient.

4

−4 →		→ ?
−3 →		→ ?
−2 →		→ ?
−1 →		→ ?
0 →	−1	→ ?
1 →		→ 0
2 →		→ ?
3 →		→ ?
4 →		→ ?

5

−4 →		→ ?
−3 →		→ −11
−2 →		→ −7
−1 →		→ ?
0 →	×4 +1	→ 1
1 →		→ ?
2 →		→ ?
3 →		→ ?
4 →		→ ?

6 Rule: $y = 4x + 1$

x	−4	−3	−2	−1	0	$\frac{1}{2}$	1	2	3	4
y					1					17

7 Rule: $y = x − 1$

x	−4	−3	−2	−1	0	$\frac{1}{2}$	1	2	3	4
y			−3						2	

This is the table of the graph of $y = 2x − 2$

x	−5	−4	−3	−2	−1	0	1	2	3	4	5
y	−12	−10	−8	−6	−4	−2	0	2	4	6	8

The gradient of the line between (−1, −4) and (4, 6) is calculated as:

$$\text{Gradient} = \frac{6 − {-4}}{4 − {-1}} = \frac{10}{5} = 2$$

According to the graph the value of *y* when *x* = − 2.5 is −7

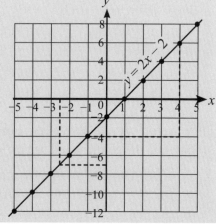

8 The rule for a line is $y = 4x − 3$

a Copy and complete the coordinate table.

x	−3	−2	−1	0	1	2	3	4
y		−11						

b Plot the points, then draw and label the line.

c Find the gradient of the line.

d The point (5, *a*) is on the line. What is the value of *a*?

9 The rule for a line is $y = 3x + 1$

x	−4	−1	0	2	3	5
y						

  a Copy and complete the coordinate table.

  b Plot the points, draw and label the line.

  c Find the gradient of the line.

  d What is the value of y when $x = 4.5$?

  e The point $(b, -8)$ is on the line. What is the value of b?

For each of these diagrams:
a Copy and join the points.
b Find a rule for the line the points lie on, work out the gradient and the y-intercept.

10

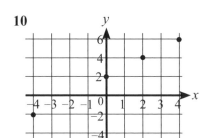

11

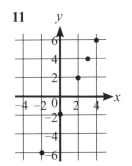

12

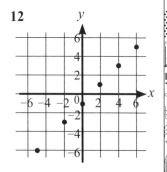

13

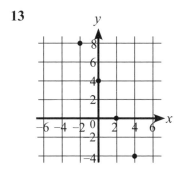

14

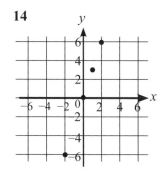

15

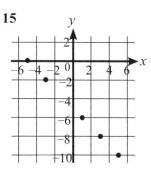

16 Draw a grid with x and y values from −10 to 10.
On this grid draw the graphs of these lines.

  $y = x + 1$ $y = x - 2$ $y = 5 - x$ $y = 2x - 4$

The steps to follow are:
  i Choose about five x-values and put them into a table;
  ii Work out the y-values;
  iii Plot these points and draw a straight line through the points;
  iv Find the gradient of each line.

17 Look at the graphs you drew in question 16.

  a Write down the coordinates of the points where the lines $y = x + 1$ and $y = 2x - 4$ cross.

  b The point $(18, 32)$ lies on which line?

EXTENSION

1 The map shows trenches of surface mining of gold. The distances are given in metres.

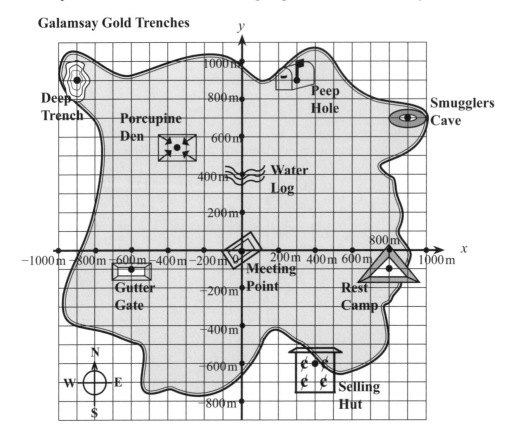

Galamsay Gold Trenches

Write the coordinate of these:

a Deep Trench   b Peep Hole   c Smugglers Cave   d Selling Hut

e Gutter Gate   f Rest Camp   g Water Log   h Porcupine Den

i What is the midpoint between Meeting Point and Smugglers Cave?

2 Each of these set of points lie on a straight line. For each set of points find an equation for the line.

A: $(-4, -18)$, $(-2.5, -12)$, $(0, -2)$, $(2, 6)$ B: $(-2, -5)$, $(0, -1)$, $(\frac{3}{4}, \frac{1}{2})$, $(5, 9)$

C: $(-3, -6)$, $(-1, 0)$, $(\frac{2}{3}, 5)$, $(3, 12)$ D: $(-1\frac{1}{3}, 8)$, $(\frac{1}{3}, 3)$, $(1\frac{1}{2}, -\frac{1}{2})$, $(-\frac{1}{2}, 5\frac{1}{2})$

3 a On a coordinate grid with x-axis labelled from −4 to 4 and the y-axis labelled from −6 to 6 draw these graphs: i $y = 2x + 1$ ii $y = -x - 2$

b Write the coordinate of the points where the two lines cross.

4 a Draw a coordinate grid with values for x from 4 to 4 and values of y from −13 to 12.

b On the grid draw the graphs of: i $y = 3x - 1$ ii $x = 3.5$

c Write the coordinate of the points where the two lines cross.

5 a Write the coordinates at the midpoint of PQ   **b** Work out the gradient of line PQ.

   i P(1, 3) and Q(2, 5)   **ii** P(0, 4) and Q(4, 0)   **iii** P(−7, 8) and Q(9, −8)

   iv P(1, 6) and Q(0, 2)   **v** P(−20, 9) and Q(3, −20)   **vi** P(9, −30) and Q(12, 2)

6 Decide whether the point (120, 703) lies on the line $y = 6x − 17$. Give reasons for your answer. What is the gradient of the line?

An **Intersection** is the set of points where two lines or curves meet.

7 These two lines intersect at (1, 2).
Find the equation of each line.
(Hint: It may help to complete a table of values.)

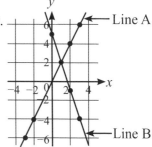

8 On a journey Sade travelled at a steady 60 kilometres per hour. The table shows how far Sade travelled every hour.

  a Copy and complete the table.

Time taken in hours, t	0	1	2	3	4	5	6
Distance travelled (km) d,		60			240		

b Use the table to plot a graph of distance against time.
Draw the axes as shown.
Use a scale of 2 cm to 1 hour on the time axis
and 1 cm to 20 km on the distance axis.

c Use the graph to answer these questions:
  i How far had Sade travelled in $1\frac{1}{2}$ hours.
  ii How long did it take Sade to travel 290 km?
  iii How long did it take Sade to travel 178 km?
  iv How far had Sade travelled in 4h 46 min.?

d Find the equation of the line.

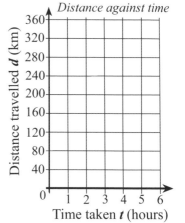

9

Load N (Newton)	10	20	30	40	50	60
Length (cm)		33	36	39		

The table above gives the length of a stretched spring when different loads hang on it.

a Copy and complete the table.

b Draw the graph.
Use a scale of 1 cm to 5 N for the load
and 1 cm to 5 cm for the length.

c How long is the spring before stretching?

d How long is the spring when a load of:
  i 25 N   **ii** 47.5 N hangs from it?

e What load is needed to stretch the spring to 43.5 cm?

f Find the equation of the line.

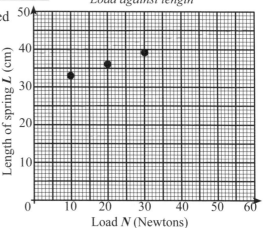

Number plane	A **number plane** is a flat surface on which every point is related to a pair of numbers called coordinates.
Coordinates	The two numbers or letters used to describe the position of a point in space are called the **coordinates** of the point.
Cartesian	The coordinate system is called **Cartesian** because it was developed by the French mathematician René Descartes.
Abscissa	The horizontal ("x") value in a pair of coordinates: how far along the point is.
Ordinate	The vertical ("y") value in a pair of coordinates: how far up or down it is.
x and y axis	$x \longrightarrow$ The left-right (horizontal) direction is commonly called **x-axis**.
	$y \uparrow$ The up-down (vertical) direction is commonly called **y-axis.**

Writing Coordinates	Coordinates are always written in a certain order: the horizontal direction first, then the vertical direction. This is called an "**ordered pair**" - a pair of numbers in a special order. Coordinates are separated by a comma and parentheses are put around the whole thing. For example, **(5, 3)** means 5 units to the right and 3 units up.
The Origin	The point (0, 0) is given the special name 'The Origin' and it is sometimes given the letter "O".
Quadrants	The x-axis and the y-axis divide the space into four quadrants.

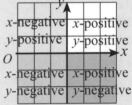

	y	
x-negative y-positive		x-positive y-positive
O		$\rightarrow x$
x-negative y-negative		x-positive y-negative

Gradient	The **gradient** or *slope* of a line is the measurement of how fast the line is rising or falling. The gradient of a line tells you how steep a line is. It is defined as the amount the line rises vertically divided by the distance moved horizontally. A gradient is usually represented by the letter **m**.

$$\text{Gradient} = \frac{\text{difference in } y\text{-coordinates}}{\text{difference in } x\text{-coordinates}}$$

The gradient of line AB $= \dfrac{BC}{AC} = \dfrac{6}{2} = 3$

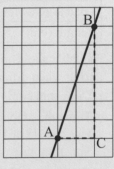

The gradient of a straight line is the same no matter which points on the line are chosen as A and B.

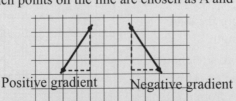

Positive gradient   Negative gradient

y-intercept	The y value at the point where the line meets the y-axis is called the **y-intercept**. **The general rule of a straight line graph is written as $y = mx + c$ where m is the gradient and c is the y-intercept i.e. where the line crosses the y-axis.**

Quadrilaterals

EXTENSION

SUMMARY

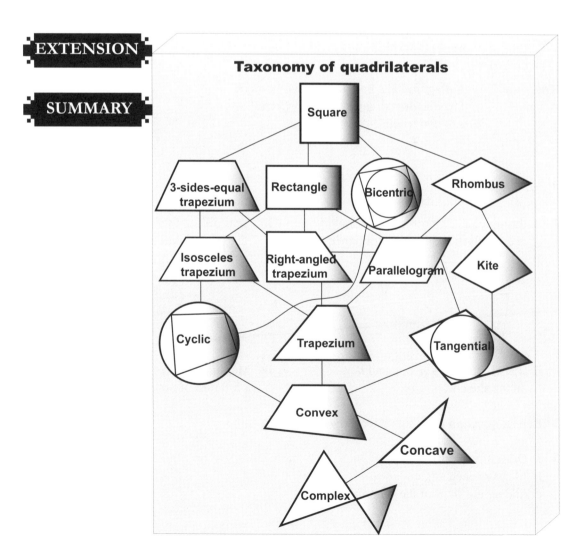

Taxonomy of quadrilaterals

1   What is a quadrilateral?

The face of most computer hardware has four sides. The face of each key on the keyboard has four sides. The flash drive slots into a four-sided opening. Even one pixel, which is a minute area of illumination on a display screen, has four sides.

Quadrilateral A **quadrilateral** is a polygon with four sides (or 'edges') and four vertices or corners. The word quadrilateral is made of the words **quad** (meaning 'four') and **lateral** (meaning 'of sides'). These shapes are examples of quadrilaterals.

A quadrilateral which has four unequal sides is called an **irregular quadrilateral**.

Diagonal A **diagonal** is a line joining two vertices. The diagonal divides the quadrilateral into two triangles.

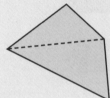

Exercise 10:1

1 **i** Using your own dimensions draw a quadrilateral on a piece of paper.

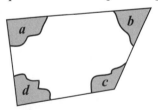

   ii Label the angles *a*, *b*, *c* and *d* as in the sketch.

   iii Tear off the fours corners and put the angles together at a common point.

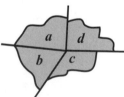

   iv Measure to make sure that they make a full turn of 360°.

2 Repeat **question 1** with another three quadrilaterals.

3 **a** Draw any quadrilateral.
   b Measure each angle.
   c Add up the sizes of the four angles.

4 Copy and complete these:

a The sum of the angles at a point = $\boxed{?}$

b The sum of the interior angles of a quadrilateral = $\boxed{?}$

5 **i** Draw any quadrilateral in your exercise book.

ii Join any pair of opposite vertices with a diagonal to form two triangles.

iii Shade the three angles of one of the triangles and mark the angles of the other triangle in a different way.

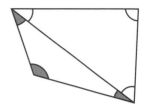

Copy and complete these:

a The three shaded angles add up to $\boxed{?}^{\text{O}}$

b The three marked angles add up to $\boxed{?}^{\text{O}}$

c The sum of the angles of a triangle = $\boxed{?}^{\text{O}}$

d The sum of the angles of two triangles = $\boxed{?}^{\text{O}}$

e The sum of the angles of a quadrilateral = $\boxed{?}^{\text{O}}$

Tessellate quadrilaterals

a Sketch two copies of this quadrilateral.
b Rotate the second shape 180° clockwise.
c Join the edges of the two shapes.
d Repeat **a**, **b** and **c** above five times to obtain the shape shown below.

> **Tessellations** are produced when congruent shapes fit together without any gaps or overlaps.

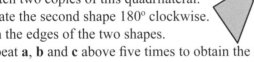

e Continue the process to obtain the first row of the shape 'Bell' shown below.
f Tessellate to produce the shape.
g Repeat the process and produce the shapes 'Arrow' and 'Stump'.

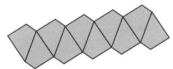

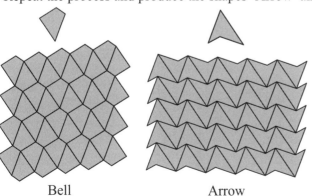

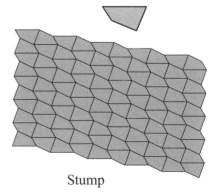

Bell   Arrow   Stump

2 Angles in a quadrilateral

The sum of the four angles of a quadrilateral is 360°.
This is true of any quadrilateral whatever its shape or size.

Example Find the angle marked β.

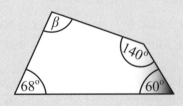

$$\beta + 140° + 60° + 68° = 360°$$
$$\beta + 268° = 360°$$
$$\beta = 360° - 268°$$
$$\beta = 92°$$

Exercise 10:2

Find the size of the angle marked β.

1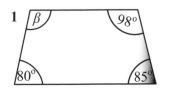

2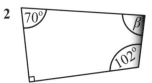

3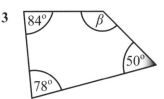

4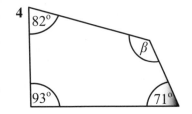

5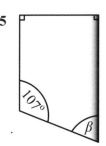

6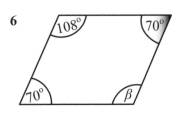

7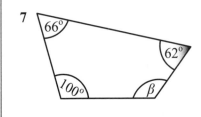

8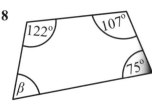

9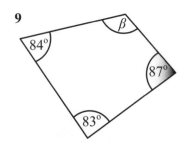

10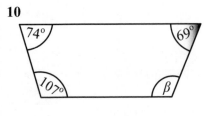

11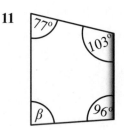

12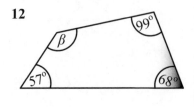

3 Properties of quadrilaterals

These are the properties of quadrilaterals with special names:

Square

Four equal sides
All angles are 90°
Four lines of symmetry
Diagonals bisect at right angles
Rotational symmetry of order four

Rectangle

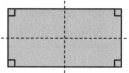

Two pairs of equal and parallel sides
All angles are 90°
Diagonals bisect each other
Two lines of symmetry
Rotational symmetry of order two

Rhombus

Four equal sides
Opposite sides parallel
Diagonals bisect at right angles
Diagonals bisect angles of rhombus
Two lines of symmetry
Rotational symmetry of order two
Opposite angles are equal

Parallelogram

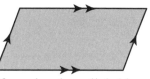

Two pairs of equal and parallel sides
Opposite angles are equal
No lines of symmetry (in general)
Rotational symmetry of order

Kite

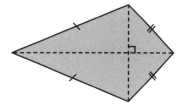

Diagonals meet at 90°
One line of symmetry
Two pairs of equal sides
One pair of equal angles

Trapezium

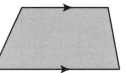

One pair of parallel lines

Isosceles trapezium

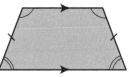

One pair of parallel lines
One pair of opposite sides are equal
One pair of equal equal angles
One line of symmetry

Arrowhead or Delta or Re-entrant kite

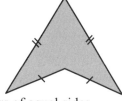

Two pairs of equal sides
One interior angle larger than 180°
One line of symmetry
Diagonals cross at right angles
outside the shape.
One pair of equal angles

Right trapezium

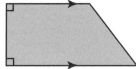

One pair of right angles
One pair of parallel lines

Exercise 10:3

1 What words go in the gaps? Choose from these words.

all   four   parallel   sides   two   unequal   parallelogram   irregular   one

a Quadrilaterals have _____ sides.

b A kite has two pairs of equal _____.

c A trapezium has two _____ sides.

d A square has _____ lines of symmetry.

e A parallelogram has _____ pairs of _____ sides and _____ sides.

f An isosceles trapezium has _____ pair of parallel sides.

g A square is a _____ with _____ its sides and _____ its angles equal.

h A quadrilateral with all its sides _____ is called an _____ quadrilateral.

2 Copy the graph, join the points and give the exact name of each of these quadrilaterals.

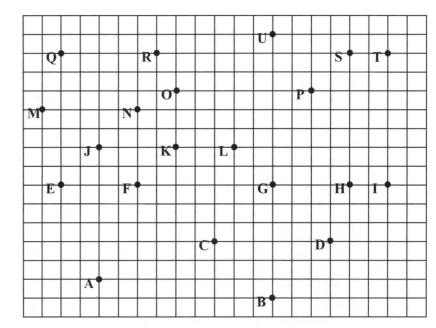

a HITS

b POKL

c QMNR

d CBDG

e JEAF

f HEOP

g DUCB

Parallelogram   Kite   Rhombus   Trapezium

3 From this list name the shapes which have:

a diagonals perpendicular   b just one axis of symmetry

c opposite angles equal   d just one pair of parallel sides

e equal diagonals   f one pair of parallel sides and one pair of right angles

4 Look at the grid on the right. Use the letters within the shapes to answer the following questions.

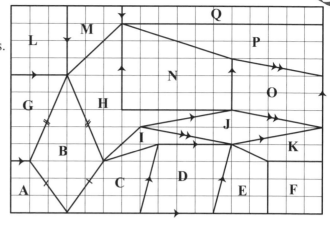

  a List all the irregular quadrilaterals.

  b Which shape is a kite?

  c List all the right trapezia.

  d List all the rectangles.

  e Which shape is a square?

  f List all the parallelograms.

5 Copy each diagram on squared paper. Mark with a cross the fourth vertex.

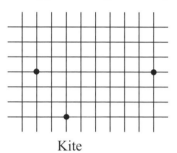

Kite

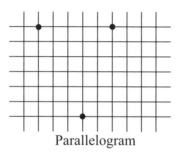

Parallelogram

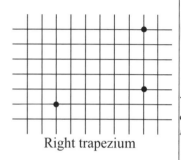

Right trapezium

Examples   Find the angle marked α and give reasons in each case.

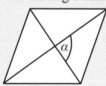

$\alpha = 90°$
Reasons: diagonals of a rhombus bisect at right angles.

$\alpha = 45°$
Reasons: diagonals of a square bisect the right angles.

Exercise 10:4

Find the angle marked α.

1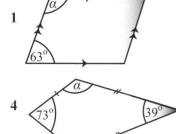

2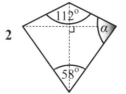

3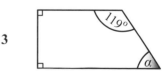

4

5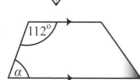

6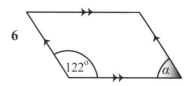

213

Example   The diagram shows a parallelogram *ABCD*. Find the size of the angles marked α, β, θ and ε.

In $\triangle BCD$ $\theta + 31° + 88° = 180°$

$$\theta + 119° = 180°$$
$$\theta = 180° - 119°$$
$$= 61°$$

In the parallelogram ABCD $\alpha = \theta$

$\alpha = 61°$ (opposite angles of a parallelogram are equal)

$\varepsilon = 31°$ (BC $\parallel$ AD, alternate angles)

$$\beta + 31° = \varepsilon + 88°$$
$$\beta + 31° = 31° + 88°$$
$$\beta = 31° + 88° - 31°$$
$$\beta = 88°$$

Alternatively: $\beta = 88°$ (AB $\parallel$ DC $\therefore$ alternate angles)

Exercise 10:5

In these questions sketch the diagrams and put the letters around the shapes in alphabetical order. Give reasons where possible to support your answers.

1 In a rhombus *PQRS*, $P\hat{Q}R = 68°$, calculate:

   a $Q\hat{R}S$ **b** $Q\hat{R}P$ **c** $P\hat{S}R$

2 In a rhombus *VWXY*, $V\hat{W}Y = 36°$, work out: **a** $W\hat{Y}X$ **b** $V\hat{X}Y$

3 In the parallelogram *ABCD*, $BD = AD$ and $B\hat{A}D = 73°$.

   Calculate: **a** $D\hat{B}A$,

                b $A\hat{B}C$

                c $B\hat{D}A$

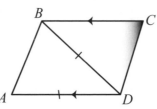

4 In a kite *EFGH*, $EF = EH$, $FG = GH$, $G\hat{E}H = 42°$ and $G\hat{F}H = 60°$.

   Work out: **a** $F\hat{E}G$ **b** $F\hat{G}E$ **c** $E\hat{H}G$

5 In a kite *JKLM*, $JK = JM$, $KL = LM$, $K\hat{L}M = 50°$ and $K\hat{J}M = 96°$. Find $J\hat{K}L$.

6 In a trapezium *PQRS*, *PQ* is parallel to *SR*, $PQ = PS$, $QS = SR$ and $Q\hat{P}S = 124°$.

   Work out: **a** $P\hat{Q}S$ **b** $Q\hat{S}R$ **c** $Q\hat{R}S$

7 Work out the angles marked θ.

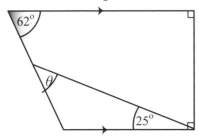

8 Work out the angles marked β and θ.

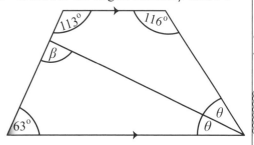

9 The figure below shows a kite. Find the angles marked α, β and θ.

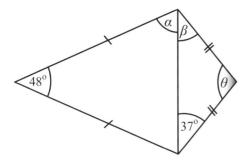

10 Work out the angles β and θ.

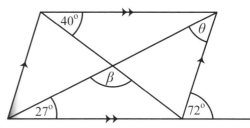

12 ABCD is a rhombus whose side is 14 cm long. BE is 8.4 cm and angle ABD is 58°. Find the size of ∠BDC, ∠ADC and ∠BAD.

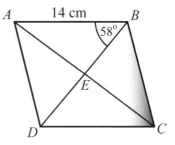

11 Find the size of the angles marked α, β and θ in the trapezium.

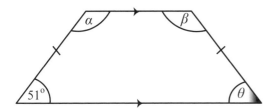

13 *PQRS* is a quadrilateral $\hat{P} = 106°$ and $\hat{Q} = 82°$. The diagonal *PR* cuts $S\hat{P}Q$ in half and *PR = PS*. Work out $Q\hat{R}S$.

*14 In quadrilateral *VWXY*, $V\hat{W}X = V\hat{X}Y = 90°$, $W\hat{X}V = 55°$ and *WX = XY*.

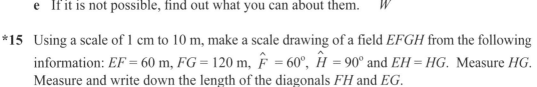

   a Find $W\hat{V}X$.
   b Find the angles of △ *WXY*.
   c *WY* and *VX* cut at *Z*. Find all the angles of △*WZV*.
   d If it is possible, find all the angles of △ *VZY.*
   e If it is not possible, find out what you can about them.

*15 Using a scale of 1 cm to 10 m, make a scale drawing of a field *EFGH* from the following information: *EF* = 60 m, *FG* = 120 m, $\hat{F}$ = 60°, $\hat{H}$ = 90° and *EH = HG*. Measure *HG*. Measure and write down the length of the diagonals *FH* and *EG*.

215

INVESTIGATION

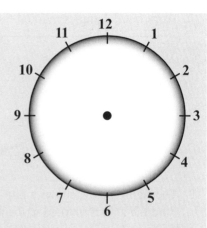

1 Draw a round clockface as shown with radius of 4 cm.
Join the following points, using a different coloured
pen or pencil for each diagram.

  a **i** $2 \Rightarrow 4 \Rightarrow 8 \Rightarrow 10 \Rightarrow 2$

     ii $1 \Rightarrow 3 \Rightarrow 5 \Rightarrow 11 \Rightarrow 1$

     iii $2 \Rightarrow 6 \Rightarrow 10 \Rightarrow 12 \Rightarrow 2$

     iv $12 \Rightarrow 3 \Rightarrow 6 \Rightarrow 9 \Rightarrow 12$

     v $11 \Rightarrow 1 \Rightarrow \text{Centre} \Rightarrow 9 \Rightarrow 11$

  b Label each quadrilateral with its special name.

2 a Draw and cut out two copies of these special quadrilaterals.

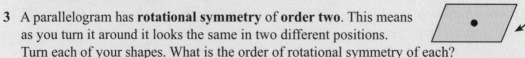

  b A square has four lines of symmetry.
    Fold your square in half along each mirror line shown.
    Check how many lines of symmetry these quadrilaterals have:
    Rectangle Parallelogram Trapezium Rhombus Kite

3 A parallelogram has **rotational symmetry** of **order two**. This means
as you turn it around it looks the same in two different positions.
Turn each of your shapes. What is the order of rotational symmetry of each?

4 Copy and complete this table:

Quadrilateral	Square	Rectangle	Parallelogram	Rhombus	Trapezium	Kite
Number of lines of symmetry	4					
Order of rotational symmetry						

5 Draw the diagonals on each of the special quadrilaterals.
  i Measure the diagonals on each to see if they are equal.
  ii Measure the angles between the diagonals.
  iii Measure to see if the diagonals cut each other in half.
  iv Measure to see if the diagonals cut the angles at the corners in half.

  v Copy and complete this table:

Quadrilateral	Diagonals cross at right angles	Diagonals cut each other in half	Diagonals cut the angles in half
Square	yes		
Rectangle			
Parallelogram			
Rhombus			
Trapezium			
Kite		no	

INVESTIGATION

TAKE-AWAY MATCHES

In this investigation you will need matchsticks, squared paper or squared dotted paper. Only closed squares are allowed.

1 Here 17 sticks are used to make six squares.

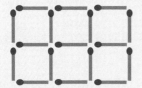
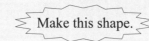

Make this shape.

2 Remove matchsticks and count the number of squares left.

Two sticks can be removed to leave five squares

Four sticks can be removed to leave four squares.

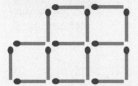
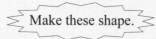
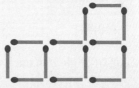

Make these shape.

3 Investigate other possibilities and record your solutions on squared or dotted paper.

4 Work on these solutions systematically. Make all these shapes and record your results.

remove one	**remove three**	**remove four**

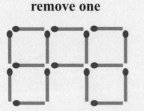
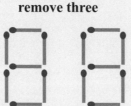
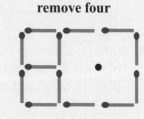

5 Find one more shape by: **a** 'remove three';　**b** 'remove five';　**b** 'remove six'.

6 Continue with this solution up to ten matchsticks removed.

7 Try starting with 24 matchsticks making nine squares.

8 Try different arrangements.

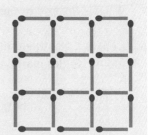

9 Record your results as shown:

Number of matchsticks	17	....			
Number of squares	9	....			

10 Investigate with 32 matchsticks making 12 squares.

EXTENSION

1 Sketch these shapes and find angles α, β, or θ.

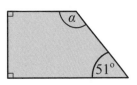 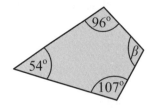 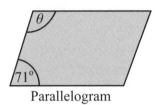

Parallelogram

2 Sketch these shapes, finding the sides and angles α, β, θ, or ε.

i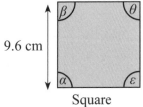

9.6 cm

Square

ii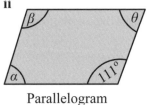

Parallelogram

iii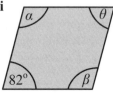

Rhombus

3 Find the value of angle ε in each of these shapes.

i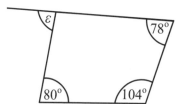

ii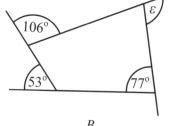

4 $ABCD$ is a kite.
Angle $BAD = 90°$ and angle $BCD = 38°$.
Work out the size of angle ADC.

5 In a quadrilateral one angle is equal to $57°$. The other three angles are equal.
What is the size of the equal angles?

6 $JKLM$ is a quadrilateral.
Find the angles marked α, β, and θ.

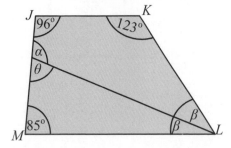

7 $MNOP$ is a rhombus.
If $\beta = 28°$ find ε.

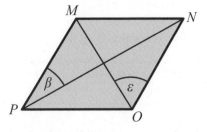

8 Three interior angles of a quadrilateral measures $107°$, $81°$ and $96°$. What is the size of the fourth angle?

9 One angle of a parallelogram measures $69°$. Write the sizes of the other three angles.

10 A diagonal of a rectangle makes an angle of $27°$ with a long side of the rectangle:
 a What angle does the diagonal make with a short side?
 b Work out the acute angle between the diagonals.
 c Work out the obtuse angle between the diagonals.

11 The figure is an arrowhead.
Find the angles marked α, β and θ.

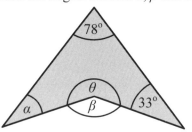

12 Work out the angles marked α, β and θ.

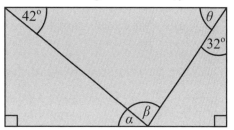

13 Find the angles marked α, β and θ.

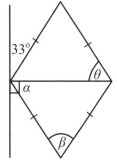

14 Find the angles marked α, β and θ.

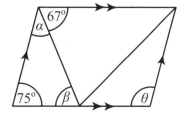

15 The figure shows the plan of a school compound.
 a Using a scale of 1 cm to 20 m, draw the field.
 b A post is placed at the intersection of the bisector of
 $Q\hat{R}S$ and the perpendicular bisector of RS. Show the position of the post and mark it T.
 c Using your scale drawing find the distance of R to T.
 d Measure RQ and QP.

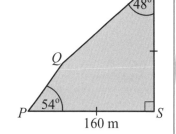

16 The figure represents the plan of a village.
 a Using a scale of 1 cm to 40 m, make an accurate scale drawing of the village.
 b Draw the diagonals JL and KM and state their lengths.
 c At the intersection of these diagonals a mobile phone mast is to be sited. Write down the distance between the mobile phone mast and the corner M of the region.

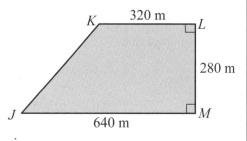

SUMMARY

Quadrilateral A quadrilateral is a polygon with four sides (or 'edges') and four vertices or corners. The word quadrilateral is made of the words **quad** (meaning 'four') and **lateral** (meaning 'of sides').

Diagonal A **diagonal** is a line joining two vertices. The diagonal divides the quadrilateral into two triangles.

The sum of the four angles of a quadrilateral is 360°.
This is true of any quadrilateral whatever its shape or size.

These are the properties of quadrilaterals with special names:

Square
Four equal sides
All angles are 90°
Four lines of symmetry
Diagonals bisect at right angles
Rotational symmetry of order four

Rectangle
Two pairs of equal and parallel sides
All angles are 90°
Diagonals bisect each other
Two lines of symmetry
Rotational symmetry of order two

Rhombus
Four equal sides
Opposite sides parallel
Diagonals bisect at right angles
Opposite angles are equal
Diagonals bisect angles
Two lines of symmetry
Rotational symmetry of order two

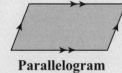

Parallelogram
Two pairs of equal and parallel sides
No lines of symmetry (in general)
Rotational symmetry of order two

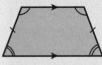

Trapezium
One pair of parallel lines

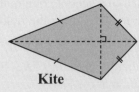

Kite
Diagonals meet at 90°
One line of symmetry
Two pairs of equal sides
One pair of equal angles

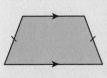

Isosceles trapezium
One pair of opposite sides are equal
One line of symmetry
One pair of parallel lines
Two pairs of parallel sides

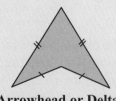

Arrowhead or Delta or Re-entrant kite
Two pairs of equal sides
One interior angle larger than 180°
One line of symmetry
Diagonals cross at right angles outside the shape
One pair of equal angles

Right trapezium
One pair of right angles
One pair of parallel lines

Ratio and proportion

CORE

EXTENSION

SUMMARY

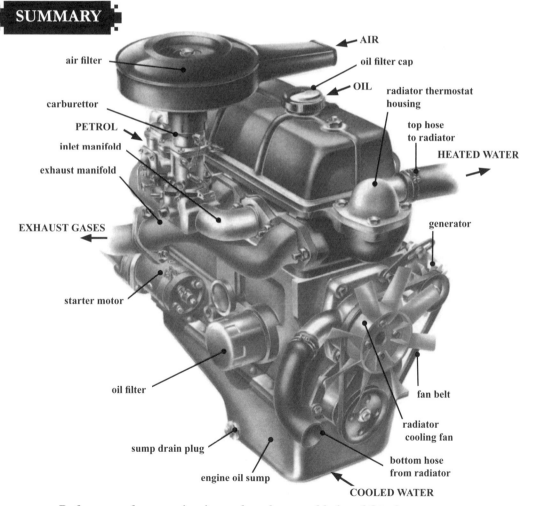

AIR

air filter

oil filter cap

OIL

radiator thermostat housing

carburettor

top hose to radiator

PETROL

HEATED WATER

inlet manifold

exhaust manifold

EXHAUST GASES

generator

starter motor

oil filter

fan belt

radiator cooling fan

sump drain plug

bottom hose from radiator

engine oil sump

COOLED WATER

Before a real car engine is produced, assembled and fitted,
a smaller scale model is usually made as a prototype.

1 Introduction to ratio

Ratio

A ratio is a way of comparing two or more quantities. The quantities must be in the same units. The numbers in the ratio are separated by a colon (:).

The ratio of A is to B is pronounced 'A to B' or $A : B$

Antecedent   Consequent

Examples

a Osei is 6 years old and Badu is 18 years old. The ratio of their ages is written as: Osei's age is to Badu's age which is 6 : 18.

b  The ratio of four black beads compared to three white beads is 4 : 3.

c The ratio of black tiles to white tiles is 5 : 11

Exercise 11:1

1 To make MixOrange drink, water and concentrated orange drink are mixed together.
Draw 7 copies of this container.
On each, shade the following mixtures of MixOrange.
Shade MixOrange one colour and water another colour.

MixOrange

i a 1 part of concentrated orange to 7 parts of water.
  b 2 parts of concentrated orange to 6 parts of water.
  c 3 parts of concentrated orange to 5 parts of water.
  d 4 parts of concentrated orange to 4 parts of water.
  e 5 parts of concentrated orange to 3 parts of water.
  f 6 parts of concentrated orange to 2 parts of water
  g 7 parts of concentrated orange to 1 part of water.

ii a If each drink was stirred, which would taste the strongest?
  b Which would taste the weakest?
  c Both **1c** and **1e** have 3 parts of one and 5 parts of the other. Will these taste the same? Explain.

2 For each of these tile patterns write the ratio of black tiles to white tiles.

a   **b**   **c**   **d**   **e**
  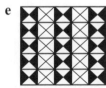

3 Write each of these as a ratio:

a 20 mm compared to 3 cm
b ¢1.20 compared to 93 p
c 900 g compared to 1.35 kg
d 2 hours compared to 90 min
e 18 months compared $2\frac{1}{2}$ years
f 3 feet compared to 57 inches

4 Find the ratio of shaded areas compared to unshaded areas for each of these diagrams.

a   b   c   d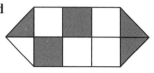

5 In a school there are 300 pupils and 15 teachers. How many teachers would you expect in a school of 700 pupils?

6 Write the ratio of black beads compared to white beads in each of these:

a    b    c   d

7 A builder uses 5 buckets of sand and 2 buckets of cement to make concrete. How many buckets of cement will he need if he uses:

   a 15 buckets of sand   b 35 buckets of sand   c 80 buckets of sand

8 The builder prepares 60 kg of mortar by mixing 10 kg of cement with 5 kg of lime and 45 kg of sand. How much cement, lime and sand does he use to prepare:

   a 15 kg of mortar   b 120 kg of mortar   c 300 kg of mortar

Here is a list of ingredients for Kubé cake

9 a Rewrite the ingredients for this recipe to make Kubé cake to serve 12 people.
   b If you used 500 g of grated ginger:
     i how much dark rum would you need?
     ii how much cane sugar would you need?

Kubé Cake - serves 8

grated coconut   500 g
grated ginger   200 g
dark rum drink   200 ml
cane sugar   315 g

10 Brass is an alloy (mixture) of zinc and copper in the ratio of 3 : 7. How much copper is in a brass pot which contains 450 g of zinc?

11 For each of these questions, write how many times as big the first quantity is compared with the second.

   a 70, 14   b ¢396, ¢18   c 6 h, 48 min   d 165 mm, 3.3 cm
   e 2 yrs, 8 months   f 1m 8 cm, 18 cm   g 5.4 kg, 720 g   h 5.81 *l*, 83 *cl*

12 For each of these write how many times as long the first drawing is compared with the second (give answers to 2 d.p.).

   a

   b

   c

2　Simplifying ratios

Ratios can be written in an easier form. To simplify ratios, convert quantities to the same units. Convert units using this list of measurements.

1 cm = 10 mm	1 g = 1000 mg	1 minute = 60 seconds
1 m = 100 cm	1 kg = 1000 g	1 hour = 60 minutes
1 km = 1000 m	1 t = 1000 kg	1 l = 1000 ml

Exercise 11:2

Convert these units from:

1　3 m to cm

2　5 t to kg

3　7 km to m

4　$2\frac{1}{2}$ hours to min

5　9.5 m to mm

6　$8\frac{1}{2}$ kg to g

7　5 l to ml

8　150 cm to m

9　$10\frac{1}{2}$ hours to min

10　1 kg 850 g to g

11　2 h 45 min to min

12　15 m 8 mm to mm

13　$2\frac{3}{4}$ min to seconds

14　1m 850 mm to cm

15　14 m 305 mm to cm

These ratios are equivalent.
The relationship between each
pair of numbers is the same.

20 : 40
15 : 30
6 : 12
2 : 4

20 : 40 can be worked out as: $\frac{20}{40} = \frac{1}{2}$

This is the simpler form of the ratios　1 : 2

You can simplify a ratio by dividing the numbers by a common factor.

Examples　　Simplify these

a 6 : 18　　　**b** 10 min : 2 h　　　**c** 100 cm : 60 cm : 40 cm

$$\overset{\div 6}{\frown}$$

a　6 : 18　　=　　1 : 3

$$\overset{\text{change to minutes}}{\frown}\qquad\overset{\div 10}{\frown}$$

b　10 min : 2 h　　=　　$\boxed{10 \text{ min} : 120 \text{ min}}$　　=　　1 : 12

$$\overset{\div 20}{\frown}$$

c　100 cm : 60 cm : 40 cm　=　5 : 3 : 2

Exercise 11:3

Simplify these ratios:

1 8 : 24

2 15 : 20

3 24 : 36

4 25 : 40

5 15 : 4

6 3 : 2 : 4

7 2 cm : 8 cm

8 32 p : 96 p

9 5 ml : 25 ml

10 ¢160 : ¢75

11 2 kg : 75 g

12 75 mm : 6 cm

13 350 g : 1.4 kg

14 $1\frac{3}{4}$ h : 49 min

15 $2\frac{1}{2}$ km : $1\frac{1}{2}$ km

16 5.1 m : 25.5 m

17 250 ml : 70cl : 1.5 l

18 0.05 kg : 300 g : 0.15 kg

19 10 cm : 40 mm : 2 m

20 65 t : 650 kg : 3.9 t

21 2 h 51 min: 1 h 35 min

22 0.05 l : 0.5 l : 3 l

23 $2\frac{1}{2} : 3\frac{1}{2} : 4\frac{1}{2}$

24 $\frac{6}{7} : 1\frac{2}{7} : 2\frac{3}{21}$

Examples   **a** Find the ratio of the lengths of the sides of the triangle below.

Ratio of the lengths = 4.8 cm : 3.6 cm : 3.2 cm

$$= 4.8 : 3.6 : 3.2 \quad \left(\begin{array}{l}\text{multiply by 10}\\ \text{and divide by 4}\end{array}\right)$$
$$= 48 : 36 : 32$$
$$= 12 : 9 : 8$$

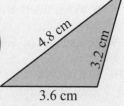

4.8 cm

3.2 cm

3.6 cm

b Ajoa walks 2 km to school in 40 minutes and Akosua cycles 5 km to school in 15 minutes. Find and simplify the ratio of :
a Ajoa's distance to Akosua's distance
b Ajoa's time : Akosua's time

a Ajoa's distance to Akosua's distance = 2 : 5

b Ajoa's time : Akosua's time = 40 min : 15 min
$$= 8 : 3 \quad \text{(divide through by 5)}$$

Exercise 11:4

In each of these questions give the answer in its simplest form.

1 A triangle sides 12 cm, 9 cm and 15 cm. Find the ratio of the three

2 A couple have 9 grandsons and 6 granddaughters.
   a Find the ratio the number of grandsons to that of granddaughters.
   b Find the ratio of the number of granddaughters to that of grandchildren.

3 In a group of 35 pupils 20 are female. Find the ratio of :
   a the number of female pupils to the number of male pupils;
   b the number of female to the total number of pupils.

4 Amisah made a model plane from paper. The model is 30 cm long
  and the actual plane is 27 m long. Find the ratio of the length of
  the model to the length of the actual plane.

5 A recipe for Palava sauce needs 250 g of meat, 125 g of smoked herring and 750 g of
  chopped spinach. Find the ratio of the weights of the ingredients to one another.

6 Two angles of a triangle are 60° and 72°. Find the ratio of the size of the third angle to the
  sum of the two.

7 A length of wood is cut into two pieces in the ratio 4 : 9. What fraction of the original
  length is the longer piece?

8 One morning a farmer notices that his hens Akopanin and Akokakra have laid eggs in the
  ratio 2 : 3.
   a What fraction of the eggs did Akopanin lay?
   b What fraction of the eggs did Akokakra lay?

9 In a school of 378 pupils, 21 are prefects. What is the ratio of prefects to non-prefects?

10 In a certain region of Ghana it was decided that schools with 500 children should have 25
   teachers and that the ratio of children to teachers should be the same in the region.
    a What is the ratio in its simplest form?
    b Would the headmaster of the school with 380 and 20 teachers have to employ more
       teachers? If so how many?

11 A nurse diluted a drug with water in the ratio of 1 : 6. If 50 ml of drug was used,
    a How much water was used?
    b How much solution was made up altogether?

12 In the figure the triangle ABC is mapped
   onto triangle A'B'C' by an enlargement
   centre O. Write down the ratio of :
    a A'C' : AC
    b Find the lengths of BC and AB.

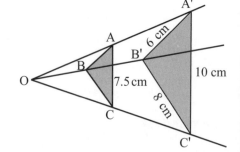

13 One rectangle is 7 cm long by 5.5 cm wide and another one is of length 8 cm and width
   5 cm. Taking them in the order given, find the ratio of their:
    a lengths   b widths   c perimeters   d areas

14 In the table the ratio of each top number to the number below it is exactly the same.
   Copy and complete the table.

6	12		$3\frac{1}{2}$		4a		4x + 2y
9		45		25.2		57	

3 Sharing in ratios

Sometimes we need to divide up an amount according to a given ratio. The method is to add up all parts of the ratio first and find the value of one 'share'. Then we multiply this up to solve the problem.

Examples

a Share 40 kg in the ratio 2 : 3

The ratio is 2 : 3
2 + 3 = 5
Divide 40 up into 5 'shares'
40 ÷ 5 = 8
∴ 1 share is equal to 8 kg
2 shares equal 16 kg
3 shares equal 24 kg

b Two girls share 96 sweets in the ratio 5 : 7

Divide 96 into (5 + 7) parts
So there are 12 parts
Each part is 96 ÷ 12 = 8
So 5 parts = 5 × 8 = 40 sweets
7 parts = 7 × 8 = 56 sweets

c Divide 28 in the ratio $1\frac{1}{4} : 2\frac{3}{4}$

Divide 28 into $(1\frac{1}{4} + 2\frac{3}{4})$ parts
There are 4 parts
Each part is 28 ÷ 4 = 7
$1\frac{1}{4}$ parts = $1\frac{1}{4} \times 7 = 8\frac{3}{4}$
$2\frac{3}{4}$ parts = $2\frac{3}{4} \times 7 = 19\frac{1}{4}$

d Share 78 kg in the ratio 2 : 3 : 8

Divide 78 into (2 + 3 + 8) parts
There are 13 parts
Each part is 78 ÷ 13 = 6
So 2 parts = 2 × 6 = 12 kg
3 parts = 3 × 6 = 18 kg
8 parts = 8 × 6 = 48 kg

Exercise 11:5

1 Share these quantities in the ratios given:

a 12 mangoes between Ampadu and Serwaah, ratio 2 : 1.

b 15 oranges between Kujo and Ama, ratio 3 : 2.

c 30 tomatoes between Kwamina and Haji, ratio 3: 7.

d 27 pineapples between Asare and Dadze, ratio 5 : 4.

2 Split the quantities in the ratios given.

a 64 m in the ratio 3 : 5   **b** ¢2500 in the ratio 4 : 1

c ¢2550 in the ratio 11 : 4   **d** 66 kg in the ratio 6 : 3 : 2

e 560 ml in the ratio 4 : 3 : 1   **f** 1.2 kg in the ratio 1 : 2 : 3

3 286 marbles are to be divided in the ratio of 7 : 4. Work out the size of each part.

4 Akosua and Akua have a total of ¢6000 between them. Akua has three times as much money as Akosua. How much does Akosua have?

5 Copy and complete this table.
The first one has been done for you.

Quantity	Divide in the ratio		
	4 :	3 :	2
36 kg	16	12	8
27 in			
81 lbs			
117 tonnes			
¢144			
108 volts			
162 Hz			
12690 bytes			

6 A line 3.2 m long is to be divided into three parts in the ratio 1 : 3 : 4. Work out each part.

7 An alloy consists of copper, zinc and tin in the ratio 2 : 3 : 5. Find the amount of each metal in 105 kg of the alloy.

8 Two points X and Y are 84 cm apart. Find the lengths XZ and ZY if Z divided XY in the ratio 4 : 3.

9 Share 60 sweets among three children in the ratio 7 : 5 : 3.

10 An aircraft carries fuel in three tanks whose capacities are in the ratio 3 : 4 : 5. The capacity of the smallest tank is 840 litres. Work out :
a the capacity of the largest tank;
b the total capacity of the three tanks.

11 Minka weighs 62 kg and Kankam weighs 58 kg. Divide 240 g of chocolate between them in the ratio of their weights.

12 The angles of a triangle are in the ratio 5 : 4 : 3. Find each angle.

13 Bonsu, Bawa and Dumfe are in a Lotto syndicate. Each week Bonsu pays ¢30, Bawa ¢10 and Dumfe pays ¢40. They agree to split the winnings in the same ratio. Calculate how much each person receives if they win: **a** ¢100　　　**b** ¢660　　　**c** ¢12 000

14 Profits from a business are shared between three shareholders. They are shared in the ratio 5 : 7 : 11.　　**a** What fraction of the profit does each person get?
b If the profit is ¢4370, find out how much each person gets.

15 Magnesium combines with Oxygen in the ratio 3 : 2 by weight.
a How much magnesium would be needed to combine with 2.3 kg of oxygen?
b What would be the weight of the substance formed?

16 Divide $360°$ into four angles in the ratio : $1\frac{1}{2} : 2\frac{1}{2} : 3\frac{1}{2} : 4\frac{1}{2}$.

17 Divide ¢4500 in the ratio $1\frac{3}{4} : \frac{2}{5} : \frac{17}{20}$

18 There is four times as much nitrogen as oxygen in the air. How much oxygen is there in 55 litres of air?

19 Who receives more land: a junior partner in a ratio of 3 : 2 share out of 0.095 km², or senior partner in a ratio 4 : 1 share out of 0.055 km²? Give the difference. (ratio senior : junior)

20 Share ¢1265 among these people according to age; Atta ($15\frac{1}{2}$), Kanu (18) and Anto ($21\frac{1}{2}$).

4   Direct proportion

Another word for comparing quantities is **proportion**. For example if an amount of petrol is purchased, the total cost is proportional to the volume of fuel bought; double the amount of petrol and the cost doubles, quadruple the mount of petrol and the cost quadruples and so on.

Rate   **Rate** is the ratio between two quantities with different units.

Direct proportion   Two quantities are said to be in **direct proportion** if they increase or decrease at the same rate.

Example   A car does 40 km on 5 litres of diesel. How far will it go on 16 litres?

The unitary method

5 litres make 40 km

1 litre makes 40 ÷ 5 = 8 km

16 litres make 16 × 8 = 128 km

The ratio method

Let x be the number of kilometres that make 16 litres

$$\frac{x}{16} = \frac{40}{5}$$

$5x = 16 \times 40$ (cross multiply)

$5x = 640$ km

$x = 128$

A simple rule of thumb method to check whether one quantity is directly proportional to another is to try two tests:

■ If one quantity is zero, is the other also zero?

■ If one quantity doubles does the other quantity also double?

Exercise 11:6

1   A minibus does 22 km on 5 litres of petrol. How far will it go on 128 litres?

2   A train travels 250 km in $4\frac{1}{2}$ hours. If it travels at the same speed, how long will it take to complete a journey of 300 km?

3   A bricklayer can lay 112 blocks in 4 hours. How many blocks can he lay in $6\frac{1}{4}$ hours?

4   A metal wire 47 cm long has a mass of 799 g. What is the mass of 25 cm of this wire?

5   The length of the shadow of a tree is directly proportional to the height of the tree.
    At 3 pm a tree 18 m tall casts a shadow 12 m long. Another tree casts a shadow 14.5 m long at the same time of day. How tall is this tree?

6   3 books weigh 654 g. What is the weight in kilograms of 24 similar books?

7   A minibus is driving at a constant speed of 30 kilometres in 20 minutes. How far will it travel in 62 minutes?

229

8   A water tank is being filled. The depth of the water is directly proportional to the time for which the tap has been running. 10 minutes after the start it is 30 cm deep. How deep will it be 29 minutes after the start?

9   The amount of fertiliser required to improve crops in an area of 36 m² is 1.35 kg.
   a How much is needed to fertilise 20 m²?   **b** What area will 15 kg fertilise?

10 Grumah covered 75 kilometres on a bicycle in 4 h 30 min. If he continues at the same speed how long will he take to complete his 100 kilometre journey?

11 In a mix for making mortar 80 kg of sand is mixed with 18 kg of cement.
   a How much sand is needed to mix with 55 kg of cement?
   b How much cement is needed to mix with 2600 kg of sand?

12 If Ansah sells 9 litres of bottled water for ¢5.40. Find the cost of 54 litres.

13 The cost of electricity to run a refrigerator for 2.8 hours is 63p. What is the cost of running the refrigerator for one hour?

14 The cost of 0.5 kg of mushrooms is ¢0.23, find the cost of 8.9 kg.

15 The fare for a train journey of 270 km costs ¢78. At the same rate per kilometre:
   a what would be the cost of travelling 153 kilometres?
   b How far could you travel on a fare of ¢65?

16 The rates of currency exchange published in a newspaper on a certain day showed 14 dollars could be exchanged for 18 euros. How many euros could be obtained for:
   a 133 dollars   **b** 49 dollars   **c** 312 dollars   **d** 455 dollars?

17 If a 2 kg bag of sugar contains 9×10^6 crystals. How many crystals are there in:
   a 1.5 kg   **b** 4.9 kg   **c** 0.003 kg   **d** 14.14 kg?

18 The air resistance of a moving car is proportional to the speed at which the car is travelling. When a car is moving at 30 km/h it is subject to air resistance of 1500 newtons. Work out the speed if the car is subject to air resistance of 3500 newtons.

19 Two quantities σ and τ are directly proportional. Copy and complete this table.

σ	1.5	3	7	13.5				σ Sigma
τ	12.78				50	80	160	τ Tau

20 In a certain country the voting system is based on proportional representation. This means that the number of seats for a given political party is directly proportional to the number of votes cast in the election. There are 120 seats. Copy and complete the table.

	Democratic Party	Progress Party	Patriotic Party	Liberal Party	Labour Party
Number of votes	14 725	3100	23 250	17 825	34 100
Number of seats					

5 Inverse proportion

The grass of a large school field needs to be cut. The headteacher wants it cut as efficiently as possible. She makes this analysis: 1 man will take 16 hours

2 men will take 8 hours

3 men will take 5 hours 20 minutes

4 men will take 4 hours

As the number of men increases the time decreases. This is an example of inverse proportion.

Inverse proportion — Two quantities are said to be **inversely proportional** if an increase in one quantity causes a decrease in the other.

Examples — A poultry farmer feeds 36 chickens on a special food for 30 days (d). If he buys an extra 12 chickens how long will the feed last?

Unitary method

36 chickens can be fed for 30 days

1 chicken can be fed for 30×36 (a longer time)

48 chickens can be fed for

$\dfrac{30 \times 36}{48} = 22\frac{1}{2}$ days

Constant product method

Let d be the required number of days

Then $48 \times d = 36 \times 30 = 1080$

$d = \dfrac{1080}{48} = 22\frac{1}{2}$ days

Two quantities A and B are in inverse proportion if by whatever A changes, B changes by the multiplicative inverse or the reciprocal of that factor.

Example — Mr Asamoah lives 60 kilometres away. If he drives at a speed of 60 km/h his journey time will be 1 hour. If he drives at a speed of 30 km/h his journey time will be 2 hours. 15 km/h will be 4 hours journey time. Therefore his speed changes by a factor of $\frac{1}{2}$, since 60 km/h times $\frac{1}{2}$ is 30 km/h.

Exercise 11:7

1 Which of these quantities are:

i directly proportional ii inversely proportional iii not related?

a The volume of a tube and the height of the tube.
b The thickness of a mathematics book and the number of pages.
c The ages of pupils and their mathematics test marks.
d The length of any trench and the time taken by one person to dig it.
e The number of a particular make of shoes bought and the cost of the shoes.
f The height of a man and the number of people in his family.
g The number of people doing a job and the time taken to finish it.
h The speed of a car and the time it takes to cover a fixed distance.

2 A contractor estimates that he can carry out the fencing of a large garden in 9 days if he employs 4 labourers.

a How many labourers would be needed to complete the work in 6 days?
b How long would 3 labourers take to do the job, assuming that all the labourers work at the same rate?

231

3 In an examination hall there are 16 rows and 9 desks in each row.
  a How many desks are there?
  b If the layout is changed so that each row contains eight desks, how many rows would there have to be?

4 An agricultural supplier delivers regular quantities of rice to a school. This quantity lasts for 21 days when there are 260 pupils.
  a How long does the quantity last for 20 pupils?
  b If the school admitted 13 extra pupils, for how many days would this same quantity of rice last last for the whole school?

5 Five men building a wall take 15 days to complete it. How long would it take 3 men to complete it?

6 Obeng bought a number of stamps which were arranged in 14 columns of 22 stamps each. If this same number of stamps were arranged in 11 columns, how many rows would there be?

7 A plane flies from Kumasi to Accra in 45 minutes at 720 m.p.h. How long would the journey take at 600 m.p.h?

8 The length of a newspaper article is 114 lines with an average of 8 words per line. If it is reset with an average of 12 words per line, how many lines will be needed?

9 If there is enough food in an emergency pack to last 8 hunters for 3 days, how long would the food last if there were 4 hunters?

10 In a factory bars of soap are packed in cartons so that there are 12 rows of 12 bars in each carton. If the same number of bars of soap are to be packed into a carton in nine rows, how many bars of soap will there be in each row?

11 Bonah is organising a coach excursion for club members. It costs ¢160 to hire the coach, which can take up to 40 people. The amount he will charge will have to depend on the number of people who want to go. He is not to make a profit.
  Let p stand for the number of people who want to go.
  Let c stand for the cost per person in ¢.

  a Copy and complete the table of values of p and c.

p	2	4	5	8	10	16	20	32	40
c	80	40							

  b What can you say about the product pc for every pair of values in the table?
  c What happens to the value of c when p doubles?

12 The frequency of a wave is inversely proportional to its wavelength. The Capital Radio transmitter sends out waves of wavelength 285 m and frequency of 1098 kHz (kilohertz). If the local station Capital Radio local sends out waves of wavelength 1600 m, find the frequency.

6 The symbol ∝

The symbol ∝ means 'is proportional to'

A statement like: height, '*h* is proportional to time, *t*' is written as $h \propto t$

In the same way the stopping distance, *d*, of a car is proportional to the square of its speed, s^2, is written as $d \propto s^2$.

The statement: pressure, *p*, is inversely proportional to volume, *V*, is written $p \propto \dfrac{1}{V}$

Examples   **a** *y* is proportional to *x*. Given that $y = 12$ when $x = 4$, calculate the value of *y* when $x = 15$

$y \propto x$ (proportional statement)

$y = kx$ (proportionality equation where *k* is a constant of proportionality)

$y = 12$ when $x = 4$

so $12 = 4k$ $(k = y \div x)$

∴ $k = 3$ $(k = 12 \div 4)$

The proportionality equation is $y = 3x$

When $x = 15$ $y = 3 \times 15 = 45$

b The volume, *V* of a cylinder is proportional to the square of the height, *h*.
$V = 10$ when $h = 5$
i Find the proportionality equation that connects *V* and *h*.
ii Use your equation to find *V* when $h = 4$.

i $V \propto h^2$

$V = kh^2$ where *k* is the constant of proportionality $(k = V \div h^2)$

$V = 10$ when $h = 5$ so $10 = k \times 5^2 = 25k$

∴ $k = 0.4$ $(10 \div 25)$

ii When $h = 4$ $V = 0.4 \times 4^2$
$= 0.4 \times 16$
$V = 6.4$

c *p* is inversely proportional to *q* so that when $p = 6$ the value of $q = 12$.
Work out the value of *p* when $q = 10$.

$p \propto \dfrac{1}{q}$

$p = \dfrac{k}{q}$

$k = pq$ where *k* is a constant

$p = 6$ when $q = 12$ ∴ $k = 6 \times 12 = 72$

The proportionality equation is $p = \dfrac{72}{q}$

When $q = 10$ $p = \dfrac{72}{10}$

$= 7.2$

Exercise 11:8

1 Express these statements by using: **i** the $\propto$ notation and **ii** a constant of proportionality.

   a The velocity V, of a particle is proportional to the time, t.

   b The stopping distance d, of a car is proportional to the square of its speed, s.

   c The circumference c, of a circle is proportional to its radius, r.

   d A quantity x is inversely proportional to the quantity y.

   e The distance d, to the horizontal is proportional to the square root of the observer's height h, above the surface of the sea.

2 Express these as statements:

   a $P \propto \dfrac{1}{m}$ **b** $A \propto \sqrt{x}$ **c** $S \propto \dfrac{1}{\sqrt{x}}$ **d** $B \propto \sqrt[3]{t}$

3 Express each of the following as an equation using the constant of proportionality.

   a $m^2 \propto \dfrac{1}{p}$ **b** $d \propto \dfrac{1}{g^2}$ **c** $V^2 \propto t^3$ **d** $A \propto \dfrac{1}{x^3}$

4 y is directly proportional to x. $y = 12$ when $x = 2$. Find the value of y when $x = 5$.

5 p is directly proportional to q so that $p = 148$ when $q = 12$. Find the value of p when $q = 7$.

6 K is inversely proportional to m. $K = 10$ when $m = 5$. Find the value of K when $m = 4$.

7 A is inversely proportional to b. $A = 12$ when $b = 2$. Work out the value of A when $b = 8$.

8 G is inversely proportional to z. $G = 16$ when $z = 0.3$. Work out the value of G when $z = 0.5$.

9 $x \propto \dfrac{1}{y}$ and $x = 3$ when $y = 4$. Find x when $y = 8$.

10 **a** If $y \propto x$ copy and complete the table.

   b If $y = kx^3$ what is the value of k?

x	2	6	8		
y	0.1			12.8	68.5

11 Some corresponding values of p and q are shown in the table. Which of the following could be true?

q	1	5	10	20
p	5	125	500	2000

   i $p \propto q^2$ **ii** $p = 5q$ **iii** $p = 5q^2$ **iv** $p = 30q - 25$

12 The heating power P, (in watts) of an electrical fire is proportional to the square of the current, i, flowing through it. When the power is 1000 watts the current is 5 amps. Work out the power when the current is 4 amps.

13 Given that $y \propto \dfrac{1}{x^2}$

Copy and complete the table shown.

x	20	17	14		8
y		240		600	

14 For a fixed distance, speed is inversely proportional to time. When an object is travelling at 300 km/h it takes 2 hours to cover a fixed distance. How long would it take to travel the same distance at 200 km/h?

15 The length of a pendulum l is directly proportional to the square of the period for which the pendulum swings (T). Given that a pendulum which has a period of 3 seconds is 2.25 metres long,

calculate the length of the pendulum which has a period of:

a 2 seconds **b** 2.5 seconds **c** 12 seconds

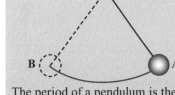

B   A

The period of a pendulum is the time it takes to go from A to B and from B to A (i.e. to complete the cycle).

16 The electrical resistance R, in a fixed length of wire varies inversely to the square of the diameter. If the diameter is 5 mm the resistance is 0.08 ohms. Find the resistance if the diameter is 4 mm.

*17 Two quantities j and p that can vary in value are inversely proportional.
Copy and complete the table.

j	12.5	8			0.01
p	6		25	70	

*18 The air pressure from a bicycle pump is inversely proportional to the square of the diameter of the pump. If the pressure of 7 N/m² is available from a pump of diameter 20 mm, find:

a the pressure available from a pump of diameter 28 mm;

b the diameter of the pump which can deliver 16 N/m² of pressure. (Give answers to 2 d.p.)

*19 The number of coins, N, with the diameter d cm and a fixed thickness that can be made from a given volume of metal, can be found by using the formula $N = \dfrac{k}{d^2}$ where k is

constant. **a** Given that 5000 coins of diameter 2.5 cm can be made from the volumes of metal, find the value of k.

    b Work out how many coins of diameter 2 cm can be made from an equal volume of metal.

    c Rearrange the formula to make d the subject.

    d 3500 coins are to be made using an equal volume of metal. Work out the diameter of these coins (to 2 d.p.).

*20 The intensity I, of a light on an object is inversely proportional to the square of the distance d, of the object from the light. If the intensity of the light is 12 candela at a distance of 6 metres, find:

a the intensity at a distance of 4 metres;

b the distance when the light intensity is 15 candela (to 2 d.p.).

7   Application of proportion

There are many examples in the real world where one variable is affected by another.
These graphs show different variations.

The time it takes for a material to decay.

The more goods you sell the more profit you make.
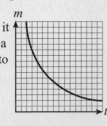

Constant speed of a car.
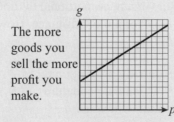

The higher the speed of a car the less time it takes to get to its destination.
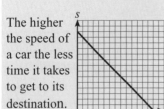

The more solar panels installed the more solar energy generated.
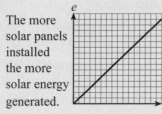

The number of bacteria in a colony with respect to time.
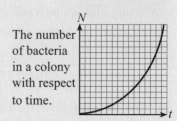

Example   **a**   18 cm³ of paper weighs 162 g. What is the weight of 26 cm²?

18 cm³ weighs 162 g

1 cm³ weighs $\dfrac{162}{18} = 9$ g

∴   26 cm² weighs $26 \times 9 = 234$ g

b   When knitting a scarf 45 stitches wide, one ball of wool gives a width of 18 cm. If the scarf had been 54 stitches wide instead, how wide a scarf would the same ball knit?

45 stitches = 18 cm wide

∴ 54 stitches will give $54 \times 18 \div 45 = 21.6$ cm

Exercise 11:9

1   If 32 matches weigh 45 g, what would 40 matches weigh?

2   5 people can clean a school in 4 hours. How long would it take 8 people to clean the school?

3   Ten grains of rice weigh 1.5×10^{-3} kg. What is the weight of 4800 grains of rice?

4   The distance a cyclist travels is directly proportional to to the number of revolutions of the front wheel of the bicycle. The cyclist travels 36 m for 15 revolutions of the front wheel.
   a   How far does the cyclist travel for 200 revolutions?
   b   How many revolutions are needed to travel 1.5 km

5   Yakubu uses 46 ml of ink in his fountain pen to write an average of 2500 characters.
   What volume of ink would he need to write 7000 characters?

6 An ink cartridge in a photocopy machine will last 20 days when an average of 50 sheets of paper are printed each day. How long will a cartridge last when the average number of sheets printed per day is increased to 80?

7 For planting 30 seedlings 204 cm² of space is needed.
  a How much space would be needed for 48 seedlings?
  b How many seedlings could be planted in a space of 1664 cm²?

8 If 17.5 metres of material makes 10 skirts, how much material should a tailor allow for making 26 skirts?

9 Which of these graphs are proportional quantities? Explain your answer.

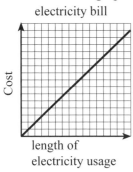
electricity bill

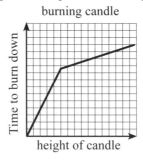
burning candle

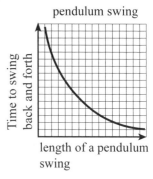
pendulum swing

10 Describe two practical examples of each of these graphs.

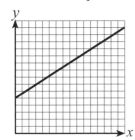

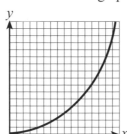

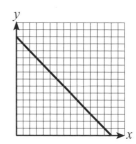

11 An electric fire uses 16 units of electricity in 6.8 hours:
  i How many units does it use in: **a** 51 min   **b** 1.7 h   **c** 2.4 h?
  ii How many hours does it take to use: **a** 50 units   **b** 18 units   **c** 63 units?
    (Round your answers to 2 d.p.)

12

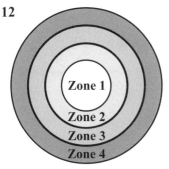
Zone 1
Zone 2
Zone 3
Zone 4

Buaben Distributers sell plastic goods. The company charges to deliver goods to customers' homes. The delivery charge depends on the zone in which the customer lives.
The diagram shows how the zones are numbered.
The delivery charge is directly proportional to the zone number.
The delivery charge for zone 2 is ¢17.
¢C is the delivery charge. Z is the zone number.
  a Write down a formula which expresses C in terms of Z.
  b Work out **i** the delivery charge for zone 4.
          ii the delivery charge for zone 3

Proportionality and music

When a guitar is plucked, it produces a musical note which may be a high or low note. High notes have high frequencies and low notes have low frequencies. The frequencies (hertz or Hz) of the notes produced by each string on a guitar depend on how tight the string is, the length of the vibrating part of the string and the thickness/density of the string.

The guitar player tunes the guitar by adjusting the tightness of each string.

By altering the length of the vibrating part with his or her fingers the player can choose a higher note.

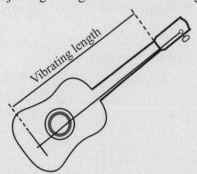

The *frequency* of a note is inversely proportional to the *length* of the vibrating string:

$$f \propto \frac{1}{l}$$

Example   If a string of 80 cm has been 'tuned' to produce a note whose frequency is 110 Hz. Work out the length of string which will produce a frequency of 185 Hz.

$$f \propto \frac{1}{l} \quad \Rightarrow \quad f = \frac{k}{l} \quad \Rightarrow \quad k = fl = 110 \times 80 = 8800$$

$$f = \frac{8800}{l} \quad \Rightarrow \quad \frac{8800}{185} = 47.6 \text{ cm (to 1 d.p.)}$$

Exercise 11:10

1   A string of 65 cm has been tuned to produce a note whose frequency is 150 Hz. Work out the length which will produce a note of frequency 175 Hz. (Give answer to 1 d.p.)

2   A string of 66 cm has been tuned to produce a note whose frequency is 110 Hz. Work out the length of string which will produce a frequency of 200 Hz.

3   A string which is being played can produce the note *C*. *C* has a frequency of 141 Hz. The table shows the frequencies of other notes produced on this string by altering the length. If the string produces *C* at 55 cm work out the length of the string to produce each of the notes in the table.

Note	A	B	C	D	E	F	G
Frequency	120	134	141	157	175	185	206
Length			55				

8 Scale Drawing

Scale 1 : 1 000 000

This simplified map shows some road networks and landmarks of Sunyani area in the Brong Ahafo region of Ghana.

Ratio can be written in the form 1 : n

Example   Write in the form 1 : n

        a 5 : 16   **b** 25 cm : 10 km

   a $5 : 16 = 1 : \dfrac{16}{5} = 1 : 3.2$

   b 10 km = 1 000 000
        25 cm : 10 km = 25 : 1 000 000
                 = 1 : 40 000

A scale drawing is the same shape as the original but different in size.

Scale   The scale of a drawing is the ratio between the length on a map or drawing and that of the real thing.

In a scale drawing:

■ all the measurements must be in proportion to the corresponding measurement of the original object

■ all the angles must remain the same as the corresponding angles of the original object

■ scales are often given as a ratio: for example 1 cm to 1 m

■ when the units in a ratio are the same, they are normally not given. For example, 1 cm to 1000 cm is written as 1 cm : 1000 cm or 1 : 1000

Examples   **a** 1 : 500 000 means 1 cm on the map represents 500 000 cm on the land.

           b 1 : 200 000 means 1 cm represents 200 000 cm or 2 km.

           c 1 : 750 000 means 1 cm represents 750 000 cm or $7\frac{1}{2}$ km.

           d 1 : 1000   means 1 cm represents 1000 cm or 10 m.

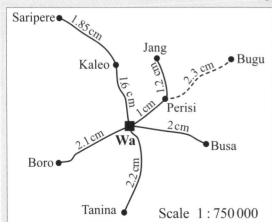

Scale 1 : 750 000

e   The map of Wa area is drawn to a scale of 1 cm to 750 000 cm. This means that a distance of 1 cm on the map represents a distance of 7.5 km on the ground.

The actual distance between:

i Wa and Kaleo is: 1.6 × 7.5 = 12 km

ii Wa and Bugu is: (1 + 2.3) × 7.5
                = 3.3 × 7.5
                = 24.75 km

Exercise 11:11

1 Write each of these ratios in the form 1 : *n*

   a 3 : 18   **b** 16 : 216   **c** 8.5 : 1275   **d** $4\frac{3}{5}$: 2760   **e** 25 : 375 000

2 Using the map of the Wa area in **example e**, find the distance between:

   a Saripere and Kaleo   **b** Wa and Tanina   **c** Tanina and Bugu via Wa and Perisi

   d Wa and Busa   **e** Boro and Jang   **f** Saripere and Busa via Kaleo and Wa

3 The scale is 1 cm to 4 m. Measure and write down the length each line represents:

   a _____   **b** _____

   c _____   **d** _____

   e _____   **f** _____

4 The scale is 1 cm to 5 km. Write down the length each line represents:

   a _____   **b** _____

   c _____   **d** _____

   e _____   **f** _____

5 Draw lines to represents these lengths. Use the scale given for each one.

	Length	Scale			Length	Scale
a	6 km	1 : 200 000		**d**	84 m	1 : 2400
b	24 km	1 : 600 000		**e**	220 km	1 : 5 000 000
c	150 m	1 : 2500		**f**	660 km	1 : 15 000 000

6 This is the plan of a garden.

   Scale 1 : 100

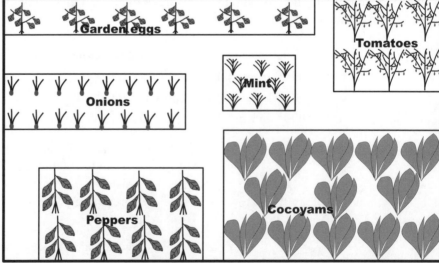

Copy and complete the table for all the fruits and vegetables. Take the length as the horizontal measurement.

Patch	Length (m)	Width (m)
Garden eggs		
Tomatoes		
......		

7 A ladder leans against a wall and makes an angle of 64°
   with the ground. The foot of the ladder is 2.5 m from the wall.

   a Use a scale of 1 : 50 and make a scale drawing of the diagram.

   b How long is the ladder?

   c How high up the wall does it reach?

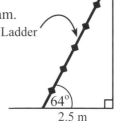

Ladder

64°

2.5 m

8 The diagram shows a sketch of one end of a garden shed.

   a Using a scale of 1 : 25 draw the front elevation of the shed.

   b Find the height of the shed from your scale drawing.

   c What is the actual height of the shed?

   d What is the topmost angle of the gable?

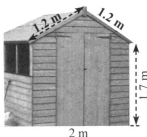

1.2 m 1.2 m

1.7 m

2 m

9 A model aeroplane is made using the scale 1: 125

   a The model is 30 cm long. How long is the real aeroplane?

   b Its cabin is 3.2 cm wide. How wide is the real cabin?

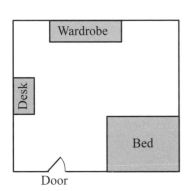

Wardrobe

Desk

Bed

Door

10 This is a scale drawing of Ametifi's bedroom. He has
    drawn it so that 1 cm on the diagram represents 2 m in
    his bedroom.

    a Write the scale in the form of a ratio.

    b Measure the length and width of the actual bedroom.

    c Draw the bedroom to scale of 1:275.

11 Look at the map of a village drawn to
    scale of 1 : 8500.
    To the nearest metre, state the actual
    distance from:
    a Kotia to Ejom
    b Sreso to Pataso
    c Beposo to Ejom
    d Pataso to Kotia via Ejom
    e Beposo to Kotia via Krofrom and Ejom

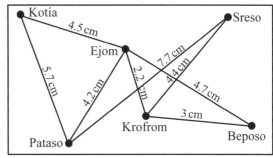

Kotia   Sreso
         4.5 cm
              Ejom
5.7 cm   7.7 cm
                        4.4 cm
      4.2 cm   2.2 cm   4.7 cm
                         3 cm
                   Krofrom
Pataso   Beposo

Curved lines

The length of a curved line can be calculated by using a piece of string provided the drawing has a scale.

To measure the distance between Afevi and Dzana place the string end at Afevi.

Follow the path with the string until you get to Dzana and mark the string.

Measure the marked length of the string against the given scale.

Map of south Kpando and lake Volta estuaries

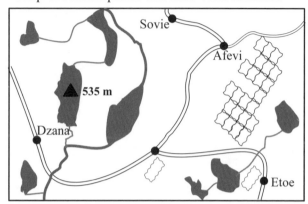

Scale 1 : 250 000

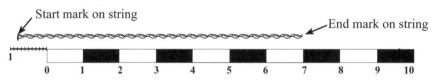

The string is 7.8 cm. It represents $7.8 \times 250\,000 = 1\,950\,000$ cm or 19.5 km

12 Using the map of south Kpando above estimate the distance between:

    a Afevi and Etoe   **b** Dzana and Etoe

    c Sovie and Etoe via Afevi   **d** Dzana and Sovie via Afevi

13 These footpaths are drawn to scale of 1 cm to 1 km. Estimate the lengths these represent.

14 This is the scale drawing of a water park.

    The scale is 1 : 32 000

    Estimate the length of the path around the main lake.

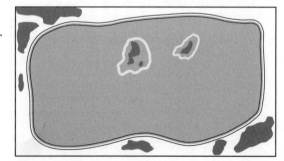

242

15 a Calculate the approximate distance by rail between Sekondi-Takoradi and Kumasi.

b Calculate the approximate road distance between Bolgatanga and Yendi via Tamale.

c Calculate the approximate shortest distance between Navrongo and Ho via Tamale.

d Esaase (west of Kumasi) is 310 km from Accra. How long (in cm) will this be on the map?

e How long in kilometres is the entire railway shown on the map?

f Copy and complete this distance chart.

Scale 1 : 9 000 000

———————— Major roads

|||||||||||||||||||||| Railway

══════════ Border

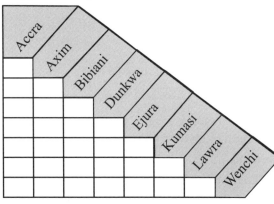

16 Using a scale of 1 : 80 000 000 on a world map copy and complete this table:

Distance between	Length on map	Actual distance
Lagos and London	6.25	5000
Accra and New York		8560
Paris and Moscow		2480
London and Hong Kong	12	
Nairobi and Singapore		7460
Accra and Sydney via London	27.61	

17 The diagram shows part of a flight of steps.

The scale is 1 cm : 100 cm

Each step is 22.5 cm deep.

a How many steps are there?

b If the total height is 5.504 m work out the height of each step.

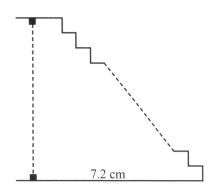

7.2 cm

EXTENSION

1 Nimoh, Yamoah and Ohemah want to share ¢400 in the ratio 1 : 2 : 5
   a What fraction of the ¢400 will each person receive?
   b How much will each person receive ?

2 In a mathematics course 70% of the final marks are for written examination papers. The other 30% are from coursework assignments.
   a Write the ratio of the examination marks to coursework marks in its simplest form.
   b Amoako scored a final percentage of 63. The ratio of his examination marks to course work marks was 7 : 2. How many coursework marks did he get?

3 Afrifa sells three types of soap in his shop: Lux, Key and Premier. In one week he sells 532 boxes of soap in the ratio 1 : 2 : 4.
   a What fraction of the total sales is Key soap ?
   b How many boxes of Lux soap does he sell ?
   c If he makes ¢8 profit on each box sold, how much profit does he make altogether from the two best-selling soaps?

4 At 9 am a 12-metre high tree casts a shadow 10 metres long. The length of the shadow (l metres) is directly proportional to the height (h metres) of a tree.
   a Find a rule connecting h and l.   b Find h when l is 15 metres.
   c Find l when h is 15 metres   d Find l when h is 18.85 metres.

5 The voltage (V) across a resistor is directly proportional to the current (I) flowing through it.
   a Find the rule connecting the voltage and current.
   b Calculate the current in amps when the voltage increases to 12.42 volts.

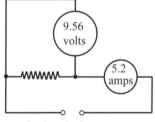

6 Given that $r \propto t$ and $r = 2.4$ when $t = 12.8$, find correct to two decimal places:
   a r when $t = 8.9$ b t when $r = 3.1$ c r when $t = 18.75$

7 A gang of four villains robbed a bank but got caught. On passing sentence the judge said to the first villain, 'as gang leader you will serve the longest sentence'. To the next, 'as second in charge you will serve the next longest sentence'. To the fourth robber he said, 'you were led astray by the others so I will give you the shortest sentence. He finally said, 'I sentence you all to a total of 122 years in prison to be served in the ratio $1 : \frac{1}{2} : \frac{1}{3} : \frac{1}{5}$'. Work out how long each person's prison sentence was.

8 This is a recipe for Palaver sauce.
   a Find the ratio of spinach, meat and herrings.
   b Write a recipe for a party of 26 people.

Palaver Sauce - serves 4	
Spinach 750 g	Red chilli peppers 3
Palm oil 250 g	Smoked herrings 125 g
Onions 4-medium	Prawns 200 g
Tomatoes 4-large	Egushi 100 g
Meat 250 g	

9 Write these ratios in the form $1 : n$

a $\frac{1}{8} : \frac{3}{4}$ b $1\frac{3}{7} : 4\frac{2}{3}$ c $6\frac{2}{5} : 3\frac{1}{3}$ d $9\frac{8}{9} : 112\frac{2}{3}$

10 The variables A and B are related by $A \propto \dfrac{1}{B}$

When $A = 30$, $B = 3$. Work out the value of A when $B = 8$.

11 Using this scale find the values of a, b, and c in kilometres.

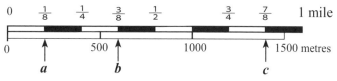

12 The extension, E, of a spring is proportional to the mass, m, hung from the spring. A mass of 2 kg gives an extension of 5 cm.

  a Find the relationship between E and m.

  b Use this relationship to find the mass needed to give an extension of 42.5 cm.

13 Two variables, x and y, vary in such a way that y is inversely proportional to the square of x.

  a When $x = 4$ $y = 5$. Find the formula giving y in terms of x.

  b Find the value y when $x = 5$.

14

radius = 2 cm

radius = 5 cm
volume of liquid = 500 ml

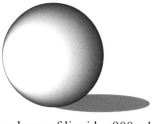
volume of liquid = 900 ml

These spheres are filled with liquid. The volume of liquid in each varies as the cube of the radius.

  a Find the volume of the liquid in the small sphere.

  b Find the radius of the large sphere.

15 The frequency of radio waves varies as the wavelength. Radio South broadcasts on a wavelength 212 metres and frequency of 1.42×10^6 cycles per second.

  a Radio North broadcasts on wavelength of 384 m. What frequency is this?

  b For Radio Central, the frequency is 6.2×10^5 cycles per second. What wavelength is this?

16 Two towns, Nabon and Shieni, whose vertical heights differ by 30 metres are shown 3.55 cm apart on a map of scale $1 : 160\,000$.

  a Measure and work out the direct distance (in metres) between Nabon and Shieni.

  b If the road connecting Nabon and Shieni slopes uniformly, work out the distance between Nabon and Shieni along the slope.

  c Work out the gradient of the road and express it as a percentage, correct to 1 d.p.

SUMMARY

Ratio	A ratio is a way of comparing two or more quantities. The quantities must be in the same units. The numbers in the ratio are separated by a colon (:).
	Ratios can be written in an easier form. To simplify ratios convert quantities to the same units.
Sharing in ratios	Sometimes we need to divide up an amount according to a given ratio. The method is to add up all parts of the ratio first and find the value of one 'share'. Then multiply this up to solve the problem.

Example   Share 40 kg in the ratio 2 : 3

The ratio is 2 : 3
$2 + 3 = 5$
Divide 40 up into 5 'shares'
$40 ÷ 5 = 8$
$\therefore$ 1 share is equal to 8 kg
2 shares equal 16 kg
3 shares equal 24 kg

Direct proportion	Two quantities are said to be in **direct proportion** if they increase or decrease at the same rate.
Inverse proportion	Two quantities are said to be **inversely proportional** if an increase in one quantity causes a decrease in the other.

The symbol $\propto$ means 'is proportional to'

A statement like: height, 'h is proportional to time, t' is written as $h \propto t$

In the same way the stopping distance d, of a car is proportional to the square of its speed s^2, is written as $d \propto s^2$.

Ratio can be written in the form 1 : n

Example   Write 5 : 16 in the form 1 : n

The ratio $5 : 16 = 1 : \dfrac{16}{5} = 1 : 3.2$

Scale   The scale of a drawing is the ratio between the length on a map or drawing and that on the real thing.

The length of a curved line can be calculated by using a piece of string provided the drawing has a scale.

To measure the distance between two places A and B put the string, end at A. Follow the path with the string until you get to B. Mark the string. Measure the marked length of the string against the given scale and work out the actual distance.

Mapping

EXTENSION

SUMMARY

The pressure in a cooking pot depends on the steam temperature; the area of a circle depends on its radius.

In each case, the value of one variable quantity (let us call it y) depends on the value of another quantity (x). Since the value of y is completely determined by the value of x, we say that y is a function of x.

A **function** from a set D to a set R is a rule that assigns a single element of R to each element in D.

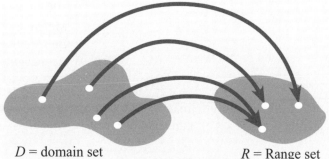

D = domain set R = Range set

A flow diagram for a function f.

A function is like a machine that assigns an output to every allowable input.

Relation   A **relation** is the connection between members of two sets.
The relations between sets are shown by arrow diagrams.

Arrow   An **arrow diagram** is a diagram in which relations are shown by lines with
diagram   arrow heads.

These are examples of phrases to show the relation between sets:

'is above'
'is equal to'
'is bigger than'
'is further away than'

Examples   **a** In this example we have two
sets: insects and their length
in millimetres.
The relationship between
the two sets can be shown
on a **relation diagram**.

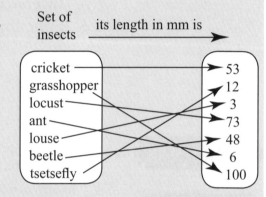

b This arrow diagram
represents the relation
'is located in'.

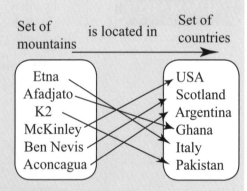

While members of two sets are linked by a relation, it is also possible to have a relation
between members of the set of numbers.

Example   This arrow diagram
represents the relation
'is a multiple of'.

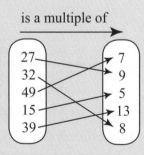

Exercise 12:1

Copy and complete each of these diagrams to show the given relation for the two sets:

1

Set of body parts — *is part of* → Set of body parts

sole	mouth
palm	eye
tooth	stomach
navel	hand
pupil	foot

2

Set of cities — *is the capital of* → Set of countries

Cairo	Germany
London	Brazil
Brasilia	Egypt
Abuja	England
Berlin	Nigeria

3

Set of animals — *wears* → Set of body coverings

cat	scale
fish	shell
snail	fur
parrot	feather

4

Set of elements — *has a chemical symbol of* → Set of chemical symbols

hydrogen	O
carbon	N
oxygen	Au
nitrogen	C
gold	H

5

Set of animals — *is smaller than* → Set of animals

tiger	tiger
cat	cat
rat	rat
goat	goat

6

is bigger than

7	7
8	8
9	9
10	10

7

is a third of

8	12
2	27
11	21
9	6
7	24
4	33

8

is the number of prime factors of

1	30
2	31
3	32
4	33
5	34
	35
	36

9

is a sixth of

0.2	33
1	48.6
5.5	44.4
7.3	6
7.4	1.2
8.1	43.8

10

is the square root of

0.7	4.84
1	5.76
1.3	0.49
2.2	8.41
2.4	1.69
2.9	1

249

Exercise 12:2

In these questions show each relation on an arrow diagram. Use the rule which relates them.

1 A = {21, 22, 23, 24, 25, 26}
   B = {20, 22, 18, 23, 19, 21}
   Relation: 'is 3 less than' from set A to B.

2 D = {36, 1, 9, 49, 4, 25, 16}
   E = {1, 2, 3, 4, 5, 6, 7}
   Relation: 'is the square of' from set D to E.

3 M = {15, 17, 20, 23, 27, 29}
   N = {87, 81, 45, 69, 51, 60}
   Relation: 'is multiplied by 3' from set M to N.

4 P = {0.81, 0.01, 9, 1, 0.04, 0.25}
   Q = {0.1, 0.2, 0.5, 0.9, 1, 3}
   Relation: 'is the square of' from set P to Q.

5 R = {−9, 0, 5, −3, 8, −5}
   S = { −8, 2, −12, −3, −6, 5}
   Relation: 'is three less than' from set R to S.

*6 T = {43, 17, 11, 29, 23, 7}
   U = {115, 58, 133, 51, 215, 33}
   Relation: 'is the square of ' from set U to T.

7 A = {20, 30, 40, 50, 60, 70}   Relation: 'is 17 less than' from set A to B.

8 D = {mm, cm, m, km}   Relation: '1 unit is bigger than' from D to D.

9 P = {Neptune, Earth, Uranus, Pluto, Mars, Mercury}
   Relation: 'is nearer the Sun than' from set P to P.

10 a B = {Jojo, Ebo, Ekow, Fifi, Kofi, Ato}
   D = {Saturday, Friday, Tuesday, Monday}
   Relation: 'was born on' from set B to set D.
   b Repeat **a** with E = {Kwasi, Kojo, Kwaku, Yaw}

> Jojo and Kojo were born on Monday and Ebo was born on Tuesday. Kwaku was born on Wednesday, Ekow and Yaw were born on Thursday, Fifi and Kofi were born on Friday. Ato was born on Saturday and Kwasi was born on Sunday.

11 U = {kilogram, dollar, °Celsius, hour, metre, litre}
   M = {length, volume, money, mass, time, temperature}
   Relation: 'is a unit of' from set U to M.

12 Write a relation that is true for all pairs of numbers that are linked in each arrow diagram.

a
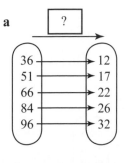

b

c
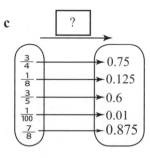

*13 Show this relation on a diagram:
   X = {1.7 × 2.8, 4.2 × 2.75, 3.8 × 9.2, 5.67 × 1.41, 0.3 × 99.2, 4.78 × 7.92}
   Y = {30, 5, 38, 35, 8, 12}
   Relation: 'has a rounded answer of' from set X to Y.

2 Mapping

Mapping A **mapping** is a rule that can be applied to a set of numbers to give another set of numbers. Mapping is represented by an arrow.

A maps B is written as: $A \longrightarrow B$ or $A \longmapsto B$

Examples Draw a mapping diagram to illustrate these relations:

a $x \longrightarrow x + 3$ **b** $k \longrightarrow 2k - 1$ **c** $n \longrightarrow n^2 - 2$

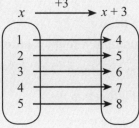 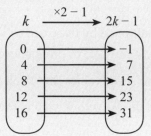 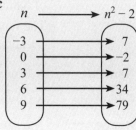

Exercise 12:3

Copy and complete these mapping diagrams:

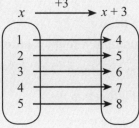

1 $x \xrightarrow{+5} x + 5$

2	?
3	8
5	?
6	?
9	?
11	?

2 $c \xrightarrow{-7} c - 7$

20	13
28	?
31	?
37	?
43	?
59	?

3 $m \xrightarrow{\times 6} 6m$

5	30
7	?
11	?
17	?
23	?
29	?

4 $p \xrightarrow{\times \frac{2}{3}} \frac{2n}{3}$

9	?
?	4
18	?
?	72
3	?
?	54

5 $t \xrightarrow{\times 4 - 3} 4t - 3$

?	9
13	?
$2\frac{1}{2}$	?
?	101
4	?
?	74

6 $b \xrightarrow{\times \frac{1}{3} + 11} \frac{b}{3} + 11$

9	?
?	18
89	?
18	?
?	28
45	?

Draw arrow diagrams to represent these mappings. Use the set: $x = \{-8, -3, 2\frac{1}{3}, 4, 15, 28\}$

7 $x \longmapsto 4x - \frac{1}{2}$

8 $x \longmapsto 15 - 6x$

9 $x \longmapsto 12x + 24$

10 $x \longmapsto x^2 + 5$

11 $x \longmapsto \frac{3}{5}x + 9$

12 $x \longmapsto 2x^2 + 3x$

251

3 Rule for mapping

Rule A **rule** describes the link between objects or numbers. For example a rule linking 3 and 9 could be ×3 or +6 or ÷$\frac{1}{3}$ or −(−6).

Function A **function** is a relation between two sets of numbers. Each member of one set of numbers is related to one member of another set of numbers by a rule. This is called a **one-to-one mapping**.

The rule for $y = 2x + 1$ relates the set of numbers $x = 1, 2, 3, 4, ...$ to the set of numbers $y = 3, 5, 7, 9, ...$

The function multiplied by three can be written in the form:

$x \longmapsto 3x$ or $f(x) = 3x$, or pronounced **'the function f maps x onto $3x$'**.

Domain A **Domain** is the set of values for which a function is defined.

Codomain A **Codomain** is the set within which the values of a function lie.

Range The **range** is the set of values that the function actually takes.

We write 'y is a function of x' as $y = f(x) = 3x$

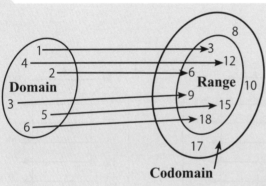

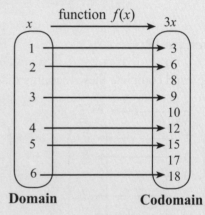

We read $f(x)$ as 'f of x'.

Domain ➡ { 1, 2, 3, 4, 5, 6}
Function ➡ $f(x) = 3x$
Range ➡ {3, 6, 9, 12, 15, 18}
Codomain ➡ {3, 6, 8, 9, 10, 12, 15, 17, 18}

Examples Draw mapping diagrams to show the function:

a $f(x) = x + 13$ using the domain {3, 4, 5, 8, 10, 12}

b $f(x) = 2x - 1$ using the domain {10, 12, 14, −2, −6, 48}

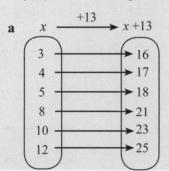

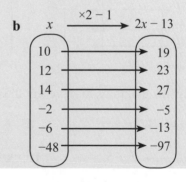

Exercise 12:4

Draw a mapping diagram to show each of these:

1 Function $f(x) = x + 1$ using the domain $\{4, 5, 6, 7, 8, 9, 10\}$.

2 Function $f(x) = 3x + 4$ using the domain $\{0, 4, 6, 8, 10, 12\}$.

3 Function $g(x) = 2x - 3$ using the domain $\{-2, 5, -8, 10, 11, 15\}$.

4 Function $g(x) = 8x$ using the domain $\{14, 12, 10, 8, 6, 4\}$.

5 Function $p(x) = -2x + 3$ using the domain $\{-5, -3, -1, 0, 1, 3\}$.

6 Function $q(x) = 5x - 6$ using the domain $\{1, 6, 11, 19, 29, 40\}$.

7 Function $T(n) = 8n - 3$ using the domain $\{12, 7, 2, -3, -8, -13\}$.

8 Function $B(n) = -11n + 11$ using the domain $\{-1, 3, 5, 8, -2, 10\}$.

9 Function $A(c) = 4c - 8$ using the domain $\{-5, -7, -9, -11, -13, -15\}$.

10 Function $A(n) = \frac{n}{3} + 5$ using the domain $\{2, 3, 8, 10, 24, 38\}$.

11 Function $f(n) = \frac{n}{3} - 4$ using the domain $\{6, 10, 19, -27, -51, -81\}$.

12 Function $f(c) = 3c^2 + 1$ using the domain $\{4, 5, -4, -5, 9, -9\}$.

13 Function $q(x) = x^2 + 2x$ using the domain $\{3, 2, 1, 6, 7, 9\}$.

14 Function $A(n) = 5 - n^2$ using the domain $\{-7, -2, 0, 6, 8, 10\}$.

*15 Function $X(t) = \frac{t}{4} - t^2$ using the domain $\{4, 6, 10, -6, -1, \frac{1}{2}\}$.

Example   For $f(x) \longmapsto 2x + 7$

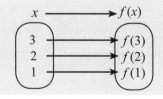

$f(3) = 2 \times (3) + 7 = 13$

$f(2) = 2 \times (2) + 7 = 11$

$f(1) = 2 \times (1) + 7 = 9$

16 For $f(x) \longmapsto 4x + 10$, find: **a** $f(2)$ **b** $f(-5)$ **c** $f(\frac{1}{2})$ **d** $f(a)$

17 For $g(x) \longmapsto 2 - x^2$, find: **a** $g(8)$ **b** $g(-12)$ **c** $g(2\frac{1}{2})$ **d** $g(b)$

*18 If $h(x) = 6x - 4$, find x when: **a** $h(x) = 15$ **b** $h(x) = 17$ **c** $h(x) = 28$ **d** $h(x) = -36$

253

Exercise 12:5

Copy, find the function $f(x)$ and complete of each of these mapping diagrams:

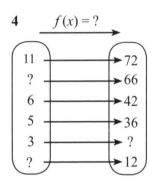

1 $f(x) = ?$

1	→ −5
3	→ −3
7	→ 1
?	→ 5
17	→ ?
?	→ 17

2 $f(x) = ?$

4	→ 18
5	→ ?
7	→ 33
?	→ 21
8	→ 38
9	→ ?

3 $f(x) = ?$

4	→ 11
11	→ 25
23	→ ?
?	→ 77
43	→ ?
59	→ 121

4 $f(x) = ?$

11	→ 72
?	→ 66
6	→ 42
5	→ 36
3	→ ?
?	→ 12

*5 $f(x) = ?$

1	→ 0.25
3	→ ?
?	→ 6
10	→ 2.5
1.2	→ ?
99	→ ?

*6 $f(x) = ?$

2	→ ?
3	→ ?
4	→ 64
0.5	→ 0.125
?	→ 216
0.1	→ ?

Copy and complete the mapping diagram in each question so that the pairs of elements that are linked by arrows are linked by the same rule.

7 $f(x) = ?$

1, −2	→ ?
?	→ −2, 1
6, 3	→ −6, −3
−2, −5	→ 2, 5
?	→ 0, 3
7, 4	→ ?

8 $f(x) = ?$

?	→ 6, 18
−5, −15	→ 10, −30
?	→ 20, 60
18, 56	→ 36, 112
31, 63	→ ?
?	→ −4, 12

9 If the range of each of these functions is {−6, −4, −2, 0, 2, 4, 6}, find the domain set.

   a $x \longmapsto \dfrac{x}{2}$ **b** $x \longmapsto 2x + 1$ **c** $x \longmapsto x - 3$

10 If the range of each of these functions is {5, 10, 15, 40, 25, 3}, find the domain set.

   a $x \longmapsto x + 3$ **b** $x \longmapsto \frac{2}{5}x$ **c** $x \longmapsto \frac{3}{5}x + 10$

11 If the range of each of these functions is {2, 6, 10, 18, 24, 56}, find the domain set.

   a $x \longmapsto 4x$ **b** $x \longmapsto 10x$ **c** $x \longmapsto 3x - 3$

4   Inverse mapping

Inverse mapping   In inverse mapping the function maps the range onto the domain.

In arithmetic operation: the inverse of addition is subtraction
the inverse of subtraction is addition
the inverse of multiplication is division
the inverse of division is multiplication
the inverse of squaring is square rooting
the inverse of square rooting is squaring.

The inverse of $f(x)$ is written as $f^{-1}(x)$.

If $f(x) = x + 3$ $f^{-1}(x) = x - 3$ If $f(x) = 6x^2$ $f^{-1}(x) = \sqrt{\dfrac{x}{6}}$

To find $f^{-1}(x)$: interchange x and y, solve for y and replace y by $f^{-1}(x)$.

Examples   **a** Find the inverse of $f(x) = y = 5x - 2$

$$f(x) = y = 5x - 2 \implies x = 5y - 2 \implies y = \frac{x+2}{5} \implies f^{-1}(x) = \frac{x+2}{5}$$

b Find the inverse of $f(x) = y = 3 - x^2$

$$f(x) = y = 3 - x^2 \implies x = 3 - y^2 \implies y = \sqrt{3 - x} \implies f^{-1}(x) = \sqrt{3 - x}$$

Using the set $\{1, 4, 5, 8, 9, 10\}$, find the inverse mapping of these functions:

c $x \longmapsto x - 5$ **d** $x \longmapsto 2x$

$f(x) = x - 5$ $\therefore f^{-1}(x) = x + 5$ $f(x) = 2x$ $\therefore f^{-1}(x) = \frac{1}{2}x$

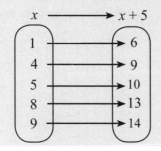

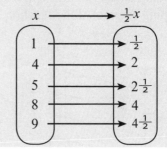

Exercise 12:6

Find the inverse function (f^{-1}) of each of these:

1 $f(x) = x + 1$ **2** $f(x) = x - 7$ **3** $f(x) = 2x$ **4** $f(x) = 5x$

5 $f(x) = 2x - 4$ **6** $f(x) = \dfrac{2x}{3}$ **7** $f(x) = 3x^2$ **8** $f(x) = 2x^2 + 4$

9 $f(x) = 2x - 4$ **10** $f(x) = \dfrac{1}{\sqrt{x}} + 10$ **11** $f(x) = 18 - 2x$ **12** $f(x) = 2x^2 + 4$

13 $f(x) = \frac{2}{7}x - 9$ **14** $f(x) = 24 + \frac{1}{5}x$ **15** $f(x) = 6 + \dfrac{5}{2}x$ **16** $f(x) = 9x^2 + 11$

⊕

Exercise 12:7

1 Using the set $\{-4, 2, 6, 10, 18, 2\}$, draw the inverse mapping diagrams of these functions:

   a $x \longmapsto 3x$ **b** $x \longmapsto 6 - x$ **c** $x \longmapsto \frac{1}{2}x + 6\frac{1}{2}$

2 Using the set $\{20, 32, 44, 56, 68\}$, draw the inverse mapping diagrams of these functions:

   a $x \longmapsto 2x + 3$ **b** $x \longmapsto 2x$ **c** $x \longmapsto \frac{3}{8}x$

3 Using the set $\{-4, 1, 2\frac{5}{8}, 6, 25\}$, draw the inverse mapping diagrams of these functions:

   a $x \longmapsto 7x + \frac{1}{3}$ **b** $x \longmapsto -x - 5$ **c** $x \longmapsto 2 - \frac{11}{12}x$

4 Using the set $\{-3, 0, 2\frac{1}{2}, 6\frac{7}{8}, 50\}$, draw the inverse mapping diagrams of these functions:

   a $n \longmapsto 10n + 6$ **b** $n \longmapsto \dfrac{2}{n} - 3$ **c** $n \longmapsto n^2$

5 Using the set $\{100, 200, 300, 400, 500, 600\}$ draw the inverse mapping diagram of each of these functions:

   a $x \longmapsto 50x$ **b** $x \longmapsto 100 - x$ **c** $x \longmapsto 2\frac{1}{2}x$

6 Draw the inverse mapping diagram to represent the function $x \longmapsto \frac{1}{2}(x + 1)$ for the domain $\{-3, -2, -1, 0, 1, 2, 3\}$

Mapping can be thought of as a 'number machine' with inputs and outputs.

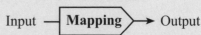

Input   **Mapping**   → Output

This diagram shows the input and output mapping diagram of the function.

$x \longmapsto x + 3$

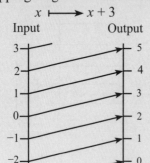

This diagram shows the input and output mapping of the **inverse function**.

$x \longmapsto x - 3$

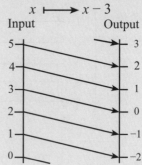

7 Draw two parallel scales, one for inputs and one for outputs, each marked from -1 to 5.

   a Draw arrows to illustrate the function $x \longmapsto x - 5$

   b Draw the input and output mapping diagram for the inverse of the function $x \longmapsto x - 5$.

*8 Draw input and output mapping diagrams to show the inverse function $f(x) = (2x - \frac{1}{2})$ for the domain $\{-\frac{1}{2}, 2\frac{1}{2}, 10\frac{7}{10}, 20, -6, 100\}$

*9 Using the set $\{-6\frac{1}{2}, -2, 0, 7\frac{1}{4}, \frac{2}{5}, 1\frac{7}{8}\}$ draw the input and output mapping diagrams for these functions:

   a $x \longmapsto 5x - 6$ **b** $f^{-1}(x) = \frac{1}{2}x$ **c** $f^{-1}(x) = 2x$ **d** $f^{-1}(x) = \sqrt{x}$

5   Functions: table of values

Mapping diagrams can be represented by a table of values when the function is given.
Substitute each value into the function and work out the answer.

Examples   **a**   If $f(x) = 3x^2$ find the value of $f(4)$

$$f(x) = 3 \times (4)^2$$
$$= 3 \times 16$$
$$= 48$$

b   Draw the table of values $f(n) = n + 6$ for $n = -10, 0, 5, 7$

Method 1 $f(n) = n + 6$:

$f(-10) = -10 + 6;$ $f(0) = 0 + 6;$
$\quad = -4$ $\quad = 6$

$f(5) = 5 + 6;$ $f(7) = 7 + 6$
$\quad = 11$ $\quad = 13$

n	-10	0	5	7
$f(n)$	-4	6	11	13

Method 2 $f(n) = n + 6$:

$n \longmapsto n + 6$

n	$n + 6$	$f(n)$
-10	$-10 + 6$	-4
0	$0 + 6$	6
5	$5 + 6$	11
7	$7 + 6$	13

Exercise 12:8

1   If $f(x) = 6x$ find the values of :   **a** $f(1)$ **b** $f(-2)$ **c** $f(5)$ **d** $f(11)$

2   If $f(x) = 4 + x$ find the values of :   **a** $f(4)$ **b** $f(-1)$ **c** $f(5)$ **d** $f(9)$

3   If $f(n) = 3n + 2$ find the values of :   **a** $f(5)$ **b** $f(8)$ **c** $f(-8)$ **d** $f(12)$

4   If $f(n) = 3n^2 + n$ find the values of : **a** $f(0)$ **b** $f(-3)$ **c** $f(10)$ **d** $f(5)$

5   Draw the table of values of $f(x) = 10x + 9$ for $x = -14, 2\frac{1}{2}, -5, -3, 0, 15$.

6   Draw the table of values of $f(x) = 2(3x - 2)$ for $x = -13, -5\frac{3}{10}, 0, 10, 15$.

In questions 7-10 find the function that links x and $f(x)$.

7

x	2	5	-1	17
$f(x)$	6	15	-3	51

8

x	-5	-10	20	30
$f(x)$	-18	-33	57	87

9

x	-1	0	1	2
$f(x)$	6	5	6	9

10

x	6	7	8	9
$f(x)$	13	12	11	10

11   Write these sets of coordinates in a table and construct a mapping diagram. Find each
function: **a** $(1, -3)$ $(2, -1)$ $(3, 1)$ $(4, 3)$ **b** $(-2, -6)$ $(0, -2)$ $(2, 2)$ $(6, 10)$
c $(4, 7)$ $(8, 19)$ $(12, 31)$ $(16, 43)$ ***d** $(\frac{1}{5}, 3)$ $(\frac{4}{5}, 6)$ $(1, 7)$ $(3, 17)$

EXTENSION

Copy and complete these arrow diagrams:

1 is the biggest prime factor of

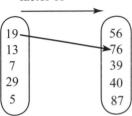

2 is $3\frac{4}{5}$ more than

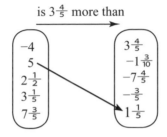

3 is a third of

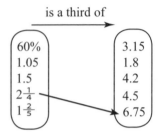

4 is multiplied by $2x$

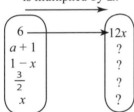

5 is $2x + 1$ less than

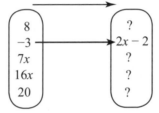

6 is $x - 1$ more than

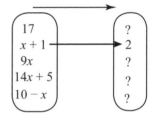

In questions 7 - 10 two sets are given a rule which relates to them. Show each relations on an arrow diagram.

7 $A = \{\frac{1}{4}, 7\frac{1}{2}, 2\frac{1}{2}, 1\frac{2}{5}, 2\frac{1}{3}\}$ B $\{5\frac{4}{9}, \frac{1}{16}, 6\frac{1}{4}, 56\frac{1}{4}, 1\frac{24}{25}\}$

Relation : 'is the square root of' from A to B.

8 X = {calories, litres, Hertz, Decibels, Watts}
Y = {frequency, electricity, Volume, Energy, Sound}
Relation: 'is the unit of' from X to Y.

9 A = {989, 95, 72, 500, 104, 273}   B = {18, 39, 19, 26, 125, 43}

Relation: 'is a multiple of' from A to B.

10 J = { 1.5, 0.4, 1.4, 2.5, 0.7, 0.125}   K = $\{\frac{49}{100}, 2\frac{1}{4}, \frac{1}{64}, \frac{4}{25}, 1\frac{24}{25}, 6\frac{1}{4}\}$

Relation : 'is a the square root of' from J to K.

11 Make these follow the rule 'multiply by 3 and then subtract 7'.

   a $9 \longrightarrow ?$ **b** $-5 \longrightarrow ?$ **c** $11 \longrightarrow ?$ **d** $-11 \longrightarrow ?$

12 Make these follow the rule 'multiply by 5 and then add 4'.

   a $19 \longrightarrow ?$ **b** $-13 \longrightarrow ?$ **c** $? \longrightarrow 74$ **d** $? \longrightarrow -2$

13 Make these follow the rule 'divide by 2 and then subtract 7':

a $10 \longrightarrow ?$ **b** $? \longrightarrow 31$ **c** $-13\frac{1}{2} \longrightarrow ?$ **d** $? \longrightarrow 3.605$

14 Decide what rule is for each of the following relations. Write down your rule, then copy and complete the box.

Box A		Box B		Box C		Box D	
$101 \longrightarrow$	50.5	$2 \longrightarrow$	8	$4 \longrightarrow$	6	$20 \longrightarrow$	40
$17.5 \longrightarrow$	8.75	$1 \longrightarrow$	1	$10 \longrightarrow$	15	$1 \longrightarrow$	59
$2.25 \longrightarrow$	1.125	$? \longrightarrow$	1000	$20 \longrightarrow$	$?$	$-8 \longrightarrow$	68
$78 \longrightarrow$	$?$	$3 \longrightarrow$	27	$? \longrightarrow$	66	$17 \longrightarrow$	$?$
$? \longrightarrow$	48.39	$6 \longrightarrow$	$?$	$80 \longrightarrow$	$?$	$? \longrightarrow$	-32
$? \longrightarrow$	7.345	$11 \longrightarrow$	$?$	$? \longrightarrow$	1500	$x \longrightarrow$	$?$

15 Draw a mapping diagram to illustrate the following. Give your answer to 1 d.p.

a Function $f(n) = \sqrt{n^2 - 4n}$ using the domain $\{7, -3, -10, 12, 4, -1\}$.

b Function $f(a) = a^3 + a$ using the domain $\{15, 10, -11, 9, 1.2, 0.5\}$.

16 Find $f^{-1}(x)$ of each of these: **a** $f(x) = 18x - 18$ **b** $f(x) = x^2 + 2$ **c** $f(x) = \frac{3x}{2} + \frac{1}{2}$

17 Using the set $\{0.1, 0.2, 0.3, 0.4, 0.5\}$ draw the inverse mapping diagram for these functions:

a $f(x) = x - 0.62$ **b** $f(x) = 3x + 0.35$ **c** $f(x) = \frac{1}{2}x^2 - 3$ **d** $f(x) = \frac{3}{x} + 2x$

18 If $f(x) = 3x + 0.4$ find the values of:

a $f(0.25)$ **b** $f(6.1)$ **c** $f(-0.7)$ **d** $f(2.4)$ **e** $f(-6.8)$

*19 Find the function that links x, $f(x)$ and $f^{-1}(x)$ in these tables:

a

x	0	1	2	3	4
$f^{-1}(x)$	3	4	5	6	7

b

x	1	2	3	4
$f^{-1}(x)$	-2	$-1\frac{1}{2}$	-1	$-\frac{1}{2}$

*20 The graph represents the function $x \longmapsto 4 - 3x$.

a Use the graph to find:

   i $f(3)$ **ii** $f(0)$ **iii** $f(-4)$

   iv $f^{-1}(4)$ **v** $f^{-1}(0)$ **vi** $f^{-1}(3)$

b By finding some more number pairs $(x, f^{-1}(x))$, draw the graph of f^{-1}.

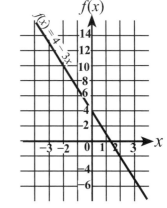

SUMMARY

Relation	A **relation** is the connection between members of two sets. The relations between sets are shown by arrow diagrams.
Arrow diagram	An **arrow diagram** is a diagram in which relations are shown by lines with arrow heads.

These are examples of phrases to show the relation between sets:

'is above'
'is equal to'
'is bigger than'
'is further away than'

Mapping	A **mapping** is a rule that can be applied to a set of numbers to give another set of numbers. Mapping is represented by an arrow.

A maps B is written as: $A \longrightarrow B$ or $A \longmapsto B$

Rule	A rule describes the link between objects or numbers. For example a rule linking 3 and 9 could be $\times 3$ or $+6$ or $\div \frac{1}{3}$.
Function	A **function** is a relation between two sets of numbers. Each member of one set of numbers is related to one member of another set of numbers by a rule. This is called a **one-to-one mapping**.

The rule for $y = 2x + 1$ relates the set of numbers $x = 1, 2, 3, 4, \ldots$ to the set of numbers $y = 3, 5, 7, 9, \ldots$

The function 'multiplied by three' can be written in the form:

$x \longmapsto 3x$ or $f(x) = 3x$ or pronounced **'the function f maps x onto $3x$'**.

Domain	A **Domain** is the set of values for which a function is defined.
Codomain	A **Codomain** is the set within which the values of a function lie.
Range	The **range** is the set of values that the function actually takes.

Inverse mapping	In inverse mapping the function maps the range onto the domain.

In arithmetic operation: the inverse of addition is subtraction
the inverse of subtraction is addition
the inverse of multiplication is division
the inverse of division is multiplication
the inverse of squaring is square rooting
the inverse of square rooting is squaring.

Mapping can be thought of as a 'number machine' with inputs and outputs.

Input ──┤ **Mapping** ╲──→ Output

Mapping diagrams can be represented by a table of values when the function is given. Substitute each value into the function and work out the answer.

Area and volume

CORE

EXTENSION

SUMMARY

Earth means many things to the people who live and move upon it. To a farmer, earth is rich soil. To a road builder, earth means mountains of hard rock. For a sailor, earth is water as far as he can see. A pilot's view of earth may include part of an ocean, a mountain and patches of farmland.

The Earth is a huge ball covered with water, rocks and soil and surrounded by air. It is one of nine planets that travels through space around the sun. The planet Earth is only a tiny part of the universe, yet it is the home of man and so many other living things.

The earth is not perfectly round

The Earth at a glance

Equatorial diameter - 12756.32 km   **Polar diameter** - 12713.54 km

Weight - 6 600 000 000 000 000 000 000 tons   **Age**: 4 500 000 000 years

Total surface area - 509 917 870 km²   **Motion**: Rotation - 23 hours,

Land area - 148 350 000 km²   56 min, 4.09 sec

Water area - 361 563 400 km²   **Revolution** - 365 days, 6 hours

Highest land - Mount Everest - 8848 m   9 min, 9.54 sec

Lowest land - The shore of the Dead Sea - 396 m below sea level

1 Area of irregular shapes

Which of these two carpets takes up more floor space? To answer this question we need to measure the amount of surface covered by each carpet so that we can compare them.

Area **Area** is the amount of surface that something takes up.
There is a rule for finding the area of a rectangle.

Area of a rectangle

Area = *l*ength × *w*idth   The formula is $A = l \times w$ or $A = lw$

The length of this square is 1 cm.
Area = 1 cm × 1 cm
= 1 cm²
= 1 square centimetre

1 cm

$$1\ \text{cm} \times 1\ \text{cm}$$

10 mm

10 mm

10 mm

Units of area Area is measured in:
square millimetres, mm² = 1 mm × 1 mm   = 1 mm²
square centimetres, cm² = 10 mm × 10 mm   = 100 mm²
square metres,   m² = 100 cm × 100 cm = 10 000 cm²
square kilometres,   km² = 1000 m × 1000 m = 1 000 000 m²
1 are = 100 m²   1 hectare, ha = 10 000 m²

Estimating area We can use a square grid on a flat surface and count the squares inside the surface to estimate its area. If the squares do not fit exactly, count the complete squares, combine the smaller squares to make up complete squares and add them up.

This is an outline of a sycamore leaf. It is drawn on 1 cm squared paper.

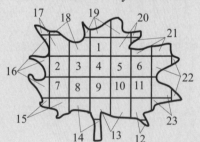

Complete squares = 11 cm²
Small squares   = 12 cm²   (12 - 23 inclusive)
Total area   = 23 cm²

Exercise 13:1

1 Estimate the area of these shapes by counting the centimetre squares.

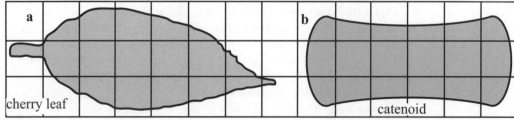

cherry leaf

catenoid

c

cusp

d

maple leaf

2 Which of the shapes in **question 1** has: **a** the smallest area; **b** the largest area?

These diagrams are traditional Ashanti symbols drawn on a 5 mm squared paper.

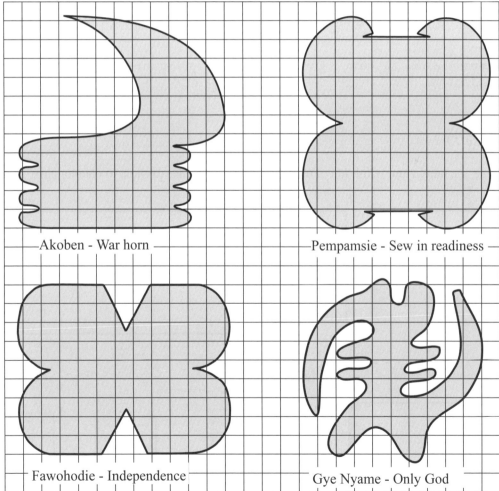

Akoben - War horn

Pempamsie - Sew in readiness

Fawohodie - Independence

Gye Nyame - Only God

3 **a** In each symbol find the total number of 5 mm squares covered by the symbol.
   b How many 5 mm squares make one square with an area of 1 cm²?
   c Estimate the total area of each symbol.

2 Area of a rectangle

The length of the rectangle is 5 cm.
The width of the rectangle is 3 cm.
The area of the rectangle = *length* × *width*

$$A = lw$$
$$= 5 \times 3$$
$$= 15 \text{ cm}^2$$

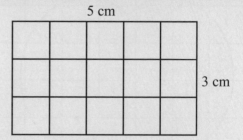

5 cm

3 cm

Note that length and width must be measured in the same unit.

A **square** is a special rectangle whose sides are equal.
A square whose side is 3 cm is filled with 9 squares
each with a side of 1 cm.

Example   Find the area of the square shown.

$$\text{Area} = 3 \text{ cm} \times 3 \text{ cm}$$
$$= 9 \text{ cm}^2$$

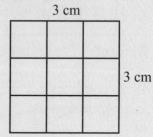

3 cm

3 cm

In general the area of a square is given by: Area = (length of side)^2 = *l* × *l.*
$$A = l^2$$

Exercise 13:2

Measure the height and width in cm of each of these. Use the formula to calculate the areas.

1   a   b   c

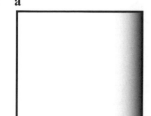      

2   Calculate the areas of these squares in cm².

a

3.8 cm

b

24 mm

c

1.7 cm

d

12 mm

Calculate the area of the shape described in each question.

3 A rectangle of length 14 mm and width 9 mm.

4 A square of side 0.75 m.

5 A rectangle measuring 2.62 cm by 8.74 cm.

6 A square of side 13.13 cm.

Work out the area of each of these rectangles:

7
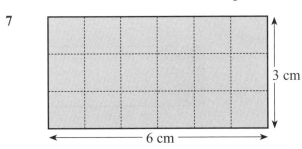
3 cm
6 cm

8
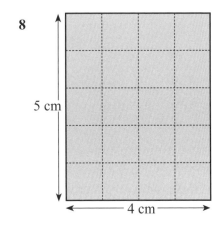
5 cm
4 cm

9
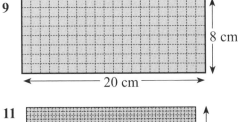
8 cm
20 cm

10
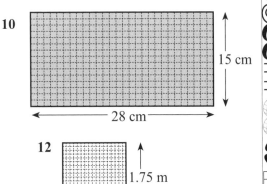
15 cm
28 cm

11
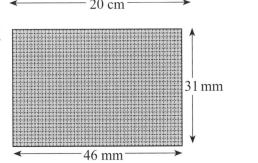
31 mm
46 mm

12
1.75 m
1.75 m

13
6 m
3.5 m

14
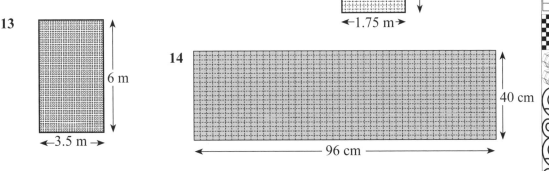
40 cm
96 cm

15 Copy and complete this table. (Hint: make all units the same before doing calculations.)

	Length	Width	Area
a	6 cm	8 cm	.... cm²
b	56 cm	480 mm	.... m²
c	1 cm	2.4 cm	.... mm²

	Length	Width	Area
d	4.9 m	16 cm	.... m²
e	750 m	1.85 km	.... km²
f	520 m	0.2 km	.... m²

The length or width of a rectangle can be calculated if the area is known.

Example   **a** Find the width of this rectangle:

Area = length × width
width = Area ÷ length
= 48 ÷ 8
= 6 cm

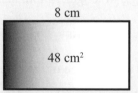

8 cm

48 cm²

b Find the length of this rectangle:

Area = length × width
length = Area ÷ width
= 27.04 ÷ 3.2
= 8.45 cm

27.04 cm²   3.2 cm

Exercise 13:3

Find the missing length or width of these rectangles:

1

36 cm²

5cm

2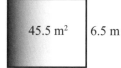

45.5 m²   6.5 m

3

187.69 m²

13.7 m

4

120 mm

264 cm²

5 The area of the page of a book is 609 cm². Find the length if the width is 21 cm.

6 The area of a dining table is 2.42 m². Find the width if the length is 1.1 m.

7 The area of a hockey pitch is 5005 m². Find its length if its width is 55 m.

*8 The area of a side-view mirror of a car is 142.5 cm². Find its length in millimetres if the height is 95 mm.

10 mm = 1 cm ➡ 10 mm × 10 mm = 1 cm × 1 cm = 100 mm²   = 1 cm²
100 cm = 1 m ➡ 100 cm × 100 cm = 1 m × 1 m   = 10 000 cm² = 1 m²
1000 m = 1 km ➡ 1000 m × 1000 m = 1 km × 1 km = 1 000 000 m² = 1 km²

Exercise 13:4

1 Draw a square 2 cm by 2 cm. Find the area in square millimetres.

2 Change each of these areas into square centimetres:
  a 4 m²   **b** 8 m²   **c** 3552 mm²   **d** 0.79 m²   **e** 486 mm²   **f** 0.063 m²

3 Change each of these areas into square metres:
  a 4750 cm²   **b** 60 000 cm²   **c** 2 km²   **d** 7.83 km²   **e** 0.3907 km²

4 Change each of these areas into square kilometres:
  a 60 000 m²   **b** 8 600 000 m²   ***c** 1 000 000 000 m²   ***d** 14 580 000 m²

3 Area of a parallelogram

Parallelogram   A **parallelogram** is a four-sided shape in which both pairs of opposite sides are parallel and equal.

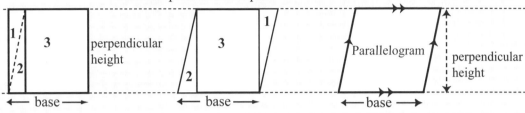

Area of a parallelogram = *A*rea of a rectangle
= *b*ase × perpendicular *h*eight
A = bh

> Sometimes the base of the parallelogram may be viewed from a different angle.

Examples   Find the area of these parallelograms:

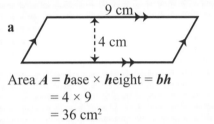

a   9 cm, 4 cm

Area *A* = *b*ase × *h*eight = *bh*
= 4 × 9
= 36 cm²

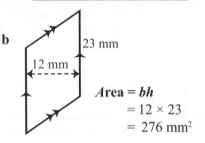

b   23 mm, 12 mm

Area = *bh*
= 12 × 23
= 276 mm²

Exercise 13:5

Find the areas of these parallelograms:

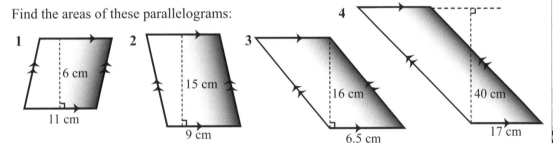

1.   6 cm, 11 cm

2.   15 cm, 9 cm

3.   16 cm, 6.5 cm

4.   40 cm, 17 cm

Measure the base and height of each of these parallelograms and find their areas:

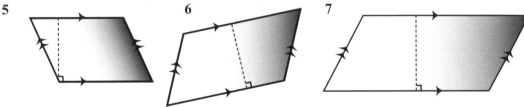

5.

6.

7.

Find the missing lengths of these parallelograms. The areas are given.

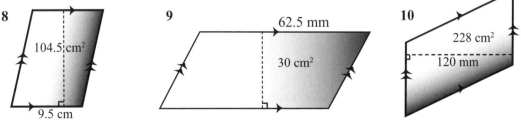

8.   104.5 cm², 9.5 cm

9.   62.5 mm, 30 cm²

10.   228 cm², 120 mm

4   Area of a triangle

This is an illustration of the plan of a new school. The architect needs to know the area of the piece of land in order to design the classrooms, offices, laboratories, the library and other buildings.

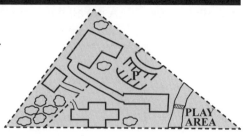

PLAY AREA

We can think of a triangle as half of a rectangle or parallelogram.

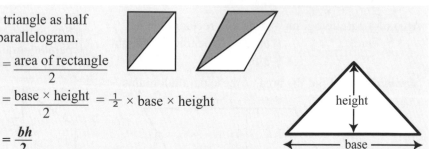

Area of a triangle $= \dfrac{\text{area of rectangle}}{2}$

$= \dfrac{\text{base} \times \text{height}}{2} = \frac{1}{2} \times \text{base} \times \text{height}$

$= \dfrac{bh}{2}$

height

base

When we talk about the height of a triangle we mean its perpendicular height.

Example   Find the area of this triangle:

Area of triangle $= \dfrac{\text{base} \times \text{height}}{2}$

$= \dfrac{10 \times 7}{2}$

$= 35 \text{ cm}^2$

7 cm

10 cm

Exercise 13:6

Find the areas of these triangles:

1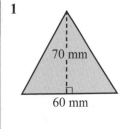
70 mm
60 mm

2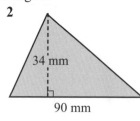
34 mm
90 mm

3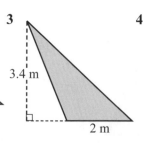
3.4 m
2 m

4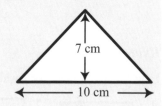
8 cm
9.6 cm

5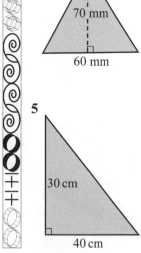
30 cm
40 cm

6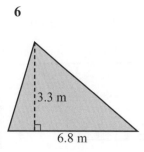
3.3 m
6.8 m

7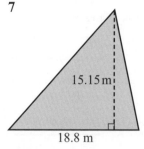
15.15 m
18.8 m

8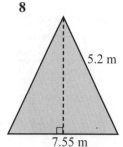
5.2 m
7.55 m

Sometimes the triangle can be on its side or upside down. Perpendicular height is measured from the base of the triangle. If the base is not obvious turn the page round and look at the triangle from a different direction.

Exercise 13:7

1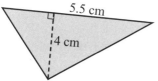
5.5 cm
4 cm

Copy and complete the following:

Area of the triangle = $\dfrac{\text{base} \times \text{height}}{2}$

$= \dfrac{\text{.....} \times \text{.....}}{2}$

$= \text{.....} \ \text{cm}^2$

2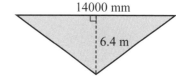
14000 mm
6.4 m

Area of the triangle = $\dfrac{\text{base} \times \text{height}}{2}$

$= \dfrac{6.4 \times \text{.....}}{2}$

$= \text{.....} \ \text{m}^2$

Find the areas of these triangles:

3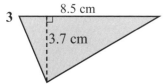
8.5 cm
3.7 cm

4 2.4 m
3.8 m

5 18 cm · 20 cm

6 750 mm
750 mm

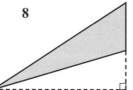

Measure these shapes to the nearest centimetre and find the areas:

7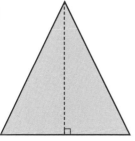

8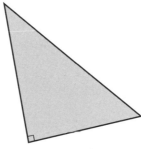

9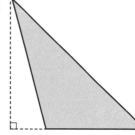

10

11

12

13 The following are dimensions of triangles. Copy and complete the tables:

	Base length	Vertical height	Area
a	6 cm	8 cm	
b		7 m	43.5 m²
c	0.9 m		4.5 m²

	Base length	Vertical height	Area
d	160 mm	110 mm	
e		15 m	240 m²
f	7.8 m		20.28 m²

5   Area of a circle

Circle   A **circle** is a set of points which are
of equal distance from a fixed point.

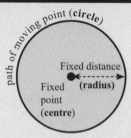

The circle can be cut up into narrow slices (called **sectors**) and placed together as shown.
The shape produced is nearly a rectangle of length πr and r.

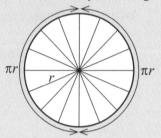

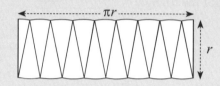

The narrower the sectors are the nearer the shape becomes a rectangle. The area of the
'rectangle' is $\pi r \times r$. This is the area of the circle from which it was made.

Hence, area of a circle of radius r is $A = \pi \times$ **radius** $\times$ **radius**

$$= \pi \times r \times r$$
$$= \pi r^2$$

The Area of a Sector

A sector of a circle is the portion bounded by an arc and two radii.

The area of a sector is part of the area of the whole circle and that
part is determined by the angle at the centre compared with 360°.

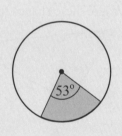

The area A of the sector in the diagram is $A = \dfrac{53}{360} \times \pi r^2$

In general, **for a sector with centre angle $x°$** : $A = \dfrac{x}{360} \times \pi r^2$

Examples   Find the area of the circles shown. Take π as 3.14.

a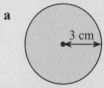

b 15 cm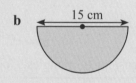

Area $= \pi r^2$

$= 3.14 \times 3 \times 3$

$= 28.36$ cm^2

Area $=$ half of circle

$= \frac{1}{2} \times \pi r^2$

$= \frac{1}{2} \times \pi \times 7.5 \times 7.5$

$= 88.3125$ cm^2

Angle of a
semicircle is
180°
$\therefore$ angle ratio is
$180 \div 360$ or $\frac{1}{2}$.
$r = d \div 2$

Exercise 13:8

Measure and work out the area of each circle. Use π as 3.14 and give your answer to 2 d.p.

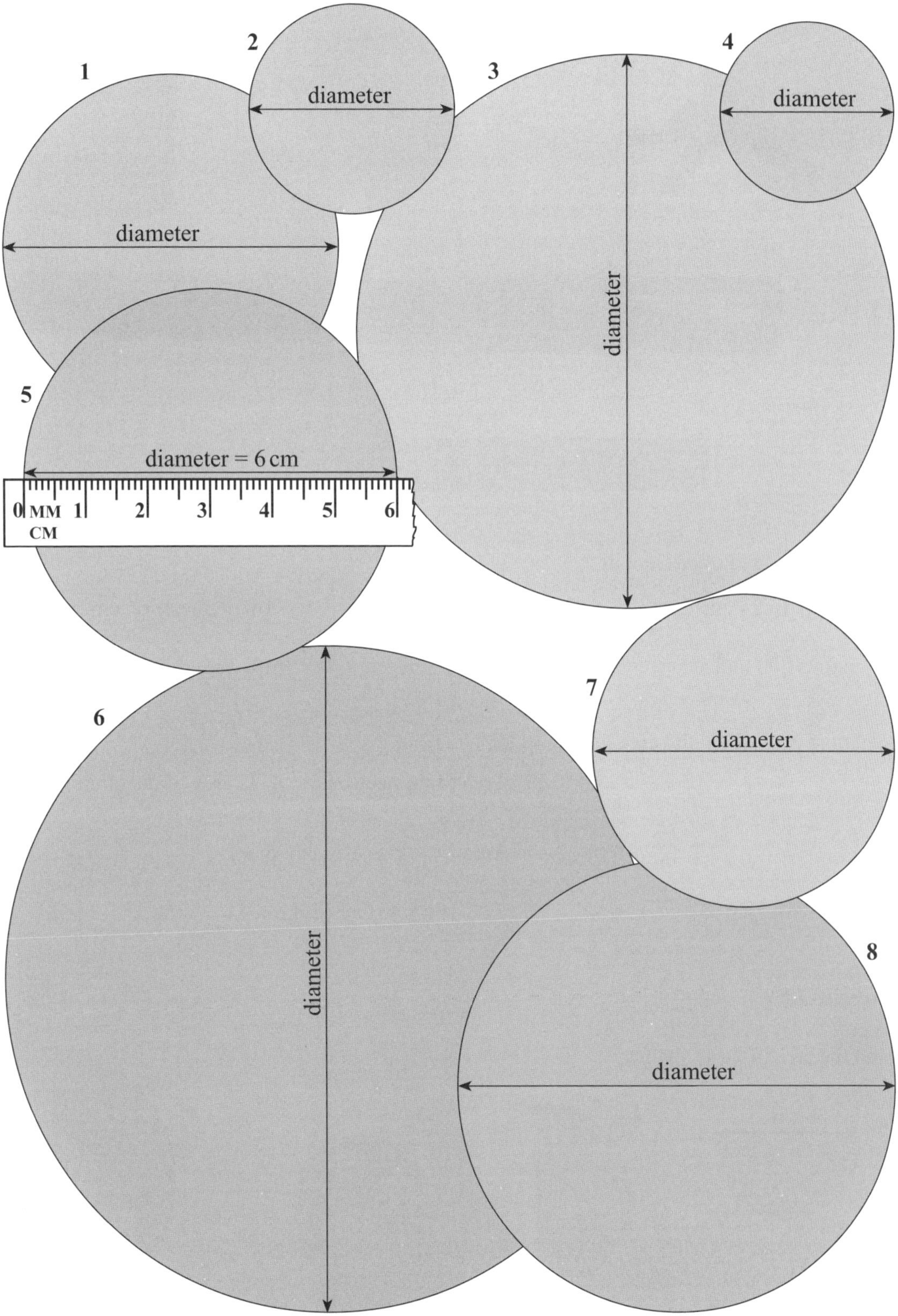

1

2
← diameter →

3

4
← diameter →

← diameter →

diameter

5
← diameter = 6 cm →

0 MM 1   2   3   4   5   6
CM

6

7
← diameter →

diameter

8

← diameter →

diameter

13

Work out the areas of the top of these items:

9
140 cm

10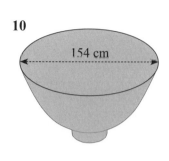
154 cm

11
3.5 cm

12 1 cm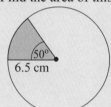

13 7 mm

Work out the area of circle with:

14 radius 16.24 cm

15 radius 3.5 mm

16 diameter 66 cm

17 radius 200 mm

18 diameter 1.5 m

19 radius 58 cm

Example Find the area of this sector.

Area of the sector is $\frac{50}{360}$ of area of the circle.

$$\text{Area} = \frac{50}{360} \times 3.14 \times 6.5^2$$

$$= 18.43 \text{ cm}^2 \text{ (2 d.p.)}$$

50°
6.5 cm

Exercise 13:9

Find the area of these shapes:

1   8 cm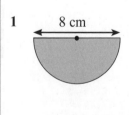

2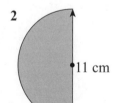
11 cm

3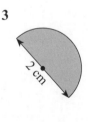
2 cm

4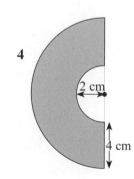
2 cm
4 cm

Find the area of each of the shaded sectors.

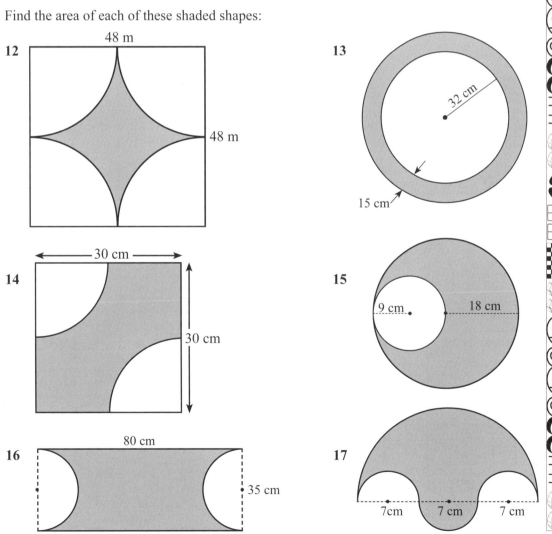

5 50° 7.5 cm

6 14.4 cm 95°

7 150° 66 cm

8 1.5 m

9 240° 87 cm

10 15.5 m

11 The diameter of the centre circle of a football pitch is 18.288 metres. What is the area of the circle? Give answer to 3 d.p.

Find the area of each of these shaded shapes:

12 48 m, 48 m

13 32 cm, 15 cm

14 30 cm, 30 cm

15 9 cm, 18 cm

16 80 cm, 35 cm

17 7cm, 7 cm, 7 cm

6 Volume of cubes and cuboids

Volume The amount of space that an object takes up is called **volume**.

Units of volume The common units of volume are based on units of length i.e. mm, cm, m and km. The volume of an object is found by seeing how many cubic units it contains.
1 cubic millimetre is the volume contained inside a cube having an edge of 1 millimetre long.

1 cubic millimetre = 1 mm³   1 cubic metre = 1 m³

1 cubic centimetre = 1 cm³   1 cubic kilometre = 1 km³

Cube A **cube** is a solid shape with all six square faces equal.

This is **1 cubic centimetre**.

This table occupies a space of about **1 cubic metre**.

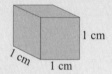
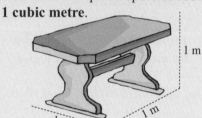

Exercise 13:10

Each cube is 1 cm³. What is the volume of each of these models?

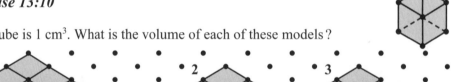

Cuboid

A **cuboid** is a solid shape whose faces are six rectangles.

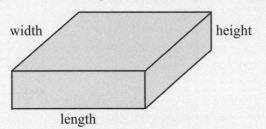

width   height

length

The volume of a cuboid is given by this formula.

Volume of cuboid = *l*ength × *w*idth × *h*eight

$$= l \times w \times h$$
$$V = lwh$$

Example

Find the volume of a cuboid with length 8 cm, width 6 cm and height 4 cm.

Volume = length × width × height

$$= 8 \times 6 \times 4$$

$$= 192 \text{ cm}^3$$

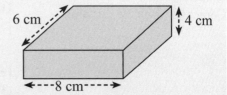

6 cm   4 cm

8 cm

Exercise 13:11

Find the volume of these cuboids:

1

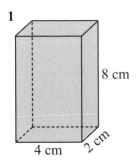

8 cm

4 cm   2 cm

2

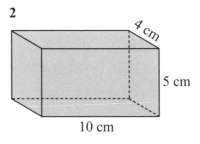

4 cm

5 cm

10 cm

3

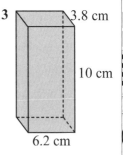

3.8 cm

10 cm

6.2 cm

4

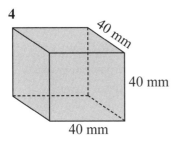

40 mm

40 mm

40 mm

5

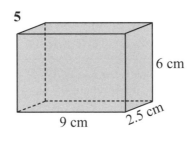

6 cm

9 cm   2.5 cm

6

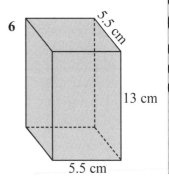

5.5 cm

13 cm

5.5 cm

275

13

Find the volume of these cuboids.

7

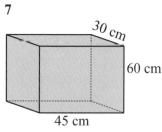

30 cm
60 cm
45 cm

8

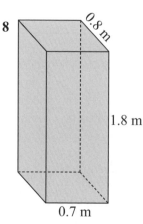

0.8 m
1.8 m
0.7 m

9

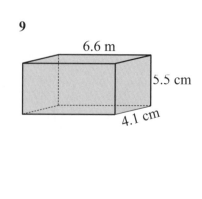

6.6 m
5.5 cm
4.1 cm

This table contains the dimensions of various cuboids.
Copy and complete the table.

	Length	Width	Height	Volume
10	5 cm	4 cm	9 cm	
11	10 m	2 m		133 m³
12		4 cm	14 cm	336 cm³
13	400 cm		10 m	200 m³
14	3 cm	4.4 cm	2.1 cm	
15	8 m		2.5 m	4.4 m³

16 What are the volumes of cuboids having these measurements?

a 10 cm by 3 cm by 6 cm

b $5\frac{1}{2}$ mm by 2 mm by 4 mm

c 2.5 cm by 2.5 cm by 10 cm

d 3.1 m by 6 m by 2.8 m

17 A long jump pit is constructed 12 m long, 3 m wide and 0.5 m deep. How many cubic metres of sand will be required to fill it?

18 Give the volume of the cuboid in each of the following cases:

a The area of the base is 60 cm² and the height is 6 cm.

b The base has one side 12 cm, the width is 2 cm longer and the height is 5 cm.

c The area of the top is 27 cm² and the depth is 8 cm.

*19 How many rectangular packets measuring 8 cm by 6 cm by 4 cm, can be packed in a rectangular cardboard box measuring 30 cm by 24 cm by 16 cm?

*20 Rectangular tiles measure 30 cm by 20 cm by 35 mm. How many of these tiles can be packed into a cube-shaped box whose edge is 1 metre?

*21

The formula obtained by the American Lung Capacity for **theoretical lung capacity** is:
$V = 0.041h - 0.018a - 2.69$ (litres) where h = height in centimetres, a = age

a Use the formula to work out the volume of your theoretical lung capacity.

b Use the formula to work out the theoretical lung capacity of Mr Asamoah who is 1.72 m tall and age 24 years.

7 Compound solid shapes

Compound solid shapes are different solid shapes put together.

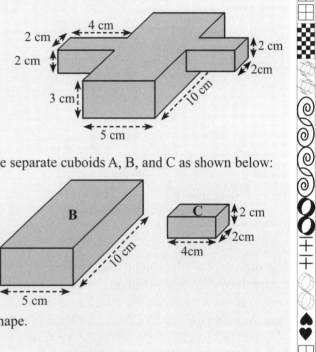

To work out the total volume of a compound solid shape:

* decide whether you are adding cuboids or taking away;
* make a sketch of the shape and mark all the measurements;
* put on an extra lines to show where the shape is being split up;
* work out any extra measurement you need;
* calculate the volume of each cuboid;
* add or subtract to get the final answer.

Example   Work out the volume
of this compound shape:

The shape is split into three separate cuboids A, B, and C as shown below:

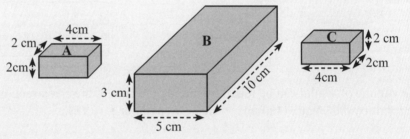

Find the volume of each shape.

Volume of A $= l \times w \times h$
$= 4 \times 2 \times 2$
$= 16 \text{ cm}^3$

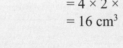

Volume of B $= l \times w \times h$
$= 10 \times 5 \times 3$
$= 150 \text{ cm}^3$

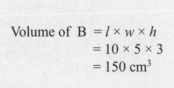

Volume of C $= l \times w \times h$
$= 4 \times 2 \times 2$
$= 16 \text{ cm}^3$

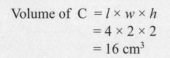

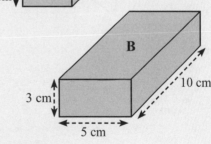

Total volume $=$ volume of A $+$ volume of B $+$ volume of C
$= 16 + 150 + 16$
$= 182 \text{ cm}^3$

Exercise 13:12

Find the volume of each of these compound shapes:

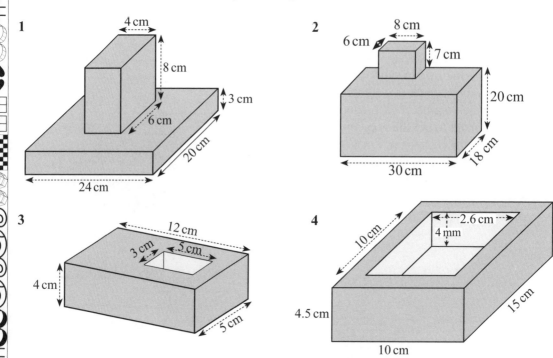

1 4 cm, 8 cm, 3 cm, 6 cm, 20 cm, 24 cm

2 8 cm, 6 cm, 7 cm, 20 cm, 30 cm, 18 cm

3 12 cm, 3 cm, 5 cm, 4 cm, 5 cm

4 2.6 cm, 4 mm, 10 cm, 4.5 cm, 15 cm, 10 cm

The volume of a solid can be found by finding the area of the cross-section and multiplying the result by the length. (*Volume* = *Area* × *Length*, or *V* = *AL*).

Find the volume of each of these compound shapes:

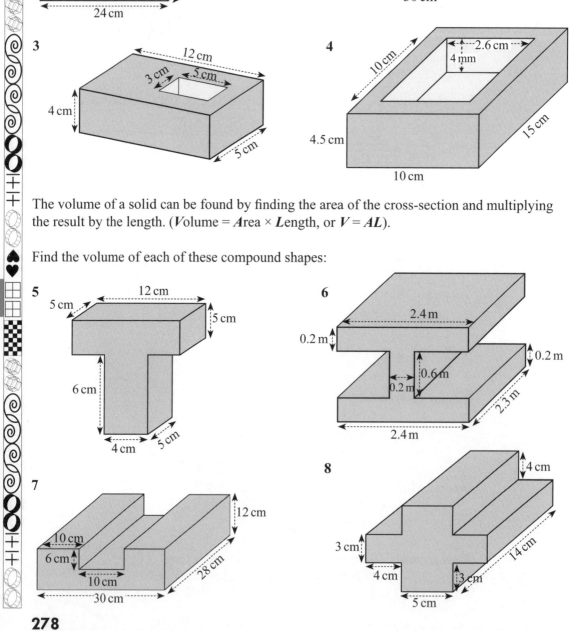

5 12 cm, 5 cm, 5 cm, 6 cm, 4 cm, 5 cm

6 2.4 m, 0.2 m, 0.2 m, 0.6 m, 0.2 m, 0.2 m, 2.3 m, 2.4 m

7 12 cm, 10 cm, 6 cm, 10 cm, 28 cm, 30 cm

8 4 cm, 3 cm, 4 cm, 3 cm, 14 cm, 5 cm

8 Volume of a prism

Prism A **prism** is a three-dimensional (3-D) shape whose ends are equal and parallel.

Properties of a prism are:
- It has the same length all the way through;
- Its sides are parallel;
- It has the same shape of its ends;
- It has a constant cross-section.

Wherever you cut a slice through the prism it is the same size and shape. The shape of the slice is called the **cross-section**.

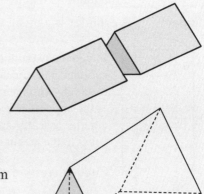

Volume of a prism = Area of cross-section × length

Example   Find the volume of the triangular prism

$$\text{Volume} = \text{Area of cross-section} \times \text{length}$$
$$= (\tfrac{1}{2} \times 12 \times 15) \times 18$$
$$= 90 \times 18$$
$$= 1620 \text{ cm}^3$$

15 cm   18 cm   ←--- 12 cm ---→

Exercise 13:13

Find the volume of these prisms:

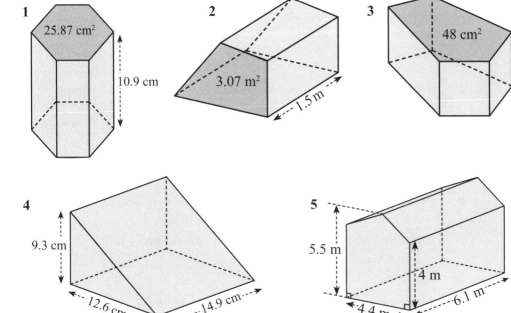

1   25.87 cm²   10.9 cm

2   3.07 m²   1.5 m

3   48 cm²   17 cm

4   9.3 cm   12.6 cm   14.9 cm

5   5.5 m   4 m   4.4 m   6.1 m

9 Surface area and volume of a cylinder

Cross-section The **cross-section** of a solid object is obtained when the solid is sliced in a particular direction.

Prism A prism is a three-dimensional (3-D) shape having the same cross section throughout its length.

Cylinder A **cylinder** is a prism whose cross-section is a circle.

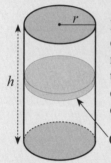

Imagine unwrapping the cylinder. This creates a rectangle with length equal to the circumference of the circular base $2\pi r$ and width equal to the height, h.

Circular cross-section

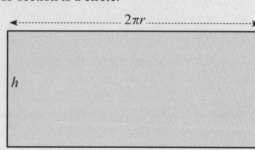

The area of the rectangle is length ($2\pi r$) × height (h). This is equal to $2\pi r \times h$, which is the curved surface area from which it was formed.

$$\text{The curved surface area of a cylinder} = 2\pi rh$$

The total surface area of a closed cylinder which has a top and a base = $2\pi rh + \pi r^2 + \pi r^2$

$$\text{The total surface area of a cylinder} = 2\pi rh + 2\pi r^2 = 2\pi r(h + r)$$

Volume

A solid has a constant cross-section and is therefore a circular prism.

The volume of the cylinder = Area of a circle × vertical height

$$= \pi r^2 \times h$$

$$V = \pi r^2 h$$

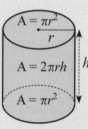

Examples **a** Calculate the curved surface area and volume of the cylinder whose height is 8 cm and whose radius is 3 cm.

Area	$= 2\pi rh$	Volume	$= \pi r^2 h$
	$= 2 \times 3.14 \times 3 \times 8$		$= 3.14 \times 3^2 \times 8$
	$= 150.72 \text{ cm}^2$		$= 226.08 \text{ cm}^3$

b Calculate the total surface area and volume of a cylinder that has a circular base of radius 3 cm and a height of 10 cm.

Total surface area	$= 2\pi r(h + r)$	Volume	$= \pi r^2 h$
	$= 2 \times 3.14 \times 3(10 + 3)$		$= 3.14 \times 3^2 \times 10$
	$= 244.92 \text{ cm}^2$		$= 282.6 \text{ cm}^3$

The formula: curved surface area = $2\pi rh$ is used for an open cylinder.

The formula: surface area = $2\pi r(h + r)$ is used for a cylinder which has a top and a base.

Exercise 13:14

1 Find the curved surface area and volume of the cylinder whose height h, and radius r, are:

   a $r = 2$ cm $h = 6$ cm   **b** $r = 5$ cm $h = 8$ cm   **c** $r = 6$ cm $h = 6$ cm

   d $r = 3$ cm $h = 4.5$ cm   **e** $r = 30$ cm $h = 9$ cm   **f** $r = 4.8$ cm $h = 6.5$ cm

2 Find the area of the paper label covering the outside of a tomato tin (not the top or base) of height 13.6 cm and radius 3.9 cm, given that there is an overlap of 1 cm.

3 A cylindrical steel shaft has a diameter of 72 mm and is 5 m long. Calculate its volume.

4 Calculate the volume of a cylinder: **a** of radius and height 13 cm;

                                         b of diameter 12 cm and height 15 cm.

5 A cylindrical tin has radius 6 cm and height 15 cm. What is the total surface area of the metal needed to manufacture this tin?

Example   A tomato-paste tin has a radius of 3 cm and a height of 10 cm.
Find the total surface area of the metal needed to make this tin.

              Area of the base $= \pi r^2$

                         $= 3.14 \times 3^2 = 28.26$ cm^2

              Area of the top $= 28.26$ cm^2

              Curved surface area $= 2\pi rh$

                         $= 2 \times 3.14 \times 3 \times 10$

                         $= 188.4$ cm^2

          Total surface area $=$ top $+$ base $+$ curved surface

                             $= 28.26 + 28.26 + 188.4$

                             $= 244.92$ cm^2

         OR $2\pi r(h + r)$ $= 2 \times 3.14 \times 3\,(10 + 3) = 244.92$ cm^2

KOOL Tomato Paste 3 cm 10 cm

Work out the curved surface area, the total surface area and the volume of each of these with the given diameters and heights:

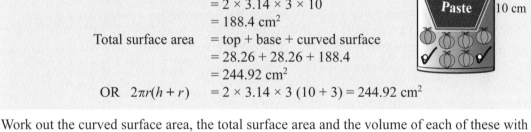

6 5 cm 3 cm   7 7.5 cm 6 cm   8 14 cm   9 4.7 cm 20 cm 1 cm

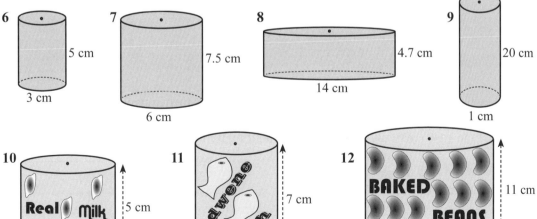

10 Real milk 5 cm 4 cm   11 Adwene Fish 7 cm 6 cm   12 BAKED BEANS 11 cm 8 cm

13

13 The radius of a closed cylinder is 35 mm and its height is 100 mm. Find:

    a the area of its curved surface   **b** the area of its base   **c** the total outer surface area

14 A cylindrical water filtration butt has a diameter of 92 cm and is 70 cm high. It has a removable flat circular lid.

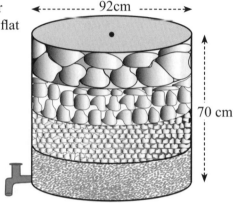

    a What is the outer surface area of the butt:

      i without the lid

      ii with the lid on?

    b Work out the volume of the water butt.

15 The inside of a cylindrical water tank is 1.75 m high and its radius is 75 cm.
Find the volume inside the tank in cubic centimetres.

16 The internal radius of a cylindrical water tank is 42 cm.
Find: **a** in cm^3 **b** in m^3
the amount of water in the tank when the depth of water is 24 cm. (Give answer to 2 d.p.)

Example   Find the radius of a cylinder with height 8 cm and volume 140 cm^3, giving the answer to 2 d.p.

$$V = \pi r^2 h$$

$$\therefore 140 = \pi r^2 \times 8$$

$$r^2 = \frac{140}{8\pi}$$

$$r = \sqrt{\frac{140}{8\pi}} = \sqrt{\frac{140}{8 \times 3.14}} = 2.36 \text{ cm}$$

17 A plastic cylinder of length 32 cm and diameter 6 cm is melted down and cast into a cylindrical plastic rod of diameter 2 cm. How long is the rod?
(**Cast** - to cast a material is to shape it by pouring it into a mould whilst molten.)

18 A metal rod is in the form of a cylinder.
The rod has a diameter of 4 cm and is
86 cm long. Work out the volume of the metal rod.

    4 cm

19 The rod above is melted down and re-cast as a cube. During the melting process none of the metal is lost. Work out the length of an edge of the cube.

20 The table gives information about various cylinders.

Copy and complete the table.

	Radius	Height	Volume
a	10 cm		2024 cm³
b	4.4 mm	16.45 mm	
c		30 cm	6028.8 cm³
d		18 cm	1998 cm³
e	1.3 cm		48 cm³

21 A wire has a circular section.
The diameter of the wire is 0.4 cm
The volume of the wire is 18.84 cm³.
Find the length of the wire.

22 Make h the subject of the formula $A = 2\pi rh + 2\pi r^2$
Thus, find the height of the cylinder which has a total surface area of 32 m² and a diameter of 3 m.

23 One cubic metre of kerosene fills a cylindrical barrel of radius 40 cm. What is the height of the barrel?

24 Which of these tins needs the most sheet metal in its construction?

a

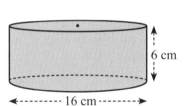

6 cm

16 cm

b

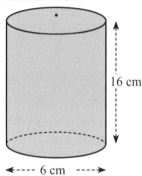

16 cm

6 cm

25 A large box is a cube with sides of length 80 cm. Smaller boxes, which are also cubes, have sides of length 20 cm.
a What is the volume of the larger box?
b What is the volume of the smaller box?
c How many small boxes will fit in the larger box?

26 Find the total surface area and the volume of these solids. Give your answer to 1 d.p.

a

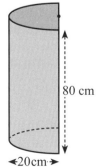

80 cm

20 cm

b

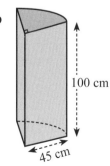

100 cm

45 cm

283

10 Units of volume and capacity

Capacity   The **capacity** of a container is the amount of liquid it will hold.

Volume   The **volume** is a measure of space occupied by a 3-D shape.

Metric capacity measure

10 millilitres (m*l*) = 1 centilitre (c*l*)		10 litres	= 1 decalitre (da*l*)
10 centilitres = 1 decilitre (d*l*)		10 decalitres	= 1 hectolitre (h*l*)
10 decilitres = 1 litre (*l*)		10 hectolitres	= 1 kilolitre (k*l*)

The most commonly used units of capacity are millilitre, centilitre and litre.

      $1\ l = 100\ cl = 1000\ ml$

A small amount of liquid is usually measured in millilitres.

      $10\ \text{mm} = 1\ \text{cm}$

Volume: $10\ \text{mm} \times 10\ \text{mm} \times 10\ \text{mm} = 1\ \text{cm} \times 1\ \text{cm} \times 1\ \text{cm}$ **$1000\ \text{mm}^3 = 1\ \text{cm}^3$**

$100\ \text{cm} = 1\ \text{m}$

Volume: $100\ \text{cm} \times 100\ \text{cm} \times 100\ \text{cm} = 1\ \text{m} \times 1\ \text{m} \times 1\ \text{m}$ **$1\,000\,000\ \text{cm}^3 = 1\ \text{m}^3$**

$1000\ \text{mm} = 1\ \text{m}$

Volume: $1000\ \text{mm} \times 1000\ \text{mm} \times 1000\ \text{mm} = 1\ \text{m} \times 1\ \text{m} \times 1\ \text{m}$ **$1\,000\,000\,000\ \text{mm}^3 = 1\ \text{m}^3$**

Changing Volumes

This cube is filled with water. The volume of water is 1 millilitre.
1 millilitre is the same as 1 centimetre cubed (cc).

    $1\ ml = 1\ \text{cm}^3$ $(1\ \text{cm} \times 1\ \text{cm} \times 1\ \text{cm} = 1\ \text{cm}^3 = 1\ \text{cc} = 1\ \text{centimetre cubed})$

    $1\,l\ = 1000\ \text{cc}$ $(10\ \text{cm} \times 10\ \text{cm} \times 10\ \text{cm})$ $1000\ l = 1\ \text{m}^3$

To change from a smaller unit to a larger unit, divide.
To change from a larger unit to a smaller unit, multiply.

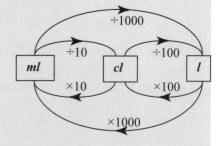

Examples
a   Change 3.5 litres to centilitres   **b**   Change 600 millilitres into litres.

           $3.5\ l = 3.5 \times 100$ $600\ ml = 600 \div 1000\ ml$

                 $= 350\ cl$ $= 0.6\ l$

c   Change 80 cm³ to mm³   **d**   Change 68 mm³ to cm³.

      $80\ \text{cm}^3 = 80 \times 1000\ \text{mm}^3$ $68\ \text{mm}^3 = 60 \div 1000$

               $= 80\,000\ \text{mm}^3$ $= 0.068\ \text{cm}^3$

Exercise 13:15

1 Change these to cm³: **a** 4000 mm³   **b** 5000 mm³   **c** 125 mm³

2 Change these to mm³: **a** 2.8 cm³   **b** 7 cm³   **c** 0.85 cm³

3 Change these to cm³: **a** 1.4 litres   **b** 0.64 litres   **c** 0.028 litres

4 Change these to litres: **a** 1900 cm³   **b** 2.4 m³   **c** 380 c*l*
                          d 300 m³   **e** 1298 cc   **f** 10 m³

5 Change these to m³: **a** 6 000 000 cm³   **b** 75 cm³   **c** 9 200 000 cm³

6 Change these to m³: **a** 860 c*l*   **b** 73 900 m*l*   **c** 45 200 000 mm³

7 Each row represents the same amount of liquid.

   Copy and complete the table.

8 m*l*	**9** c*l*	**10** *l*	**11** cm³	**12** m³
4000				
		3.8		
				4.2
			1600	
		24.47		
	70			
15				
			803	
				0.109
794.8				

Volumes of different containers can be added or subtracted.

Examples   Work out the following. Give your answers in the units shown in brackets.

a 4.7 *l* + 3.05 *l* (*l*)   **b** 168 c*l* + 1.2 *l* + 3.24 *l* (*l*)   **c** 675 m*l* − 0.493 *l* (m*l*)

$$
\begin{array}{r}
4.7 \\
+\ 3.05 \\
\hline
7.75\,l
\end{array}
\qquad
\begin{array}{r}
1.68 \\
1.2 \\
+\ 3.24 \\
\hline
6.12\,l
\end{array}
\qquad
\begin{array}{r}
675 \\
-\ 493 \\
\hline
182\ \text{m}l
\end{array}
$$

Work out these giving your answers in the units shown in brackets.

13 75 c*l* + 18 c*l* − 0.83 *l*   (*l*)   14 46 *l* − 46 c*l* − 460 c*l*   (c*l*)

15 1.5 c*l* − 9 m*l*   (m*l*)   16 1.2 *l* + 34 c*l* + 1450 m*l*   (*l*)

17 2 *l* + 440 m*l* + 895 m*l*   (*l*)   18 5 *l* − 50 c*l* − 500 m*l*   (c*l*)

19 44 *l* − 900 c*l* − 5700 m*l*   (*l*)   20 1.05 *l* + 85 c*l* − 900 m*l*   (m*l*)

EXTENSION

1 Estimate the areas of these shapes:

1 cm

1 cm

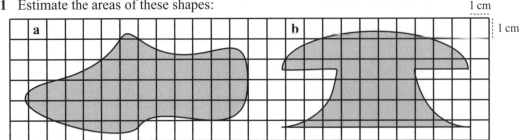

2 a Work out the length AB.
  b Work out the area of the triangle AED.

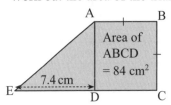

3 A gold ingot is in the shape of a trapezoidal prism. The area of the cross-section is 144 cm² and the ingot is 24 cm long.
  a Find the volume of the ingot.
  b If the gold weighs 19.2 g per cm³, find the weight of the ingot in kg.

4 The surface area of a sphere with radius r is $4\pi r^2$.

The volume of a sphere is given by the formula, $V = \frac{4\pi r^3}{3}$

The radius of the earth is 6378 km.
Work out: **a** The surface area of the earth.
          b The volume of the earth.

Work out the area of the shaded part of these shapes:

5

15 cm

6 cm

6

14 cm

←----14 cm ---→

7

8.8 cm

8 The diagram shows a rectangular garden. A concrete driveway crosses the garden forming a lawn on one side and a triangular flower bed on the other. Calculate:
  a The area of the driveway;
  b The area of the lawn;
  c The area of the flower bed.

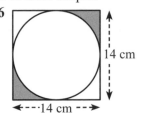

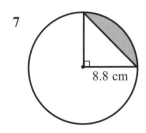

9 The volume V, of cube of edge $e,$ is given by $V = e^3$. Find the volume of a cube whose edges are: **a** 3 cm   **b** 0.2 m   **c** 14 cm   **d** 5.5 cm

10 The area of one face of a cube is 0.49 m². What is the volume of the cube?

11 A block of lead is hammered out to form a square sheet 10 mm thick. The original dimensions of the block were 30 cm × 12 cm × 18 cm. Find the area of the square sheet.

12 A solid wooden cylinder of length 20 cm and base radius 4 cm is cut exactly in half to form two cylinders. How much bigger is the total surface area of the two cylinders than the total surface area of the original cylinder?

13 A rectangular medicine bottle is 7.5 cm wide, 12 cm high and 4 cm thick. **a** Work out its capacity in millilitres.
  b How many 5 ml dosages can be obtained from a full bottle?

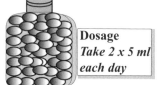

Dosage
Take 2 x 5 ml each day

14 Work out the shaded area shown in the diagram.

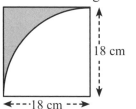

18 cm

18 cm

15 A triangular piece of cloth is shown. It has an area of 9.5 m². Work out the length AC.

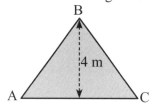

B

4 m

A   C

16 The net given below can be used to form the cylinder shown.

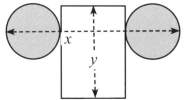

x

y

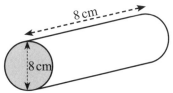

8 cm

8 cm

Work out: **a** the circumference of the shaded face;   **b** the area of the shaded face;
  c the total surface area of the cylinder;   **d** the volume of the cylinder;
  e the lengths marked x and y.

17 How many litres of water are required to fill a rectangular washing bath 1.5 m long and 0.56 m wide which is 0.46 m deep?

18 Twelve circular discs, each of diameter 8 cm, are stamped out of the rectangular sheet of metal shown in the diagram. Find the area of the metal sheet that is waste.

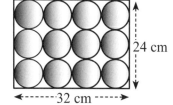

24 cm

32 cm

19 The capacity of an oil barrel of height 86 cm is 58 litres. What is its radius?

20 A concrete shape consists of a cubical base of edge 0.4 m, surmounted by a cylinder of radius 0.2 m. If the total height of the shape is 1 m find the volume of the concrete used in making it.

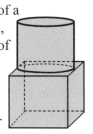

21 In a cylindrical block of wood, radius 12 cm and height 30 cm, a cylindrical hole of radius 3 cm is drilled as shown. What is the volume of wood remaining?

18 cm

287

SUMMARY

Area	Area is the amount of surface that something takes up. There is a rule for finding the area of a rectangle.
Area of a rectangle	$Area = length \times width$ The formula is $A = l \times w$ or $A = lw$

The length of this square is 1 cm.
$$Area = 1 \text{ cm} \times 1 \text{ cm}$$
$$= 1 \text{ cm}^2$$
$$= 1 \text{ square centimetre}$$

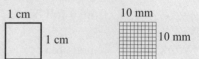

Units of area   Area is measured in:

square millimetres, $mm^2 = 1mm \times 1$ mm $= 1$ mm^2
square centimetres, $cm^2 = 10$ mm $\times 10$ mm $= 100$ mm^2
square metres, $m^2 = 100$ cm $\times 100$ cm $= 10\,000$ cm^2
square kilometres, $km^2 = 1000$ m $\times 1000$ m $= 1\,000\,000$ m^2

Area of a triangle $= \dfrac{\text{area of rectangle}}{2} = \frac{1}{2} \times \text{base} \times \text{height}$

Area of a circle with radius r, is $A = \pi \times radius \times radius = \pi \times r \times r = \pi r^2$

For a sector with centre angle x^o : Area $= \dfrac{x}{360} \times \pi r^2$

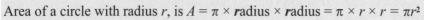

Capacity	The **capacity** of a container is the amount of liquid it will hold.
Volume	The amount of space that an object takes up is called **volume**.
Units of volume	The common units of volume are based on units of length i.e. mm, cm, m and km. The volume of an object is found by seeing how many cubic units it contains.

1 cubic millimetre is the volume contained inside a cube having an edge of 1 millimetre long.

Volume of a cuboid $= length \times width \times height$
$$= l \times w \times h$$
$$V = lwh$$

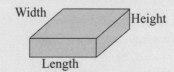

Cross-section	The **cross-section** of a solid object is a shape which is obtained when the solid is sliced in a particular direction.

Volume of a prism = Area of cross-section × length

Prism	A prism is a three-dimensional (3-D) shape having the same cross-section throughout its length.
Cylinder	A **cylinder** is a prism whose cross-section is a circle.

The volume of the cylinder = Area of a circle × vertical height
$$= \pi r^2 \times h$$
$$V = \pi r^2 h$$

The formula: **curved surface area** $= 2\pi rh$ is used for an open cylinder.

The formula: **surface area** $= 2\pi r(h + r)$ is used for a cylinder which has a top and a base.

Rates

EXTENSION

SUMMARY

Workers such as civil servants, doctors and secretaries are paid a monthly salary. Workers such as waiters, bricklayers, labourers and machinists are paid a weekly wage.

Tax is a system of raising money to finance government services and activities. Governments use the tax revenue to pay for the police force, health, schools, roads, national defence and many other public services.

People earn money in different ways:

Payment by the hour

Overtime

Piecework

Commission

Pension fund

Interest rates

Buying and selling

Wages and salaries

If money is invested with a bank, interest is paid to the investor. If money is borrowed then the borrower will be charged interest on the loan.

1 Exchange rates

CITY FOREX BUREAU

Today's Rate

Currency	We Buy	We Sell
US Dollar $1	¢1.45	¢1.51
Pound Sterling £1	¢2.19	¢2.25
Euro €1	¢1.82	¢1.88
Yuan ¥1	¢0.21	¢0.25

Exchange all major currencies

The official currency of Ghana is the Cedi (¢)

1 Cedi = 100 pesewas

¢1= 100 p

When people visit Ghana they need to change their foreign money into cedis before they are able to buy goods and services.

Foreign exchange

An institution or system for dealing in the currencies of other countries is called a **foreign exchange**.
Forex is an abbreviation for foreign exchange.

Exchange rate

The ratio at which the unit of currency of one country is exchanged for the unit of currency of another country is called the **exchange rate**.

'**We Buy**' means the bureau company buys your foreign currency. To change foreign currencies into cedis use the 'We Buy' column.

'**We Sell**' means the bureau company sells you the foreign currency. To change cedis into foreign currencies use the 'We Sell' column.

Examples

Use the advert above to answer these questions:

a   If ¢1.82 = €1, find the value of €2.50 in cedis.

$$€2.50 = 2.50 × 1.82$$
$$= ¢4.55$$

Note
Money is always calculated to 2 d.p.

b   Change ¢64.40 to euros.

$$¢64.40 = 64.40 ÷ 1.88$$
$$= ¢34.26$$

Exercise 14:1

Using the bank's exchange rate (We Buy) given above, work out (to the nearest pesewa):

1   The number of euros equivalent to ¢32.

2   The number of pounds sterling equivalent to ¢157.

3   The number of Chinese yuan equivalent to ¢18.

4   The number of US dollars equivalent to ¢2.80.

5   The number of US dollars equivalent to ¢78.20.

6   Agyekum travelled from New York via London to Ghana. He wanted to change his travel cheques which consisted of £50 and $85. How many cedis did he get?

7   Find the total of each of these people's shopping lists in cedis:

Shirt	£20
Trousers	$32
Shoes	¥5.50
Cufflinks	£5

Mr Ayi

Skirt	$30
Blouse	£18
Sandals	¥112.50
Earrings	¢3.69

Mr Nti

Scarf	¢4.99
Pack of pens	$1.10
Novel	¥57
Calculator	£8.99

Ms Mia

8   Change these amounts from cedis into euros:

   a ¢38.50   b ¢165   c ¢100   d ¢262.90   e ¢860.80

9   Change these amounts: a $250 to pounds sterling   b ¢929 to US dollars
                              c ¢150.40 to yuan   d ¥72.50 to pounds sterling

10 Using the exchange rate in **question 11** below copy and complete this table. The value of each row is the same.

¢	$	£	€	¥
160				
			700	
		27		
				3500
	1350			

11 The following table gives the equivalent of ¢1 in various currencies.

¢	Euro €	Pound Sterling £	Yuan ¥	US dollar $
1	0.55	0.45	4.76	0.70

Use the table to calculate (to the nearest pesewa) the cedi equivalent of these items:

a   £12.99

b   ¥204
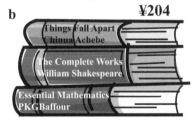

c   €29.99

d $13

e   €10.99

f   £129

2   Rate as ratio

Rate   **Rate** is a ratio between two quantities with different units. Rate is usually expressed as an amount of one quantity with respect to one unit of another.

Fuel consumption is the rate at which fuel is used. For vehicles it is usually expressed as kilometres per gallon, (km.p.gal or km gal^{-1} or km/gal)

Speed is the rate at which a moving object covers a distance. It is given as the distance covered in a unit of time, for instance, kilometres per hour (km.p.h, or km h^{-1} or km/h).

Basic units of conversion

Length	**Weight**	**Capacity**
1 inch = 25.4 mm	1 lb = 0.45 kg	1 gal = 4.456 l

Basic formulas

$$\text{Speed} = \frac{\text{distance}}{\text{time}} \qquad \text{Density} = \frac{\text{mass}}{\text{volume}} \qquad \text{Fuel consumption} = \frac{\text{distance}}{\text{capacity}}$$

Example   Express a fuel consumption of 50 km/gal in km/l using 1 gallon ≈ 4.5 litres.

$$50 \text{ km/gal} = 50 \div 4.5$$
$$= 11.\dot{1} \text{ km/}l$$

Exercise 14:2

In these questions give answers correct to 1 d.p.

1   Express a fuel consumption of 60 km/gal in km/l.

2   Express a speed of 30 miles per hour in kilometres per hour using 8 km ≈ 5 miles.

3   Express 50 miles per hour in kilometres per hour.

4   Express 20 litres/second in litres per hour.

5   Express 50 m²/litre in m²/gal using 1 gallon ≈ 4.5 litres.

6   Express 128 m²/litre in m²/gal.

7   To cover an area of 48 m², 3 litres of paint are needed. Give the coverage in l/m².

8   A car consumes 1 gallon of petrol in 42 kilometres. The driver puts 30 litres of petrol into the tank. How far can he expect to travel?

To change from say km/h to m/s, we need to change one unit and then change the other.

km/h is expressed as $\dfrac{\text{kilometre}}{\text{hour}}$ so change kilometres into metres and change hours into seconds.

Example   Express 50 km/h in m/s.

$$50 \text{ km/h} = \frac{50 \times 1000}{60 \times 60} \qquad (1 \text{ km} = 1000 \text{ m}; \ 1 \text{ h} = 60 \text{ min and } 1 \text{ min} = 60 \text{ sec})$$

$$= 13.9 \text{ m/s}$$

Exercise 14:3

1 Express a speed of 80 km/h in m/s.

2 Express a speed of 68 km/h in m/s.

3 Express 80 lb/sq in kg/cm².

4 Express 60 m²/*l* in sq ft/gal.

5 The front tyre pressure of a car should be 2.1 kg/cm² yet the pressure gauge at the local automobile garage measures pressure in lb/sq in. What should the gauge read to give the correct pressure ?

6 This is the speedometer of a vehicle.

Calculate the speed in km/h
indicated by: A, B, C, D, E and F.

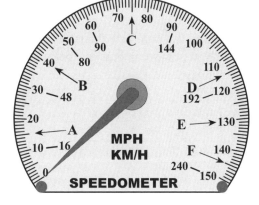

7 The density of gold is 19.3 g/cm³. Given 1 oz = 28.3 g, find the the density of gold in oz/in³.

8 A petrol pump can deliver petrol at a rate of 1.5 litres/second. How long does it take to fill a tank of : **a** 5 gallons   **b** 11.5 gallons   **c** 14 gallons ?

Convert these units:

9 Fuel consumption **a** 12 mi/gal to km/*l*   **b** 22 mi/gal to km/*l*   **c** 48 mi/gal to km/*l*

                                d 15 km/*l* to mi/gal   **e** 35 km/*l* to mi/*l*   **f** 67 km/gal to mi/*l*

10 Carbon emission **a** 165 g/km to oz/km   **b** 140 g/km to oz/km   **c** 60 oz/km to g/km

                              d 120 oz/km to g/m   **e** 225 g/km to g/mi   **f** 400 g/km to oz/mi

11 Speed   **a** 250 km/h to m/s   **b** 250 m/s to km/h   **c** 20 m/s to mi/h

293

INVESTIGATION

MOBILE PHONE RATES

People using mobile phones can use 3 rates of charges.

Investigate the three schemes to find out which is the best rate to choose.

Scheme 1	Scheme 2	Scheme 3
A payment of ¢15 per month for the line rental, plus 30p per minute, or part of a minute for each call made.	A payment of ¢24 per month for the line rental, plus 20p per minute, or part of a minute for each call made.	A payment of ¢31 per month for the line rental, plus 10p per minute, or part of a minute for each call made.

Any rate of charge for a mobile phone follows the rule:

A fixed amount of money for the monthly line rental,
plus the cost per minute or part of a minute is rounded to a minute.

There can be many other rates of charges for a mobile phone.

1 Copy and complete the table.
   (Note: charge in pesewas per minute is p/min).

No. of minutes	1	2	3	4	5	6	7	8	9	10	n^{th} min.
Scheme 1 rate (p/min)	30	80									$30n$
Scheme 2 rate (p/min)	20	40									
Scheme 3 rate (p/min)	10										

2 Write down the general formula for the cost in scheme 1, 2 and 3.

3 Plot the values for *time* against *cost* for all three phones on the same graph.

4 Compare the rate of charges *n* p/min (e.g. 30p/min) after 10, 20, 30, 50, 100 and 200 minutes.

5 Which scheme gives the best value?

6 **Investigate** rates of charges.

   In your investigation: **i** vary the line rental
   ii vary the cost of each call
   iii make comparisons
   iv make generalisations

3 Simple interest

Interest	**Interest** is money paid regularly at a particular rate when money is lent or invested. The rate of interest is usually written as a percentage.
Simple interest (S.I.)	The amount of interest earned per year, when a given amount of money is invested. The interest earned is the same each year. If the money is invested for 2 years the amount of interest will be doubled. If the money is invested for three years the amount of interest will be trebled.
Principal (P)	The original sum of money borrowed, lent or invested is called the **principal**.
Rate of interest (R)	The *rate of interest* is a fixed price paid or charged. It is expressed as a percentage per annum. *Per annum* **(p.a.)** is a Latin phrase meaning *throughout the year* usually used in a financial context.
Time (T)	The time in years over which the money is lent, borrowed or invested.

Example

¢250 is invested at 6% p.a.

a Work out the interest at the end of 1 year.
b How much will be earned at the end of 5 years?

a Amount of interest = 6% of ¢250

$$= \frac{6}{100} \times 250$$

$$= ¢15$$

b Amount of interest after 5 years = 5 × 15
$$= ¢75$$

Simple interest formula

From **example 1** we see that the amount of interest can be calculated from:

$$\text{S.I.} = \frac{PRT}{100} \quad \text{(R is expressed as a fraction with denominator of 100)}$$

Example

Awuah borrowed ¢600 for a period of 4 years at 7% simple interest per annum. Work out the amount of interest payable on the loan.

We are given that P = ¢600, R = 7% and T = 4 years

$$\text{S.I.} = \frac{P \times R \times T}{100}$$

$$= \frac{600 \times 7 \times 4}{100}$$

$$= ¢168$$

Banks and financial institutions have different interest rates on different accounts.

Exercise 14:4

Work out the amount of simple interest (S.I.) for each of these (P = principal. R - Rate % p.a. Time - T in years):

	P	R	T
1	¢100	5%	2
2	¢100	7%	3
3	¢75	4%	4
4	¢100	5%	4
5	¢150	6%	5
6	¢260	7%	3
7	¢80	$6\frac{1}{2}$%	4
8	¢180	5%	5
9	¢600	6%	6
10	¢468	8%	4

	P	R	T
11	¢288	10%	6
12	¢725	$4\frac{1}{2}$%	4
13	¢330	$5\frac{3}{4}$%	2
14	¢426	7%	12
15	¢500	8%	11
16	¢1625	$3\frac{3}{4}$%	3
17	¢2700	$7\frac{1}{2}$%	$6\frac{1}{2}$
18	¢7400	$6\frac{1}{4}$%	$8\frac{1}{2}$
19	¢480	7%	4
20	¢1250	$6\frac{3}{4}$%	10

Work out the simple interest on each of the following. Give your answers correct to the nearest pesewa.

21 ¢2300 invested for 3 years at 7% p.a.

22 ¢1600 borrowed for 4 years at 15% p.a.

23 ¢5200 invested for 5 years at $9\frac{1}{4}$% p.a.

24 ¢9990 lent for 6 years at 13% p.a.

25 ¢3400 lent for 4 years at $5\frac{1}{4}$% p.a.

26 ¢1600 invested for 12 years at $8\frac{3}{4}$% p.a.

If we know any three of the quantities I, P, R and T then it is possible to find the fourth quantity. To do this we transpose the simple interest formula to give:

$$P = \frac{100I}{RT} \quad \text{or} \quad R = \frac{100I}{PT} \quad \text{or} \quad T = \frac{100I}{PR} \qquad \textbf{(I = Interest)}$$

Example   ¢500 is invested for 6 years. At the end of this time the simple interest amounts to ¢255. Work out the rate of simple interest.

We are given P = ¢500 T = 6 years and I = ¢255

We use the formula $R = \dfrac{100I}{PT}$

$R = \dfrac{100 \times 255}{500 \times 6} = 8.5$ Hence the interest rate is 8.5%.

The total amount received, paid or invested (*A*) is the sum of the principal and interest.

We obtain the formula *A = P + I* or the amount received = Principal + Interest

Exercise 14:5

Calculate the total amounts received if:

1 Principal = ¢160, Interest = ¢13.79

2 Principal = ¢210, Interest = ¢15.09

3 Principal = ¢456.89, Interest = ¢25.70

4 Principal = ¢78.67, Interest = ¢8.50

5 Principal = ¢602.65, Interest = ¢55.77

6 Principal = ¢799.99, Interest = ¢76.35

7 Find the rate per cent per annum simple interest for ¢205.50 to be the interest on ¢685 for 4 years.

8 Find the length of time for ¢282.10 to be the interest on ¢650 invested at 6.2% p.a.

9 Find the rate per cent per annum simple interest when ¢151.29 is the interest on ¢820 for 3 years.

10 Find the length of time for ¢74 to be the interest on ¢729.64 invested at 5% p.a.

11 Find the principal required for the simple interest to be ¢500 on money borrowed for 3 years at 8% p.a.

12 Find the principal required for the simple interest to be ¢334 on money lent for $2\frac{1}{2}$ years at 9% p.a.

13 Find the rate per cent per annum simple interest when ¢392.60 is the interest on ¢755 for $2\frac{1}{2}$ years.

14 Find the rate per cent per annum simple interest when ¢245.70 is the interest on ¢700 for $4\frac{1}{2}$ years.

15 Find the length of time when ¢242.52 is the interest on ¢430 borrowed at 9.4% p.a.

16 Find the principal required for the simple interest to be ¢1200 on money lent for $5\frac{1}{2}$ years at 12.3% p.a.

Calculate the total amount received from these investments:

17 ¢700 for 3 years at 10% p.a.

18 ¢3250 for 4 years at 8.5% p.a.

19 ¢981 for $7\frac{1}{2}$ years at 12% p.a.

20 ¢5000 for $6\frac{1}{2}$ years at 9.5% p.a.

21 ¢543 for 5 years at $7\frac{3}{4}$% p.a.

22 ¢976 for $6\frac{1}{2}$ years at 9.5% p.a.

23 ¢3400 for $7\frac{1}{2}$ years at 8.3% p.a.

24 ¢6789 for $8\frac{1}{2}$ years at $6\frac{3}{4}$% p.a.

25 ¢4560 for $4\frac{3}{4}$ years at $5\frac{1}{3}$% p.a.

26 ¢7044 for $7\frac{2}{3}$ years at $7\frac{3}{4}$% p.a.

4   Discount

Discount   The amount of money taken off the value of something is called a **discount**. The discount rate is most often given as a percentage.

Example   A radio is offered for sale at ¢48. If a customer is offered 10% discount, how much does the customer actually pay?

Method 1

Percentage of the amount to be paid = 100% − 10%
= 90%
Amount paid = 90% of ¢48
$= \frac{90}{100} \times 48$
= ¢43.20

Method 2

Discount = 10% of ¢48
$= \frac{10}{100} \times 48$
= ¢4.80
Amount paid = ¢48 − ¢4.80
= ¢43.20

Method 3

Amount paid
= (100% − 10%) × 48
= (1 − 0.10) × 48
= 0.90 × 48
= ¢43.20

Any one of the three methods can be used.

Exercise 14:6

Work out the amount paid in the following sales:

1   ¢100 at a discount of 5%
2   ¢850 at a discount of 7%
3   ¢250 at a discount of 12%
4   ¢748 at a discount of 15%
5   ¢3554 at a discount of 10%
6   ¢1296 at a discount of 20%
7   ¢8087 at a discount of 25%
8   ¢5914 at a discount of $18\frac{1}{2}$%
9   ¢1006 at a discount of $24\frac{1}{2}$%
10   ¢2999 at a discount of 12%

Finding the discount rate

Example   Mathematical Set: Cost Price @ ¢18.00 Selling Price @ ¢15.30

$$\text{Discount rate} = \frac{\text{Cost price} - \text{Selling Price}}{\text{Cost Price}} \times 100$$

$$= \frac{18 - 15.30}{18} \times 100$$

$$= 15\%$$

Work out the percentage discount rate of these items. Give your answers to 1 d.p.

11   **Cake**: Cost price @ ¢6.40
        Selling price @ ¢5.90
12   **Toothpaste**: Cost price @ ¢3.15
        Selling price @ ¢2.90

13   **Soft drink**: Cost price @ ¢0.57
        Selling price @ ¢0.48
14   **Cutlery set**: Cost price @ ¢30.00
        Selling price @ ¢27.50

15   **Milk**: Cost price @ ¢1.20
        Selling price @ ¢1.05
16   **Soap pack**: Cost price @ ¢4.30
        Selling price @ ¢3.87

5 Commission

Commission A fee or percentage allowed to sales people or agents for their services is called a **commission**.

Workers are normally paid a basic weekly wage or a salary; the commission is extra money to encourage them to sell more.

Where a commission is *charged* in a transaction the amount is taken away. For example a bank may charge a commission for exchanging money.

Gross wage A **gross wage** is an amount that a person earns before any deductions are made.

Example In addition to a basic weekly wage of ¢120. Kuffour receives a commission of 2% for selling textbooks. Work out his gross wage for a whole week if he sells textbooks to the value of ¢860.

Basic wage = ¢120   Commission on ¢860 at 2% = $\frac{2}{100} \times 860 = ¢17.20$

Gross wage for the week = Basic wage + Commission
= ¢120 + ¢17.20
= ¢137.20

Exercise 14:7

Find the commission at 3% on goods worth:

1 ¢50   2 ¢102   3 ¢360   4 ¢850.50   5 ¢700

Find the commission at $5\frac{1}{2}$% on goods worth:

6 ¢125.80   7 ¢200.10   8 ¢3680   9 ¢499   10 ¢999.95

Work out the gross wages for the following:

	Basic weekly wage	Value of goods sold	Commission rate		Basic weekly wage	Value of goods sold	Commission rate
11	¢80	¢100	3%	16	¢85	¢450	6%
12	¢105.50	¢60.50	4%	17	¢60	¢200	8%
13	¢110	¢400	$2\frac{1}{2}$%	18	¢128	¢185	$8\frac{1}{2}$%
14	¢125	¢550	$4\frac{1}{2}$%	19	¢78.60	¢100	$4\frac{3}{4}$%
15	¢64	¢60.50	5%	20	¢213.28	¢345	$6\frac{3}{4}$%

21 Mrs Asantewaah earns ¢240 per month and receives $8\frac{1}{2}$% commission on goods sold. Work out her gross earning for July if her sales total ¢490 in July.

22 Mrs Yarko is paid a wage of ¢38 and a commission at $14\frac{4}{5}$%. Mrs Sakyi is paid ¢75 plus a commission at $9\frac{1}{2}$%. Who earned the most and by how much, from selling goods worth ¢828?

23 Muntari, who works as a salesman in an ironmongers, is paid a basic wage of ¢186. In one week he earns $8\frac{2}{5}$% commission for selling ¢790 worth of nails, $7\frac{1}{2}$% commission for selling ¢180 worth of wire and $6\frac{3}{4}$% commission for selling ¢350 worth of iron rods. Work out his total wage that week.

6   Taxes

The government spends a large amount of money each year on health, education, defence, roads, transport, social services and so on. Much of this money comes from income tax. The amount which anyone has to pay depends on how much they earn.

Tax   **Tax** is a compulsory financial contribution levied by a government to raise revenue. There are two types of taxes: direct tax and indirect tax.

Direct tax   A tax imposed directly on taxpayers' incomes or profits is called **direct tax**. Examples are income tax, health tax and corporation tax.

Indirect tax   A tax imposed on goods or services rather than on income or profits is called **indirect tax**. Examples are value added tax (VAT), excise duty and road tax.

Income tax   A tax levied directly on personal income is called **income tax**. The rate at which income tax is calculated is announced by the government minister of finance. The rate can vary from year to year. Examples are wages, salaries, dividends, rent and interest.

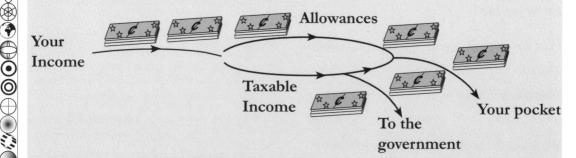

Allowance   Money provided for a particular purpose such as clothing, food and travel expenses is called an **allowance**.

Gross income   The amount a person earns in a week, month or year is called **gross income**.

Net income   When all the tax deductions and other contributions have been taken away from the income, what remains is called **net income** or **take home pay**.

Taxable income = gross income − tax allowance

The percentage of taxable income must be paid in tax.
The percentage payable is called the **tax rate**.

**Value added   Value Added Tax (VAT) is tax imposed by government at each stage in the
tax (VAT)**   production of goods or services. It is calculated at a rate fixed by the government (at the time of writing this book VAT is 12.5% in Ghana). VAT is added to the basic cost of goods and services.

Examples   **a** Karkari earns ¢368 per week. He pays ¢25.20 in health insurance, ¢19.56 towards his pension fund and his income tax amounts to ¢44.70. Work out his gross pay.

Total deductions = ¢25.20 + ¢19.56 + ¢44.70
= ¢89.46

Net pay   = gross pay − deductions
= ¢368 − ¢89.46
= ¢278.54

b Akoto earns ¢185 per month. She pays 6% on health insurance, 3% toward her pension and ¢2.10 for her union membership fee. If her income tax amounts to ¢27.75, work out her net wage.

Health insurance = 6% of ¢185   Pension = 3% of ¢185
= 0.06 × 185   = 0.03 × 185
= ¢11.10   = ¢5.55

Total deductions = ¢5.55 + ¢11.10 + ¢27.75
= ¢46.50

Net pay   = gross pay − deductions
= 185 − 46.50
= ¢138.00

Exercise 14:8

Copy and complete this table which gives details of the pay earned by these employees in one week.

| Employee | Gross pay | Deductions | | | Net pay |
		Health insurance	Income Tax	Pension contribution	
1	Badu	¢29.40	¢0.88	¢2.69	¢1.86	
2	Marfo	¢14.80	¢0.44	¢1.33		¢12.36
3	Owusu	¢35.44	¢1.06	¢3.54	¢1.77	
4	Duah		¢0.23	¢0.70	¢0.39	¢6.49
5	Kwame	¢52.00		¢4.68	¢2.60	¢43.22
6	Asare	¢68.95	¢2.07		¢3.44	¢57.28

7 Akua earns ¢37.80 per week. Her deductions are health insurance (¢3.02), income tax (¢6.27) and pension contribution (¢2.27). Work out her take home pay.

8 A woman's taxable income is ¢86. If tax is paid at 26% of the taxable income, work out the amount of income tax paid.

9 When income tax was levied at 28% a man paid ¢14.75 in tax. What was his taxable income?

10 Ofori's salary is ¢2580.50 per annum and his total tax-free allowances are ¢309.76.

   a Work out his taxable income.

   b If income tax is levied at 24%, work out the amount of tax paid.

11 Mintah is paid ¢1.15 per hour for a 40-hour week.

   a Work out his gross weekly wage.

   b He pays health insurance at 2.58% of his gross wage. How much per week does he pay in health insurance contributions?

   c If in addition he pays ¢4.42 per week in income tax, work out his net weekly wage.

*12 In the United Kingdom in 2006 the rates of taxable income per annum were as follows:

on the first £2020	10%	(the starting rate)
on the next £29380	22%	(the basic rate)
on any income over £31400	40%	(the higher rate)

   a Elizabeth earned a gross salary of £16800 per annum and her tax-free allowance amounted to £1521. Work out the amount of income tax that she paid.

   b Andrew earned a salary of £20500. Work out the amount of income tax he paid.

   c Charlene earned a gross salary of £36650 per annum and her tax-free allowable amount to £2888. Work out the amount of income tax that she paid.

   d Work out the net pay for: **i** Elizabeth   **ii** Andrew   **iii** Charlene

*13 Kurt from Germany earns €32500 per annum and his wife has an annual salary of €15600. Allowance and income tax are calculated on their combined salaries. The information below shows their tax-free allowances.

   Husband's personal allowance €3600
   Allowance on wife's earnings €2300
   Both pension contribution payments €2800

   The rates of tax for married couples are as follows:
   On first €15668 - tax free
   Income up to €52152 - 40%

   Work out: **a** their total allowance
   b their taxable income
   c the total amount of tax payable
   d their net income

Adding Value Added Tax to purchases

Example Work out the total purchase price of an umbrella which costs ¢8.50 and has 12.5% VAT added.

Method 1

VAT at 12.5% of ¢8.50 = 0.125 × 8.50
= ¢1.0625
Customer pays = ¢8.50 + ¢1.0625
= ¢9.56
[or in short: 8.50 + (0.125 × 8.50)]

Method 2

The price includes VAT
∴ customer pays:
= (100% + 12.5%) of ¢8.50
= 1.125 × 8.50
= ¢9.56

Exercise 14:9

Find the total purchase price of each of these items. Take VAT as 12.5%.

1 Digital alarm clock costing ¢8.85

2 Stereo amplifier costing ¢225.90

3 Metal gate costing ¢165

4 Mobile phone costing ¢57.50

5 Double bed costing ¢41

6 Holiday in England ¢2880

7 Hotel bill costing ¢189.50

8 Calculator costing ¢11.90

9 Pair of shoes costing ¢28.90

10 Television set costing ¢657.99

In each of these bills work out the subtotal cost, find the VAT and calculate the final cost.

11

Addae Trading Stores	Amount ¢
2 loaves of bread	2.88
Lux soap	0.50
1 Dozen eggs	1.80
Box of sugar	0.89
5 kg bag of rice	6.90
2L UHT milk	0.64
6L Spring water	2.40
SUB-TOTAL	
VAT @ 12.5%	
FINAL	

12

Gyasi Car Repairs	
Service	Amount ¢
2 Front Tyres @ ¢87.60	175.20
5*l* Engine Oil	2.49
Wheel Balance	4.00
Thermostat	6.45
Brake Pads	50.68
Engine Tune	29.90
General Service	55.00
SUB-TOTAL	
VAT @ 12.5%	
FINAL	

13

Dibi Restaurant	Amount ¢
Jolof Rice x 2	1.56
Palaver Sauce	1.18
Fried Yam	0.90
Palm-nut Soup	0.84
Pawpaw cocktail	0.78
2 x Malt Beer Drink	1.26
2*l* Voltic Water	0.96
Pack of doughnuts	0.48
SUB-TOTAL	
VAT @ 12.5%	
FINAL	

14

Dayie Hotel	
Description	Amount ¢
Accommodation 13th - 26th	189.00
Room Service	70.00
Food	112.63
Laundry Service	38.00
Drinks	19.60
Telephone Calls	18.89
Transport	50.00
Miscellaneous	98.90
SUB-TOTAL	
VAT @ 12.5%	
FINAL	

INVESTIGATION

CALCULATING OUR CARBON FOOTPRINT

Greenhouse gas (GHG) is a gas that traps heat in the atmosphere e.g. carbon dioxide (CO_2), methane (CH_4) and nitrous oxide (N_2O).

A **carbon footprint** is the total amount of greenhouse gases produced to directly or indirectly support human activities. It is expressed in terms of the amount of carbon dioxide emitted in kilograms.

Boeing 747 Aeroplane travel
Accra to London - 5105 km
Litres of fuel used - 61260 l
Type of fuel - kerosene

Toyota Corolla car travel
Engine size - 1.4 litres
Fuel - Diesel
Fuel consumption - 17 km per litre
Estimated number of kilometres per year - 12000 km

Miscellaneous
1 kWh electricity from the national grid produces 0.5 kg of CO_2.
1 litre diesel fuel produces 2.68 kg of CO_2.
1 litre of kerosene produces 3.155 kg of CO_2.
1 kg of wood charcoal produces 2.41 kg of CO_2.
1 kg of butane for cooking produces 1.74 kg of CO_2.
Butane gas is bought in 80 kg cylinders.

Example The carbon footprint on the usage of 16 litres of kerosene is calculated as follows:
1 litre = 3.155 of CO_2
16 litres = 16 × 3.155 = 50.48 kg of CO_2.

Use the above information to work out the total carbon footprint of the following families' activities:

▶ Mr Kessi, a businessman lives on his own. He:
* Travels from Accra to London on Boeing 747 aeroplane three times a year.
* Uses his Toyota Corolla car (diesel), an average of 16 km per day for 320 days in a year.
* Uses butane gas cylinders for cooking. 18 cylinders are used per year.
* Uses electricity of 150 kWh per month.

▶ Mrs Domfe runs a family business making and selling small cakes from home:
* She uses an electric oven and consumes 85 kWh electricity per week.
* Her Toyota van runs on petrol and delivers cakes. It averages 28 km per day.
* Her family uses 1 kg wood charcoal per day for their own cooking.

▶ Mr Abu cares for a family of 8:
* Cooking uses 2 kg of wood charcoal per day.
* Their house is lit with 2 lanterns. They burn 0.8 litres of kerosene per night.
* The family travels by minibus and the combined consumption of minibus fuel averages 80 litres per week.

■ Which family has the highest carbon footprint?
■ Now work out the carbon footprint of your family.

EXTENSION

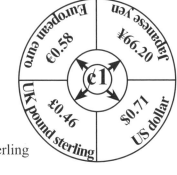

1   Use the foreign exchange rate to change the following:

   a ¢30.28 into euros   **b** $417 into cedis

   c ¥1250 into euros   **d** £100 into yen

   e ¢320 into pounds sterling   **f** ¥750 into cedis

   g ¥6000 into dollars   **h** £2930 into cedis

   e £250 into dollars   **j** $3400 into pounds sterling

2   Akosua and Kushiato went on holiday to UK. Akosua changed ¢5935 into pounds
   sterling and Kushiato had $520 .

   a How many more pounds sterling did Akosua have than Kushiato?

   b What was their total money worth in euros?

3   A company exporting goods to Holland is paid in euros and receives a cheque for
   €1500. How much in cedis will be the company receive from its bank if the bank charges
   a commission of $6\frac{1}{2}\%$?

4   Akosah bought 500 US dollars thinking that the exchange rate was $1 to ¢1.38.
   The exchange rate was in fact $1 to ¢1.41. If the bank commission was 1%, did Akosah
   pay more or less than he expected and by how much?

5   Bemah changed ¢250 into pounds sterling for a business trip to the UK but did not spend
   any of the money. On return she changed the pounds sterling back into cedis.
   If 2% commission was deducted on each transaction, how much did she lose?

6   The price of fuel is ¢2.37 a gallon. How much is this per litre?

7   Express: **a** 1 km/h in m/s   **b** 70 km/h in m/s   **c** 30m/s in km/h

8   On a journey from London to Accra, a Boeing 767 aeroplane cruises at 880 km/h above
   the Sahara desert. Express 880 km/h in m/s and m.p.h.

9   How many years will it take ¢1700 to double its value when invested at 6% simple interest?

10 ¢657 is invested in a savings account and increases by a simple interest of 5.25% each year.
   How much will it be worth:

   a in 2 years;   **b** in 5 years;   **c** in $8\frac{1}{2}$ years?

11 What sum of money will yield a simple interest of ¢100 at 9.3% per annum for $4\frac{1}{2}$ years?

12 Mr Boahene earns ¢27.50 per week plus a commission of $6\frac{3}{4}\%$. If he sells goods worth
   ¢86, find his total earnings for the week.

13 Find the total purchase price of a saucepan marked ¢2.50 plus VAT at $12\frac{1}{2}\%$.

14 A set of four stainless steel saucepans sells for ¢20.70. The price includes VAT at 15%.
  a Find the price excluding VAT.
  b Find the new selling price if the value added tax is reduced from 15% to $12\frac{1}{2}\%$.

15 A bicycle salesman is paid a basic salary of ¢86 per month plus a commission of ¢1.50 for each bike that he sells.

  a In June he sells 52 bikes. How much salary does he receive?

  b He needs to earn at least ¢200 a month. How many bikes must he aim to sell?

  c What will be his new basic salary after a 6% pay rise?

16 Ayew sells car insurance. His company pays him ¢20 per day. They also pay him a commission of 12% on all the sales he makes. In December and January he worked 36 days and sold ¢467 worth of insurance. Calculate his pay for the two months.

17 The first ¢100 of a sum of money is taxed at 25% and the remainder, if any, is taxed at 35%. Work out: **a** the tax on ¢140   **b** the sum where the tax is: **i** ¢60   **ii** ¢36.

18 The average fuel consumption of a car is measured in kilometres per litre.
  a Work out the average fuel consumption of a car that travels 250 km on 18 litres.

  b Hassan sets off with a full tank of petrol on a 300 km journey. When he arrives, his fuel gauge indicates $\frac{1}{8}$ full. His car's full tank holds 48 litres.
    i Work out the average fuel consumption for his journey.
    ii If the average fuel consumption remains the same, how much further can he travel before he runs out of petrol?

19 At a steady speed of 30 km per hour, the fuel consumption of Okai's car is 12 km per litre of diesel.
  a How far will his car travel on 30 litres of diesel at 30 km per hour?
  b How much diesel will his car use on a journey of 180 miles, where the average speed is 30 km per hour?
  c How far does he travel on 10 gallons of diesel at a steady speed of 30 km.p.h.?

20 Water is leaking from a storage tank of volume 4 m³ at a rate of 0.6 litres per minute. How long will it take a full tank of water to leak away?. Give your answer in hours and minutes.

21 **a** Water comes out of a tap at a rate of 14 litre/min. Copy and complete this table.

Time in minutes	0	0.5	1	1.5	2	3	4	5	10	20	30
Amount in litres	0		14								

  b Draw a graph of time against amount.
  c Use the graph to find the time taken to fill a tank which can hold 100 litres.

22 This is the (time, temperature) graph representing the rate at which a stove cools.

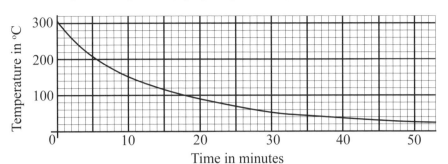

Work out the average rate that the temperature falls (in deg./min) between:

a 0 min to 20 min   **b** 20 min to 50 min

23 This is the recommended gear change at various speeds when driving a car.
Copy the table and complete the bottom row. Write your values to the nearest whole number.

Speed	1st gear	2nd gear	3rd gear	4th gear	5th gear
mph	0 - 15	10 - 20	20 - 35	30 - 50	> 50
km/h					

24 **VO2 max** is the maximum rate at which the heart, lungs and muscles effectively use oxygen during exercise. Change these VO2 max values:

a 30 ml/kg/min to ml/kg/s   **b** 50 ml/kg/min to ml/kg/s

25 Nkrumah and Boateng are running round a field together. Boateng soon gets ahead of Nkrumah. Boateng runs at 6 metres per second (m/s). Nkrumah runs at 5 metres per second. They each work out a rule for the distance they run.

a Write Boateng's rule in algebra using the letters d for distance and t for time.

b Copy this table for each value of Boateng's rule.
Use your formula to fill it in.

Number of seconds	10	20	30	40	50	60	70	80	90	100
Distance										

c Draw a graph for this table.

d Write Nkrumah's rule in algebra.

e Make a table for Nkrumah's distances.
Draw the graph on the same diagram as Boateng's

f Describe the differences between the two graphs.
Explain why the graphs are different.

g A photographer is waiting 480 m from the start to take a picture of each man as they pass. How long must he wait for each man?

SUMMARY

Foreign exchange	An institution or system for dealing in the currencies of other countries is called **foreign exchange**. **Forex** an is abbreviation for foreign exchange.
Exchange rate	The ratio at which the unit of currency of one country is exchanged for the unit of currency of another country is called the **exchange rate**.
Rate	**Rate** is a ratio between two quantities with different units. Rate is usually expressed as the amount of one quantity with respect to one unit of another.
Interest	**Interest** is money paid regularly at a particular rate when money is lent or invested. The rate of interest usually is written as a percentage.
Rate of interest (R)	This is a fixed price paid or charged. It is expressed as a percentage per annum. *Per annum* **(p.a.)** is a Latin for *throughout the year*.
Simple interest (S.I.)	The amount of interest earned per year, when a given amount of money is invested. The interest earned is the same each year. If the money is invested for 2 years the amount of interest will be doubled. If the money is invested for three years the amount of interest will be trebled.
Principal (P)	The original sum of money borrowed, lent or invested is called the **principal**.
Time (T)	The time in years over which the money is lent, borrowed or invested.
Discount	The amount of money taken off the value of something is called a **discount**. Discount rate is most often given as a percentage.
Commission	A fee or percentage allowed to sales people or agents for their services is called a **commission**. Workers are normally paid a basic weekly wage or a salary; the commission is extra money to encourage them to sell more.
Allowance	Money provided for a particular purpose such as clothing, food and travel expenses is called an **allowance**.
Tax	**Tax** is a compulsory financial contribution levied by a government to raise revenue. There are two types of taxes: direct tax and indirect tax.
Direct tax	A tax imposed directly on taxpayers' income or profit is called **direct tax**. Examples are income tax, health tax and corporation tax.
Indirect tax	A tax imposed on goods or services is called **indirect tax**.
Income tax	A tax levied directly on personal income is called **income tax**.
Net income	When all the tax deductions and other contributions have been taken away from the income, what remains is called **net income** or **take home pay**.
Gross income	The amount a person earns in a week, month or year is called **gross income**.
Value added tax (VAT)	Value Added Tax (**VAT**) is a tax imposed by government at each stage in the production of goods or services.

Probability

EXTENSION

SUMMARY

Probability emerged in the 17th century. The word probability derives from the Latin *probare* (to prove or to test). Probability gives us a measure for the likelihood that something will happen. However it must be appreciated that probability can never predict the number of times that an occurrence actually happens.
Being able to quantify the likely occurrence of an event is important because most of the decisions that affect our daily lives are based on likelihoods and not absolute certainties.

This is a **roulette wheel**.
It is a gambling game in which a ball is dropped in a revolving wheel with numbered compartments.
The players bet on the number where the ball will come to rest.

The gambler may bet:
Straight up - a single number bet.
Split - a bet on 2 adjoining numbers.
First 18 numbers, last high eighteen numbers, even or odd numbers.
What other bets can you think of ?

1 Probability scales

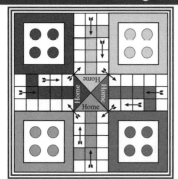

If you play the Ludo board game you will see that the chance of getting a specific number in order to move a counter can be frustrating. A player may say 'I only need to get a 4 on the dice to send this counter home'. But this 4 can take a long time to come.

What chance has this player got?

In probability we ask questions like: 'What are the chances of ...... ?'
'How likely is it .... ?'

Here are more specific questions to which we do not know the answers:
'Who will win the league?'
'If I toss a coin will it land heads up?'
'What is the likelihood of rain tomorrow?'
'Is there a risk that her company will be in debt next year?'
'What chance does Ghana have to win the next football world cup?'

Probability   In mathematics **probability** means how likely something is to happen.
The probability of an event occurring is measured on a scale with
'impossible' at one end and 'certain' at the other.

Here is a probability scale:

b				**c**				**a**
impossible	very unlikely	unlikely		even chance		likely	very likely	certain

We have shown by writing over the scale:

a It will be dark by midnight tonight.

b If you throw an ordinary six-sided dice it will show a 7.

c A newly-born baby will be a girl.

Exercise 15:1

For each question below, draw a probability scale. Show by writing over the scale **a**, **b** and **c** how likely you think each one is.

1 a You will have mathematics homework tonight.
b Someone in your class is left handed.
c You will live to be 100 years old.

2 a A newly-born baby will be a boy.
b You will walk from Axim to Kulungugu in one day.
c A cockerel will crow at 3.30 a.m. tomorrow morning.

3 **a** You will have yams to eat today.
  b It will rain on Eid Day where you live.
  c You will be late for school at least once this term.

4 **a** The sun will rise tomorrow morning.
  b Someone in your family will win the lottery on Saturday.
  c It will be dark at midnight tonight.

5 **a** You will jump up and stay in the air for ten seconds.
  b A dog will wag its tail when food is coming to it.
  c You will blink your eyes in the next minute.

6 **a** A coin thrown in the air will land on its edge and remain there.
  b Ghana will win a gold medal in the men's 4 × 100 metres at the next Olympic Games.
  c The day after Saturday will be Sunday.

Random	If an item is chosen at **random** it means that every item has an equal chance of being chosen. '**At random**' means 'without looking' or 'not knowing which of the choices will be made in advance.'

7 **a** A book chosen at random from your teacher's table will be the class register.
  b An item chosen at random from your school bag will be a blue pen.
  c An item chosen at random from your pocket will be money.

8 **a** An item chosen at random from the shop shelf will be a tin of milk.
  b An item chosen at random from a shoe shine box will be a duster.
  c An item chosen at random from your house kitchen will be a spoon.

Probability as a number

People in different countries have different words for saying how likely or unlikely any particular event is to occur.

Probability is measured accurately using numbers. We use 0 for 'impossible' and 1 for 'certain'. If something is not certain to happen it must have a probability less than 1. Probabilities are written as fractions, decimals or percentages. It is written between 0 to 1. A probability scale looks like this:

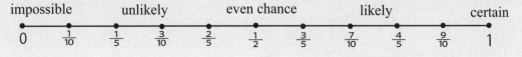

| impossible | | unlikely | | even chance | | likely | | certain |

$$0 \quad \tfrac{1}{10} \quad \tfrac{1}{5} \quad \tfrac{3}{10} \quad \tfrac{2}{5} \quad \tfrac{1}{2} \quad \tfrac{3}{5} \quad \tfrac{7}{10} \quad \tfrac{4}{5} \quad \tfrac{9}{10} \quad 1$$

Exercise 15:2

1 Redraw your answers from questions 1 to 8 on probability scales like the one shown above.

2 For each letter you have marked, give an estimate of the probability.
  Write your answer as: **i** decimal   **ii** fraction   **iii** percentage

2 Experimental probability

Event A thing that happens or takes place is called an **event**.

Outcome The result of an event is called an **outcome**.

Trial A **trial** is an action which results in one of several possible outcomes.

Dice Dice are small cubes used in games.
They are usually numbered 1 to 6 on the faces.

Experiment An **experiment** consists of a number of trials.
The chance of certain events occurring can be predicted. For example, if an ordinary dice is thrown, there are six possible outcomes. These are 1, 2, 3, 4, 5 and 6. An experiment could be throwing dice to see what numbers will show. The list 1, 2, 3, 4, 5, 6 is called the **set of all possible outcomes**.

Experimental probability An estimate of probability, made by doing trials or experiments, is called **experimental probability**.

Example How many possible outcomes are there for choosing one letter from the vowels of the alphabet?
List of possible outcomes: a, e, i, o, u
Number of possible outcomes: 5

Coin A coin is a piece of money which can be thrown (called *tossing* or *spinning*) and has equal probabilities of landing on each of its two sides.

Head The **head** is the name of one side of a coin usually having the picture of a head on it. This side of the coin is also known the **obverse**.

Tail The **tail** of a coin is the side which is not a head. It is also known as the **reverse**.

Exercise 15:3

How many possible outcomes are there for these experiments?
In each case, write down the list of all possible outcomes.

1 Throwing a dice.

2 Choosing one even number from the first ten positive whole numbers.

3 Getting two heads when throwing two coins.

4 Taking the cards T or I from a bag containing the cards **U T I L I T I E S**.

5 Choosing one number at random from the first 4 prime numbers.

6 Choosing the counters M or T from the counters **M A T H E M A T I C S**.

7 Choosing the letters S or I from the word **P O S S I B I L I T I E S**.

3 How probability theory works

If you throw an ordinary dice you are likely to get 1, 2, 3, 4, 5 or 6. All outcomes are equally likely. If you want to calculate the probability of getting a five, there is only one outcome that is possible.

There is only one 5 and six numbers. So we say there is a 1 in 6 (or 1 out of 6) chance of getting a five. We say that the probability of throwing a five is $\frac{1}{6}$.

This can be written more briefly as P(throwing a five) = $\frac{1}{6}$.

The mathematical way of writing it is P(5) = $\frac{1}{6}$.

$$\text{Probability of an event} = \frac{\text{Number of ways the event can happen}}{\text{Total number of possible outcomes}}$$

Examples

a A bag contains three white counters and two black counters. What is the probability of picking a black counter?

There are two black counters out of five

$\therefore$ P(black) = $\frac{2}{5}$

b A dice is thrown. What is the probability of getting an even number?

There are three even numbers out of six numbers

$\therefore$ P(even number) = $\frac{3}{6}$ = $\frac{1}{2}$

c A letter is chosen at random from the letters of the word TOGETHER. What is the probability that the letter E will be chosen?

There are 2 ways of choosing the letter E and there are 8 letters in TOGETHER.

$\therefore$ P(E) = $\frac{2}{8}$ = $\frac{1}{4}$

Exercise 15:4

1 Find the probability of throwing a dice and getting:
   a an odd number   b a 2   c a prime number
   d a 1 or a 3   e 4 or more   f a factor of 77 that is greater than 1

2 A box of 10 pens of primary and other colours sits on a desk. What is the probability of picking a red pen at random?

3 What is the probability of choosing a prime number from the numbers 5, 6, 7, 8, 9, 10, 11.?

4 A letter is chosen at random from the word PROBABILITY. What is the probability that T is chosen?

5 Assume that a coin cannot land on its edge. What is the probability of a coin landing so that it shows: a a head   b a tail?

6 A bag contains 14 blue beads and 6 red beads. What is the probability of choosing a blue bead?

7 There are 5 sweets in a bag. Copy the scale, write down the probability and put the labels in the correct boxes. Mint ◆ Ginger ◇

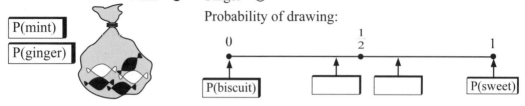

Probability of drawing:

P(mint)

P(ginger)

8 There are 10 sweets in a bag. Copy the scale, write down the probability and put the labels in the correct boxes. Mint ◆ Ginger ◇ Toffee ◆

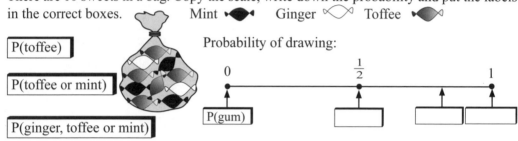

Probability of drawing:

P(toffee)

P(toffee or mint)

P(ginger, toffee or mint)

9 There are 15 balls in a bag. Copy the scale, write down the probability and put the labels in the correct boxes.

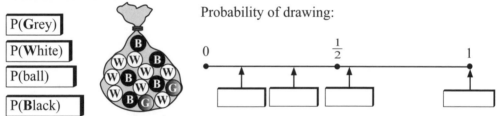

Probability of drawing:

P(**Grey**)

P(**White**)

P(ball)

P(**Black**)

10 There are 20 tickets in a bag. Copy the scale, write down the probability and put the labels in the correct boxes.

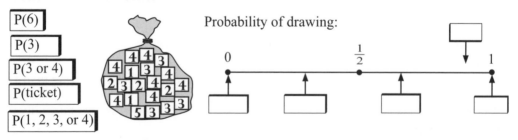

Probability of drawing:

P(6)

P(3)

P(3 or 4)

P(ticket)

P(1, 2, 3, or 4)

11 There are 15 beads in a bag. Copy the scale, write down the probability and put the labels in the correct boxes.

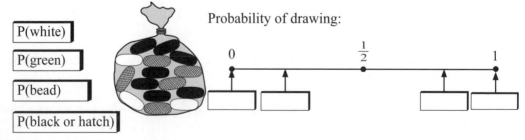

Probability of drawing:

P(white)

P(green)

P(bead)

P(black or hatch)

12 A pencil case contains 6 red pens and 5 blue pens. Tetteh takes out a pen without looking at it. What is the probability that he takes out:

    a a red pen   **b** a blue pen   **c** a black pen ?

13 A bag contains 40 beads. Ten are black, 12 are green and the rest are red. Foriwaah takes a bead from the bag at random. What is the probability that she takes:

    a a black bead   **b** a green bead

    c a bead that is not red   **d** a bead that is black or red?

14 One letter is chosen at random from the word POSSIBILITIES.

    What is the probability that it is: **a** the letter I   **b** the letter S   **c** a vowel ?

15 A book of 180 pages has a picture on each of 35 pages. If one page is chosen at random, what is the probability that it has a picture on it?

P(event *not* happening) = 1 − P(event happening)

Example   In a bag there are 9 marbles of which 5 are brown. One is drawn at random. What is the probability that the marble drawn is not brown ?

$$P(\text{not brown}) = 1 - P(\text{brown})$$
$$= 1 - \tfrac{5}{9}$$
$$= \tfrac{4}{9}$$

16 In a bag there are 10 marbles. Four are red. One marble is drawn at random. What is the probability of picking a marble that is not red out of the bag?

17 Ten cards numbered 2, 2, 3, 3, 5, 6, 7, 8, 9, 9 are placed in a bag. One card is selected at random. Find the probability that it is:

    a an odd number   **b** not an odd number   **c** a seven   **d** not a seven

18 A **raffle** is a means of raising money by selling numbered tickets, one or more of which are subsequently drawn at random, whereupon the holder or holders of such tickets win a prize. If you bought 15 raffle tickets and a total of 450 were sold, what is the probability that you win the first prize ?

19 One letter is chosen at random from the letters of the alphabet. What is the probability that it is a consonant?

20 A number is chosen at random from the set of two-digit whole numbers (i.e. the numbers 10 to 99). What is the probability that it is exactly divisible by both 3 and by 4 ?

21 In a snack bar the probability of a customer buying a cake is 0.74. What is the probability of a customer not buying a cake?

*22 What is the probability of getting a double 5 when two dice are thrown?

PLAYING CARDS

Playing cards are specially prepared from heavy paper
or thin cardboard and have distinguishing motifs.
The complete set is called a **pack** of cards or **deck**.
A deck of cards may be used for playing a variety
of card games. Playing cards probably originated
in Hindustan (India) around AD 800.
The cards are typically palm-sized for convenient
handling. For most games cards are put into
random order by **shuffling**.

		PACK OF CARDS										Court cards		
BLACK	**Clubs**	Ace	2	3	4	5	6	7	8	9	10	Jack	Queen	King
	Spades	Ace	2	3	4	5	6	7	8	9	10	Jack	Queen	King
RED	**Diamonds**	Ace	2	3	4	5	6	7	8	9	10	Jack	Queen	King
	Hearts	Ace	2	3	4	5	6	7	8	9	10	Jack	Queen	King

Examples   A pack of cards is shuffled and then one card is chosen at random.

   a What is the probability that it is a 7 of hearts?

   There is only one seven of hearts and there are 52 cards

   $\therefore$ P(7 of hearts) $= \dfrac{1}{52}$

   b What is the probability that it is an ace?

   There only four aces and there are 52 cards

   $\therefore$ P(one ace) $= \dfrac{4}{52}$ or $\dfrac{1}{13}$

Exercise 15:5

1 Using the information above on the pack of cards copy and complete these. There are ...
   a ...... cards in the pack   **b** ...... queens in the pack   **c** ...... 8s in the pack
   d ...... red court cards   **e** ...... black cards in the pack   **f** ...... hearts in the pack
   g ...... 10s in the pack   **h** ...... court cards in the pack   **i** ...... 2s in the pack

A pack of cards is shuffled and then one card is chosen at random.

2 Find the probability that it is:
   a a king   **b** a queen of diamonds   **c** a club   **d** the jack of hearts
   e a 10 of hearts **f** not a spade   **g** an eight   **h** a picture card

3 What is the probability of choosing:
   a a red card   **b** a numbered card   **c** a red ace   **d** a lettered card
   e a nine   **f** a black numbered card   **g** a heart   **h** a 2?

*4 Work out the probability of these:
   a P(diamond or club)   **b** P(red or black card)   **c** P(club, heart or spade)
   d P(jack, 10 or ace)   **e** P(number greater than 8)   **f** P(3, 5, 7 or jack)
   g P(queen or jack)   **h** P(king of clubs or spade)   **i** P(2, 3 or a picture card)

4 Relative frequency

If you drop a drawing pin it is just as likely to land point up as point down.

Trials	Tally	Frequency
Point up	ⵑ卌 卌 卌 卌 卌 卌 Ⅰ	31
Point down	卌 卌 卌 ‖‖	19

Bar chart showing pin dropping

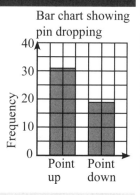

Frequency   The **frequency** of an event is the number of times that it happens.

Relative frequency   The **relative frequency** of an event $= \dfrac{\text{frequency of an event}}{\text{total frequency}}$

The relative frequency gives an *estimate* of the probability.

Using a survey or an experiment we can determine the probability for an event. From these probabilities we can predict how many times we would expect a particular event to occur for a certain number of trials.

In the experiment above, the pin was dropped 50 times.

Relative frequency of point up $= \dfrac{\text{number of landings point up}}{\text{total number of drops}} = \dfrac{31}{50} = 0.62$

Relative frequency of point down $= \dfrac{\text{number of point down landings}}{\text{total number of drops}} = \dfrac{19}{50} = 0.38$

We can get a stronger result for the probability by repeating the experiment many more times.

Exercise 15:6

A motoring organisation's survey asks which cars have the most reliable brake system.

Model	Cars with faulty brake system	Cars with good brake system	Total number of cars
Tinee	1340	965	2305
Nitran	847	2432	3279
Minti	378	406	784
Caraca	996	851	1847
Victory	1824	314	2138

1 a Work out $\dfrac{378}{784}$ to 2 decimal places.

b Work out the relative frequency of each model having a faulty brake system to 2 d.p.

c Write the five relative frequencies as percentages.

d Which model has the greatest relative frequency of faulty brake systems?

2 A firm making ball point pens carries out tests on four types of pen. Any pen which writes less than 800 m is substandard. The table shows the results of the test.

Type of pen	Number of substandard	Number OK	Total
Ball point	17	567	584
Roller tip	28	482	555
Fountain	73	1050	1123
Gel	40	528	568

a What is the relative frequency (in percentages) of substandard pens among:

    i Ball point   **ii** Roller tip   **iii** Fountain   **iv** Gel?

b If you buy a new pen of each type, which would be the most likely to be substandard? (Assume that the pens tested are typical.)

A **fair** or **unbiased coin** is a coin which is not bent or deliberately weighted. The chances of getting a head or tail are equal.

3 Essien tosses a coin 100 times. This is his data.

    a Find the relative frequency of

        i heads   **ii** tails

    b Is the coin fair? Explain your answer.

Outcome	Frequency
heads	42
tails	58

4 Ajara collects data on types of vehicles passing the school gate. Her results are shown in the table:

Type	Tally	Frequency
Taxi	卌 卌 卌 卌 |||	23
Bus	卌 卌 卌		16
Private Car	卌 卌 卌 卌 卌 卌 ||	32
Van	卌 卌 ||||	14
Long vehicle	卌 卌		11
Other	||||	4

a How many vehicles does Ajara include in her survey?

b What is the relative frequency of a private car passing the gate? Give your answer as:

    i a fraction   **ii** a decimal   **iii** a percentage.

c What is the relative frequency of a long vehicle passing the gate? Give your answer as:

    i a fraction   **ii** a decimal   **iii** a percentage.

d What type of vehicle is most likely to pass the school gate next?

e Write down an estimate for the probability that the next car will be a taxi. Give your answer as a fraction.

f How can the estimate for the probability of a taxi be made reliable?

Research   Sometimes you can use data collected by someone else. The data may have been collected over a number of years, such as how often it rains in Kumasi on Independence Day. Finding data this way is called **research**.

Exercise 15:7

For each of the these questions, say which method you would choose to work out the probability.

Method 1   Use probability theory to calculate it.
Method 2   Collect your own data or do an experiment.
Method 3   Research to find data.

If you decide to use method 2, say what you would do. Also say how much data you would collect or how many times you would repeat the experiment.

1   The probability that a person chosen at random in a school will be left-handed.

2   The probability that the next car passing your school will be a green car.

3   The probability that the CO_2 emissions in Ghana next year will reach 6 tonnes per capita.

4   The probability of winning the lottery next Saturday.

5   The probability that a car is stolen on a Friday night in Tema.

6   The probability that the jack of clubs will be chosen from a pack of cards.

7   The probability that if someone is chosen at random from your class, their favourite football team will be BA United.

8   The probability that a volcano will erupt next week in a particular country.

9   The probability that a new drug will cure malaria.

10   The probability that a shoe pushed off a table will land the right way up.

11   The probability that a new ¢2 coin will land tails up.

12   The probability that the temperature on 14th August will be 23°C.

13   The probability that the next item chosen from a lady's bag will be a lipstick.

14   The probability that the next person entering a hospital suffers from an ulcer.

15   The probability that the sunset on 5th March will be at 5.28 p.m.

16   The probability that households using mosquito nets have fewer cases of malaria than those not using mosquito nets.

EXTENSION

1 A bag contains 5 red, 4 blue and 18 green balls. If a ball is chosen at random find the probability that it is not red.

2 A number is chosen at random from the whole numbers 1 to 50 inclusive. Find the probability that it is a prime number.

3 Duah has a box of 15 coloured light bulbs. Six are blue, seven are white and two are green. What is the probability that it is: **a** green   **b** either blue or green?

4 On a combination lock there are two rings.
There are three digits on each ring: 1, 2, 3.
Each combination is a two-digit number e.g. 3, 1

   a List all the possible combinations.

   b What is the probability that a lock has the combination 3, 1?

   c What is the probability that two rings of the combination lock are the same?

5 A fair dice is rolled 540 times. How many times would you expect to roll:

   a a two   **b** an odd number   **c** a number less that 3?

6 'You should eat snails when there is an r in the month'. The name of the month is chosen at random. Find the probability that it contains an R.

7 A coin is biased so that the probability of tossing a 'head' is 0.57.
   a How many 'heads' would you expect when the coin is tossed 200 times?
   b How many 'tails' would you expect when the coin is tossed 1100 times?

8 A shopkeeper is keen to sell his stock of left-handed scissors. He has read that 7% of the population is left-handed. What is the probability that the next person to enter his shop is right-handed?

9 A bag contains 8 red balls and x green ones. A ball is chosen at random; the probability that it is red is found to be 0.2. Work out the value of x.

10 A spinner is divided into 12 equal sectors.
It is spun 600 times. How often would you expect to spin:

   a a shaded sector   **b** an even number

   c a vowel   **d** a prime number?

11 There are 30 counters in a box. $\frac{2}{5}$ are red, $\frac{1}{3}$ are green and the rest are blue.

   a How many are blue?

   b A counter is taken out of the box without looking. What is the probability that it is:
      i blue   **ii** yellow   **iii** green   **iv** red?

12 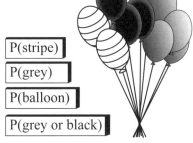 There are 9 balloons hanging. Donkor wants to pull one balloon string. He gets that balloon. Copy the scale, write down the probability and put the labels in the correct boxes.

P(stripe)

P(grey)

P(balloon)

P(grey or black)

Probability of drawing:

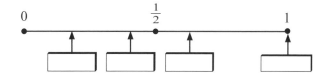

13 If the traffic lights show green for 45 seconds, amber for 3 seconds, red for 50 seconds and red and amber together for 2 seconds, what is the probability that a car will have to stop? (Note that when the green light shows it means go.)

14 If the probability of a bus being early is $\frac{1}{10}$ and the probability that it arrives late is $\frac{3}{5}$, what is the probability that it arrives on time?

15 The table gives the ages of pupils in a school.

Age next birthday	12	13	14	15	16	17
Number of boys	50	85	80	76	84	60
Number of girls	90	72	83	81	64	75

If one of the pupils had their birthday announced in the local radio:

a What is the probability that it is a boy who would be 17 years old on his birthday?

b What is the probability that it is someone under 14 years of age?

c What is the probability that it is a girl?

16 The table shows the results of rolling a dice 600 times.

Score	1	2	3	4	5	6
Frequency	83	91	106	120	101	99

a Show this information on a suitable line graph.

b Work out the relative frequency of each score. Give your answer as a fraction.

c Comment briefly whether you think this is an unbiased dice or not.

17 Abdul and Jamela have collected some data about a spinner on which the score is always 0 or 1. Abdul has spun the spinner 100 times and Jamela spun it 400 times.

	Number of 0s	Number of 1s
Abdul	66	34
Jamela	168	232

a Work out the experimental probability of getting a 1, using Abdul's results.

b Repeat this calculation using Jamela's result instead.

c Explain briefly which of the answers is more reliable.

d Suggest a way of obtaining an even more reliable answer.

SUMMARY

Probability	In mathematics **probability** means how likely something is to happen. The probability of an event occurring is measured on a scale with 'impossible' at one end and certain at the other.

Here is a probability scale:

impossible   very unlikely   unlikely   even chance   likely   very likely   certain

Random	If an item is chosen at **random** it means that every item has an equal chance of being chosen. '**At random**' means 'without looking' or 'not knowing what the outcome is in advance'.

Probability as a number

Probability is measured accurately using numbers. We use 0 for 'impossible' and 1 for 'certain'. If something is not certain to happen it must have a probability less than 1.

A probability scale looks like this:

impossible   unlikely   even chance   likely   certain

0 $\frac{1}{10}$ $\frac{1}{5}$ $\frac{3}{10}$ $\frac{2}{5}$ $\frac{1}{2}$ $\frac{3}{5}$ $\frac{7}{10}$ $\frac{4}{5}$ $\frac{9}{10}$ 1

Event	A thing that happens or takes place is called an **event**.
Outcome	The result of an event is called the **outcome**.
Trial	A **trial** is an action which results in one of several possible outcomes.
Dice	**Dice** are small cubes used in games. The faces are usually numbered 1 to 6.
Experiment	An experiment consists of a number of trials. The chance of certain events occurring can be predicted. For example if an ordinary dice is thrown, there are six possible outcomes. These are 1, 2, 3, 4, 5 and 6. The act of throwing the dice is called an experiment. The list 1, 2, 3, 4, 5, 6 is called the **set of all possible outcomes**.
Experimental probability	An estimate of probability, made by doing trials or experiments is called **experimental probability**.

Coin	A coin is a piece of money which can be thrown (called *tossing* or *spinning*) and has equal probabilities of landing on each of its two sides.
Head	The **head** is the name of one side of a coin usually having the picture of a head on it. This side of the coin is also known as **obverse**.
Tail	The **tail** of a coin is the side which is not a head. It is also known as the **reverse**.

$$\text{Probability of an event} = \frac{\text{Number of ways the event can happen}}{\text{Total number of possible outcomes}}$$

P(event not happening) = 1 − P(event happening)

Frequency	The **frequency** of an event is the number of times that it happens.
Relative frequency	The **relative frequency** of an event $= \dfrac{\text{frequency of an event}}{\text{total frequency}}$

Research	Sometimes you can use data collected by someone else. The data may have been collected over a number of years, such as how often it rains in Kumasi on Independence Day. Finding data this way is called **research**.

322

16 Vectors

EXTENSION

SUMMARY

RADAR is a mnemonic for **RA**dio **D**etection **A**nd **R**anging. It is an aerial on ships, ports and aerodromes. A signal like a radio or light wave is sent out from the aerial. It bounces off any object it meets, picked up again by the aerial and appears on a *radar screen* in the form of a bright spot of light. The actual screen is like a television set except that it has angles and concentric circles marked on it as shown below. Radar can detect objects as small as an insect or as large as a mountain.

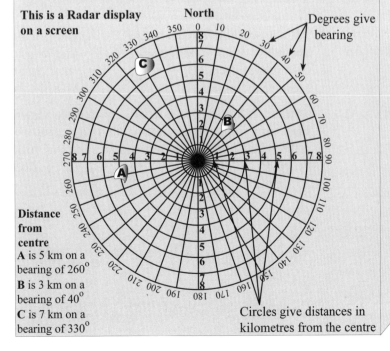

This is a Radar display on a screen

Degrees give bearing

Distance from centre
A is 5 km on a bearing of 260°
B is 3 km on a bearing of 40°
C is 7 km on a bearing of 330°

Circles give distances in kilometres from the centre

1 Bearings

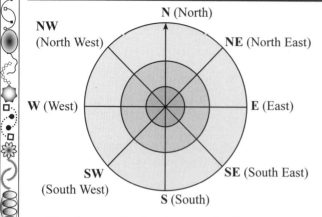

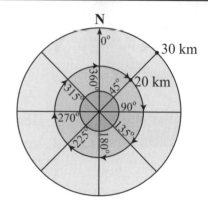

The four cardinal points are North, South, East and West. The directions **NE**, **SE**, **SW** and **NW** are frequently used.

The position of an object in an area can be described by giving its bearing and its distance from a central point.

Bearing

A **bearing** is an angle expressed in three digits to indicate direction.
Bearings are always measured clockwise starting from north.
If the angle is less than 100° put a zero as the first digit. For example 058° is the bearing for an angle of 58° clockwise from north.

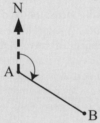

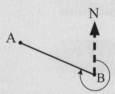

The *bearing of B from A* means that you are at A. You start at A. You face north. You turn clockwise until you are facing B. Measure the angle.

The *bearing of A from B* means that you are at B. You start at B. You face north. You turn clockwise until you are facing A. Measure the angle.

Note that if a bearing is measured from A the angle itself must be at A.
The bearing can be measured anything up to 360°.
A three-figure bearing is sometimes called a **circular bearing** or an **absolute bearing**.

Example

In each diagram give the bearing of B from A.

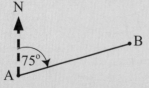

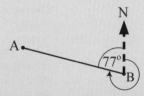

The bearing of B from A is 075°

The bearing of A from B is 283°
(Angle B = 360 − 77 = 283°)

Exercise 16:1

For each diagram give the bearing of B from A.

1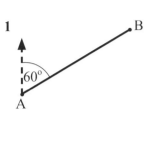

2

3

4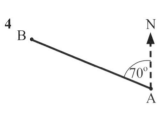

5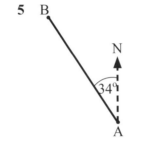

6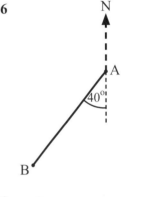

7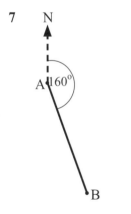

8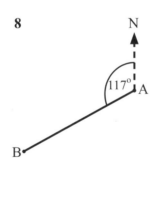

9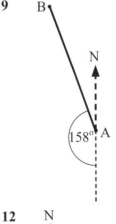

10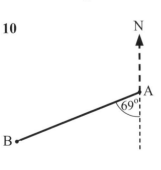

11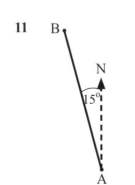

12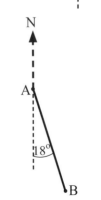

Example   Work out: **a** the bearing of B from A

b the bearing of A from B

A

•B

a Draw a north line at A
Join A to B with a straight line.

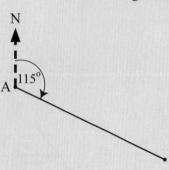

Measure clockwise from north
to the line joining A to B.

The bearing is 115°.

b Draw a north line at B

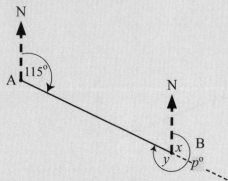

Measure the bearing clockwise from this
North line. The angle is $p°$.

Angle $p°$ is made up of angle x and angle y.
Angle x is 115° because the two north
lines are parallel.
Angle y is 180° because it is on a straight
line.
The bearing of A from B is $p°$.
∴ the bearing of A from B = 115 + 180
                          = 295°

Exercise 16:2

1 What is the bearing of:
  a B from P;
  b B from A ?

2 What is the bearing of:
  a Q from O;
  b T from O ?

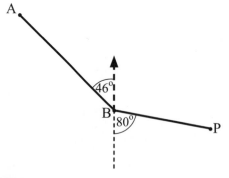

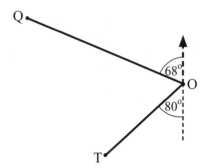

3 What is the bearing of:
 a V from E
 b E from W

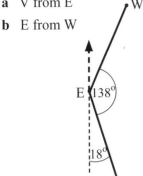

4 What is the bearing of:
 a D from J
 b J from Y

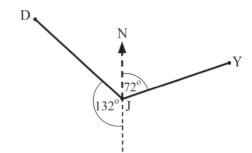

5 What is the bearing of:
 a X from Y
 b X from Z
 c Z from Y

6 What is the bearing of:
 a L from J
 b L from K
 c J from K

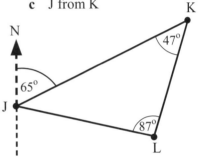

Back bearing In the diagram the bearing of
B from A is 68°.
The bearing of A from B is then
called the **back bearing**
(or **reverse bearing**).

In the diagram the back bearing
is 248° (or 180° + 68°).

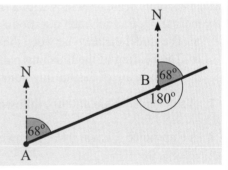

Here the bearing of A from B is given. Find the bearing of B from A (or back bearing).

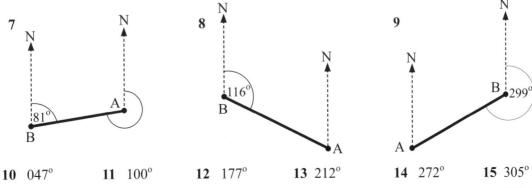

10 047°   **11** 100°   **12** 177°   **13** 212°   **14** 272°   **15** 305°

327

Example Brofoyedru is 10 km from Kejetia on a bearing of 062°. Dompoase is 6.5 km on a bearing of 188° from Brofoyedru. Using a scale drawing of 1 cm to 2 km find: **a** The direct distance from Kejetia to Dompoase.
b The bearing of Dompoase from Kejetia.
c The bearing of Kejetia from Brofoyedru.
d The bearing of Kejetia from Dompoase.

Use the information to sketch.

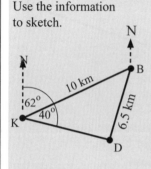

The problem is analysed by drawing to scale and using the properties of corresponding, alternate and straight angles to work out the angles.

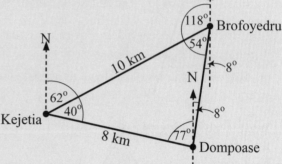

a The distance from Kejetia and Dompoase is measured as 8 km.

b The bearing of Dompoase from Kejetia = 62 + 40 = 102°.

c The bearing of Kejetia from Brofoyedru = 180 + 8 + 54 = 242°.

d The bearing of Kejetia from Dompoase = 180 + 103 = 283°.

Exercise 16:3

Make accurate scale drawings with a scale of 1 cm to 1 km, unless told otherwise.
By measuring, find for each question:
   a The direct distance between the starting point and the finishing point.
   b The bearing of the finishing point from the starting point.
   c The bearing of the starting point from the finishing point.

1 A ship sailed 6 km at 090°, followed by 5 km at 045°.

2 A ship sailed 3 km at 045°, followed by 8 km at 135°.

3 A ship sailed 4 km due east, followed by 4 km due north.

4 A ship sailed 4 km at 270°, followed by 3 km at 000°.

5 A ship sailed 5 km at 135°, then 9 km at 045°, then 8 km at 180°.

6 A ship sailed 3 km at 000°, then 10 km at 090°, then 6 km at 180°.

7 A ship sailed 150 km at 336°, then 150 km at 198°, then 65 km at 137°. (Use a scale of 1 cm to 20 km).

8 A ship sailed 66 km at 312°, then 88 km at 108°, then 56 km at 000°. (Use a scale of 1 cm to 10 km).

328

Draw to scale beginning with a small sketch.

9 Daban is 9 km from Kejetia on a bearing of 186°. Sofoline is 5 km at a bearing 274° from Kejetia. Find: **a** the direct distance from Daban to Sofoline.
  b the bearing of Sofoline from Daban.

10 A ship sails 10 km on a bearing 090° and then a further 7 km on a bearing 050°. How far is the ship now from its starting point?

11 A ship sails 6 km on a bearing 160° and then a further 10 km on a bearing 240°.
  a How far is the ship now from its starting point?
  b On what bearing must the ship sail so that it returns to its starting point?

12 A pilot makes a two-stage journey. Stage 1: 500 km on a bearing of 060°.
  Stage 2: 300 km on a bearing of 150°.
  Using a scale of 1 cm : 100 km work out the distance and bearing if the journey started at the end of stage 2 to the beginning of stage 1.

13 (500, 090) stands for a journey of 500 km on a bearing of 090°. Using your own scale find the direct journey represented by: (500, 090°) followed by (375, 250°).

14 Q and R are both 100 km from P.
  R is on a bearing of 225° from Q.

  Find by scale drawing:

  a The size of the angle PQR

  b The bearing of P from Q

  c The bearing of R from P

  d The bearing of P from R

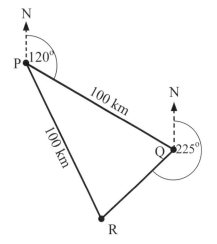

15 A helicopter sets out at point P and flies due north to a point Q at a distance of 120 km. It then flies due east to a point R. If the bearing of R from P is 037°, find:
  a the distance QR **b** the distance PR

16 Point B is 10 km from A on a bearing from 052°. Point C is 4 km from A on a bearing 107°. **a** How far is B from C?
  b What is the bearing of B from C?

Measuring Distances and Bearings

Exercise 16:4

Find the actual distance and the bearing of the Ahenfie Palace from each of the landmarks. You will need to measure with a ruler and use the scale at the bottom of the map to find the actual distances in kilometres. The dotted line is to help you position your protractor.

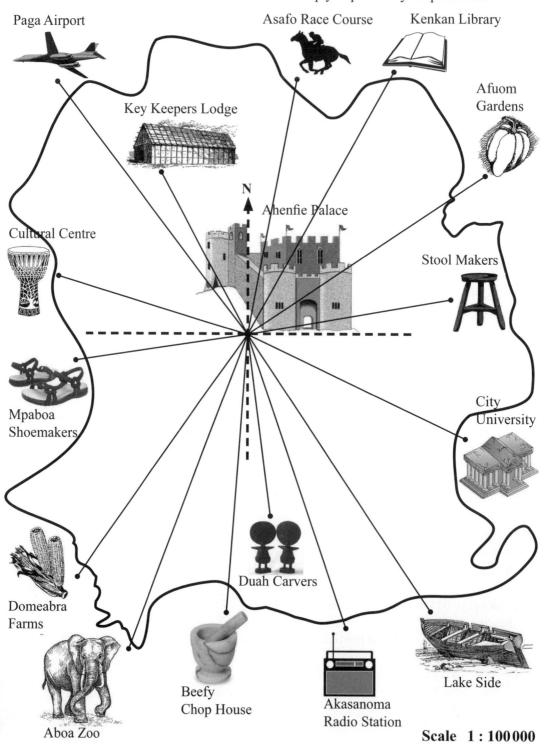

Paga Airport

Asafo Race Course

Kenkan Library

Afuom Gardens

Key Keepers Lodge

N

Ahenfie Palace

Cultural Centre

Stool Makers

Mpaboa Shoemakers

City University

Domeabra Farms

Duah Carvers

Beefy Chop House

Akasanoma Radio Station

Lake Side

Aboa Zoo

Scale   1 : 100 000

2   Vector notaton

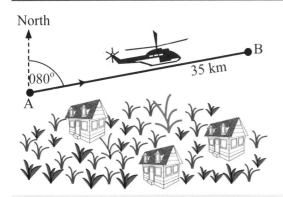

North

080°

35 km

A

B

A helicopter sets out from point A on this map and travels in a straight line to point B. The distance from A to B is 35 km and the bearing is 080°.
The line going from A to B in the direction of the arrow is called a **displacement vector** or simply a **vector**.

Scalar   Quantities which just have size are called **scalar** quantities. Examples of scalar are: mass (e.g. 20 kg) or length (e.g. 14 cm).

Displacement   The distance of an object measured from a given point in a given direction is called **displacement**.

Vector   Quantities which have both size and direction are called **vector** quantities. Examples of vector are force (e.g. 8 N acting upwards) or velocity (e.g. 30 km/h due south).

Vector quantities are usually represented by a line. The length of the line represents the size of the vector.
An arrow is placed on the line to show the direction of the vector e.g. $\overrightarrow{AB}$.

Example   The vector in the diagram starts at A and ends at B. The symbol for the vector from A to B is $\overrightarrow{AB}$. We can describe the vector $\overrightarrow{AB}$ completely by giving its length (35 km) and its direction (bearing - 080°). Sometimes vectors are written in bold type, vector $\overrightarrow{AB}$ as **a** (or <u>a</u>).

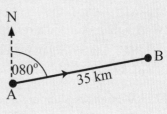

N

080°

35 km

A

B

Exercise 16:5

Draw these vectors using a scale of 1 cm : 1 m. Label each vector correctly.

1 $\overrightarrow{AB}$ 3 m due north   **2** $\overrightarrow{MN}$ 10 m due east   **3** $\overrightarrow{XY}$ 8 m due west

4 $\overrightarrow{ST}$ 7.5 m due south-east   **5** $\overrightarrow{PQ}$ 5 m due north-west   **6** $\overrightarrow{UV}$ 8.8 m due south-west

Draw these vectors using a scale 1 cm : 10 km. Label each vector.

7 $\overrightarrow{EF}$ is 42 km on a bearing of 200°.   **8** $\overrightarrow{WA}$ is 85 km on a bearing of 116°.

9 $\overrightarrow{HO}$ is 62 km on a bearing of 079°.   **10** $\overrightarrow{GA}$ is 100 km on a bearing of 172°.

11 $\overrightarrow{AS}$ is 94 km on a bearing of 254°.   **12** $\overrightarrow{WR}$ is 78 km on a bearing of 349°.

If P and Q are two points, then the vectors $\overrightarrow{PQ}$ and $\overrightarrow{QP}$ are in the opposite directions and have different bearings.

This diagram shows a vector $\overrightarrow{PQ}$ and its bearing.

This diagram shows $\overrightarrow{QP}$ and its bearing.

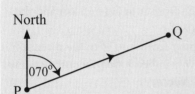

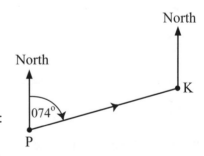

The bearing is always measured at the starting point of the vector.

13 A boat starts at a point P and travels along the vector $\overrightarrow{PQ}$ (40 km, bearing 040°). From Q it travels along the vector $\overrightarrow{QR}$ (55 km, bearing 130°).

  a Draw the vectors $\overrightarrow{PQ}$ and $\overrightarrow{QR}$ to scale.

  b Measure the length and bearing of the vector $\overrightarrow{PR}$.

14 A boat sails A to B, then from B to C. $\overrightarrow{AB}$ is 62 km on a bearing 100°. $\overrightarrow{BC}$ is 28 km on a bearing 200°. Find from a scale drawing the length and bearing of the vector $\overrightarrow{AC}$.

15 A boat sails on a triangular course XYZ. $\overrightarrow{XY}$ is 60 km on a bearing 165°. $\overrightarrow{YZ}$ is 70 km on a bearing 265°. Find from a scale drawing the length and bearing of $\overrightarrow{ZX}$.

16 A light motorised aircraft flies on a triangular course GEF. $\overrightarrow{GF}$ is 37 km on a bearing 295°. $\overrightarrow{FE}$ is 62 km on a bearing 080°. Find from a scale drawing the length and bearing of $\overrightarrow{EG}$.

17 Kwamena is planning a search for his missing friend. Searchpoint A is 500 m from the start on a bearing of 075°. Searchpoint B is 700 m from A on a bearing of 170°.

  a Make a scale drawing showing the positions of A and B. Use a scale of 1 cm = 100 m.

  b Find the distance and the bearing of the start from Searchpoint B.

18 Use the diagram shown to answer these questions

  a If the bearing of $\overrightarrow{PK}$ is 074° work out the bearing of $\overrightarrow{KP}$.

  b Draw a sketch of a vector $\overrightarrow{PK}$ whose bearing is 138° and work out the bearing of $\overrightarrow{KP}$.

  c Repeat **question a** for when the bearing of $\overrightarrow{PK}$ is:
    i 194°   **ii** 248°   **ii** 300°.

  d Can you find any rule for working out the bearing of $\overrightarrow{KP}$ when you are given the bearing of $\overrightarrow{PK}$?

3 Column vectors

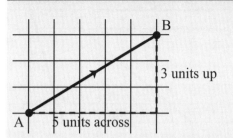

Vectors drawn on a grid can be described by giving the position of the end point in relation to the start point. The vector $\overrightarrow{AB}$ can be described by using two numbers.

The number of units across : 5

The number of units up   : 3

We write the two numbers one above the other in brackets.

$$\overrightarrow{AB} = \begin{bmatrix} 5 \\ 3 \end{bmatrix} \begin{matrix} \leftarrow \text{Across} \\ \leftarrow \text{Up} \end{matrix} \qquad \begin{bmatrix} 5 \\ 3 \end{bmatrix} \text{ is called a } \textbf{column vector.}$$

The two numbers are written in a column.

Across to the **right** is **positive** and to the **left** is **negative**.

Upwards is **positive** and **downwards** is **negative**.

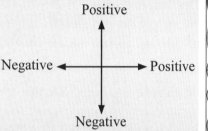

Examples $\overrightarrow{CD} = \begin{bmatrix} 3 \\ -4 \end{bmatrix}$ means 3 to the right
                                      4 down

$\underline{m} = \begin{bmatrix} -3 \\ -5 \end{bmatrix}$ means 3 to the left
                         5 down

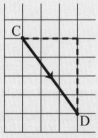

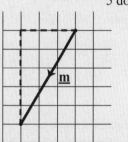

Exercise 16:6

Write these vectors as column vectors.

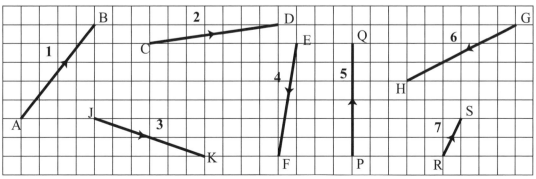

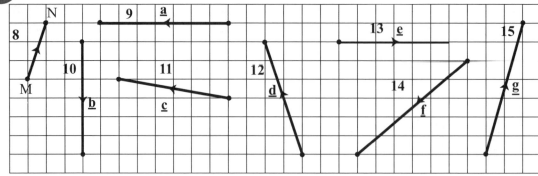

Exercise 16:7

Draw these vectors

1 $\overrightarrow{UT} = \begin{bmatrix} 1 \\ 5 \end{bmatrix}$ 2 $\overrightarrow{VW} = \begin{bmatrix} -2 \\ 4 \end{bmatrix}$ 3 $\overrightarrow{XY} = \begin{bmatrix} -6 \\ -5 \end{bmatrix}$ 4 $\overrightarrow{AS} = \begin{bmatrix} 3 \\ -4 \end{bmatrix}$

5 $\overrightarrow{PE} = \begin{bmatrix} 4 \\ 4 \end{bmatrix}$ 6 $\overrightarrow{IN} = \begin{bmatrix} 0 \\ -5 \end{bmatrix}$ 7 $\overrightarrow{TO} = \begin{bmatrix} -5 \\ 7 \end{bmatrix}$ 8 $\overrightarrow{UP} = \begin{bmatrix} -4 \\ -2 \end{bmatrix}$

9 $\underline{i} = \begin{bmatrix} 7 \\ 8 \end{bmatrix}$ 10 $\underline{j} = \begin{bmatrix} 6 \\ -4 \end{bmatrix}$ 11 $\underline{k} = \begin{bmatrix} -7 \\ 0 \end{bmatrix}$ 12 $\underline{l} = \begin{bmatrix} -3 \\ 2 \end{bmatrix}$

13 $\underline{m} = \begin{bmatrix} -3 \\ -4 \end{bmatrix}$ 14 $\underline{n} = \begin{bmatrix} -2 \\ 8 \end{bmatrix}$ 15 $\underline{p} = \begin{bmatrix} 6 \\ -7 \end{bmatrix}$ 16 $\underline{q} = \begin{bmatrix} -5 \\ -9 \end{bmatrix}$

17 $\underline{r} = \begin{bmatrix} -1 \\ -8 \end{bmatrix}$ 18 $\underline{s} = \begin{bmatrix} -5 \\ 5 \end{bmatrix}$ 19 $\underline{t} = \begin{bmatrix} -3 \\ 7 \end{bmatrix}$ 20 $\underline{u} = \begin{bmatrix} -8 \\ -2 \end{bmatrix}$

21 a   Stage one of the journey from Fort Metal Cross to Agona School can be written as $\begin{bmatrix} 5 \\ 0 \end{bmatrix}$.
The second stage is $\begin{bmatrix} 1 \\ 5 \end{bmatrix}$. Write the other stages in this way to complete the journey.

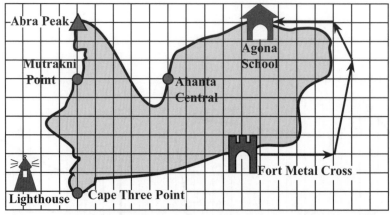

  b   Write down some vectors for a journey i   from Ahanta Central to Abra Peak
                                            ii   from Cape three Point to Fort Metal Cross
  c   Give your partner a starting point and some vectors and ask him for the destination.

4 Equal vectors

Equal vectors Vectors are **equal** if they have the same length and are in the same direction. Equal vectors have the same column vector.

In this diagram $\overrightarrow{PQ} = \overrightarrow{RS}$ because both of them are equal to $\begin{bmatrix} 4 \\ 2 \end{bmatrix}$.

$\overrightarrow{PQ}$ is not equal to $\overrightarrow{TU}$, because the column vector of $\overrightarrow{TU}$ is $\begin{bmatrix} -4 \\ 2 \end{bmatrix}$.

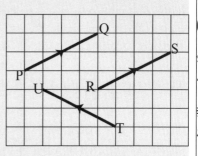

Exercise 16:8

1 Write down the equal vectors and their column vectors.

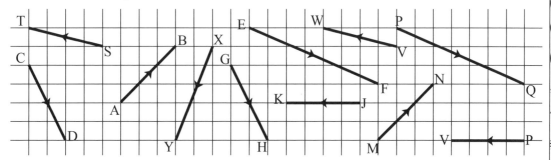

Inverse vector

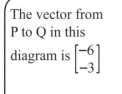

The vector from P to Q in this diagram is $\begin{bmatrix} -6 \\ -3 \end{bmatrix}$

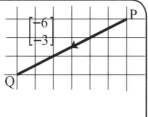

The vector which takes you back from Q to P is $\begin{bmatrix} 6 \\ 3 \end{bmatrix}$

$\begin{bmatrix} -6 \\ -3 \end{bmatrix}$ is called the **inverse** of $\begin{bmatrix} 6 \\ 3 \end{bmatrix}$

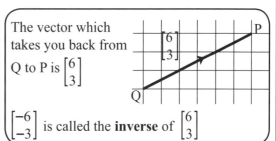

2 Draw and write down the inverse of each of these vectors:

a $\begin{bmatrix} -7 \\ 3 \end{bmatrix}$ b $\begin{bmatrix} 6 \\ 1 \end{bmatrix}$ c $\begin{bmatrix} -5 \\ 0 \end{bmatrix}$ d $\begin{bmatrix} 1 \\ -4 \end{bmatrix}$ e $\begin{bmatrix} 0 \\ -4 \end{bmatrix}$

f $\begin{bmatrix} 5 \\ -6 \end{bmatrix}$ g $\begin{bmatrix} -2 \\ 7 \end{bmatrix}$ h $\begin{bmatrix} 4 \\ -4 \end{bmatrix}$ i $\begin{bmatrix} 2 \\ -5 \end{bmatrix}$ j $\begin{bmatrix} 1 \\ 2 \end{bmatrix}$

3 Write the inverse of these vectors:

a $\begin{bmatrix} 10 \\ -16 \end{bmatrix}$ b $\begin{bmatrix} -9 \\ 23 \end{bmatrix}$ c $\begin{bmatrix} -20 \\ -37 \end{bmatrix}$ d $\begin{bmatrix} 47 \\ -16 \end{bmatrix}$ e $\begin{bmatrix} 100 \\ -16 \end{bmatrix}$

5 Addition of vectors

In the diagram, $\overrightarrow{AB} = \begin{bmatrix} 4 \\ 1 \end{bmatrix}$ and $\overrightarrow{BC} = \begin{bmatrix} 2 \\ 3 \end{bmatrix}$

The two vectors can be added like this:

$\overrightarrow{AB} + \overrightarrow{BC} = \begin{bmatrix} 4 \\ 1 \end{bmatrix} + \begin{bmatrix} 2 \\ 3 \end{bmatrix}$

Notice the direction of the arrows.

$= \begin{bmatrix} 4+2 \\ 1+3 \end{bmatrix}$ ⟵ The top numbers add up to 6
⟵ The bottom numbers add up to 4

The result $= \begin{bmatrix} 6 \\ 4 \end{bmatrix}$ is the column vector of $\overrightarrow{AC}$ (dotted line).

Examples **i** If $\overrightarrow{DE} = \begin{bmatrix} -2 \\ 3 \end{bmatrix}$ and $\overrightarrow{EF} = \begin{bmatrix} 6 \\ 2 \end{bmatrix}$ work out $\overrightarrow{DE} + \overrightarrow{EF}$.

$$\overrightarrow{DE} + \overrightarrow{EF} = \begin{bmatrix} -2 \\ 3 \end{bmatrix} + \begin{bmatrix} 6 \\ 2 \end{bmatrix} = \begin{bmatrix} -2+6 \\ 3+2 \end{bmatrix} = \begin{bmatrix} 4 \\ 5 \end{bmatrix}$$

ii If $\underline{a} = \begin{bmatrix} 5 \\ 2 \end{bmatrix}$ and $\underline{b} = \begin{bmatrix} 3 \\ 4 \end{bmatrix}$ work out $\underline{a} + \underline{b}$

$$\underline{a} + \underline{b} = \begin{bmatrix} 5 \\ 2 \end{bmatrix} + \begin{bmatrix} 3 \\ 4 \end{bmatrix} = \begin{bmatrix} 5+3 \\ 2+4 \end{bmatrix} = \begin{bmatrix} 8 \\ 6 \end{bmatrix}$$

Zero vector A **zero vect**or is a vector of length 0 and size 0. Zero vector is also called a **null vector**.

$\underline{w} = \underline{u} + \underline{v}$ If $\underline{u} = \begin{bmatrix} 3 \\ 4 \end{bmatrix}$ and $\underline{v} = \begin{bmatrix} -3 \\ -4 \end{bmatrix}$ $\underline{u} + \underline{v} = \begin{bmatrix} 3 \\ 4 \end{bmatrix} + \begin{bmatrix} -3 \\ -4 \end{bmatrix} = \begin{bmatrix} 0 \\ 0 \end{bmatrix}$

$\underline{w} = \begin{bmatrix} 0 \\ 0 \end{bmatrix}$ $\therefore \underline{w}$ is a zero vector

Exercise 16:9

Add these vectors:

1 $\begin{bmatrix} 4 \\ 6 \end{bmatrix} + \begin{bmatrix} 5 \\ 2 \end{bmatrix}$ **2** $\begin{bmatrix} 3 \\ 1 \end{bmatrix} + \begin{bmatrix} 4 \\ 4 \end{bmatrix}$ **3** $\begin{bmatrix} 1 \\ -5 \end{bmatrix} + \begin{bmatrix} -1 \\ 2 \end{bmatrix}$ **4** $\begin{bmatrix} -3 \\ -6 \end{bmatrix} + \begin{bmatrix} -2 \\ 5 \end{bmatrix}$

5 $\begin{bmatrix} 7 \\ 2 \end{bmatrix} + \begin{bmatrix} -6 \\ 6 \end{bmatrix}$ **6** $\begin{bmatrix} 9 \\ -5 \end{bmatrix} + \begin{bmatrix} -4 \\ -5 \end{bmatrix}$ **7** $\begin{bmatrix} -5 \\ 8 \end{bmatrix} + \begin{bmatrix} -8 \\ -9 \end{bmatrix}$ **8** $\begin{bmatrix} -1 \\ -5 \end{bmatrix} + \begin{bmatrix} -2 \\ 0 \end{bmatrix}$

9 $\begin{bmatrix} -9 \\ -7 \end{bmatrix} + \begin{bmatrix} -2 \\ 9 \end{bmatrix}$ **10** $\begin{bmatrix} -8 \\ 1 \end{bmatrix} + \begin{bmatrix} 0 \\ -11 \end{bmatrix}$ **11** $\begin{bmatrix} -2 \\ -7 \end{bmatrix} + \begin{bmatrix} 0 \\ 7 \end{bmatrix}$ **12** $\begin{bmatrix} -3 \\ -4 \end{bmatrix} + \begin{bmatrix} 4 \\ -3 \end{bmatrix}$

13 $\begin{bmatrix} 24 \\ 9 \end{bmatrix} + \begin{bmatrix} 16 \\ -7 \end{bmatrix}$ **14** $\begin{bmatrix} -29 \\ 17 \end{bmatrix} + \begin{bmatrix} 35 \\ -19 \end{bmatrix}$ **15** $\begin{bmatrix} 27 \\ -27 \end{bmatrix} + \begin{bmatrix} -27 \\ 28 \end{bmatrix}$ **16** $\begin{bmatrix} 6 \\ -7 \end{bmatrix} + \begin{bmatrix} -36 \\ 28 \end{bmatrix}$

For each of the diagrams given write the vector sum that is shown as a dotted line:

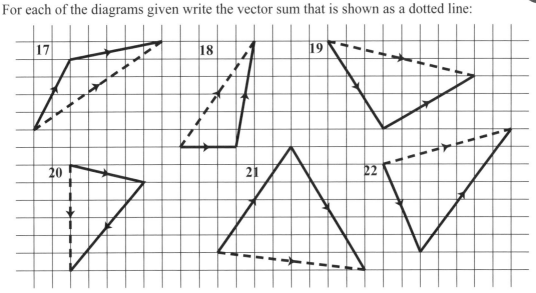

Add the given pairs of vectors and draw the result on a square grid.

23 $\begin{bmatrix} 2 \\ 3 \end{bmatrix} + \begin{bmatrix} 4 \\ 4 \end{bmatrix}$ **24** $\begin{bmatrix} -2 \\ -3 \end{bmatrix} + \begin{bmatrix} -4 \\ -1 \end{bmatrix}$ **25** $\begin{bmatrix} 7 \\ 0 \end{bmatrix} + \begin{bmatrix} -3 \\ 6 \end{bmatrix}$ **26** $\begin{bmatrix} -4 \\ -1 \end{bmatrix} + \begin{bmatrix} -2 \\ -3 \end{bmatrix}$

27 $\begin{bmatrix} 1 \\ -5 \end{bmatrix} + \begin{bmatrix} -1 \\ 2 \end{bmatrix}$ **28** $\begin{bmatrix} 4 \\ 6 \end{bmatrix} + \begin{bmatrix} 2 \\ -3 \end{bmatrix}$ **29** $\begin{bmatrix} 0 \\ -4 \end{bmatrix} + \begin{bmatrix} -6 \\ 6 \end{bmatrix}$ **30** $\begin{bmatrix} -5 \\ -5 \end{bmatrix} + \begin{bmatrix} 6 \\ 6 \end{bmatrix}$

Work out and draw diagrams to show $\overrightarrow{AB} + \overrightarrow{BC}$

31 $\overrightarrow{AB} = \begin{bmatrix} 4 \\ -2 \end{bmatrix}$ and $\overrightarrow{BC} = \begin{bmatrix} -1 \\ -3 \end{bmatrix}$ **32** $\overrightarrow{AB} = \begin{bmatrix} 3 \\ -7 \end{bmatrix}$ and $\overrightarrow{BC} = \begin{bmatrix} -5 \\ 2 \end{bmatrix}$

33 $\overrightarrow{AB} = \begin{bmatrix} 5 \\ 1 \end{bmatrix}$ and $\overrightarrow{BC} = \begin{bmatrix} 5 \\ 1 \end{bmatrix}$ **34** $\overrightarrow{AB} = \begin{bmatrix} -1 \\ -4 \end{bmatrix}$ and $\overrightarrow{BC} = \begin{bmatrix} 5 \\ -2 \end{bmatrix}$

35 $\overrightarrow{AB} = \begin{bmatrix} -3 \\ -5 \end{bmatrix}$ and $\overrightarrow{BC} = \begin{bmatrix} 1 \\ 5 \end{bmatrix}$ **36** $\overrightarrow{AB} = \begin{bmatrix} -6 \\ -1 \end{bmatrix}$ and $\overrightarrow{BC} = \begin{bmatrix} 12 \\ 2 \end{bmatrix}$

$\begin{bmatrix} -7 \\ -2 \end{bmatrix}$ represents 7 steps west and 2 steps south. Copy and complete these:

37 $\begin{bmatrix} -9 \\ 1 \end{bmatrix} + \begin{bmatrix} -3 \\ -5 \end{bmatrix}$ represents

—— steps —— and

—— steps ——

followed by —— steps —— and

—— steps —— .

makes —— steps —— .

38 $\begin{bmatrix} 16 \\ -4 \end{bmatrix} + \begin{bmatrix} 11 \\ 15 \end{bmatrix}$ represents

—— steps —— and

—— steps ——

followed by —— steps —— and

—— steps ——

makes —— steps —— .

337

6 Subtraction of vectors

If $\overrightarrow{AB} = \begin{bmatrix} 4 \\ 2 \end{bmatrix}$ the inverse of $\overrightarrow{AB}$ is written as $-\overrightarrow{AB} = \begin{bmatrix} -4 \\ -2 \end{bmatrix}$ $\therefore$ $-\overrightarrow{AB} = \overrightarrow{BA}$

Let $\overrightarrow{AB} = \begin{bmatrix} 4 \\ 2 \end{bmatrix}$ and $\overrightarrow{BC} = \begin{bmatrix} 3 \\ 4 \end{bmatrix}$

$\overrightarrow{AB} - \overrightarrow{BC} = \begin{bmatrix} 4 \\ 2 \end{bmatrix} - \begin{bmatrix} 3 \\ 4 \end{bmatrix} = \begin{bmatrix} 4-3 \\ 2-4 \end{bmatrix} = \begin{bmatrix} 1 \\ -2 \end{bmatrix}$

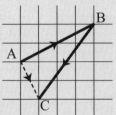

$-\overrightarrow{BC}$ is the inverse of $\overrightarrow{BC}$

With ordinary numbers, 'subtract 4' is the same as 'add −4'.

Similarly with vectors, 'subtract $\underline{q}$ is the same as 'add $-\underline{q}$'

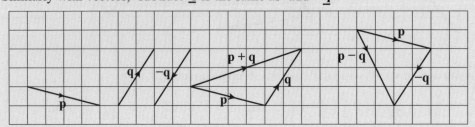

Exercise 16:10

Work out these:

1 $\begin{bmatrix} 7 \\ 2 \end{bmatrix} - \begin{bmatrix} 6 \\ 0 \end{bmatrix}$
2 $\begin{bmatrix} 4 \\ 5 \end{bmatrix} - \begin{bmatrix} 3 \\ 2 \end{bmatrix}$
3 $\begin{bmatrix} 5 \\ 6 \end{bmatrix} - \begin{bmatrix} 5 \\ 3 \end{bmatrix}$
4 $\begin{bmatrix} 8 \\ -9 \end{bmatrix} - \begin{bmatrix} 6 \\ 1 \end{bmatrix}$

5 $\begin{bmatrix} 2 \\ 5 \end{bmatrix} - \begin{bmatrix} 4 \\ 4 \end{bmatrix}$
6 $\begin{bmatrix} -1 \\ -3 \end{bmatrix} - \begin{bmatrix} 3 \\ 5 \end{bmatrix}$
7 $\begin{bmatrix} 0 \\ 4 \end{bmatrix} - \begin{bmatrix} -1 \\ -4 \end{bmatrix}$
8 $\begin{bmatrix} 7 \\ -2 \end{bmatrix} - \begin{bmatrix} 3 \\ -1 \end{bmatrix}$

9 $\begin{bmatrix} -10 \\ 5 \end{bmatrix} - \begin{bmatrix} 7 \\ 14 \end{bmatrix}$
10 $\begin{bmatrix} -9 \\ -13 \end{bmatrix} - \begin{bmatrix} -8 \\ 19 \end{bmatrix}$
11 $\begin{bmatrix} 2 \\ 12 \end{bmatrix} - \begin{bmatrix} 0 \\ -17 \end{bmatrix}$
12 $\begin{bmatrix} -17 \\ -7 \end{bmatrix} - \begin{bmatrix} -5 \\ -5 \end{bmatrix}$

Work out and draw diagrams to show $\overrightarrow{AB} - \overrightarrow{BC}$

13 $\overrightarrow{AB} = \begin{bmatrix} 4 \\ -1 \end{bmatrix}$ and $\overrightarrow{BC} = \begin{bmatrix} 2 \\ 3 \end{bmatrix}$
14 $\overrightarrow{AB} = \begin{bmatrix} 6 \\ 6 \end{bmatrix}$ and $\overrightarrow{BC} = \begin{bmatrix} 5 \\ 2 \end{bmatrix}$

15 $\overrightarrow{AB} = \begin{bmatrix} 0 \\ -4 \end{bmatrix}$ and $\overrightarrow{BC} = \begin{bmatrix} -4 \\ 0 \end{bmatrix}$
16 $\overrightarrow{AB} = \begin{bmatrix} -9 \\ 10 \end{bmatrix}$ and $\overrightarrow{BC} = \begin{bmatrix} -2 \\ -2 \end{bmatrix}$

17 $\overrightarrow{AB} = \begin{bmatrix} 4 \\ 0 \end{bmatrix}$ and $\overrightarrow{BC} = \begin{bmatrix} 3 \\ 0 \end{bmatrix}$
18 $\overrightarrow{AB} = \begin{bmatrix} -8 \\ -7 \end{bmatrix}$ and $\overrightarrow{BC} = \begin{bmatrix} -6 \\ -5 \end{bmatrix}$

19 $\overrightarrow{AB} = \begin{bmatrix} -5 \\ 8 \end{bmatrix}$ and $\overrightarrow{BC} = \begin{bmatrix} 7 \\ 8 \end{bmatrix}$
20 $\overrightarrow{AB} = \begin{bmatrix} 4 \\ -9 \end{bmatrix}$ and $\overrightarrow{BC} = \begin{bmatrix} -1 \\ 3 \end{bmatrix}$

7 Multiples of vectors

You can multiply a vector by a scalar. If a vector $\overrightarrow{AB}$ is 5 km due East, then the vector $3\overrightarrow{AB}$ is 15 km due East.

In general: **if k is any number the vector $k\overrightarrow{AB}$ is a vector in the same direction as $\overrightarrow{AB}$ whose length is k times the length of $\overrightarrow{AB}$.**

Examples If $\overrightarrow{PQ} = \begin{bmatrix} 3 \\ -5 \end{bmatrix}$, find: **a** $2\overrightarrow{PQ}$ **b** $-3\overrightarrow{PQ}$

$$\textbf{a } 2\overrightarrow{PQ} = 2\begin{bmatrix} 3 \\ -5 \end{bmatrix} = 2 \times \begin{bmatrix} 3 \\ -5 \end{bmatrix} = \begin{bmatrix} 2 \times 3 \\ 2 \times -5 \end{bmatrix} = \begin{bmatrix} 6 \\ -10 \end{bmatrix}$$

$$\textbf{b } -3\overrightarrow{PQ} = -3\begin{bmatrix} 3 \\ -5 \end{bmatrix} = -3 \times \begin{bmatrix} 3 \\ -5 \end{bmatrix} = \begin{bmatrix} -3 \times 3 \\ -3 \times -5 \end{bmatrix} = \begin{bmatrix} -9 \\ 15 \end{bmatrix}$$

If $\underline{v} = \begin{bmatrix} 6 \\ 4 \end{bmatrix}$, find: **c** $\frac{1}{2}\underline{v}$ **d** $-\frac{3}{2}\underline{v}$

$$\textbf{c } \tfrac{1}{2}\underline{v} = \tfrac{1}{2}\begin{bmatrix} 6 \\ 4 \end{bmatrix} = \tfrac{1}{2} \times \begin{bmatrix} 6 \\ 4 \end{bmatrix} = \begin{bmatrix} \tfrac{1}{2} \times 6 \\ \tfrac{1}{2} \times 4 \end{bmatrix} = \begin{bmatrix} 3 \\ 2 \end{bmatrix}$$

$$\textbf{d } -\tfrac{3}{2}\underline{v} = -\tfrac{3}{2}\begin{bmatrix} 6 \\ 4 \end{bmatrix} = -\tfrac{3}{2} \times \begin{bmatrix} 6 \\ 4 \end{bmatrix} = \begin{bmatrix} -\tfrac{3}{2} \times 6 \\ -\tfrac{3}{2} \times 4 \end{bmatrix} = \begin{bmatrix} -9 \\ -6 \end{bmatrix}$$

Exercise 16:11

1 If $\overrightarrow{AB} = \begin{bmatrix} 2 \\ 6 \end{bmatrix}$ find: **a** $2\overrightarrow{AB}$ **b** $5\overrightarrow{AB}$ **c** $\frac{1}{2}\overrightarrow{AB}$

2 If $\overrightarrow{PQ} = \begin{bmatrix} 4 \\ -1 \end{bmatrix}$ find: **a** $3\overrightarrow{PQ}$ **b** $-2\overrightarrow{PQ}$ **c** $7\overrightarrow{PQ}$

3 If $\underline{r} = \begin{bmatrix} -5 \\ 4 \end{bmatrix}$ find: **a** $-\underline{r}$ **b** $-3\underline{r}$ **c** $5\underline{r}$

4 If $\underline{v} = \begin{bmatrix} 8 \\ 6 \end{bmatrix}$ find: **a** $-3\underline{v}$ **b** $\frac{3}{2}\underline{v}$ **c** $\frac{3}{4}\underline{v}$

5 If $\underline{x} = \begin{bmatrix} 4 \\ 2 \end{bmatrix}$, $\underline{y} = \begin{bmatrix} -3 \\ 4 \end{bmatrix}$ and $\underline{z} = \begin{bmatrix} -8 \\ -6 \end{bmatrix}$ work out:

a $\frac{3}{2}\underline{z}$ **b** $2(\underline{x} - \underline{z})$ **c** $4(\underline{z} + 2\underline{y})$ **d** $\frac{1}{2}\underline{z} + \underline{x}$ **e** $\frac{1}{2}(-\underline{x} - \underline{z})$ **f** $6(\frac{1}{2}\underline{z} - 3\underline{x})$

6 If $\underline{i} = \begin{bmatrix} 0 \\ -1 \end{bmatrix}$, $\underline{j} = \begin{bmatrix} 5 \\ 4 \end{bmatrix}$ and $\underline{k} = \begin{bmatrix} -3 \\ -3 \end{bmatrix}$ work out:

a $\frac{4}{5}\underline{j}$ **b** $2(4\underline{i} - \underline{j})$ **c** $2(\underline{j} - \underline{k})$ **d** $\frac{1}{2}(\underline{i} + \underline{k})$ **e** $3(\underline{k} - \underline{j}) - \underline{i}$ **f** $\frac{2}{3}\underline{i} + \frac{3}{4}\underline{j}$

EXTENSION

1 State whether each of these is scalar or vector quantity:
  a a force of 40 N   b a mass of 58 kg   c an acceleration of 6 m/s²
  d a distance of 3 km   e time of 9 sec   f a change of position of 23 km due west

2 Mark a point P near the centre of a page in your exercise book then mark the north line.
  Using a scale of 1 cm to 1 km plot these points.

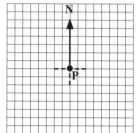

	Place	Distance from P (km)	Bearing
a	Nsuta	7.0	066°
b	Tetrem	5.6	270°
c	Jamasi	2.9	199°
d	Wiamoase	9.3	325°
e	Kwaman	8.5	154°

3 The bearing of A from B is given. Find the bearing of B from A.

a 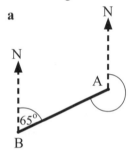   b 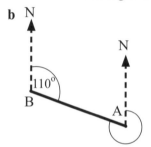   c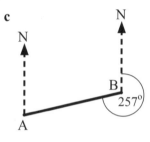

4 A **ferryboat** is a boat used regularly to convey people or goods over a short distance.
  A ferryboat is sailing on a bearing of 128°. Another is sailing in exactly the opposite
  direction. On what bearing is this second ferry sailing?

  Starboard is the right-hand side and **port** is the left-hand side of a ship or aircraft.

5 A ship sails 8 km on a bearing of 064°. Find its new bearing after 6 km if it turns through:
  a 95° to starboard   b 123° to port   c 180° to starboard   d 25° to port

6 An aeroplane flies 40 km on a bearing of 267°. Find its new bearing after 60 km if it turns:
  a 218° to starboard   b 180° to port   c 40° to starboard   d 108° to port

7 (60, 050°) stands for a journey of 60 km on a bearing of 050°. Find the single journey
  represented by (60, 050°) followed by (40, 325°) followed by (46, 265°).

8 Find the bearing of: a Q from P
                         b R from P
                         c P from Q
                         d Q from R

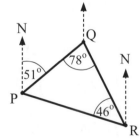

9 A helicopter pilot is to make a 'round trip' calling at three hilltops, Soro, Bepo and Anim, before returning to base at Efie. The diagram shows a sketch of the route he takes.

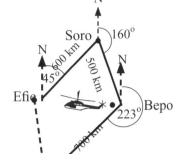

  a Draw the diagram to scale.
  b Which hilltop is nearest to Efie?
  c What bearing must the pilot take to return straight from Anim to Efie?
  d What is the distance from Bepo to Efie?

10 In the given vector sums, find the missing component:

  a $\begin{bmatrix} 5 \\ -3 \end{bmatrix} + \begin{bmatrix} ? \\ ? \end{bmatrix} = \begin{bmatrix} 7 \\ 7 \end{bmatrix}$ **b** $\begin{bmatrix} 5 \\ -3 \end{bmatrix} + \begin{bmatrix} ? \\ ? \end{bmatrix} = \begin{bmatrix} -8 \\ -5 \end{bmatrix}$ **c** $\begin{bmatrix} -8 \\ 2 \end{bmatrix} + \begin{bmatrix} ? \\ ? \end{bmatrix} = \begin{bmatrix} -7 \\ 0 \end{bmatrix}$

11 If $\overrightarrow{MT} = \begin{bmatrix} -5 \\ 6\frac{1}{5} \end{bmatrix}$, find: **a** $3\overrightarrow{MT}$ **b** $-2\overrightarrow{MT}$ **c** $-10\overrightarrow{MT}$ **d** $\frac{5}{7}\overrightarrow{MT}$

12 Make two copies of the diagram.

  a On the first copy show $\overrightarrow{AB} + \overrightarrow{AC}$

  b On the second copy show $\overrightarrow{AB} - \overrightarrow{AC}$

13 Write down the vector columns you will use to make these journeys:

  a from Akwantonbra to Wiawso

  b from Asanteya to Edukrom

  c from Bodi to Dadieso

  d from Sankore to Akwantonbra

  e from Edukrom to Asanteya

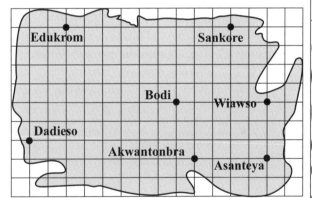

14 If $\underline{v} = \begin{bmatrix} 3 \\ -4 \end{bmatrix}$ and $\underline{w} = \begin{bmatrix} -5 \\ -15 \end{bmatrix}$ find:

  a $3\underline{v} + \underline{w}$ **b** $\underline{v} - \frac{2}{5}\underline{w}$ **c** $4(\underline{v} + \underline{w})$ **d** $5\underline{w} - 6\underline{v}$ **e** $\frac{1}{12}\underline{v} - \frac{1}{100}\underline{w}$

15 Given that $\begin{bmatrix} 2 \\ x \end{bmatrix} + \begin{bmatrix} x \\ y \end{bmatrix} = \begin{bmatrix} 7 \\ -4 \end{bmatrix}$, find the values of x and y.

16 Solve the vector equation: **a** $\begin{bmatrix} x \\ 4 \end{bmatrix} - \begin{bmatrix} -5 \\ y \end{bmatrix} = \begin{bmatrix} 6 \\ y \end{bmatrix}$ **b** $\begin{bmatrix} 2x \\ y \end{bmatrix} + \begin{bmatrix} x \\ 3y \end{bmatrix} = \begin{bmatrix} -5 \\ 6 \end{bmatrix}$

17 i Kwaku earns pocket money by selling newspapers and cleaning cars. Here is a table showing the minutes he spent on each of these jobs during one week.

	Mon	Tues	Wed	Thur	Fri	Sat	Sun
Cleaning cars	60	90	75	0	75	90	30
Selling newspapers	30	0	30	75	45	30	75

a Put these down as vector columns and find the total. The first and second are done for you:

$$\begin{bmatrix} 60 \\ 30 \end{bmatrix} + \begin{bmatrix} 90 \\ 0 \end{bmatrix} + \begin{bmatrix} \ \\ \ \end{bmatrix} + \begin{bmatrix} \ \\ \ \end{bmatrix} + \begin{bmatrix} \ \\ \ \end{bmatrix} + \begin{bmatrix} \ \\ \ \end{bmatrix} + \begin{bmatrix} \ \\ \ \end{bmatrix} = \begin{bmatrix} \ \\ \ \end{bmatrix}$$

b What information is given by the total vector?

ii On Monday the graph shows 60 minutes cleaning cars and 30 minutes selling papers. At the end of Tuesday a total of 150 minutes has been spent cleaning cars and 30 minutes selling newspapers. At the end of Wednesday there is a total of 225 minutes cleaning cars and 60 minutes selling newspapers.

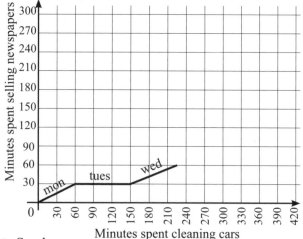

Graph of Kwaku's jobs during one week

a Copy the graph.

b Complete the line for Thursday to Sunday.

18 P is the point (1, 4), Q is the point (5, 2) and $\overrightarrow{PS} = \begin{bmatrix} 7 \\ 3 \end{bmatrix}$.

a Write down the coordinates of the point S. **b** PQRSP is a parallelogram. Find $\overrightarrow{PR}$.

19 Solve the vector equations **a** $\begin{bmatrix} x \\ 4 \end{bmatrix} - \begin{bmatrix} -5 \\ y \end{bmatrix} = \begin{bmatrix} 6 \\ y \end{bmatrix}$ **b** $\begin{bmatrix} 2x \\ y \end{bmatrix} + \begin{bmatrix} x \\ 3y \end{bmatrix} = \begin{bmatrix} -9 \\ 6 \end{bmatrix}$

20 This diagram was drawn on squared paper, but most of the squares have been rubbed out. Without using squared paper yourself, work out the column vector for:

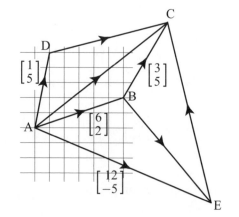

a $\overrightarrow{AC}$ **b** $\overrightarrow{DC}$

c $\overrightarrow{BE}$ **d** $\overrightarrow{EC}$

SUMMARY

Bearing	A **bearing** is an angle expressed in three digits to indicate direction. **Bearings are always measured clockwise starting from north.** If the angle is less than 100°, put a zero as the first digit. For example 058° is the bearing for an angle of 58° clockwise from north.
Scalar	Quantities which just have size are called **scalar** quantities. Examples of scalar are: mass (e.g. 20 kg) or length (e.g. 14 cm)
Displacement	The distance of an object measured from a given point in a given direction is called **displacement**.
Vector	Quantities which have both size and direction are called **vector** quantities. Examples of vector are force (e.g. 8 N acting upwards) or velocity (e.g. 30 km/h due south). Vector quantities are usually represented by a line. The length of the line represents the size of the vector. An arrow is placed on the line to show the direction of the vector e.g. $\overrightarrow{AB}$.

Column vectors

Vectors drawn on a grid can be described by giving the position of the end point in relation to the start point. The vector $\overrightarrow{AB}$ can be described by using two numbers.

The number of units across : 5

The number of units up   : 3

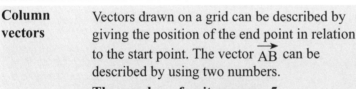

We write the two numbers one above the other in brackets. $\begin{bmatrix} 5 \\ 3 \end{bmatrix}$ is called a **column vector**.

Equal vectors   Vectors are equal if they have the same length and are in the same direction. Equal vectors have the same column vector.

Zero vector   A **zero vector** is a vector of length 0 and size 0. A zero vector is also called a **null vector**.

Addition of vectors

Two vectors can be added.

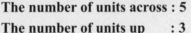

If $\overrightarrow{AB} = \begin{bmatrix} 4 \\ 2 \end{bmatrix}$ and $\overrightarrow{BC} = \begin{bmatrix} 2 \\ 3 \end{bmatrix}$ then $\overrightarrow{AB} + \overrightarrow{BC} = \begin{bmatrix} 4 \\ 2 \end{bmatrix} + \begin{bmatrix} 2 \\ 3 \end{bmatrix} = \begin{bmatrix} 4+2 \\ 2+3 \end{bmatrix}$

The result $\begin{bmatrix} 6 \\ 5 \end{bmatrix}$ is the column vector of $\overrightarrow{AC}$.

Subtraction of vectors

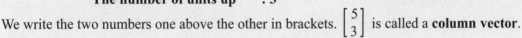

If $\overrightarrow{AB} = \begin{bmatrix} 4 \\ 2 \end{bmatrix}$ and $\overrightarrow{BC} = \begin{bmatrix} 3 \\ 4 \end{bmatrix}$ then $\overrightarrow{AB} - \overrightarrow{BC} = \begin{bmatrix} 4 \\ 2 \end{bmatrix} - \begin{bmatrix} 3 \\ 4 \end{bmatrix} = \begin{bmatrix} 1 \\ -2 \end{bmatrix}$

Multiples of vectors

A vector can be multiplied by a scalar.

In general: **if k is any number, the vector $k\overrightarrow{AB}$ is a vector in the same direction as $\overrightarrow{AB}$ whose length is k times the length of $\overrightarrow{AB}$.**

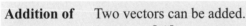

If $\overrightarrow{PQ} = \begin{bmatrix} 3 \\ -5 \end{bmatrix}$ then $2\overrightarrow{PQ} = 2\begin{bmatrix} 3 \\ -5 \end{bmatrix} = 2 \times \begin{bmatrix} 3 \\ -5 \end{bmatrix} = \begin{bmatrix} 2 \times 3 \\ 2 \times -5 \end{bmatrix} = \begin{bmatrix} 6 \\ -10 \end{bmatrix}$

2 cm squared paper

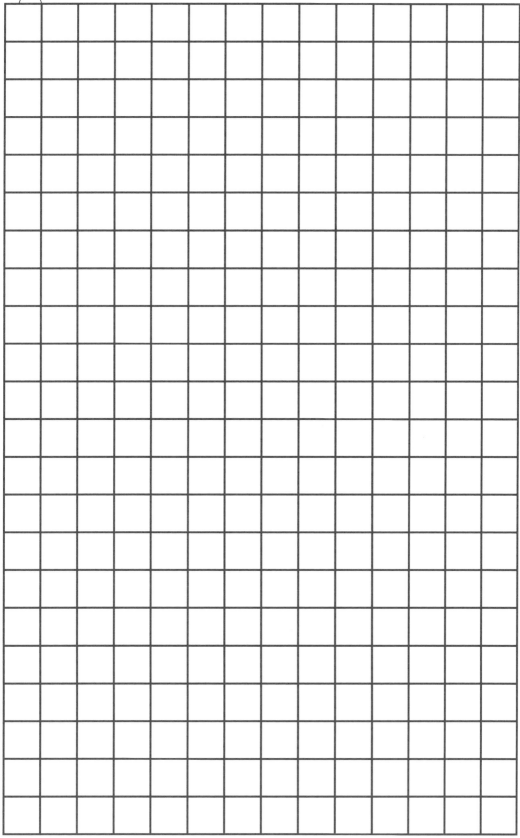

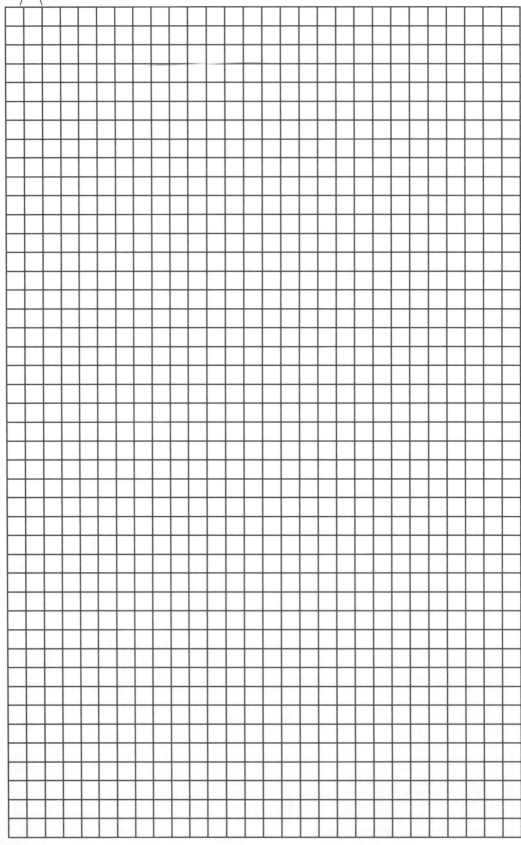

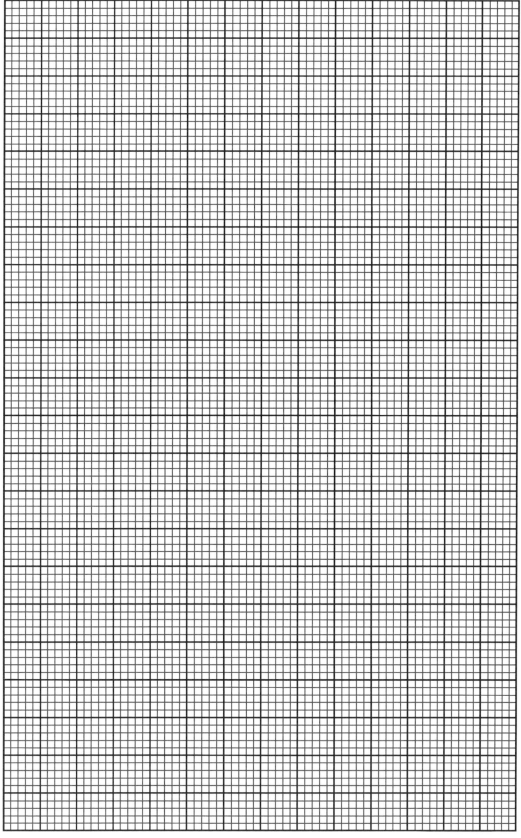

100 square grid

1	2	3	4	5	6	7	8	9	10
11	12	13	14	15	16	17	18	19	20
21	22	23	24	25	26	27	28	29	30
31	32	33	34	35	36	37	38	39	40
41	42	43	44	45	46	47	48	49	50
51	52	53	54	55	56	57	58	59	60
61	62	63	64	65	66	67	68	69	70
71	72	73	74	75	76	77	78	79	80
81	82	83	84	85	86	87	88	89	90
91	92	93	94	95	96	97	98	99	100

Measuring rule

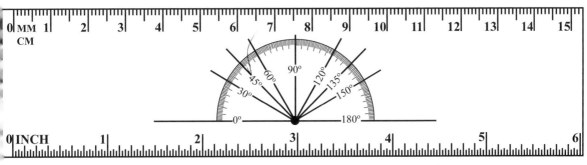

355

FORMULAE

Area of rectangle = length × width

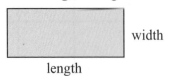

width

length

Area of triangle = $\frac{1}{2}$ × base × height

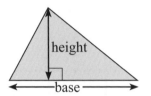

height

base

Area of parallelogram = base × height

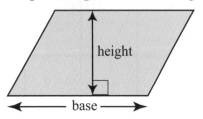

height

base

Circumference of a circle = π × diameter
= 2 × π × radius

Area = π × (radius)^2

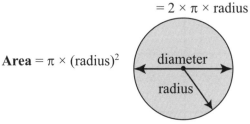

diameter

radius

Volume of cuboid = length × width × height

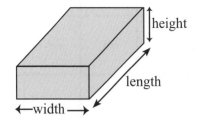

height

length

width

The value of π is approximately 3.14

$$\text{Speed} = \frac{\text{Distance}}{\text{Time}}$$

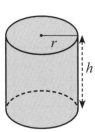

r

h

The curved surface area of a cylinder = **2πrh**
The total surface area of a cylinder = **2πr(h + r)**

Area of a prism = Area of cross-section × length

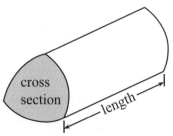

cross
section

length

Area of a sector with centre angle $x°$: $A = \dfrac{x}{360} × πr^2$

$x°$ r

Probability of an event = $\dfrac{\text{Number of ways the event can happen}}{\text{Total number of possible outcomes}}$

356

Answers

Page 3   *Exercise 1:1*

1 222 **2** 21 100 **3** 120 015 **4** 1344 **5** 320 000 **6** 110 102 **7** 102 034 **8** 2 020 207 **9** 103 145
10 1 000 042 **11** 3516 **12** 122 001 **13** 230 004 **14** 202 049 **15** 1 001 357 **16** 2 102 010

Page 3   *Exercise 1:2*

(hieroglyphic answers 1–20)

Page 4   *Exercise 1:3*

(hieroglyphic answers 1–8)

Page 5   *Exercise 1:4*

(hieroglyphic answers 1–12)

Page 7   *Exercise 1:5*

1 240 m **2** 360 m **3** 600 m **4** 960 m **5** 50 m **6** 80 m **7** 200 m **8** 165 m **9** 1 : 3.5 **10** 1 : 4 **11** 1 : 2.1
12 1 : 12.24 **13** 98.4 m

Page 9   *Exercise 1:6*

1 a 33 **b** 13 **c** 22 **d** 87 **e** 66 **f** 59 **g** 120 **h** 94 **i** 965 **j** 697 **k** 572 **l** 888 **2 a** ιε **b** κα **c** οδ
d ρμδ **e** θλε **f** φκ **g** ωε **h** ⌐Ϙθ **i** χοη **j** σξζ **k** υν **l** ⌐νγ   **3 a** 66 **b** 555 **c** 1052 **d** 2005
e 1557 **f** 123 **g** 38 **h** 1665 **i** 919 **j** 1999 **k** 1427 **l** 2009 **4 a** XVIII **b** XXIX **c** XLII
d LXVII **e** LXX **f** LXXXIX **g** CXXVII **h** CXXVII **i** CCXII **j** CCLV **k** DXXXVI **l** CMLXXXVII
m MXLV **n** MDC **o** MDCCCLII **p** MCMXXVII **q** MMCCCL **r** MMMCDXXXVI
5 a 13 **b** 17 **c** 26 **d** 41 **e** 22 **f** 58 **g** 140 **h** 45 **i** 100 **6 a** (cuneiform) **b** (cuneiform) **c** (cuneiform) **d** (cuneiform)
e (cuneiform) **f** (cuneiform) **g** (cuneiform) **h** (cuneiform)

Page 11   *Exercise 1:7*

1 a ١٤ **b** ١٥ **c** ١٦ **d** ١٨ **e** ١٩ **f** ٢٠ **2 a** ٢٥ **b** ٢٧ **c** ٣١ **d** ٣٣ **e** ٣٦ **f** ٤٤ **g** ٤٨
h ٥٣ **i** ٥٩ **j** ٦٠ **k** ٦٧ **l** ٧٤ **3 a** ٢٦; sitta wa 'ishrun **b** ٣٧; sab'a wa thalathun **c** ٧٨ thamaniya wa
sab'un **d** ٥١; wahid wa khamsun **e** ٨٨; thamaniya wa thamanum **f** ٩١; wahid wa tis'un **g** ١٢٠; mia wa
'ishrun' **h** ٢٣٧; m'iatun wa sab'a wa thalathun **i** ٣٥٠; m'ia thalath wa khamsin **j** ٤٠٠; arba'a m'ia
k ٦٤٥; sitta mi'a wa khamsa wa arba'un **l** sab'a m'ia **4 a** ٢٩ **b** ١٧ **c** ٣٨ **d** ٧٣ **e** ٨١ **f** ٥٥ **g** ٨٤
h ٦٣ **i** ٤٩ **5 a** 30 **b** 55 **c** 29 **d** 26 **e** 81 **f** 47 **g** 86 **h** 93 **i** 45 **j** 715 **k** 394 **l** 748 **6 a** ٤٩
b ١٧ **c** ٣٤ **d** ١٧٩ **e** ١٣١ **f** ٥٧٦ **g** ٢٣٣ **h** ١٦٤٠ **7 a** ١٠٧ **b** ٢٧ **c** ٤٣ **d** ٣٥٤ **e** ٣٤٠ **f** ٤٣٢
g ١١٣١ **h** ٩٠

8 a

٢١	٢٦	١٩
٢٠	٢٢	٢٤
٢٥	١٨	٢٣

b

١	١٥	١٤	٤
١٢	٦	٧	٩
٨	١٠	١١	٥
١٣	٣	٢	١٦

c

٢١	٢	٨	١٤	١٥
١٣	١٩	٢٠	١	٧
٠	٦	١٢	١٨	٢٤
١٧	٢٣	٤	٥	١١
٩	١٠	١٦	٢٢	٣

9 a MCCXXVI **b** XXXVIII **c** CXLIX **d** LXIV **e** CLXV **f** CCLXXXIV **g** DCLXIV
h MMMCXCVIII **i** CCCLXXVI

10 a 4006 **b** 9003 **c** 8002 **d** 5078 **e** 4041 **f** 7175 **g** 5966 **h** 9996 **i** 8535 **j** 4612 **k** 270 000
l 840 000 **m** 2 610 000 **n** 50 840 000 **o** 90 396 **11 a** $'\gamma\sigma$ **b** $'\delta\psi\xi$ **c** $'\theta\sigma\varepsilon$ **d** $\overset{\alpha}{M}{}'\gamma\varphi$ **e** $\overset{\varsigma}{M}{}'\varepsilon\omega\mu$
f $\overset{\eta}{M}$ **g** $\overset{\zeta}{M}{}'\theta\tau$ **h** $\overset{\iota\alpha}{M}{}'\omega$ **i** $\overset{\mu\theta}{M}{}'\theta$ **j** $\overset{\iota}{M}{}'\varepsilon\pi$ **k** $\overset{\nu\varsigma}{M}{}'\varsigma\psi$ **l** $\overset{o\zeta}{M}{}'\beta$ **m** $\overset{\rho}{M}$ **n** $\overset{\tau\iota}{M}{}'\varepsilon\varphi$ **o** $'\beta\sigma\xi\theta\,\underset{M}{}'\varsigma\psi\lambda\theta$

Exercise 1:8

1 a 14 **c** 2 groups **d** 4 **e** 24_5 **2 a** 27 **c** 5 **d** 2 **e** 52_5 **3 a** 36 **c** 7 **d** 1 **e** 121_5 **4** 4 **5** 10_5 **6** 12_5
7 24_5 **8** 20_5 **9** 31_5 **10** 42_5 **11** 32_5 **12** 101_5 **13** 112_5 **14** 123_5 **15** 200_5 **28 a** 15 **b** 35 **c** 34 **d i** 9 boxes,
2 tins over **ii** 15 boxes, 3 tins over **iii** 19 boxes, 4 tins over **iv** 27 boxes, 2 tins over **v** 52 boxes, 1 tin over

Exercise 1:9

1 13_5 **2** 11_5 **3** 11_5 **4** 110_5 **5** 130_5 **6** 123_5 **7** 1212_5 **8** 1222_5 **9** 10010_5 **10** 14333_5 **11** 4_5 **12** 13_5
13 14_5 **14** 143_5 **15** 112_5 **16** 143_5 **17** 124_5 **18** 112_5 **19** 1234_5 **20** 1124_5 **21** 2133_5 **22** 1024_5
23 413_5 **24** 1210_5 **25** 2104_5

Exercise 1:10

1 $113_5 = 33_{10}$ **2** $2041_5 = 271_{10}$ **3** $102311_5 = 3456_{10}$ **4** $21123_5 = 1413_{10}$ **5** $203120_5 = 6660_{10}$ **6** $43_5 = 23_{10}$
7 $111_5 = 31_{10}$ **8** $324_5 = 89_{10}$ **9** $321_5 = 86_{10}$ **10** $4203_5 = 553_{10}$ **11** $3143_5 = 523_{10}$ **12** $12043_5 = 898_{10}$
13 $102030_5 = 3390_{10}$ **14** $223311_5 = 7956_{10}$ **15** $421341_5 = 13971_{10}$

Exercise 1:11

1 14_5 **2** 21_5 **3** 214_5 **4** 323_5 **5** 400_5 **6** 1022_5 **7** 2430_5 **8** 3044_5 **9** 4000_5 **10** 11310_5 **11** 11124_5
12 13000_5 **13** 32342_5 **14** 134210_5 **15** 102143_5 **16** 12100_5 **17** 40400_5 **18** 12444_5 **19** 31020_5
20 100001_5 **21** 13421_5 **22** 143311_5 **23** 130412_5 **24** 30444_5 **25** 222031_5

Exercise 1:12

1 12_{10} **2** 11_{10} **3** 14_{10} **4** 23_{10} **5** 15_{10} **6** 8_{10} **7** 27_{10} **8** 26_{10} **9** 17_{10} **10** 30_{10} **11** 42_{10} **12** 57_{10} **13** 21_{10}
14 23_{10} **15** 16_{10} **16** 119_{10} **17** 38_{10} **18** 52_{10} **19** 33_{10} **20** 89_{10} **21** 109_{10} **22** 105_{10} **23** 127_{10} **24** 120_{10}
25 255_{10}

Exercise 1:13

1 111_2 **2** 1001_2 **3** 1011_2 **4** 1111_2 **5** 10111_2 **6** 11011_2 **7** 11110_2 **8** 100100_2 **9** 101000_2 **10** 1000110_2
11 1100011_2 **12** 1100101_2 **13** 10010110_2 **14** 11001000_2 **15** 1111100_2 **16** 11011110_2 **17** 100101100_2
18 101000011_2 **19** 11111010_2 **20** 101011110_2 **21** 11110100_2 **22** 101101101_2 **23** 101111110_2
24 110010111_2 **25** 111110011_2 **26** 1000010110_2 **27** 1001011000_2 **28** 1100011111_2 **29** 1110001101_2
30 1111111111_2

Exercise 1:14

1 43_5 **2** 431_5 **3** 331_5 **4** 1140_5 **5** 224_5 **6** 2010_5 **7** 1334_5 **8** 3000_5 **9** 2014_5 **10** 3044_5 **11** 10100_2
12 10101000_2 **13** 11110101_2 **14** 100001001_2 **15** 11000010_2 **16** 111001110_2 **17** 10110110_2
18 100000100_2 **19** 110000000_2 **20** 1001110000_2

1 1010_2 **2** 10010_2 **3** 10110_2 **4** 11001_2 **5** 101100_2 **6** 110100_2 **7** 10100111_2 **8** 1001101_2 **9** 1110_2

10 110001_2 **11** 1000100_2 **12** 11011_2 **13** 1_2 **14** 1_2 **15** 1101_2 **16** 1110_2 **17** 1000001_2 **18** 1010101_2

1 104_5 **2** 40_5 **3** 140_5 **4** 120_5 **5** 1024_5 **6** 431_5 **7** 1101_5 **8** 1122_5 **9** 2131_5 **10** 3020_5 **11** 44104_5

12 23010_5 **13** 2_5 **14** 101_5 **15** 104_5 **16** 324_5 **17** 10134_5 **18** 11433_5

1 072486 **2** 06166277 **3** 08155266 **4** 0044207774224 **5** 00923411483344 **6** 002333126626
7 00312048218007 **8** 0033149641254 **9** 00447887824834 **10** 00233242027779 **11** 00312076215315
12 003317579334016 **13** 009234116747742 **14** 0074952439283376 **15** 004479241729923
16 0411438244 **17** 01115144893527 **18** 0074956724030429 **19** 00442088927234 **20 a** 00447954328759
b 009234118014044 **c** 01115148921025 **d** 0049407978903682 **e** 01118457422693 **f** 003120206488713

1 a Western **b** Ashanti **c** Greater Accra **d** Northern **e** Upper East **f** Central **g** Greater Accra
h Brong Ahafo **i** Northern **j** Upper West **k** Brong Ahafo **l** Volta

1 a LW **b** SW **c** FM **d** SW **e** MW **f** LW **g** MW **h** SW **2 a** 145 kHz - 350 kHz
b 530 kHz - 1600 kHz **c** 2310 kHz - 30 MHz **d** 88 MHz - 108 MHz

1 a 60 000 metre band **b** 25 000 **c** 2000 metre band **d** 480 metre band **e** 331 metre band **f** 300 metre
band **g** 12.2 metre band **h** 4.3 metre band **i** 3.5 metre band **j** 2.3 metre band

1 520 - Astronomy and allied sciences; 523 - Specific celestial bodies and phenomena; 523.41 - Mercury
2 a $330 \rightarrow 331 \rightarrow 331.01 \rightarrow 331.011 \rightarrow 331.016 \rightarrow 331.02 \rightarrow 331.026 \rightarrow 331.04136$ **b** $310 \rightarrow 311 \rightarrow$
$311.018 \rightarrow 311.07 \rightarrow 311.0942 \rightarrow 311.116 \rightarrow 311.126 \rightarrow 311.2$ **c** $900 \rightarrow 950 \rightarrow 959 \rightarrow 959.9 \rightarrow 959.92$
$\rightarrow 959.927 \rightarrow 959.9278 \rightarrow 959.92781$ **d** $000 \rightarrow 063 \rightarrow 065 \rightarrow 065.6 \rightarrow 065.68 \rightarrow 065.687 \rightarrow 065.6878 \rightarrow$
065.68783 **3** Natural science and mathematics **b** Technology **c** The Arts **d** General knowledge, **e** Social
science **a** 523.78 - Eclipses **b** 622.07 - The study of mining **c** 709 - History of art **d** 813.54 - Four ways for
forgiveness

1 a F4/L/7073/0508 **b** M10/L/7002/0106 **c** F4/P/4915/0806 **2 a** men's shoe size 11, made in other material,
batch 5250, made in October 2010 **b** women's shoe size $6\frac{1}{2}$, plastic, batch 3029, made in November 2008,
c men's shoe size 10, made in other material, batch 800, made in January 2005 **d** women's shoe size $5\frac{1}{2}$, leather, batch 7438, made in April 2007 **e** men's shoe size 11, other material, batch 1055, made in September 2010
f women's shoe size $7\frac{1}{2}$, leather, batch 606, made in August 2008 **3 a** F580718BAN2807AH
b M750502KOB4505S **c** F691001ANS3910A **d** M870620AYE5706N **4 a** male, initials - NK, birth - 1st
September 1969, Arm, expire - September 2039 **b** female, initials - MB, birth - 15th November 1975, Sek,
expire - November 2045 **c** female, initials - ME, birth - 30th May 1956, Sul, expire - May 2026
d male, initials - IF, birth - 11th July 1980, Kuf, expire - July 2050

1  **2**   **3** 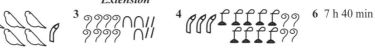 **6** 7 h 40 min

7 125 months **8** 76 days **9 a** 12 dots; 1100_2; 22_5; 12_{10} **b** 17 dots; 10001_{12}; 32_5; 17_{10} **c** 20 dots; 10100_2;
40_5; 20_{10} **d** 34 dots; 100010_2; 114_5; 34_{10} **10 a** 13000_5 **b** 34424_5 **c** 100204_5 **d** 112000_5 **e** 140404_5
f 240140_5 **11 a** $99_{10} = 344_5 = 1100011_2$ **b** $199_{10} = 1244_5 = 11000111_2$ **c** $299_{10} = 2144_5 = 100101011_2$
d $399_{10} = 3044_5 = 110001111_2$ **e** $499_{10} = 3444_5 = 111110011_2$ **f** $599_{10} = 4344_5 = 1001010111_2$

12 a 24_5 **b** 320_5 **c** 3223_5 **d** 13043_5 **e** 1021_5 **15 a** 100111_2 **b** 10001101_2 **c** 101111110_2 **d** 1101111_2
e 10010_2 **16 a** 111_5 **b** 132_5 **c** 141_5 **d** 322_5 **e** 112_5 **17 a** 36 **b i** 24 **ii** 23 **iii** 39 **iv** 116 **c i** 4 cartons
3 eggs **ii** 1 box 2 eggs **iii** 4 boxes 3 eggs **iv** 2 boxes 4 cartons 4 eggs **v** 5 boxes 1 carton 3 eggs **18 a** 21_5
b 23_5 **c** 21_5 **d** 24_5 **e** 33_5 **19 a** 2_5 **b** 1_5 **c** 4_5 **d** 13_5 **e** 4_5 **23 a** met **b** 689 **c** 3457 **d** code **e** DEAL
f form **g** Time **h** join **25 a** 2 lines **b** 4 lines **c** 8 lines **d** 16 lines **e** 32 lines **f** 64 lines

Chapter 2   Linear equations and inequalities

Page 36   *Exercise 2:1*

1 $D = ST$ **2** $A = 2t$ **3** $E = 6bm$ **4** $y = mx + c$ **5** $v = u + at$ **6** $c = 15abc$ **7** $k = \dfrac{21b}{2}$ **8** $g = \dfrac{GM}{2r}$

9 $E = \dfrac{mv}{2}$ **10** $c = 3a + 25$ **11** $Fs = \dfrac{5mv}{2}$ **12** $y = 4a + bx + c$ **13** $I = mv - mu$ **14** $v = 4u - 2ap$

Page 37   *Exercise 2:2*

  $K + (K - 2) = 12$ $E - 7 + E = 65$ where $A + 7 = E$ $l + t = 6.83$, $t = 6.83 - 3.45$

4 Total Shopping: $\dfrac{¢10 - 2 \times 1.20}{2}$ **5** Number of pupils: $\dfrac{68 - 5}{9}$ **6** House number of Mr Allotey: $73 - 39$

7 Kobi : $\dfrac{157 - 13}{2}$ Fifi : $\dfrac{157 - 13}{2} + 13$ **8** Tetteh paid: $\dfrac{86.70 - 7.50}{2}$; Sakina paid: $\dfrac{86.70 - 7.50}{2} + 7.50$

9 a $904 \div 200 = 4.52$ kg **b** $(4.52 - 0.08) \div 24 = 0.185$ kg

Page 38   *Exercise 2:3*

1 $x - 10 = 6$ **2** $x + 3 = 15$ **3** $5(x + 3) = 30$ **4** $4(x - 2) = 12$ **5** $4x - 10 = 26$ **6** $8x + 5 = 13$ **7** $\dfrac{x}{8} + 25 = 49$
8 $3(4x - 1) = 33$ **9** $2x - 5 = 20$ **10** $15 + x = 27$ **11** $4x = 24$

Page 39   *Exercise 2:4*

1 16 **2** 4 **3** 5 **4** 3 **5** 3 **6** 7 **7** $x = 11$ **8** $x = 6$ **9** $x = 3$ **10** $x = 225$ **11** $x = 3$ **12** $b = 21$ **13** $c = 4\frac{2}{5}$
14 $d = 2.5$ **15** $e = 3$ **16** $f = 7$ **17** $g = -1$ **18** $h = 12$ **19** $j = 4\frac{1}{2}$ **20** $k = 2$ **21** $x = 35$ **22** $m = 3$
23 $n = 54$ **24** $p = 12$ **25** $q = 14$ **26** $r = 6\frac{2}{7}$

Page 40   *Exercise 2:5*

1 1 **2** 3 **3** 7 **4** 16 **5** 37 **6** 9 **7** 11 **8** 9 **9** 5 **10** 20 **11** 6 **12** 108 **13** 39 **14** 10 **15** 19 **16** $5\frac{1}{2}$
17 15 **18** -20 **19** 55 **20** $\frac{1}{3}$ **21** 8 yrs **22** 37.2 **23** 64 p **24** 95 p

Page 41   *Exercise 2:6*

1 2 **2** 3 **3** 5 **4** 6 **5** 8.5 **6** 12 **7** 4 **8** 4 **9** 75 **10** 60 **11** 50 **12** 108 **13** 45 **14** 17.5 **15** 35 **16** 52
17 10 **18** 5.52 **19** 3 **20** 19.75 **21** 9 **22** 28.125 **23** 14 **24** 12 **25** $12\frac{1}{2}$ **26** 14.5 **27** 6 **28** $\frac{1}{6}$ **29** 30
30 8 **31** 2 **32** 28

Page 42   *Exercise 2:7*

1 2 **2** 3 **3** 2 **4** $5\frac{5}{7}$ **5** 9 **6** $\frac{1}{4}$ **7** 3 **8** 5 **9** 1 **10** $5\frac{1}{6}$ **11** $2\frac{1}{2}$ **12** $12\frac{1}{2}$ **13** 8 **14** 343 **15** $20\frac{2}{5}$
16 $-69\frac{1}{3}$ **17** 80 **18** 4 **19** 36 **20** 8 **21** $-10\frac{1}{2}$ **22** 60 **23** 2 **24** 6 **25** -1 **26** 0 **27** $\frac{1}{6}$ **28** $\frac{5}{9}$ **29** 17
30 2 **31** -1 **32** $\frac{5}{22}$ **33** 2 **34** $1\frac{6}{7}$ **35** $1\frac{17}{33}$ **36** 30 **37** -22 **38** 363 **39** $25\frac{2}{3}$ **40** $-2\frac{1}{2}$ **41** 1 **42** $\frac{10}{17}$
43 0.95 **44** -188

Page 43   *Exercise 2:8*

1 2 **2** 4 **3** 9 **4** 9 **5** $\frac{1}{4}$ **6** $5\frac{1}{2}$ **7** $1\frac{1}{4}$ **8** $-\frac{1}{6}$ **9** 2 **10** $4\frac{1}{2}$ **11** $3\frac{1}{2}$ **12** -2 **13** -2 **14** $3\frac{5}{6}$ **15** -4
16 $1\frac{1}{3}$

Page 43   *Exercise 2:9*

1 -7 **2** 8 **3** 3 **4** 12 **5** $4\frac{1}{2}$ **6** 10 **7** $4\frac{1}{5}$ **8** $5\frac{1}{2}$ **9** 100 **10** -3 **11** $11\frac{4}{7}$ **12** $1\frac{1}{5}$

Exercise 2:10

1 $1\frac{1}{2}$ **2** 6 **3** 5 **4** 6 **5** $5\frac{1}{8}$ **6** $6\frac{3}{8}$ **7** 2 **8** −1 **9** 8 **10** 2 **11** $14\frac{1}{3}$ **12** 4 **13** $-2\frac{5}{7}$ **14** 40 **15** 7
16 $3\frac{1}{3}$ **17** $1\frac{3}{5}$ **18** $5\frac{1}{5}$ **19** 15 **20** 21 **21** 30 **22** 17 **23** $3\frac{3}{4}$ **24** −2 **25** $5\frac{5}{11}$ **26** 1 **27** $\frac{3}{5}$
28 $8\frac{2}{3}$ **29** 1 **30** $4\frac{1}{2}$ **31** $12\frac{4}{7}$ **32** 9

Exercise 2:11

1 −0.4 **2** 2 **3** $-1\frac{1}{2}$ **4** $1\frac{1}{4}$ **5** −28 **6** $2\frac{1}{9}$ **7** $-9\frac{1}{11}$ **8** −24 **9** 65 **10** $17\frac{1}{4}$ **11** $-4\frac{2}{7}$ **12** $-\frac{3}{5}$

13 $w = 12.97$ **14** $a = 6.25$ cm **15** $x = 6$; sides: 24 cm, 13 cm, 20 cm and 17 cm **16** 44 **17** 38, 39, 40 **18** $\frac{23}{35}$

19 9, 4, 12 **20** $l = 3\frac{3}{8}$, $w = 2\frac{5}{8}$ **21** 105.56 cm^2 **22 a** $100x$ cm **b** $\frac{n}{100}$ cm **c** $1000t$ km **d** $\frac{y}{1000}$ m **23 a** $\frac{y}{8}$

b $\frac{p}{4x}$ **c** $\frac{7b}{13}$ **d** $\frac{18xy}{29w}$ **25 a** 4 **b** 1 **26** $\frac{m}{4} - 2 = \frac{m}{5}$; $m = 40$; 1st Game 10 marbles each;

2nd Game 8 marbles each **27** $\frac{x}{10} + \frac{23 - x}{15} = 2$; $x = 14$ **28 a** $\frac{y}{6}$; **b** $\frac{y}{2}$ **c** $\frac{y}{6} + \frac{y}{2} = 20$ **d** $y = 30$

29 $\frac{k}{80} + \frac{1}{2}$; $\frac{k}{60}$; $\frac{k}{80} + \frac{1}{2} = \frac{k}{60}$; $k = 120$ km **30 a** $(x + 10)$ km **b** $\frac{x}{45}$ km **c** $\frac{x + 10}{90}$ **d** $\frac{x}{45} = \frac{x + 10}{90} + \frac{1}{3}$; $x = 40$

Puzzling Algebra

1 p = 4, m = 3, n = 2, k = 5 **2** a = 3, q = 8, t = 6, u = 4; **3** b = 6, c = 4, g = 3, j = 8 **4** d = 4, f = 3, v = 9, y = 5
5 e = 14, h = 9, k = 17, m = 12, z = 6 **6** f = 11. p = 6, s = 10, u = 7, x = 8 **7** Σ = 9, π = 15, ∞ = 8, ε = 7,
= 12 **8** ¢ = 21, \$ = 15, £ = 9, ¥ = 10, ₦ = 7 **9** ♧ = 17 ♡ = 25 ◇ = 13, ◎ = 10, ♤ = 19 **10** ⊞ = 24,
⊕ = 7, ⊠ = 12, ◈ = 20, ⊹ = 16 **11** ♂ = 12, ♀ = 7, ¶ = 6, ∅ = 4 **12** σ = 15, β = 20, ψ = 9, λ = 4, δ = 6,
μ = 12, η = 23, θ = 7

Exercise 2:14

1 $x < 4$ **2** $x < 1$ **3** $x \leq 3$ **4** $x < 2$ **5** $x < \frac{3}{5}$ **6** $x \leq 3$ **7** $x > 150$ **8** $x \leq -10$ **9** $x \geq -5$ **10** $x > 2\frac{3}{7}$ **11** $x > 8$
12 $2 < x \leq 3$ **13** $1 < x < 4$ **14** $3 < x < 2$ **15** $-5 < x < 2$ **16** $-1 < x < 5$ **17** $2 < x < 5$ **18** $18 \leq x < 21$
19 $3 \leq x < 8\frac{1}{2}$ **20** $-\frac{1}{4} < x \leq 3$ **21** $\frac{1}{3} < x < 8\frac{1}{3}$ **22** $-2 < x \leq 9\frac{2}{3}$ **23** $-17 \leq x \leq -1$ **24** $6 \leq x \leq -\frac{6}{7}$

Exercise 2:15

4 a $t > 24\,^{\circ}\text{C}$ **b** $p \geq 36$ **c** $w \leq 12$ kg **d** $2n - 5 < 100$ **5 a** 1, 2, 3, 4, 5, 6 **b** −4, −3, −2, −1, 0, 1 **c** −5, −4,
−3, −2, −1, 0, 1, 2 **d** 3, 4 **e** −2, −1, 0, 1, 2, 3, 4, 5, 6, 7, 8, 9, 10 **f** 1, 2, 3, 4, 5, 6, 7

Exercise 2:16

1 B: 40.03, 39.97 H: 15.02, 14.98 D: 8.005, 7.995 **2 a** 7.36, 7.34 **b** 3.357, 3.347 **c** 6.108, 6.102
d 3.357, 3.347, **e** 3.756, 3.750 **f** 5.039, 5.029 **g** 8.556, 8.546 **h** 1.01, 1.00 **i** $47^{\circ}, 43^{\circ}$ **j** 7.29, 7.19
k 7.97, 7.79 **l** 20.05, 19.95 **m** 65.14, 64.86 **n** 10.1, 9.9 **3 a** 42.045, 42.035 **b** 17.95, 17.85 **c** 36.5015,
36.4985 **d** 3.055, 3.045 **e** 79.9125, 79.8875 **f** 93.9505, 93.9495 **4 a** 6.03 ± 0.003 **b** 14.994 ± 0.006
c 24.7 ± 0.115 **d** 17.2 ± 0.125 **e** 48.995 ± 0.045 **f** 82.5 ± 0.255

Extension

1 a $\frac{6x}{7}$; $x = 10\frac{1}{2}$ **b** $\frac{2y}{3} + 5 = 17$; $x = 18$; **c** $\frac{n - 23}{4}$; $n = 15$ **2 a** $7\frac{1}{5}$ **b** 4 **c** 1 **d** −3 **e** $-5\frac{2}{3}$ **f** $-11\frac{1}{3}$
3 a 33 **b** $5\frac{5}{11}$ **c** 10 **d** $11\frac{1}{4}$ **e** $2\frac{2}{9}$ **f** $7\frac{2}{3}$ **g** −49 **h** 8 **i** −2 **4** 47, 49, 51 **5** $21\frac{1}{3}$ m **6** ¢16.25
7 a $5c = 6c - 180$ **b** 180 ml **c** 360 ml **d** 900 ml **8 a** $x \leq -8\frac{2}{3}$ **b** $x < 1\frac{4}{11}$ **c** $x \geq 6$ **d** $x \leq -6$ **e** $x \geq -13$
f $x \leq -4\frac{4}{7}$ **9** A = 9 kg, B = 18 kg **10** $n = 9$ **11 a** $n = 13.5$ **b** $n = 9$ **c** $n = 19$ **14 a** $4p - 5$ **b** 123 **c** 155
d 37 **15 a** $7.5 + 2n$ **b** $7.5 + 2n = 25$; $n = \$8.75$ **16** $x = 12$ yrs father = 48 yrs, mother = 41 yrs

Chapter 3 Angles

Exercise 3:1

1 a $\frac{1}{4}$ turn anticlockwise **b** $\frac{1}{2}$ turn anticlockwise **c** $\frac{3}{4}$ turn clockwise **d** full turn clockwise **2 a** anticlockwise
$\frac{1}{4}$ turn, clockwise $\frac{1}{4}$turn, anticlockwise $\frac{1}{4}$ turn, clockwise $\frac{1}{4}$ turn **b** anticlockwise $\frac{1}{4}$ turn, clockwise $\frac{1}{4}$
turn, anticlockwise $\frac{1}{4}$ turn, clockwise $\frac{1}{4}$ turn. **3 a** clockwise $\frac{1}{4}$ turn, anticlockwise $\frac{1}{4}$ turn, clockwise $\frac{1}{4}$turn.
b anti clockwise $\frac{1}{4}$turn, clockwise $\frac{1}{4}$ turn, anticlockwise $\frac{1}{4}$ turn. **c** anticlockwise $\frac{1}{4}$ turn, clockwise $\frac{1}{4}$ turn,
clockwise $\frac{1}{4}$ turn, half turn, clockwise $\frac{1}{4}$turn, anticlockwise $\frac{1}{4}$turn. **d a** ↻$\frac{1}{4}$, ↺$\frac{1}{4}$, ↻$\frac{1}{4}$, **b** ↺$\frac{1}{4}$, ↻$\frac{1}{4}$,
↺$\frac{1}{4}$, **c** ↺$\frac{1}{4}$, ↻$\frac{1}{4}$, ↻$\frac{1}{4}$, half turn, ↻$\frac{1}{4}$, ↺$\frac{1}{4}$, **4** North **5** North **6 a** SE **b** NE **c** NW **d** SE

Page 58

7 $\frac{7}{8}$ turn **8 a** $\frac{1}{4}$ turn **b** $\frac{1}{2}$ turn **c** $\frac{3}{4}$ turn **d** $\frac{1}{2}$ turn **e** $1\frac{1}{2}$ turn **f** $\frac{1}{12}$ turn **g** $\frac{2}{6}$ turn **h** $\frac{7}{12}$ turn

9 a From Prempeh college turn anticlockwise onto Sunyani road, clockwise on the roundabout onto Bekwai then halfway down onto Suntreso.

b From the Officers Mess go on Cedar Ave, at the junction on Bekwai road turn anticlockwise onto the roundabout, turn clockwise onto Western Bypass then past SecTec school then clockwise into Patase.

c Get on the Bantama High Street, turn clockwise on the first roundabout onto Bekwai Road, go over the next roundabout, on the third roundabout turn clockwise onto Western Bypass then anticlockwise to the police station.

d From the hospital turn anticlockwise onto Bekwai Road. On the next roundabout turn anticlockwise onto Pine Road; go straight on and turn clockwise onto Cedar Avenue. Go straight on to the second junction and turn anticlockwise into Jackson Avenue and turn clockwise onto the Golf course.

Page 60

1 65° **2** 29° **3** 105° **4** 78° **5** 96° **6** 30° **7** 165° **8** 128° **9** 27° **10** 42° **11** 130°

Page 62

1 $\angle ABC = 90°$ **2** $\angle AOD = 56°$ **3** $\angle AOT = 10°$ **4** $\angle MAB = 137°$ **5** $\angle GYE = 147°$ **6** $\angle ZYX = 45°$
7 $\angle TOH = 169°$ **8** $\angle BED = 54°$

Page 63

1 $\angle PAT = 174°$ **2** $\angle PAL = 53°$ **3** $\angle PAB = 156°$ **4** $\angle KAD = 79°$ **5** $P\hat{A}X = 122°$ **6** $K\hat{A}S = 102°$
7 $P\hat{A}H = 86°$ **8** $K\hat{A}P = 180°$ **9** $\angle PAM = 114°$ **10** $\angle KAJ = 87°$ **11** $\angle PAY = 23°$ **12** $\angle KAN = 119°$
13 $P\hat{A}G = 108°$ **14** $K\hat{A}T = 6°$ **15** $P\hat{A}U = 15°$ **16** $K\hat{A}Y = 157°$ **17** $\angle WAT = 135°$ **18** $\angle SAT = 96°$
19 $\angle RAB = 124°$ **20** $\angle CAL = 116°$ **21** $D\hat{A}B = 55°$ **22** $M\hat{A}S = 36°$ **23** $J\hat{A}H = 7°$ **24** $Z\hat{A}U = 148°$ **25** $J\hat{A}M = 21°$ **26** $F\hat{A}D = 34°$ **27** $S\hat{A}Y = 55°$ **28** $\angle MAN = 53°$ **29** $Y\hat{A}W = 16°$ **30** $V\hat{A}Q = 142°$
31 $G\hat{A}S = 30°$ **32** $B\hat{A}R = 124°$

Page 64

1 $\angle ABE = 98°$; $\angle ANE = 63°$ **2** $\angle NGT = 53°$; $\angle GTA = 159°$ **3** $\angle PBW = 114°$; $\angle BWP = 39°$ **4** $P\hat{S}Y = 76°$;
$S\hat{P}Y = 75°$ **5** $L\hat{J}N = 106°$; $L\hat{A}N = 166°$ **6** $X\hat{L}M = 215°$; $L\hat{X}T = 27°$; $X\hat{T}M = 41°$ **7** $R\hat{G}D = 54°$;
$G\hat{D}P = 155°$; $G\hat{P}R = 49°$; $D\hat{P}R = 102°$ **8** $F\hat{Z}R = 126°$; $Z\hat{R}H = 41°$; $R\hat{H}F = 149°$; $H\hat{F}Z = 44°$

Page 67

1 a Right angle **b** Acute angle **c** Obtuse angle **d** Reflex angle **e** Straight angle **f** Reflex angle **g** Reflex angle **h** Acute angle **2 a** Reflex angle **b** Obtuse angle **c** Acute angle **d** Reflex angle **e** Acute angle
f Obtuse angle **g** Reflex angle **h** Reflex angle **i** Acute angle **j** Obtuse angle **3 a** acute **b** obtuse **c** acute
d acute **e** acute **f** reflex **g** obtuse **h** acute **i** obtuse **j** obtuse **k** acute **l** right **4 a** 157.5° **b** 81°
c 210° **d** 270° **e** 162° **f** 45° **g** 153° **h** 342° **i** 274.5° **5 a** 32° **b** 77° **c** 122° **6 3** 43° **6** 75°
к = 88° ч = 49° ъ = 123° ф = 105° ю = 34° я = 146° щ = 25° л = 147°

Page 69

1 $\angle ABC = 82°$ **2** $\angle ABC = 74°$ **3** $\angle ABC = 93°$ **4** $e = 38°$ **5** $f = 60°$ **6** $g = 48°$ **7** $h = 37°$ **8** $i = 32°$
9 $j = 18°$

Page 70

1 $g = 160°$ **2** $q = 192°$ **3** $s = 145°$ **4** $y = 28°$ **5** $k = 224°$ **6** $b = 38°$ **7** $d = 107°$ **8 a** $x = 110°$
9 a $v = 14.5°$; $v + 10 = 24.5°$; $v - 4 = 10.5°$; $10v = 145°$; $j = 53°$

Page 71

1 $a = 156°$ **2** $b = 74°$ **3** $c = 68°$; $d = 112°$ **4** $e = 114°$; $f = 114°$ **5** $g = 142°$; $h = 142°$; $i = 38°$ **6** $j = 77°$;
$k = 103°$; $l = 103°$ **7** $m = 96°$; $n = 96°$; $o = 84°$ **8** $p = 139°$; $q = 139°$; $r = 41°$ **9** $s = 16°$; $t = 112°$;
$u = 52°$; $v = 112°$ **10** $w = 57°$; $x = 55°$; $y = 68°$; $z = 57°$ **11** $\psi = 77°$; $\kappa = 86°$; $\theta = 86°$; $\xi = 17°$ **12** $\partial = 39°$;
$\varphi = 51°$; $\pi = 98°$ **13** $2\eta = 108°$; $\eta = 54°$; $\varepsilon = 54°$; $\beta = 108°$; $\alpha = 18°$ **14** $\mu = 80°$; $\gamma = 80°$; $\sigma = 50°$

Exercise 3:11

7 $a = 101°$ **8** $b = 13°$ **9** $c = 47°$ **10** $d = 59°$ **11** $e = 80°$ **12** $f = 91°$; $g = 89°$; $h = 91°$ **13** $i = 99°$; $j = 81°$
$k = 99°$ **14** $l = 67°$ **15** $m = 82°$; $n = 52°$ **16** $o = 53°$; $p = 77°$ **17** $q = 36°$; $r = 57°$ $s = 27°$; $t = 63°$
18 $u = 87°$; $v = 54°$ $w = 74°$; $x = 106°$; $y = 74°$; $z = 106°$; $a = 37°$

Exercise 3:12

1 $p = 47°$; $q = 133°$ **2** $p = 62°$; $q = 32°$ **3** $p = 60°$; $q = 120°$ **4** $p = 42°$; $q = 149°$ **5** $p = 61°$; $q = 59°$
6 $p = 47°$; $q = 107°$ **7** $l = 58°$; $z = 88°$ **8** $t = 164°$; $x = 116°$ **9** $v = 138°$; $s = 120°$ **10** $r = 115°$; $s = 65°$
$t = 31°$; $u = 124°$ **11** $d = 35°$; $n = 80°$ **12** $f = 29°$; $g = 97°$ $h = 54°$; $i = 54°$ $j = 126°$; $k = 126°$ **13** $c = 106°$;
$q = 69°$; $w = 37°$; $2w = 74°$ **14** $q = 40°$; $r = 55°$; $s = 80°$; $t = 15°$; $u = 25°$; $v = 40°$ **15** $c = 61°$; $v = 47°$;
$x = 56°$ **16** $d = 57°$; $g = 147°$; $h = 135°$; $k = 44°$; $q = 91°$; $r = 89°$; $s = 91°$; $t = 89°$; $u = 56°$; **17** $m = 60°$;
$n = 60°$; $p = 120°$; $q = 30°$; $r = 60°$; $s = 120°$ **18** $a = 137.5°$; $b = 42.5°$; $c = 42.5°$; $e = 113°$; $f = 137.5$

Exercise 3:13

2 i $a + e$ **ii** $e + c$ **iii** $b + d$ **iv** $c + f$ **v** $h + d$ **vi** $d + f$ **vii** $e + g$ **viii** $d + e$ **ix** $g + c$ **x** h and g are
supplementary **3 a** b, f, d **b** a, c, e, g **4** $a = 66°$; $b = 68°$ $c = 112°$ $d = 114°$ $e = 68°$ **5** $a = 133°$; $b = 47°$
$c = 115°$ $d = 115°$ $e = 133°$ **6** $a = 112°$; $b = 142°$ $c = 68°$ $d = 142°$ $e = 38°$ **7** $x = 56°$ **8** $a = 106°$;
$b = 106°$ $c = 106°$ $d = 106°$ $e = 74°$ **9** $a = 104°$; $b = 43°$ $c = 33°$ **10** $q = 110°$ **11** $z = 107°$ **12** $q = 58°$
13 $m = 228°$; $p = 34°$

Exercise 3:14

7 FD 10 LT 90 FD 20 LT 90 FD 30 **8** LT 90 FD 40 RT 90 FD 30 LT 90 FD 20 **9** BK 30 RT 70 FD 50
10 FD 10 RT 90 FD 30 LT 45 FD 30 **11** BK 35 LT 90 FD 48 RT 90 FD 35 RT 90 FD 48 **12** FD 67 RT 45 FD
38 RT 90 FD 38 RT 45 FD 67 RT 90 FD 54 **13 a** FD 40 RT 120 FD 40 RT 120 FD 40 RT 120 **b** FD 40 RT 90
FD 40 RT 90 FD 40 RT 90 FD 40 RT 90 **c** FD 40 RT 72 FD 40 RT 72 FD 40 RT 72 FD 40 RT 72 FD 40 RT 72
d FD 40 RT 60 FD 40 RT 60 FD 40 RT 60 FD 40 RT 60 FD 40 RT 60 FD 40 RT 60

Extension

1 a $60°$ **b** $171°$ **c** $67.5°$ **d** $186.3°$ **e** $324°$ **f** $490.5°$ **2 a** three **b** two **c** half **3 a** $15°$ **b i** 9 h **ii** 21 h
4 a $308°$ **b** $229°$ **c** $261°$ **7 a** $x = 60°$ **b** $x = 19°$; $2x = 38°$; $3x = 57°$ **c** $x = 5°$; $8x = 40°$; $9x = 45°$; $19x = 95°$
8 $p = 27.5°$; $q = 62.5°$ $r = 62.5°$ $s = 27.5°$; $t = 55°$ **9** $x = 32°$; $3x = 96°$; $5x = 160°$ **10** $x = 50°$; $y = 50°$;
11 $x = 30°$; $t = 20°$ **12** $a = 32°$; $b = 60°$ $c = 20°$ $d = 62°$; $e = 106°$; $f = 46°$; $g = 28°$ $h = 58°$; $i = 122°$;
$j = 30°$; $k = 110°$; $l = 36°$ $m = 74°$ $n = 70°$; $o = 106°$; $p = 52°$; $q = 22°$ $r = 68°$ $s = 92°$; $t = 52°$; $u = 82°$;
$v = 60°$ $w = 180°$

Chapter 4 Statistics

Exercise 4:1

1 c **2** a **3** b **4** d **5** a **6** d **7** c **8** c **9** b **10** c **11** c **12** a **13** d **14** b

Exercise 4:2

1 a quantitative **b** qualitative **c** qualitative **d** quantitative **e** qualitative **f** quantitative **2 a** discrete
b discrete **c** continuous **d** discrete **e** continuous **f** continuous **3 a** continuous **b** discrete **c** continuous
d continuous **e** continuous **f** discrete **g** continuous **h** discrete **4 a** continuous **b** continuous
c continuous **d** continuous **e** discrete **f** discrete **g** continuous **h** discrete **i** continuous **j** continuous

Exercise 4:3

1 a ii b ii c i d ii e i f i g ii h ii 2 Bus - 23; Taxi - 8; Walk - 32 Car - 11 Bike - 6
b Total - 80 **c** most people walk, few people travel by bicycle

Exercise 4:4

1 a Nowhere to place zero mark; Class boundaries not well defined if you get 30 you could be in either 20 - 30
or 30 - 40 **2** Akosuah's mistakes are: the first class should be $0 \leq marks < 10$ to include zero mark; next class
should be $10 \leq marks < 20$, etc. **3** To the nearest kilogram: $39.5 - 44.4$, $44.5 - 49.4$, $49.5 - 54.4$, $54.5 - 59.4$
4 less than 19.5 min, $19.5 - 29.4$, $29.5 - 39.4$, 39.5 or more minutes.

Exercise 4:5

1 a Ama - 150 votes; Konadu - 75 votes; Sika - 175 votes; Agyiri - 25 votes; **b** Sika won by 25 votes
3 c 142 people **4 a** Bode Food Shop sold the most root vegetables **b** 75 **c** 65 **5 c** 28%

Exercise 4:6

1 b 15% **c** You cannot tell as those who did no homework were put together with those up to 10.
d The longest time possible is 79 minutes because the last class is less than 80 minutes however you cannot tell if pupils spent more than 70 minutes. **4 c** 17% calls lasted from 11 to 15 min. **5 c** A CD of 38 min 32 s would be put in 36 - 40 minute class interval. **d** 22%

Page 100

Exercise 4:7

1 a

Stem	Leaf
12	8

b

Stem	Leaf
3	0.4

c

Stem	Leaf
14	0.3

d

Stem	Leaf
0.03	8

e

Stem	Leaf
3.01	4

f

Stem	Leaf
0.0	9

g

Stem	Leaf
7.8	0

h

Stem	Leaf
843.2	5

i

Stem	Leaf
7	$\frac{1}{2}$

j

Stem	Leaf
165	3

Page 101

Exercise 4:8

1 a 55 **b** 55 **c** 39 **2 a** 3.6 **b** 3.4 **c** 3.1 **3 a** $150 \le$ height < 155 **b** 154 **c** 156 **d** 35 **4 b i** 68%
ii 64% **iii** 72

Page 103

Exercise 4:9

1 a Median: History - 41, Physics - 44; Mode : History - 32, Physics - 54; Range: History - 59, Physics - 51
2 a Mode: Adama - none; Yeboah - 3.8, Median: Adama - 4.4; Yeboah - 4.4 **3 b** girls: median - 166, mode - 166
c boys : median - 170, mode - 170; **d** Range: girls 32 cm; boys - 35 cm **4 b** Modal group: Musah 20.0 - 20.09
Azumah 20.4 - 20.49 **c** Musah: mode - 20.13, median - 20.125, range - 1.14 **d** Azumah: mode 20.02 and
20.43, median - 20.23, range - 0.91 **e** median, as not enough repetitions to make mode meaningful.

Page 105

Exercise 4:10

1 Central - 11, Northern - 7, Volta - 4, Ashanti - 18 **2** P.E. 21, Geography 13, History - 10, Science - 11,
English - 17 **3** Corn - 100°, Rice - 60°, Beans - 72°, Maize - 40°, Onions - 88°.

Extension

Page 107 **4 a** 3 **b** 0.5 **c** 0.10 **d** 6 **e** 100 **f** 500 **7 i** Girls: median - 8.7, mode - 9.6 range - 5.5
Boys: median -10.7, mode - 10.9, range - 6 **c** The median; it reveals the weighting of the results better than the
mode **10 a** 15, 22, 51, 43, 23 **b** 36°, 50°, 119°, 101°, 54°, **11** Modal group: males $45 \le$ hours < 46; females $44 \le$
height < 45 **c** males: mode - 45.5, median 45.5, range - 5.5 **d** females: mode - 43.8, median - 44.3, range - 5

Chapter 5 Rational and irrational numbers

Page 113

Exercise 5:1

1 0.5 **2** 0.6 **3** 0.2 **4** 0.375 **5** 0.625 **6** 0.3125 **7** 0.03125 **8** 1.65 **9** $\frac{3}{5}$ **10** $\frac{7}{50}$ **11** $\frac{23}{100}$ **12** $\frac{123}{1000}$

13 $\frac{1}{8}$ **14** $\frac{17}{20}$ **15** $2\frac{3}{25}$ **16** $4\frac{11}{40}$ **17 a** $0.\dot{2}$ **b** $1.1\dot{3}\dot{5}$ **c** $6.01\dot{4}\dot{7}$ **d** $9.1\dot{4}8\dot{7}$ **e** $3.01\dot{7}47\dot{1}$

f $8.09\dot{3}32\dot{5}$ **g** $8.1\dot{1}45\dot{7}$ **h** $10.89\dot{2}\dot{1}$ **18 a** $0.\dot{3}$, $0.\dot{6}$ factor of $0.\dot{3}$ **b** $0.\dot{1}\dot{8}$ $0.\dot{2}\dot{7}$, $0.\dot{3}\dot{6}$ factor of $0.\dot{0}\dot{9}$.

c $0.\dot{2}, 0.\dot{4}, 0.\dot{6}, 0.\dot{8}$ factor of $0.\dot{2}$ **d** $0.\dot{1}4285\dot{7}$, $0.\dot{2}8571\dot{4}$, $0.\dot{4}2857\dot{1}$, $0.\dot{5}7142\dot{8}$ factor of $0.\dot{1}4285\dot{7}$

Page 114

Exercise 5:2

1 $\frac{1}{3}$ **2** $\frac{2}{3}$ **3** $\frac{7}{33}$ **4** $\frac{29}{33}$ **5** $\frac{25}{33}$ **6** $\frac{10}{11}$ **7** $\frac{2}{11}$ **8** $\frac{43}{333}$ **9** $\frac{17}{111}$ **10** $\frac{9}{101}$ **11** $2\frac{125}{999}$ **12** $4\frac{12791}{99999}$

13 a $\frac{71}{90}$ **b** $\frac{29}{90}$ **c** $\frac{8}{15}$ **d** $\frac{163}{990}$ **e** $\frac{124}{165}$ **f** $\frac{191}{330}$ **g** $\frac{292}{555}$ **h** $5\frac{119}{165}$ **i** $2\frac{409}{990}$ **j** $\frac{2729}{3330}$ **k** $\frac{347}{1110}$

l $22\frac{8467}{9990}$ **14 a** $\frac{1}{3}$ **b** $\frac{1426}{9999}$ **c** $\frac{1}{11}$ **d** $\frac{6}{11}$

Exercise 5:3

1 a $\frac{3}{5}$ b $\frac{1}{2}$ c $\frac{7}{3}$ d $\frac{105}{100}$ e $\frac{27}{10}$ f $\frac{23}{12}$ 3 a $\frac{6}{25}$ b $\frac{3}{10}$ c $\frac{1}{8}$ d $\frac{161}{200}$ e $\frac{103}{50}$ f $\frac{57}{1000}$ 5 a $\frac{1}{4}$ b $\frac{1}{5}$

c $\frac{3}{7}$ d $\frac{1}{3}$ e $\frac{2}{5}$ f $\frac{1}{4}$ 6 a, c, d, e f

Exercise 5:4

1 a $2.405 < 2.45$ b $\frac{1}{2} > \frac{1}{3}$ c $\sqrt{36} > 5.98$ d $\sqrt{1} < \sqrt{1.21}$ e $0.0025 < \sqrt{0.25}$ f $0.809 < 0.89$

g $0.3233 < \frac{34}{51}$ h $\frac{\sqrt{4}}{5} < \frac{1}{\sqrt{4}}$ i $\frac{7}{\sqrt{100}} > \frac{\sqrt{36}}{24}$ 2 a $0.087, 0.299, 0.507. 0.75, 0.802$ b $\frac{11}{110}, \frac{15}{60}, \frac{1}{3}$,

$\frac{3}{4}, \frac{4}{5}$ c $1.008, 1.08, 1.084, 1.108, 1.18$ d $\frac{6}{100}, \frac{10}{50}, \frac{1}{3}, \frac{8}{20}, \frac{3}{4}$ e $0.9, 1\frac{3}{5}, 2.5, 3\frac{3}{10}, 3.31$ f $0.1,$

$\frac{1}{8}, 0.33, \frac{1}{2}, \frac{2}{3}$ 3 a $\sqrt{1600}, \sqrt{100}, \sqrt{16}, \sqrt{0.16}, \sqrt{0.0016}$ b $0.444, 0.44, 0.404, 0.4. 0.04$ c $\frac{5}{3}, \frac{10}{9}, \frac{9}{10}$,

$\frac{4}{5}, \frac{3}{5}$ d $0.77, \frac{2}{3}, 0.616, \frac{1}{5}, 0.166$ e $3.5, 2\frac{3}{5}, 2\frac{1}{10}, 1.2, \frac{1}{10}$ f $\frac{50}{\sqrt{25}}, \sqrt{81}, (\sqrt{8})^2, \frac{\sqrt{49}}{\sqrt{100}}, \frac{\sqrt{4}}{\sqrt{9}}$

Exercise 5:5

1 5 2 5.3 3 0.07 4 $-\frac{1}{40}$ 5 $3.2\dot{7}$ 6 50 7 26 8 4.214 9 $4\frac{1}{2}$ 10 $-12\frac{1}{2}$ 11 $\frac{1}{5}$ 12 0 13 -11

14 $\frac{31}{40}$ 15 $\frac{81}{128}$

Exercise 5:6

1 a $15 = 15$; yes b $10 \neq -10$; no c $17 = 17$; yes d $5 \neq -5$; no e $-7 \neq 7$; no f $6 \neq \frac{1}{6}$, no g $51 = 51$; yes
h $3 \neq \frac{1}{3}$; no i $36 = 36$; yes j $3 \neq \frac{1}{3}$, no k $-5 \neq 5$, no l $-18 = -18$ yes 2 a $80 = 80$; yes b $2400 = 2400$; yes
c $25 = 25$; yes d $50 = 50$; yes e $-1 \neq 5$; no f $-8 \neq 2$; no g $-1 \neq 7$; no h $5 \neq 27$; no i $2.5 \neq 160$; no

j $4 \neq 16$; no k $1.\dot{7} \neq 144$; no l $-80 = -80$; yes 3 a $22 \neq 70$; + is not distributive over × b $31 \neq 221$;
+ not is distributive over × c $9 \neq 2.85$; + is not distributive over ÷ d $40 \neq 1.41$; + is not distributive over ÷
e $-47 \neq -25$; − is not distributive over × f $8 \neq 352$; − is not distributive over × g $8 \neq -0.8$;

− is not distributive over ÷ h $26.\dot{6} ; \neq 1.19$; − is not distributive over ÷ i $-66 = -66$; × is distributive over −
2 j $-190 = -190$; × is distributive over − k $\frac{6}{7} \neq 0.14$; × is not distributive over ÷ l $28 \neq 2$; × is not distributive over ÷ m $0.14 \neq 0.98$; ÷ is not distributive over × n $1.6 \neq 8$; ÷ is not distributive over × o $\frac{3}{7} \neq -0.04$; ÷ is
not distributive over − p $12 \neq -12.5$; ÷ is not distributive over − q $11 \neq 7$, + is not distributive over − r $65 \neq 5$,
+ is not distributive over − s $7 \neq 35$, − is not distributive over + t $59 \neq 159$, − is not distributive over +
u $75 = 75$, × is distributive over + v $229.5 = 229.5$, × is distributive over + w $1.17 \neq 17.01$, ÷ is not distributive over + x $0.125 \neq 1.02$, ÷ is not distributive over + 4 a odd number, b an even c odd d even e closed,
operation, addition f closed, multiplication

Exercise 5:7

1 b, d, e 2 b, d 3 b, d 4 c, e 5 a 1.41 b 2.24 c 2.65 d 3.32 e 3.61 6 a 3 b $\frac{\sqrt{2}}{9}$, irrational

c $7\sqrt{7}$, irrational d $\frac{2\sqrt{5}}{\sqrt{2}}$, irrational e 4

Exercise 5:8

1 i 2 i both ii Z iii both iv neither 3 i both ii both iii both iv neither 4 i both ii both
iii both 4 iv Z v both vi both vii neither viii neither 5 N is closed under addition and
multiplication 6 Z is closed under addition, subtraction and multiplication

Exercise 5:9

1 Q is closed under all four operations (+, −, ×, ÷ if $a \div 0$ is not included). 2 none 3 a ∈, ⊂ b ∈, ⊂ c ∉ d ∉

e ∈, ⊂ f ∉ g ⊂, ∈, = h ⊂, ⊂ or ∈, ∈ 4 i $1\frac{4}{5}$; Q ii $\frac{19}{20}$, Q iii $1\frac{1}{2}$, Q iv $2\frac{19}{20}$, Q v $1\frac{7}{20}$, Q

vi $\frac{1}{10}$, Q vii $-1\frac{1}{10}$, Q viii $\frac{83}{80}$, Q ix $\frac{\sqrt{5}}{2}$, not Q x $2\frac{1}{2}$, Q xi $\frac{16}{3}$, Q xii $\frac{4}{55}$, Q

Fractal geometry

7

Size of square	Number of squares	Area of each square	Total area of squares	Total number of squares	Fraction of the original square
32 mm by 32 mm	1	32 × 32 = 1024 mm²	1 × 1024 = 1024 mm²	1	1
16 mm by 16 mm	4	16 × 16 = 256 mm²	4 × 256 = 1024 mm²	5	¼
8 mm by 8 mm	16	8× 8 = 64 mm²	16 × 64 = 1024 mm²	21	¹⁄₁₆
4 mm by 4 mm	64	4 × 4 = 16 mm²	64 × 16 = 1024 mm²	85	¹⁄₆₄
2 mm by 2 mm	256	2 × 2 = 4 mm²	256 × 4 = 1024 mm²	341	¹⁄₂₅₆
1 mm by 1 mm	1024	1 × 1 = 1 mm²	1024 × 1 = 1024 mm²	1365	¹⁄₁₀₂₄

8 1365 **10** 6144 mm² **11 i** 1 : 1024 **ii** as in the 6th column

Extension

1 a $0.\overset{..}{27}$; recurs **b** 0.3; terminates **c** 0.375; terminates **d** $0.42857\overset{.}{1}$; recurs **e** 0.6; terminates **2** 16 **3 a** $\dfrac{1001}{9999}$

b $\dfrac{19}{99}$ **c** $5\dfrac{721}{999}$ **d** $13\dfrac{74}{99}$ **4 a** $\dfrac{53}{990}$ **b** $\dfrac{169}{330}$ **c** $\dfrac{34}{99}$ **d** $\dfrac{23082}{9999}$ **e** $\dfrac{7103}{666}$ **5** possible answers: **a** $\dfrac{16}{10}$ **b** $\dfrac{19}{5}$

c $\dfrac{7}{10}$ **d** $\dfrac{141}{200}$ **6 a** $\dfrac{1}{5}$ **b** $\dfrac{1}{3}$ **c** $\dfrac{1}{100}$ **d** $\dfrac{4}{5}$ **e** $\dfrac{1}{2}$ **7** possible answers: **a** $6 > \sqrt{37} > 7$ **b** $3.1 > \sqrt{10.23} > 3.2$

8 i N & Z are closed **ii** N & Z are closed **iii** Z is closed, N not closed **iv** N & Z are not closed **9 a** true

b true **c** false **10 a** $-7.5, -3.3, -\sqrt{7}, -2, 0, \frac{1}{3}, \sqrt{0.9}, \sqrt{3}, \sqrt{4.9}, 2\frac{1}{2}, \sqrt{21}, 5.05, 7.8, 9$

b i 9 **ii** −2, 0, 9 **iii** 9 **iv** $\sqrt{0.9}, \sqrt{3}, \sqrt{4.9}, -\sqrt{7}, \sqrt{21}$ **v** $9, \sqrt{4.9}, \frac{1}{3}, 2\frac{1}{2}, \sqrt{3}, 0, \sqrt{21}, 7.8, 5.05,$

$\sqrt{0.9}$, **vi** 9, −2 **vii** −2 **viii** $-7.5, -2, -3.3, \frac{1}{3}, 2\frac{1}{2}, 5.05, 7.8, 9$ **11** possible answers: $7 \times 5 = 35; 3 \times 5 = 15;$

$3 \times 17 = 51; 5 \times 19 = 95$ **12 a** $\dfrac{3}{2}$ **b** $\dfrac{3\sqrt{5}}{\sqrt{2}}$ **c** $\sqrt{21}$ **d** $4\sqrt{30}$

Chapter 6 Shape and space

Exercise 6:2

2 a cylinder **b** cuboid **c** cylinder **d** cube **e** sphere **f** triangular prism **3 a** 6, 12, 8 **b** 4, 6, 4 **c** 6, 12, 8
d 8, 12, 6 **e** 5, 8, 5 **f** 5, 9, 6 **4 a** 12 **b** 8 **c** 6 **d** EF, HG (or AD) **e** square **5 a** 9 **b** 6 **c** 5 **d** FA
e FD, AE **6 a** 8 **b** 5 **c** 5 **d** square **e** 4 **7** Tetrahedron - triangles; Parallelepiped - parallelograms;
Octahedron - equilateral triangles; Icosahedron - pentagons **9** E = V + F − 2

Exercise 6:3

9 a a, c, d, f - makes cubes; b, e, g, h - do not make cubes **10 a** *F* is opposite *A*; in net **c** *E* is opposite *A*;
in net **d** *C* is opposite *A*; in net **f** *D* is opposite *A*; **11 a** pentagonal pyramid **b** 6 **c** 10 **d** 6 **12 a** triangular
prism **b** *H* **c** *C & G* **d** *DC* **13 a** Cone **b** Cylinder

Extension

1 prisms: triangular based, circular based, rectangular based, hexagonal based; non prism: cone, sphere,
triangular based pyramid, square based pyramid **2** 84 cm **3 a** triangular prism **b** triangle based pyramid
c cuboid **4 a** right angle triangle **b** 9 **c** GF **d** A & E **7** semi-circular based prism, two cylinders
11 i 24 cubes **ii** 60 faces **iii** 400 cm² **iv** 24 000 cm² **v a** 4 cubes **b** 8 cubes **c** 8 cubes **d** 4 cubes

Chapter 8 Algebraic expressions

Exercise 8:1

1 19 **2** 11 **3** 18 **4** 5 **5** 3 **6** 2 **7** 16 **8** 2 **9** 6 **10** 3 **11** $\dfrac{73}{90}$ **12** 0 **13** 209 **14** $1\dfrac{3}{16}$ **15** $8\dfrac{14}{15}$
16 16 **17** 24 **18** −50 **19** 50 **20** 13 **21** $6\frac{3}{5}$

Exercise 8:2

1 $30 \div (2 + 3)$ **2** $(30 \div 2) + 3$ **3** $2 \times (3 + 4) \times 2$ **4** $(15 - 3) \div 2$ **5** $4 \times (5 - 2) \times 3$
6 $15 + (14 - 11) + (13 - 12)$ **7** $(18 - 8) \times 12 \div 3$ **8** $(6 + 2) \times (3 + 4)$ **9** $(52 \div (10 + 3) + 27 - 9$
10 $(8 \div 16) \times (43 - 19)$ **11** $(-3 + 56) + (23 - 5)$ **12** $(88 - 17) - 91 + (9 - 8)$ **13** $((7 - 15) \times 8) + 67$
14 $3 \times (20 - 14) \div (24 \div 8)$ **15** $-6 \times (-43 \div 344) \times 84$

Page 172   *Exercise 8:4*

1 –4   2 5   3 7   4 –7   5 1   6 12   7 –10   8 26

Page 173   *Exercise 8:5*

1 –12   2 –28   3 99   4 –4   5 6   6 3   7 –36   8 115   9 108   10 29.5   11 –5   12 8   13 –6a   14 4a
15 70r   16 a   17 –3a   18 4a   19 st^2 20 $8k^2$ 21 $-5p^3$ 22 –18   23 –3x   24 –5   25 –105ab
26 $-36x^2y$ 27 y^3 28 6a   29 $-5\frac{1}{2}x$ 30 –6   31 288ab   32 $-144a^2b^2$ 33 $288a^2w^2x^2$ 34 10p   35 $-3\frac{1}{2}s$
36 $\frac{1}{3}c$ 37 $30p^2$ 38 –2xz   39 $-x^2y$

Page 174   *Exercise 8:6*

1 12x + 12y   2 3x – 3y   3 20 + 30x   4 –4x – 2y   5 0.8x – 20y   6 3b – 3a   7 10x – 30 8 2axy + 4bxy
9 6 – 8m   10 ax – ay – az   11 30a + 20b – 10c   12 $\frac{1}{2}x - \frac{1}{2}$ 13 $2m + 6m^2 + 8mn$ 14 5z – x – 3y
15 32c – 24a – 28b   16 $3x^3 - 6x^2y + 3x^2y^2$ 17 1.2a – 0.12b + 0.012c   18 25z – 2.5x – 15y   19 $6p - 8p^2 + 10p^3$
20 $2a^2 + 4ab + 0.5ac$ 21 28 – 21m + 5n   22 6x + t + s   23 $\frac{2}{5}a - 2\frac{4}{5}x - 18y$ 24 49a + 28b – 63c

Page 175   *Exercise 8:7*

1 21x + 30   2 10x + 3a + 3b   3 12xy + 2x – 2y   4 11 – 14x   5 2c – a – 3b   6 12a + 8   7 –7a – 7b
8 –9a – 7   9 –19x – 19y   10 3a + 3b + 3c   11 $6q - 4q^2 - 5z$ 12 $l^2 - 36$ 13 6g – 7gf – 6f   14 $x^2 - 12x + 2$
15 $f^2 + 2$ 16 $-4 - z^2$ 17 $14xy - 31x - 26x^2 + 45y$ 18 41a + 105ab + 3b + 3   19 $-5\frac{1}{2}y - 5\frac{1}{2}x$
20 6.7y – 0.8x   21 12a + 13b   22 11 – 4a – 7b   23 3b – 5a   24 4.2x – 6y

Page 178   *Exercise 8:9*

1 2x + 2y cm   2 4x + 16 cm   3 8a + 6 cm   4 12x + 12y + 8 cm   5 19 + 4x cm   6 2x + 14y + 4 cm
7 18x + 13y – 5 cm   8 15 + 3x + 6z cm   9 8p + 8q – 6 cm

Page 179   *Exercise 8:10*

1 a 74 b 27 c 5 d 57   2 a –56   b –3 c –7 d $-\frac{1}{4}$ 3 a –33 b –31.5 c 71 d –22   4 a 74 b 251 c 4
d 3929   5 a –18 b –16 c $-30\frac{7}{12}$ d 2   6 a –200 b –7 c –60 d $196\frac{4}{5}$ 7 a –816 b –12.75 c 39 d 1181
8 a $14\frac{4}{5}$ b $-\frac{1}{2}$ c $24\frac{3}{4}$ d $8\frac{1}{2}$ 9 a 88 b 19 c 118 d –270   10 a –58 b –1 c 538 d –15   11 a 45 b –121
c $\frac{1}{6}$ d $2\frac{3}{10}$ 12 a 7.8 b –8.56 c –88.5   13 a 64.05 b 70 c 290   14 a 7 b $2\frac{1}{2}$ c $37\frac{2}{5}$ 15 78.3   16 $1\frac{1}{7}$
17 a 12 b 280 c –50   18 1051.80   19 9   20 a –6.38 °C   b –28.3 °C c –20 °C d 29.4 °C e 58.7 °C

Page 181   *Exercise 8:11*

1 8(q +2)   2 2(a + 2b)   3 4(a – 2)   4 3(4a – 3y)   5 5(2a – 1)   6 10(x – 3y)   7 3(2 – 5x)   8 x(1 – 6y)
9 xy(2 + z)   10 2y(3x – 2z)   11 x(y + 3)   12 7(a – 7b + 3c)   13 d(5 + c)   14 k(5p – q)   15 j(3k – 2)
16 11x(a + 3 – 11y)   17 3k(2j – 3)   18 4(3a + 2b)   19 17x(1 – 3y)   20 0.5x(1 – 3a – 5y)   21 5b(3a + c)
22 $\frac{1}{4}a(3c - 16)$ 23 18g(1 + 4h)   24 5(2a + b – 7ab)   25 9(8pt – 6t – 1)   26 xy(z + 5w)   27 eg(27f + 77)
28 0.8x(n – 2y + 10)   29 27(a + 3ab – 4)   30 25m(3n – 2p)   31 9y(7xz – 6)   32 $8\frac{1}{2}(6p + 2pq - 1)$

Page 182   *Exercise 8:12*

1 x(2 + 3x)   2 a(1 – a)   3 a(b – c)   4 c(8c + 1)   5 6p(3p + 2q)   6 $9e^2(c + 4)$ 7 3gh(h + 5g)
8 6d(4d + 3y)   9 $k^2(l^2 - 11j)$ 10 $a^2(1 + 5b)$ 11 $8(y^2 - 4)$ 12 $4(n^2 - 3m^2)$ 13 gh(gh – 6)   14 $2p^2q(q+3)$
15 7kl(3kl – 2)   16 16m(m + 3l)   17 $6(5a^2 - 2m^3)$ 18 $xy(16x^2 - 15)$ 19 2pqr(3p – q)   20 $3s^2(3 - 2s)$
21 $7f^2(e + 4)$ 22 9st(2s – 3t)   23 $5a^3b(b + 2)$ 24 $a(a^2 - 7a + 5)$ 25 8xy(z – 4w)   26 $x(x + 3x^2 - 5)$
27 7xy(2x – 3y)   28 $a^2x(7x^2 + a^2)$ 29 $\pi(R^2 - r^2)$ 30 $m(gh - \frac{1}{2}v^2)$ 31 $\frac{1}{2}m(u^2 - v)$ 32 4a(3 – 5ab)
33 $P(1 + \frac{RT}{100})$ 34 $\frac{1}{2}h(a - b)$ 35 $2r(h_1 - h_2)$ 36 $2p(1 - 2p + 5p^2)$ 37 $x(1 + 3x - 5x^2)$ 38 $r(\pi^2 + 5)$
39 Mn(n – M)   40 2πr(r + h)   41 3ab(1 + 2a – 3b)   42 $\frac{1}{6}bc(b - 2c)$ 43 $\pi h(r^2 + R^2)$ 44 $\frac{1}{3}\pi r^2(r - h)$

Page 183   *Extension*

1 a –12 b –3 c 36 d –0.30 e 0.0036 f 3.95   2 a –12pq b –16.9xy c $6x^2y^2$ d $-6x^3y^2$ e $1.6s^2t^2$
f 132abc   3 a 2n – 2d b 8k – 4c c 17s + 20t + 4h d 27a + 2b + 7c e 17a – 6b – 9c f 5by – 10xy – 9x
4 a 2x – 3d b 3c + 7d c –y d 7x e 30b – 20a f 10a – 5k   5 a area: $8 + 14x + 6x^2$ perimeter: 12 + 10x
b area: $16c^2 + 4cx + 2x + 8c$; perimeter: 12 + 4x + 8c   c area: $19a^2 + 25ab + 10b^2$; perimeter: 19a + 10b
d area: $6y^2 + 12xy$; perimeter: 10x + 10y   6 a 2.6 b 6.95   7 a 0.34 b 494   8 a $\frac{3}{8}$ b $\frac{101}{187}$ 9 9a + 9b

367

Chapter 8 Extension

10 $120x + 60y$ **11** $90m + 75n$ **12** $18\frac{2}{3}x - 4\frac{2}{3}y$ **14 a** 132 **b** 270 **c** 180 **d** 108.5 **e** 1008 **f** 1518 **g** 735
h 1920 **i** 2300 **j** 180 **k** −22.592 **l** 42 **m** 1550.5 **n** 119.65 **o** 973 **15 i** $5\frac{2}{3}a + 9b$ **ii** $5n + x + 5$
iii $2c + 6x + 13y$ **16 a** $3(3a + 9b + 5c)$ **b** $\frac{1}{4}n(x + 3y + 2z)$ **c** $\frac{2}{5}b(a + 1 - 2c)$ **d** $3b(5a + 6c + 7d)$
e $y(x^2y + n^2 + b^2y)$ **f** $17x(2ab + y - 3ay)$ **g** $8xy(4b + 5c - 3a)$ **h** $\frac{1}{5}y(x + 2n - 3)$ **i** $\frac{1}{3}x(y + 9 + 3x)$
18 $14 - 9a$ **b** $3a^2 - 34a - 12$ **c** $0.4x + 3.4y - 1.8$ **d** $7 - 9a$ **e** $5a + 6$ **f** $12a - 3ab - 2b$

Chapter 9 Number plane

Exercise 9:1

1 a James Fort **b** Cantonments **c** Usher Town **d** Mamobi **e** Asylum Down **2 a** (5, 4) **b** (8, 10)
c (8.5, 8.5) **d** (6.5, 4.5) **e** (5.5, 2.5) **f** (4, 3) **3 a** 2 **b** 6 **c** 4 **d** 8.5 **e** 9 **f** 7 **4 a** (5.5, 12) **b** (2.25, 2.25)
c (8, 7) **d** (5.5, 6) **e** (3, 7.5) **f** (4.5, 2) **5 a** 1.4 km **b** 1.4 km **c** 4.2 km **d** 7 km **e** 6.3 km **f** 4.9 km
6 a 20 km; 16 km² **b** 30 km; 50 km² **c** 14 km; 11.76 km² **7 a** (2, 3.5) **b** (1, 7) **c** (3, 7.5) **d** (5.5, 6)
e (5.5, 10) **f** (6, 3.5) **g** (8, 7) **h** (4.25, 4.25)

Exercise 9:2

3 i square **ii** rectangle **iii** right angle triangle **iv** hexagon **5 b** (−2, 0) **6 b** (1, 6) **7 b** (−1, 5) **8 b** (−2, 3)
9 MATHS IS THE QUEEN OF ALL SUBJECTS **10** TAKE CARE WITH X AND Y **11 i a** Sugar cane **b**
Tomatoes **c** Corn **d** Garden eggs **e** Mangoes **f** Plantain **ii a** (4, 2) **b** (6, 3) **c** (9, 1.5) **d** (6.5, 6) **e** (3, 9.5)
f (5.5, 8.5) **g** (2, 3) **h** (2.5, 4.5) **iii a** (11, 4.25) **b** (6.75, 7) **c** (7.5, 5.5) **d** (2.5, 2) **iv a** 42m **b** $37\frac{1}{2}$ **c** $43\frac{1}{2}$

Exercise 9:4

1 d i the x-coordinate of line A is always 1 **ii** the y-coordinate of line B is always 4 **4 b** A: $x = -3.5$; B: $x = 4$
C: $y = 2.5$ D: $y = -3$ E: $y = -4.5$ F: $y = 0.5$ G: $x = 2.5$ **c i** (4, 2.5) **ii** (−3.5, 4.5) **iii** (−3.5, −3) **iv** (2.5, 0)
5 b i $y = -3$ **ii** $x = -2$ **iii** $x = -5$ **iv** $y = 6.5$ **v** $y = 1$ **vi** $x = -3.5$

Exercise 9:5

1 a 2 **b** $1\frac{1}{2}$ **c** $\frac{1}{2}$ **d** 4 **e** $\frac{1}{4}$ **f** 1 **g** $1\frac{1}{2}$ **h** 4 **i** $\frac{2}{3}$ **2 a** b and g; d and h, **b** they are parallel **3** $\frac{2}{3}$ **4 a** 6
b 1 **c** $\frac{1}{6}$ **d** $1\frac{2}{7}$ **e** 3 **f** $2\frac{1}{2}$ **g** $2\frac{2}{3}$ **h** 2 **i** $-\frac{1}{4}$ **5 a** −2 **b** $-\frac{1}{2}$ **c** $-\frac{3}{4}$ **d** $-1\frac{2}{3}$ **e** −3 **f** $-\frac{2}{5}$ **g** $\frac{1}{2}$ **h** −3
6 a $-\frac{3}{5}$ **b** $-1\frac{2}{7}$ **c** $-2\frac{1}{3}$ **d** $-1\frac{2}{5}$ **e** 2 **f** $3\frac{1}{6}$

Exercise 9:6

1 A-B = 0.18; B-C = 1.67; C-D = 1.33; D-E = 1.74; E-F = 1.05 **2 b** J-K = 0.83; K-L = 0.77; L-M = 0.91;
M-N = 1.2; N-P = 0.56; D-E = 0.70; E-F = 0.68; F-G = 1.25; G-H = 1.67; H-P = 0.64 **3 a** from left to right
b path q is steeper as it crosses contour lines from 300 to 700 m; path p crossed from 300 - 500 m
d Gradients: D-E = $\frac{1}{3}$ **e** No

Exercise 9:7

2 $y = 2x$ **b** $y = 2x - 1$ **c** $y = x - 2$ **d** $y = 2x - 2$ **e** $y = 5x + 3$ **f** $y = -3x - 2\frac{1}{2}$ **4 ii** $y = x - 1$ **iv** $m = 1$
5 ii $y = 4x + 1$ **iv** $m = 4$ **8 c** $m = 4$ **d** $a = 17$ **9 c** $m = 3$ **d** $y = 14.5$ **e** $b = -3$ **10** $y = x + 2$; $m = 1$; $c = 2$
11 $y = 2x - 2$; $m = 2$; $c = -2$ **12** $y = x - 1$; $m = 1$; $c = -1$ **13** $y = -2x + 4$; $m = -2$; $c = 4$ **14** $y = 3x$; $m = 3$;
$c = 0$ **15** $y = -x - 5$; $m = -1$; $c = -5$ **16 iv** Gradients are: 1, 1, −1, 2 **17 a** (5, 6) **b** $y = 2x - 4$

Extension

1 a (−800, 900) **b** (300, 900) **c** (900, 700) **d** (400, −600) **e** (−500, −100) **f** (800, −100) **g** (0, 400) **h** (−350, 550)
i (450, 350) **2** A: $y = 4x - 2$, B: $y = 2x - 1$ C: $y = 3 - 3x$ D: $y = 4 - 3x$ **3 b** (−1, −1) **4 c** (3.5, 9.5) **5 i a** (1.5, 4);
b 2 **ii a** (2, 2); **b** −1 **iii a** (1, 0); **b** −1 **iv a** (0.5, 4); **b** 1 **v a** (−8.5, −5.5); **b** $1\frac{6}{23}$ **vi a** (10.5, −14); **b** $10\frac{2}{3}$
6 (120, 703) lies on the line $y = 6x - 17$: when $x = 120$, $y = 703$, gradients is 6. **7** Equation for line A is $y = 2x$;
equation for line B is $y = 3x + 5$ **8 c i** 90 km **ii** 4h 50 mins **iii** 2h 58 mins **iv** 286 km **d** $y = 60x$ **9 c** 30 cm
d i 37.5 cm **ii** 44.25 cm **e** 45 N **f** $y = 0.3x + 30$

Chapter 10 Quadrilaterals

Exercise 10:1
4 a 360° **b** 360° **5 a** 180° **b** 180° **c** 180° **d** 360° **e** 360°

Exercise 10:2
1 $\beta = 97°$ **2** $\beta = 98°$ **3** $\beta = 148°$ **4** $\beta = 114°$ **5** $\beta = 73°$ **6** $\beta = 112°$ **7** $\beta = 132°$ **8** $\beta = 56°$ **9** $\beta = 106°$
10 $\beta = 110°$ **11** $\beta = 84°$ **12** $\beta = 136°$

Chapter 10 Quadrilaterals

Exercise 10:3

1 a four **b** sides **c** parallel **d** four **e** two/parallel/four **f** one **g** quadrilateral/all/all **h** unequal/irregular
2 a Rectangle **b** Right trapezium **c** Parallelogram **d** Square **e** Kite **f** Trapezium **g** Kite **3 a** Kite
b Isosceles trapezium/Kite **c** Rhombus/Parallelogram **d** Trapezium **e** Rhombus **f** Trapezium

4 a M, G, N, A, C, E, K, I **b** B **c** A, M, G, N **d** Q, L **e** F **f** O, D

Exercise 10:4

1 117° **2** 95° **3** 61° **4** 124° **5** 68° **6** 58°

Exercise 10:5

1 a 112° **b** 56° **c** 68° **2 a** 36° **b** 54° **3 a** 73° **b** 107° **c** 34° **4 a** 42° **b** 30° **c** 108° **5** 107°
6 a 28° **b** 28° **c** 76° **7** $\theta = 37^{\circ}$ **8** $\beta = 83^{\circ}; \theta = 37^{\circ}$ **9** $\alpha = 66^{\circ}; \beta = 37^{\circ}; \theta = 106^{\circ}$ **10** $\beta = 113^{\circ};$
$\theta = 45^{\circ}$ **11** $\alpha = 129^{\circ}; \beta = 129^{\circ}; \theta = 51^{\circ}$ **12** $\angle BDC = 58^{\circ} \angle ADC = 116^{\circ}$ and $\angle BAD = 64^{\circ}$
13 $\angle QRS = 119^{\circ}$ **14 a** $W\hat{V}X = 35^{\circ}$ **b** angles of $\triangle WXY: Y\hat{W}X = 17.5^{\circ}; X\hat{Y}W = 17.5^{\circ}; W\hat{X}Y = 145^{\circ};$ **c** angles of
$\triangle VZY: V\hat{W}Z = 72.5^{\circ}; W\hat{Z}V = 72.5^{\circ}; W\hat{V}Z = 35^{\circ};$ **d** $V\hat{Z}Y = 107.5^{\circ}; Z\hat{V}Y = 30^{\circ}; V\hat{Y}Z = 42.5^{\circ}$
15 $HG = 7.2$ cm: 72 m; $FH = 12.4$ cm : 124 m; $EG = 10.4$ cm : 104 m

Extension

1 $\alpha = 129^{\circ}; \beta = 103^{\circ}; \theta = 109^{\circ}$ **2 i** $\alpha = \beta = \theta = \varepsilon = 90^{\circ}$ **ii** $\alpha = \theta = 69^{\circ}; \beta = 111^{\circ};$ **iii** $\alpha = \beta = 98^{\circ};$
$\theta = 82^{\circ}$ **3 i** $\varepsilon = 82^{\circ};$ **ii** $\varepsilon = 98^{\circ};$ **4** $A\hat{D}C = 116^{\circ}$ **5** 101° **6** $\alpha = 113^{\circ}; \beta = 28^{\circ}; \theta = 67^{\circ}$ **7** $\varepsilon = 62^{\circ}$ **8** 76°
9 $69^{\circ}; 111^{\circ}; 62^{\circ}$ **10 a** 63° **b** 54° **c** 126° **11** $\alpha = 33^{\circ}; \beta = 144^{\circ}; \theta = 216^{\circ}$ **12** $\alpha = 42^{\circ}; \beta = 80^{\circ}; \theta = 58^{\circ}$
13 $\alpha = 57^{\circ}; \beta = 66^{\circ}; \theta = 57^{\circ}$ **14** $\alpha = 38^{\circ}; \beta = 67^{\circ}; \theta = 105^{\circ}$ **15 c** $RT = 4.6$ cm : 92 m **d** $RQ = 8.8$ cm :
176 m; $QP = 2.6$ cm : 52 m **16 b** $JL = 17.6$ cm : 704 m; $KM = 10.6$ cm : 424 m **c** 7.1 cm : 284 m

Chapter 11 Ratio and proportion

Exercise 11:1

1 ii a g (7 parts of concentrated orange to 1 part of water) **b** a (1 part of concentrated orange to 7 parts of water)
c No **2 a** 3:13 **b** 4:5 **c** 5:7 **d** 4:14 **e** 30:70 **3 a** 20:30 **b** 120:93 **c** 900:1350 **d** 120:90 **e** 18:30
f 36:57 **4 a** 1:3 **b** 4:12 **c** 3:13 **d** 7:9 **5** 35 teachers **6 a** 5:1 **b** 5:4 **c** 1:2 **d** 2:4 **7 a** 6 **b** 14
c 32 **8 a** for 15 of mortar - 2.5:1.25:11.25 **b** for 120 of mortar - 20:10:90 **c** for 300 of mortar - 50:25:225
9 a Grated coconut 750g; grated ginger - 300g; dark rum drink - 300ml; cane sugar - 472.5g **b i** dark rum - 500ml
ii cane sugar - 787.5g **10** 1050g **11 a** 5 times **b** 22 times **c** 7.5 times **d** 5 times **e** 3 times **f** 6 times
g 7.5 times **h** 7 times **12 a** 3.46 times **b** 3.95 times **c** 5.93

Exercise 11:2

1 300 cm **2** 5000 kg **3** 7000 m **4** 150 mins **5** 9500 mm **6** 8500 g **7** 5000 ml **8** 1.5 m **9** 630 mins
10 1850 g **11** 165 mins **12** 1508 mm **13** 165 secs **14** 185 cm **15** 170.5 cm

Exercise 11:3

1 1:3 **2** 3:4 **3** 2:3 **4** 5:8 **5** 15:4 **6** 3:2:4 **7** 1:4 **8** 1:3 **9** 1:5 **10** 32:15 **11** 80:3
12 5:4 **13** 1:4 **14** 15:7 **15** 5:3 **16** 1:5 **17** 5:14:30 **18** 1:6:3 **19** 5:2:100 **20** 100:1:6
21 9:5 **22** 1:10:60 **23** 5:7:9 **24** 2:3:5

Exercise 11:4

1 4:3:5 **2 a** 3:2 **b** 2:5 **3 a** 4:3 **b** 4:7 **4** 1:90 **5** 2:1:6 **6** 4:11 **7** $\frac{9}{13}$ **8 a** $\frac{2}{5}$ **b** $\frac{3}{5}$ **9** 1:18
10 a 20:1 **b** His ratio is 19:1 so he doesn't need more teachers **11 a** 300ml of water **b** 350ml solution made up
12 a 4:3 **b** $BC = 6$ cm; $AB = 4.5$ **13 a** 7:8 **b** 5.5:5 **c** 25:26 **d** 38.5:40

Exercise 11:5

1 a 8 mangoes to Ampadu and 4 mangoes to Serwaah **b** 9 oranges to Kujo and 6 aranges to Ama
c 9 tomatoes to Kwamina and 21 tomatoes to Haji **d** 15 pineapples to Asare and 12 pineapples to Dadze
2 24m : 40m **b** ¢2000 : ¢500 **c** ¢1870 : ¢680 **d** 36kg : 18kg : 12kg **e** 280ml : 210ml : 70ml
f 0.2 kg : 0.4 kg : 0.6 kg **3** 182 : 104 **4** ¢1500 **6** 0.4 : 1.2 : 1.6 **7** copper-21kg; zinc-31.5; tin-52.5kg

8 $XZ = 48$cm, $ZY = 36$cm **9** $28 : 20 : 12$ **10 a** 1400 **b** $3360l$ **11** Minka - 124; Kankam - 116 **12** $75^\circ : 60^\circ : 45^\circ$
13 a Bonsu-¢37.50; Bawa-¢12.50; Dumfe-¢50; **b** Bonsu-¢247.50; Bawa-¢82.50; Dumfe-¢330 **c** Bonsu-¢4500;
Bawa-¢1500; Dumfe-¢6000 **14 a** $\frac{5}{23}$; $\frac{7}{23}$; $\frac{11}{23}$ **b** $950 : 1330 : 2090$ **15 a** 3.45kg **b** 5.75kg
16 $45^\circ : 75^\circ : 105^\circ : 135^\circ$ **17** ¢2625 : ¢600 : ¢1275 **18** 11 litres **19** senior partner; $0.006 \, \text{km}^2$ more
20 Atta - ¢356.50; Kanu - ¢414; Anto - ¢494.50

1 563.2km **2** 5 hrs 24 mins **3** 175 **4** 425g **5** 21.75m **6** 5.232kg **7** 93km **8** 87cm **9 a** 0.75kg **b** 400m²
10 6h **11 a** sand-244.4kg; cement-585kg **12** ¢32.40 **13** $22\frac{1}{2}$p **14** ¢4.09 **15 a** ¢44.20 **b** 225km **16 a** €171
b €63 **c** €401.14 **d** €585 **17 a** 6.75×10^6 **b** 2.205×10^7 **c** 1.35×10^4 **d** 6.363×10^7 **18** 70km/h

1 a i b **i** c **iii** d **i** e **i** f **iii** g **ii** h **ii** **2 a** 6 labourers **b** 12 days **3 a** 144 desks **b** 18 rows
4 a 273 days **b** 20 days **5** 25 days **6** 28 **7** 54 mins **8** 76 lines **9** 6 days **10** 16 bars **11** pc always = 160
c when p doubles c halves **12** 195.6 kHz

1 a i $V \propto t$ **ii** $V = kt$ **b i** $d \propto s^2$ **ii** $d = ks^2$ **c i** $c \propto r$ **ii** $c = kr$ **d i** $x \propto \frac{1}{y}$ **ii** $x = \frac{k}{y}$ **e i** $d \propto \sqrt{h}$
ii $d = k\sqrt{h}$ **2 a** P is inversely proportional to m **b** A is inversely proportional to the square root of x.
c S is inversely proportional to the square root of x **d** B is proportional to the cube root of t **3 a** $m^2 = \frac{k}{p}$
b $d = \frac{k}{g^2}$ **c** $V^2 = kt^3$ **d** $A = \frac{k}{x^3}$ **4** $y = 30$ **5** $p = 86\frac{1}{3}$ **6** $K = 12.5$ **7** $A = 3$ **8** $G = 2.4$ **9** $x = 1.5$
10 b $k = 0.0125$ **11** $p = 5q^2$ **12** 640 watts **14** 3h **15 a** 1m **b** 1.5625 m **c** 36m **16** 0.125 **18** 5 N/m²
b 93.54 mm **19 a** 31250 **b** 7812 coins **c** $\sqrt{\frac{31250}{y}}$ **d** 2.99 cm **20 a** 27 candela **b** 5.37 m

1 56.25g **2** 2.5 hrs **3** 0.72 kg **4 a** 480m **b** 625 revs **5** 128.8 ml **6** 13 days **7 a** 326.4cm² **b** 244 **8** 45.5m
11 a 2 units **b** 4 units **c** 5.65 units **ii a** 21.25 hrs **b** 7.65 hrs **c** 26.775 hrs **12 a** $c = kz$ **b i** ¢34 **ii** ¢25.50

1 55.7 cm **2** 36.3 cm

1 a 1 : 6 **b** 1 : 13.5 **c** 1 : 150 **d** 1 : 600 **e** 1 : 15 000 **2 a** 13.875km **b** 16.5km **c** 41.25km **d** 15 km
e 32.25km **f** 40.875km **3 a** 16km **b** 24.8 m **c** 22.4 m **d** 6.8m **e** 18.8m **f** 13.2 m **4 a** 26m **b** 32m
c 17.5m **d** 26m **e** 23.5m **f** 19.5m **5 a** 3cm **b** 4cm **c** 6cm **d** 3.5cm **e** 4.4cm **f** 4.4cm **7 b** 5.7m
c 5.15m **8 b** 9.45cm **c** 2.35m **d** 113° **9 a** 3750 cm **b** 400 cm **10 a** 1 : 200 **b** 4.5m by 4m **11 a** 383m
b 655m **c** 400m **d** 740m **e** 825m **12 a** 17.75km **b** 19.5km **c** 21.5km **d** 23.25km **13 a** 6.3km **b** 11.4km
c 10.6km **d** 14.5km **14** 5.696km **15 a** 279km **b** 269km **c** 675km **d** 3.44 cm **e** 580km **17 a** 32 steps
b 17.2cm

1 a Nimoh-$\frac{1}{8}$ Yamoah-$\frac{1}{4}$; Ohemah-$\frac{5}{8}$; **b** Nimoh-¢50; Yamoah-¢100; Ohemah-¢250 **2 a** 7:3 **b** 14 **3 a** $\frac{2}{7}$
b 76 **c** ¢3648 **4 a** $l = \frac{5}{6}h$ **b** $h = 18$m **c** $l = 12.5$m **d** $l = 15.71$m **5 a** $V = 1.85l$ **b** 6.71amps **6 a** $r = 1.67$
$t = 16.53$ **c** $r = 3.52$ **7** 60 years, 30 years, 20 years, 12 years **8 a** 6:2:1 **b** Spinach-4875 g, Palm oil-1625 g,
Onions-26 medium, Tomatoes-26 large, Meat-1625g, Red chilli peppers-19$\frac{1}{2}$, Smoked herrings-812.5g,
Prawns-1300g, Egushi-650g **9 a** 1 : 6 **b** 1 : 3.27 **c** 1 : 0.52 **d** 1 : 11.39 **10** $A = 11.25$ **11 a** 0.2km **b** 0.6km
c 1.4km **12 a** $E = 2.5m$ **b** 17kg **13 a** $y = \frac{80}{x^2}$ **b** 3.2 **14 a** 32ml **b** 6.08cm **15** 2.572×10^6 **b** 92.56m
16 a 4800 m **b** 5.68 km **c** 0.5%

Chapter 12 Mapping

12 a 'divided by 3 gives' **b** 'subtract 210 gives' **c** 'decimal fraction is'

16 a 18 **b** −10 **c** 12 **d** $4a + 10$ **17 a** −62 **b** −142 **c** −$4\frac{1}{4}$ **d** $2 - b^2$ **18 a** $3\frac{1}{6}$ **b** $3\frac{1}{2}$**c** $5\frac{1}{3}$ **d** −$5\frac{1}{3}$

Exercise 12:5

1 $x - 6$ **2** $5x - 2$ **3** $2x + 3$ **4** $6x + 6$ **5** $\frac{1}{4}x$ **6** x^3 **9 a** $\{-12, -8, -4, 0, 4, 8, 12\}$ **b** $\{-3.5, -2.5, -0.5, 0.5, 1.5, 2.5\}$ **c** $\{-3, -1, 1, 3, 5, 7, 9\}$ **10 a** $\{2, 7, 12, 37, 22, 0\}$ **b** $\{12.5, 37.5, 100, 62.5, 7.5\}$ **c** $\{-8\frac{1}{3}, 10, 50, 37\frac{1}{2}, -11\frac{2}{3}\}$ **11 a** $\{\frac{1}{4}, 2\frac{1}{2}, -1\frac{1}{2}, 4\frac{1}{2}, 6, 14\}$ **b** $\{\frac{1}{5}, \frac{3}{5}, 1, 1\frac{4}{5}, 2\frac{4}{5}, 5\frac{3}{5}\}$ **c** $\{31, 23, 15, 7, -1, -9, -17\}$

Exercise 12:6

1 $x - 1$ **2** $x + 7$ **3** $\frac{x}{2}$ **4** $\frac{x}{5}$ **5** $\frac{x+4}{2}$ **6** $\frac{3x}{2}$ **7** $\sqrt{\frac{x}{3}}$ **8** $\sqrt{\frac{x-4}{2}}$ **9** $10 + 5x$ **10** $\left(\frac{1}{x-10}\right)^2$ **11** $9 - \frac{1}{2}x$

12 $\frac{x-4}{2}$ **13** $\frac{7x+63}{2}$ **14** $5x - 120$ **15** $\frac{2x-12}{5}$ **16** $\sqrt{\frac{x-11}{9}}$

Exercise 12:8

1 a 6 **b** -12 **c** 30 **d** 66 **2 a** 8 **b** 3 **c** 9 **d** 13 **3 a** 17 **b** 26 **c** -22 **d** 38 **4 a** 0 **b** 24 **c** 310 **d** 80
7 $3x$ **8** $3x - 3$ **9** $x^2 + 5$ **10** $19 - x$ **11 a** $f(x) = 2x - 5$ **b** $f(x) = 2x - 2$ **c** $f(x) = 3x - 5$ **d** $f(x) = 5x + 2$

Extension

11 a 20 **b** -22 **c** 26 **d** -40 **12 a** 99 **b** -61 **c** 14 **d** -1.2 **13 a** -2 **b** 76 **c** -13 **d** 21.21

14 A $\frac{1}{2}x$ **B** x^3 **C** $\frac{3x}{2}$ **D** $60 - x$ **16 a** $\frac{x+18}{18}$ **b** $\sqrt{x-2}$ **c** $\frac{2x-1}{3}$ **18 a** 1.15 **b** 18.7 **c** -1.7 **d** 7.6

e -20 **19 a** $f(x) = x - 3$ $f^{-1}(x) = x + 3$ **b** $f(x) = 2x + 5$ $f^{-1}(x) = \frac{x-5}{2}$ **20 a i** -5 **ii** 4 **iii** 16 **iv** 0 **v** $1\frac{1}{3}$

vi $\frac{1}{3}$ **b** $f^{-1}(x) = \frac{4-x}{3}$

Chapter 13 Area and volume

Exercise 13:1

1 a 10.5 cm² **b** 11 cm² **c** 18 cm² **d** 17 cm² **2 a** cherry leaf **b** cusp **3 a** Akoben - 72; Pempamsie - 94; Fawohodie - 88; Gye Nyame - 44 **b** 4 **c** Akoben - 17.5 cm²; Pempamsie - 23.5 cm²; Fawohodie - 22 cm²; Gye Nyame - 11 cm²

Exercise 13:2

1 a 10.5 cm² **b** 7.8 cm² **c** 20.8 cm² **2 a** 14.44 cm² **b** 5.76 cm² **c** 2.89 cm² **d** 1.44 cm² **3** 126 mm²
4 0.5625 m² **5** 22.9 cm² **6** 172.37 cm² **7** 18 cm² **8** 20 cm² **9** 160 m² **10** 420 cm² **11** 1426 mm²
12 3.06 m² **13** 21 m² **14** 3840 cm² **15 a** 48 **b** 0.27 **c** 240 **d** 0.784 **e** 1.3875 **f** 104 000

Exercise 13:3

1 7.2 cm **2** 7 m **3** 13.7 m **4** 220 mm **5** 29 cm **6** 2.2 m **7** 91 m **8** 150 mm

Exercise 13:4

1 400 mm² **2 a** 40 000 cm² **b** 80 000 cm² **c** 35.52 cm² **d** 7900 cm² **e** 4.86 cm² **f** 630 cm² **3 a** 0.475 m²
b 6 m² **c** 2 000 000 m² **d** 7 830 000 m² **e** 390 700 m² **4 a** 0.06 km² **b** 8.6 km² **c** 1000 km² **d** 14.58 km²
e 14.85 km²

Exercise 13:5

1 66 cm² **2** 135 cm² **3** 104 cm² **4** 4.68 cm² **5** 4.25 cm² **6** 3.96 cm² **7** 11.25 cm² **8** 11 cm² **9** 48 cm
10 1.9 cm = 190 mm

Exercise 13:6

1 2100 mm² **2** 1530 mm² **3** 3.4 m² **4** 38.4 cm² **5** 600 cm² **6** 11.22 m² **7** 142.41 m² **8** 19.63 m²

Exercise 13:7

1 $5.5 \times 4 \div 2 = 11$ cm² **2** $6.4 \times 14 \div 2 = 44.8$ m² **3** 15.725 cm² **4** 4.56 m² **5** 180 cm² **6** 281 250 mm²
7 3.69 cm² **8** 2.34 cm² **9** 2.88 cm² **10** 6.125 cm² **11** 5.735 cm² **12** 4.725 cm² **13 a** 24 cm² **b** 12.43 m
c 10 m **d** 8800 mm² **e** 32 m **f** 5.2 m

Exercise 13:8

1 22.89 cm² **2** 8.55 cm² **3** 62.18 cm² **4** 6.61 cm² **5** 28.26 cm² **6** 88.21 cm² **7** 19.63 cm² **8** 40.69 cm²
9 15 386 cm² **10** 18 617.06 cm² **11** 9.62 cm² **12** 0.79 cm² **13** 38.47 mm² **14** 828.14 cm² **15** 31.16 mm²
16 3419.46 cm² **17** 125 600 mm² **18** 1.77 m² **19** 10 562.96 cm²

Exercise 13:9

1 25.12 cm² **2** 47.49 cm² **3** 1.57 cm² **4** 50.24 cm² **5** 24.53 cm² **6** 171.82 cm² **7** 5699.1 cm² **8** 1.77 m²
9 15844.44 cm² **10** 565.79 m² **12** 495.36 m² **13** 3720.9 m² **14** 546.75 m² **15** 763.02 cm² **16** 1838.38 cm²
17 153.86 cm²

Exercise 13:10

1 10 cm³ **2** 8 cm³ **3** 24 cm³ **4** 32 cm³ **5** 23 cm³ **6** 20 cm³

Exercise 13:11

1 64 cm³ **2** 200 cm³ **3** 235.6 cm³ **4** 64 000 mm³ **5** 135 cm³ **6** 393.25 cm³ **7** 81 000 cm³ **8** 1.008 m³
9 148.83 cm³ **10** 180 cm³ **11** 6.65 m **12** 6 cm **13** 5 m **14** 27.72 cm³ **15** 0.22 m **16 a** 180 cm³
b 44 mm³ **c** 62.5 cm **d** 52.08 m³ **17** 18 m³ **18 a** 360 cm³ **b** 840 cm³ **c** 216 cm³ **19** 60 packets
20 476 tiles **21 b** 3.93 litres

Exercise 13:12

1 1632 cm³ **2** 11 136 cm³ **3** 180 cm³ **4** 664.6 cm³ **5** 420 cm³ **6** 2.484 m³ **7** 8400 cm³ **8** 1036 cm³

Exercise 13:13

1 281.983 cm³ **2** 4.605 m³ **3** 816 cm³ **4** 872.991 cm³ **5** 127.49 m³

Exercise 13:14

1 a S.A.= 75.36 cm²; V = 75.36 cm³; **b** S.A.= 251.2 cm²; V = 628 cm³; **c** S.A.= 226.08 cm²; V = 678.24 cm³;
d S.A.= 84.78 cm²; V = 127.17 cm³; **e** S.A.= 1695.6 cm²; V = 25 434 cm³; **f** S.A.= 195.94 cm²; V = 470.25 cm³;
2 346.69 cm² **3** 20 347 200 mm³ **4 a** 6898.58 cm³ **b** 1695.6 cm³ **5** 791.28 cm² **6** 47.1 cm²; 98.91 cm²;
35.325 cm³; **7** 141.3 cm²; 197.82 cm²; 211.95 cm³; **8** 206.61 cm²; 514.332 cm³; 723.142 cm³; **9** 62.8 cm²;
64.37 cm²; 15.7 cm³; **10** 62.8 cm²; 87.92 cm²; 62.8 cm³; **11** 131.88 cm²; 188.4 cm²; 197.82 cm³; **12** 276.32 cm²;
376.8 cm²; 552.64 cm³; **13 a** 21980 mm² **b** 3846.5 mm² **c** 29673 mm² **14 a i** 26865.84 cm² **ii** 33510.08
cm² **b** 465096.8 cm³ **15** 3090937.5 cm³ **16 a** 132935.04 cm³ **b** 0. 1329 m³ **17** 288 cm **18** 1080.16 cm3
19 10.26 cm **20 a** 6.45 cm **b** 1000 mm³ **c** 8 cm **d** 5.95 cm **e** 9 cm **21** 150 cm **22** 1.90 m **23** 1.99 m
24 a 703.36 cm **b** 357.96 cm; **a** needs the most sheet metal **25** 512 000 cm³ **b** 8000 cm³ **c** 64 small boxes
26 a SA = 6280 cm²; V = 50240 cm³ **b** S.A. = 10244.25; V = 158 962.5 cm³

Exercise 13:15

1 a 4 cm³ **b** 5 cm³ **c** 0.125 cm³ **2 a** 2800 mm³ **b** 7000 mm³ **c** 850 mm³ **3 a** 1400 cm³ **b** 640 cm³
c 28 cm³ **4 a** 1.9 *l* **b** 2400 *l* **c** 3.8 *l* **d** 300 000 *l* **e** 1.298 *l* **f** 10 000 *l* **5 a** 6 m³ **b** 0.000075 m³ **c** 9.2 m³
6 a 0.0086 m³ **b** 0.0739 m³ **c** 0.0452 m³ **13** 0.1 *l* **14** 4094 c*l* **15** 6 m*l* **16** 2.99 *l* **17** 3.335 *l* **18** 400 c*l*
19 29.3 *l* **20** 1000 m*l*

Extension

1 a 38 cm² **b** 32 cm² **2 a** 9.17 cm **b** 33.9 cm² **3 a** 3456 cm³ **b** 663.552 kg **4 a** 510926783 km²
b 1 086 230 410 000 km² **5** 146.52 cm² **6** 21.07 cm² **7** 22.07 cm² **8 a** 40m² **b** 80 m² **c** 8 m² **9 a** 27 cm³
b 0.008 m³ **c** 2744 cm³ **d** 166.375 cm³ **10** 0.343 m³ **11** 648 000 cm² **12** 100.48 cm² **13 a** 360 m*l*
b 72 dosages **14** 69.66 cm² **15** 4.75 m **16 a** 25.12 cm **b** 50.24 cm² **c** 301.44 cm² **d** 401.92 cm³
e *x* = 24 cm; *y* = 8 cm **17** 386.4 *l* **18** 165.12 cm² **19** 14.65 cm **20** 0.13936 m³ **21** 13 056.12 cm³

Chapter 14 Rates

Exercise 14:1

1 a €17.58 **2** £71.69 **3** ¥85.71 **4** $1.93 **5** $53.93 **6** ¢232.75 **7** Mr Ayi - ¢102.31; Mr Nti - ¢110.24;
Ms Mia - ¢38.54 **8 a** €20.48 **b** €87.77 **c** € 53.19 **d** €139.84 **e** €457.87 **9 a** £161.11 **b** $615.23
c ¥601.60 **d** £6.77 **11 a** ¢28.87 **b** ¢42.86 **c** ¢54.53 **d** ¢18.57 **e** ¢19.98 **f** ¢286.67

Exercise 14:2

1 13.3 km/*l* **2** 48 km/h **3** 80 km/h **4** 72000 *l*/h **5** 225 m²/gal **6** 576 m²/gal **7** 0.0625 *l*/m² **8** 280 km

1 22.2 m/s **2** 18.9 m/s **3** 5.58 kg/cm^2 **4** 143.3 sq ft/gal **5** 30.80 lb/sq in **6** A - 24 km/h; **B** - 64 km/h **C** - 120 km/h **D** - 184 km/h **E** - 208 km/h **F** - 232 km/h **7** 11.39 oz/in^3 **8 a** 15 s **b** 35 s **c** 42 s **9 a** 4.3 km/l **b** 7.8 km/l **c** 17.24 km/l **d** 42.3 km/l **e** 21.7 mi/l **f** 9.1 mi/l **10 a** 5.8 oz/km **b** 4.9 oz/km **c** 1714.3 g/km **d** 3.4 g/m **e** 363 g/mi **f** 22.6 oz/mi **11 a** 69.4 m/s **b** 900 km/h **c** 44.7 mi/h

1 ¢10 **2** ¢21 **3** ¢12 **4** ¢20 **5** ¢45 **6** ¢54.60 **7** ¢ 20.80 **8** ¢45 **9** ¢216 **10** ¢149.76 **11** ¢172.80 **12** ¢130.50 **13** ¢37.95 **14** ¢357.84 **15** ¢440 **16** ¢182.81 **17** ¢1316.25 **18** ¢3931.25 **19** ¢134.40 **20** ¢843.75 **21** ¢483 **22** ¢960 **23** ¢2405 **24** ¢7792.20 **25** ¢714 **26** ¢1680

1 ¢173.79 **2** ¢225.09 **3** ¢482.59 **4** ¢87.17 **5** ¢658.42 **6** ¢876.34 **7** 7.5% **8** 7 years **9** 6.15% **10** 2.03 years **11** ¢2083.33 **12** 1484.44 **13** 20.8% **14** 7.8% **15** 6 years **16** ¢1773.84 **17** ¢910 **18** ¢4355 **19** ¢1863.90 **20** ¢8087.50 **21** ¢753.41 **22** 1578.68 **23** ¢5516.50 **24** ¢10684.19 **25** ¢5715.19 **26** ¢11228.95

1 ¢95 **2** ¢790.50 **3** ¢220 **4** ¢635.80 **5** ¢3198.60 **6** ¢1036.80 **7** ¢6065.25 **8** ¢4819.91 **9** ¢759.53 **10** ¢2639.12 **11** 7.8% **12** 7.9% **13** 15.79% **14** 8.33% **15** 12.5% **16** 10%

1 ¢1.50 **2** ¢3.06 **3** ¢10.80 **4** ¢25.52 **5** ¢21 **6** ¢6.92 **7** ¢11.01 **8** ¢202.40 **9** ¢27.45 **10** ¢55 **11** ¢83 **12** ¢107.92 **13** ¢120 **14** ¢149.75 **15** ¢67.03 **16** ¢112 **17** ¢76 **18** ¢143.73 **19** ¢83.35 **20** ¢236.57 **21** ¢281.65 **22** Mrs Nyarko by ¢6.88 **23** ¢289.49

1 ¢23.97 **2** ¢0.67 **3** ¢26.07 **4** ¢7.81 **5** ¢1.50 **6** ¢6.16 **7** ¢26.24 **8** ¢22.36 **9** ¢52.68 **10 a** ¢2270.74 **b** ¢544.98 **11 a** ¢46 **b** ¢1.19 **c** ¢40.39 **12 a** ¢3118.98 **b** £4267.60 **c** £7610.40 **d i** £13 681.02 **ii** £16 232.40 **iii** £29 039.60 **13 a** €5900 **b** €23 732 **c** £9492.80 **d** €38 607.20

1 ¢9.96 **2** ¢254.14 **3** ¢185.63 **4** ¢64.69 **5** ¢46.13 **6** ¢3240 **7** ¢213.19 **8** ¢13.39 **9** ¢32.51 **10** ¢740.24 **11** subtotal - ¢16.01; vat - ¢2.00; final cost - ¢18.01 **12** subtotal - ¢323.72; vat - ¢40.47; final cost - ¢364.19 **13** subtotal - ¢7.96 vat - ¢1.00; final cost - ¢8.96 **14** subtotal - ¢597.02; vat - ¢74.63; final cost - ¢671.65

1 €17.56 **b** ¢587.32 **c** €10.95 **d** ¥13043 **e** £147.20 **f** ¢11.33 **g** $63.35 **h** ¢6369.57 **i** $385.87 **j** £2202.82 **2 a** £2393.20 **b** €3017.51 **3** ¢2418.11 **4** Akosah paid ¢101 more **5** ¢9.90 **6** ¢0.52 **7 a** 0.28 m/s **b** 19.44 m/s **c** 108 km/h **8** 244.4 m/s; 546.8 mph **9** $16\frac{2}{3}$ years **10 a** ¢726 **b** ¢829.50 **c** ¢950.25 **11** ¢238.95 **12** ¢33.31 **13** ¢2.81 **14 a** ¢18 **b** ¢20.25 **15 a** ¢164 **b** 76 **c** ¢91.16 **16** ¢776.04 **17 a** ¢39 **b i** ¢200 **ii** ¢131.43 **18 a** 13.9 km/l **b** 7.14 km/l **ii** 42.8 km **19 a** 360 km **b** 24 l **c** 545.52 km **20** 111 h 7 min **21 c** 7.14 min **22** 10.5 deg/min **b** 2.3 deg/min **24 a** 0.5 ml/kg/s **b** 0.83 ml/kg/s **25 a** $d = 6t$ **d** $d = 5t$ **f** Boateng's graph is steeper **g** 80 s for Boateng; 96 s for Nkrumah

Chapter 15 Probability

2 a even chance **b** impossible **c** very likely **4 a** certain **b** very unlikely **c** certain **5 a** impossible **b** likely **c** very likely **6 a** very unlikely **c** certain

1 6 outcomes: 1, 2, 3, 4, 5, 6 **2** 5: 2, 4, 6, 8, 10 **3** H, H **4** 5: I, I, I, T, T **5** 4 **6** 4: M, M, T, T **7** 7: I, I, I, I, S, S, S

1 a $\frac{1}{2}$ **b** $\frac{1}{6}$ **c** $\frac{1}{2}$ **d** $\frac{1}{3}$ **e** $\frac{1}{2}$ **f** 0 **2** $\frac{1}{10}$ **3** $\frac{3}{7}$ **4** $\frac{1}{11}$ **5 a** $\frac{1}{2}$ **b** $\frac{1}{2}$ **6** $\frac{7}{10}$ **7** P(mint) = $\frac{3}{5}$ P(ginger) = $\frac{2}{5}$

8 P(toffee) = $\frac{1}{2}$; P(toffee or mint) = $\frac{4}{5}$; P(ginger, toffee or mint) = 1 **9** P(Grey) = $\frac{2}{15}$; P(white) = $\frac{8}{15}$;

373

Page 313

P(ball) = 1; P(black) = $\frac{1}{3}$; **10** P(6) = 0; P(3) = $\frac{3}{10}$; P(3 or 4) = $\frac{7}{10}$; P(ticket) = 1 P(1, 2, 3 or 4) = $\frac{9}{10}$
11 P(white) = ($\frac{1}{5}$); P(green) = 0; P(bead) = 1; P(black or hatch) = $\frac{4}{5}$ **12 a** $\frac{6}{11}$ **b** $\frac{5}{11}$ **c** 0 **13 a** $\frac{1}{4}$ **b** $\frac{3}{10}$

c $\frac{11}{20}$; **d** $\frac{7}{10}$ **14 a** $\frac{4}{13}$; **b** $\frac{3}{13}$ **c** $\frac{6}{13}$ **15** $\frac{7}{36}$ **16** P(not red) = $\frac{3}{5}$ **17 a** $\frac{3}{5}$ **b** $\frac{2}{5}$ **c** $\frac{1}{10}$ **d** $\frac{9}{10}$ **18** $\frac{1}{30}$

19 $\frac{21}{26}$ **20** $\frac{4}{45}$ **21** 0.26 **22** $\frac{1}{36}$

Page 316

Exercise 15:5

1 a 52 **b** 4 **c** 4 **d** 6 **e** 26 **f** 13 **g** 4 **h** 12 **i** 4 **2 a** $\frac{1}{13}$ **b** $\frac{1}{52}$ **c** $\frac{1}{4}$ **d** $\frac{1}{52}$ **e** $\frac{1}{26}$ **f** $\frac{39}{52}$ **g** $\frac{1}{13}$

h $\frac{3}{13}$ **3 a** $\frac{1}{2}$ **b** $\frac{9}{13}$ **c** $\frac{1}{26}$ **d** $\frac{4}{13}$ **e** $\frac{1}{13}$ **f** $\frac{9}{26}$ **g** $\frac{1}{4}$ **g** $\frac{1}{13}$ **4 a** $\frac{1}{2}$ **b** 1 **c** $\frac{3}{4}$ **d** $\frac{3}{13}$ **e** $\frac{5}{13}$ **f** $\frac{4}{13}$

g $\frac{2}{13}$ **h** $\frac{1}{26}$ **i** $\frac{5}{13}$

Page 317

Exercise 15:6

1 a 0.48 **b** Tinee: 0.581 **c** Nitran: 0.26 **d** Minti: 0.48 **e** Caraca: 0.54 **f** Victory: 0.85 **c** Tinee - 58%;
Nitran - 26%; Minti - 48%; Caraca - 54%; Victory - 85% **d** Victory **2 a i** 3% **ii** 5% **iii** 7% **iv** 7%
b The Gel pen **3 a i** 0.42 **ii** 0.58 **b** The coin lands on its tail 16% more than on its head. This seems to be

unfair or weighted. **4 a** 100 **b i** $\frac{32}{100}$ **ii** 0.32 **iii** 32% **c i** $\frac{11}{100}$ **ii** 0.11 **iii** 11% **d** Private car **e** $\frac{23}{100}$

Page 320

Chapter 15 Extension

1 a 0.81 **2** $\frac{3}{10}$ **3 a** $\frac{2}{15}$ **b** $\frac{8}{15}$ **4 a** 1,1 1,2 1,3 2,1 2,2 2,3 3,1 3,2 3,3 **b** $\frac{1}{9}$ **c** $\frac{1}{3}$ **5** 90 times

b 270 times **c** 180 times **6** $\frac{2}{3}$ **7 a** 114 **b** 473 **8** 0.93 **9** $x = 32$ **10 a** 300 **b** 200 **c** 150 **d** 150

11 a 8 **b i** $\frac{4}{15}$ **ii** 0 **iii** $\frac{1}{3}$ **iv** $\frac{2}{5}$ **12** P(stripe) = $\frac{2}{9}$ P(grey) = $\frac{4}{9}$ P(balloon) = 1 P(grey or black) = $\frac{7}{9}$

13 $\frac{11}{20}$ **14** $\frac{3}{10}$ **15 a** $\frac{1}{15}$ **b** $\frac{23}{45}$ **c** $\frac{31}{60}$ **16 b** P(score of 1) = $\frac{83}{600}$; P(score of 2) = $\frac{91}{600}$;

P(score of 3) = $\frac{53}{300}$; P(score of 4) = $\frac{1}{5}$; P(score of 5) = $\frac{101}{600}$; P(score of 6) = $\frac{33}{200}$; **c** The dice is biased

towards a 4 and away from a 1. **17 a** Abdul: P(score of a 1) = 0.34 **b** Jamela: P(score of a 1) = 0.58 **c** You
expect an outcome close to 0.5 for each event so Jamela's answer is more reliable as it is 0.08 close to 0.5 whereas
Abdul's answer is further (0.16) away from the expected answer of 0.5.

Chapter 16 Vectors

Page 325

Exercise 16:1

1 a 060° **2** 026° **3** 090° **4** 290° **5** 326° **6** 220° **7** 160° **8** 243° **9** 338° **10** 249° **11** 345° **12** 162°

Page 326

Exercise 16:2

1 a 280° **b** 134° **2 a** 292° **b** 260° **3 a** 162° **b** 204° **4 a** 312° **b** 252° **5 a** 144° **b** 071° **c** 212° **6 a** 111°
b 198° **c** 245° **7** 279° **8** 244° **9** 061° **10** 313° **11** 260° **12** 183° **13** 148° **14** 088° **15** 055°

Page 328

Exercise 16:3

1 a 10.2 km **b** 070° **c** 250° **2 a** 85 km **b** 114° **c** 295° **3 a** 5.65 km **b** 045° **c** 225° **4 a** 5 km **b** 307°
c 127° **5 a** 11.1 km **b** 118° **c** 298° **6 a** 10.5 km **b** 107° **c** 287° **7 a** 79 km **b** 230° **c** 050° **8 a** 81 km
b 025° **c** 205° **9 a** 10.1 km **b** 337° **10** 16.1 km **11** 12.5 km **b** 033° **12** 585 km; 271° **13** (200, 308)
14 a 75° **b** 300° **c** 150° **d** 330° **15** 92 km **b** 150 km **16 a** 84 km **b** 030°

Page 330

Exercise 16:4

Asafo Race Course (6.9, 011°); Kenkan Library (8, 029°); Afuom Gardens (7.7, 056°); Stool Makers (5.5, 080°);
City University (6.5, 115°); Lake Side (8.9, 146°); Akasanoma Radio Station (8.3, 161°); Dual Carvers (4.9, 173°);
Beefy Chop House (7.5, 184°); Aboa Zoo (9, 200°); Domeabra Farms (7.9, 216°); Mpaboa Shoemakers (4.8, 261°);
Cultural Centre (5.4, 287°); Paga Airport (8.5, 322°); Key Keepers Lodge (4.9, 332°)

Page 331

Exercise 16:5

13 (69 km, 094°) **14** (64 km, 125°) **15** (83 km, 040°) **16** (39 km, 227)° **17 b** (820 km, 313°) **18 a** 254°
b 318° **c i** 014° **ii** 068° **iii** 120° **d** If PK < 180° then KP = PK + 180°, If PK > 180° then KP = PK − 180°

1 $\overrightarrow{AB} = \begin{bmatrix} 4 \\ 5 \end{bmatrix}$ 2 $\overrightarrow{CD} = \begin{bmatrix} 7 \\ 1 \end{bmatrix}$ 3 $\overrightarrow{JK} = \begin{bmatrix} 6 \\ -2 \end{bmatrix}$ 4 $\overrightarrow{EF} = \begin{bmatrix} -1 \\ -6 \end{bmatrix}$ 5 $\overrightarrow{PQ} = \begin{bmatrix} 0 \\ 6 \end{bmatrix}$ 6 $\overrightarrow{GH} = \begin{bmatrix} -6 \\ -3 \end{bmatrix}$

7 $\overrightarrow{RS} = \begin{bmatrix} 1 \\ 2 \end{bmatrix}$ 8 $\overrightarrow{MN} = \begin{bmatrix} 1 \\ 3 \end{bmatrix}$ 9 $\underline{a} = \begin{bmatrix} -7 \\ 0 \end{bmatrix}$ 10 $\underline{b} = \begin{bmatrix} 0 \\ -6 \end{bmatrix}$ 11 $\underline{c} = \begin{bmatrix} -6 \\ 1 \end{bmatrix}$ 12 $\underline{d} = \begin{bmatrix} -2 \\ 6 \end{bmatrix}$ 13 $\underline{e} = \begin{bmatrix} 6 \\ 0 \end{bmatrix}$

14 $\underline{f} = \begin{bmatrix} -6 \\ -5 \end{bmatrix}$ 15 $\underline{g} = \begin{bmatrix} 2 \\ 7 \end{bmatrix}$

1 a $\begin{bmatrix} -1 \\ 2 \end{bmatrix}, \begin{bmatrix} 0 \\ -3 \end{bmatrix}$ b i $\begin{bmatrix} -1 \\ 0 \end{bmatrix} \begin{bmatrix} 0 \\ 3 \end{bmatrix} \begin{bmatrix} -4 \\ 0 \end{bmatrix}$ ii $\begin{bmatrix} 9 \\ 1 \end{bmatrix}$

1 $\overrightarrow{ST} = \overrightarrow{VW} = \begin{bmatrix} -4 \\ 1 \end{bmatrix}$ $\overrightarrow{AB} = \overrightarrow{MN} = \begin{bmatrix} 3 \\ 3 \end{bmatrix}$ $\overrightarrow{CD} = \overrightarrow{GH} = \begin{bmatrix} 2 \\ -4 \end{bmatrix}$ $\overrightarrow{KJ} = \overrightarrow{ST} = \begin{bmatrix} -2 \\ 0 \end{bmatrix}$ $\overrightarrow{EF} = \overrightarrow{PQ} = \begin{bmatrix} 7 \\ -3 \end{bmatrix}$

2 a $\begin{bmatrix} 7 \\ -3 \end{bmatrix}$ b $\begin{bmatrix} -6 \\ -1 \end{bmatrix}$ c $\begin{bmatrix} 5 \\ 0 \end{bmatrix}$ d $\begin{bmatrix} -1 \\ 4 \end{bmatrix}$ e $\begin{bmatrix} 0 \\ 4 \end{bmatrix}$ f $\begin{bmatrix} -5 \\ 6 \end{bmatrix}$ g $\begin{bmatrix} 2 \\ -7 \end{bmatrix}$ h $\begin{bmatrix} -4 \\ 4 \end{bmatrix}$ i $\begin{bmatrix} -2 \\ 5 \end{bmatrix}$ j $\begin{bmatrix} -1 \\ -2 \end{bmatrix}$ 3 a $\begin{bmatrix} -10 \\ 16 \end{bmatrix}$

b $\begin{bmatrix} 9 \\ -23 \end{bmatrix}$ c $\begin{bmatrix} 20 \\ 37 \end{bmatrix}$ d $\begin{bmatrix} -47 \\ 16 \end{bmatrix}$ e $\begin{bmatrix} -100 \\ 16 \end{bmatrix}$

1 $\begin{bmatrix} 9 \\ 8 \end{bmatrix}$ 2 $\begin{bmatrix} 7 \\ 5 \end{bmatrix}$ 3 $\begin{bmatrix} 0 \\ -3 \end{bmatrix}$ 4 $\begin{bmatrix} -5 \\ -1 \end{bmatrix}$ 5 $\begin{bmatrix} 1 \\ 8 \end{bmatrix}$ 6 $\begin{bmatrix} 5 \\ -10 \end{bmatrix}$ 7 $\begin{bmatrix} -13 \\ -1 \end{bmatrix}$ 8 $\begin{bmatrix} -3 \\ -5 \end{bmatrix}$ 9 $\begin{bmatrix} -11 \\ 2 \end{bmatrix}$ 10 $\begin{bmatrix} -8 \\ -10 \end{bmatrix}$

11 $\begin{bmatrix} -2 \\ 0 \end{bmatrix}$ 12 $\begin{bmatrix} 1 \\ -7 \end{bmatrix}$ 13 $\begin{bmatrix} 40 \\ 2 \end{bmatrix}$ 14 $\begin{bmatrix} 6 \\ -2 \end{bmatrix}$ 15 $\begin{bmatrix} 0 \\ 1 \end{bmatrix}$ 16 $\begin{bmatrix} -30 \\ 21 \end{bmatrix}$ 17 $\begin{bmatrix} 7 \\ 5 \end{bmatrix}$ 18 $\begin{bmatrix} 4 \\ 6 \end{bmatrix}$ 19 $\begin{bmatrix} 8 \\ -2 \end{bmatrix}$ 20 $\begin{bmatrix} 0 \\ -6 \end{bmatrix}$

21 $\begin{bmatrix} 8 \\ -1 \end{bmatrix}$ 22 $\begin{bmatrix} 7 \\ 2 \end{bmatrix}$ 23 $\begin{bmatrix} 6 \\ 7 \end{bmatrix}$ 24 $\begin{bmatrix} -6 \\ -4 \end{bmatrix}$ 25 $\begin{bmatrix} 4 \\ 6 \end{bmatrix}$ 26 $\begin{bmatrix} -6 \\ -4 \end{bmatrix}$ 27 $\begin{bmatrix} 0 \\ -3 \end{bmatrix}$ 28 $\begin{bmatrix} 6 \\ 3 \end{bmatrix}$ 29 $\begin{bmatrix} -6 \\ 2 \end{bmatrix}$ 30 $\begin{bmatrix} 1 \\ 1 \end{bmatrix}$

31 $\begin{bmatrix} 3 \\ -5 \end{bmatrix}$ 32 $\begin{bmatrix} -2 \\ -5 \end{bmatrix}$ 33 $\begin{bmatrix} 10 \\ 2 \end{bmatrix}$ 34 $\begin{bmatrix} 4 \\ -6 \end{bmatrix}$ 35 $\begin{bmatrix} -2 \\ 0 \end{bmatrix}$ 36 $\begin{bmatrix} 6 \\ 1 \end{bmatrix}$

1 $\begin{bmatrix} 1 \\ 2 \end{bmatrix}$ 2 $\begin{bmatrix} 1 \\ 3 \end{bmatrix}$ 3 $\begin{bmatrix} 0 \\ 3 \end{bmatrix}$ 4 $\begin{bmatrix} 2 \\ -10 \end{bmatrix}$ 5 $\begin{bmatrix} -2 \\ 1 \end{bmatrix}$ 6 $\begin{bmatrix} -4 \\ -8 \end{bmatrix}$ 7 $\begin{bmatrix} 1 \\ 8 \end{bmatrix}$ 8 $\begin{bmatrix} 4 \\ -1 \end{bmatrix}$ 9 $\begin{bmatrix} -17 \\ -9 \end{bmatrix}$ 10 $\begin{bmatrix} -1 \\ -32 \end{bmatrix}$ 11 $\begin{bmatrix} 2 \\ 29 \end{bmatrix}$

12 $\begin{bmatrix} -12 \\ -2 \end{bmatrix}$ 13 $\begin{bmatrix} 2 \\ -4 \end{bmatrix}$ 14 $\begin{bmatrix} 1 \\ 4 \end{bmatrix}$ 15 $\begin{bmatrix} 4 \\ -4 \end{bmatrix}$ 16 $\begin{bmatrix} -7 \\ 12 \end{bmatrix}$ 17 $\begin{bmatrix} 1 \\ 0 \end{bmatrix}$ 18 $\begin{bmatrix} -2 \\ -2 \end{bmatrix}$ 19 $\begin{bmatrix} -12 \\ 0 \end{bmatrix}$ 20 $\begin{bmatrix} 5 \\ -12 \end{bmatrix}$

1 a $\begin{bmatrix} 4 \\ 12 \end{bmatrix}$ b $\begin{bmatrix} 10 \\ 30 \end{bmatrix}$ c $\begin{bmatrix} 1 \\ 3 \end{bmatrix}$ 2 a $\begin{bmatrix} 12 \\ -3 \end{bmatrix}$ b $\begin{bmatrix} -8 \\ 2 \end{bmatrix}$ c $\begin{bmatrix} 28 \\ -7 \end{bmatrix}$ 3 a $\begin{bmatrix} 5 \\ -4 \end{bmatrix}$ b $\begin{bmatrix} 15 \\ -12 \end{bmatrix}$ c $\begin{bmatrix} -25 \\ 20 \end{bmatrix}$ 4 a $\begin{bmatrix} -24 \\ -18 \end{bmatrix}$

b $\begin{bmatrix} 12 \\ 9 \end{bmatrix}$ c $\begin{bmatrix} 6 \\ 4\frac{1}{2} \end{bmatrix}$ 5 a $\begin{bmatrix} -12 \\ -9 \end{bmatrix}$ b $\begin{bmatrix} 24 \\ 16 \end{bmatrix}$ c $\begin{bmatrix} -56 \\ 8 \end{bmatrix}$ d $\begin{bmatrix} 0 \\ -1 \end{bmatrix}$ e $\begin{bmatrix} 2 \\ 2 \end{bmatrix}$ f $\begin{bmatrix} -96 \\ -54 \end{bmatrix}$ 6 a $\begin{bmatrix} 4 \\ 3\frac{1}{5} \end{bmatrix}$ b $\begin{bmatrix} -10 \\ -16 \end{bmatrix}$

c $\begin{bmatrix} 16 \\ 14 \end{bmatrix}$ d $\begin{bmatrix} -1\frac{1}{2} \\ -2 \end{bmatrix}$ e $\begin{bmatrix} -24 \\ -20 \end{bmatrix}$ f $\begin{bmatrix} 3\frac{3}{4} \\ 2\frac{1}{3} \end{bmatrix}$

1 a vector b vector c vector d scalar e scalar f vector 3 a $295°$ b $250°$ c $077°$ 4 $308°$ 5 a $078°$ b $085°$ c $110°$ d $048°$ 6 a $237°$ b $223°$ c $333°$ d $253°$ 7 $(72, 342°)$ 8 a $051°$ b $107°$ c $231°$ 9 b Anim c $346°$ d 610 km d $333°$ 9 b $348°$ d 570 km 10 a $\begin{bmatrix} 2 \\ 10 \end{bmatrix}$ b $\begin{bmatrix} -13 \\ -2 \end{bmatrix}$ c $\begin{bmatrix} 1 \\ -2 \end{bmatrix}$ 11 a $\begin{bmatrix} -15 \\ 18\frac{3}{5} \end{bmatrix}$ b $\begin{bmatrix} 10 \\ -12\frac{2}{5} \end{bmatrix}$ c $\begin{bmatrix} 50 \\ -62 \end{bmatrix}$

d $\begin{bmatrix} -3\frac{4}{7} \\ 4\frac{3}{7} \end{bmatrix}$ 13 a $\begin{bmatrix} 4 \\ 3 \end{bmatrix}$ b $\begin{bmatrix} -11 \\ 7 \end{bmatrix}$ c $\begin{bmatrix} -8 \\ -2 \end{bmatrix}$ d $\begin{bmatrix} -2 \\ -7 \end{bmatrix}$ e $\begin{bmatrix} 11 \\ -7 \end{bmatrix}$ 14 a $\begin{bmatrix} 4 \\ -27 \end{bmatrix}$ b $\begin{bmatrix} 5 \\ 2 \end{bmatrix}$ c $\begin{bmatrix} -8 \\ -76 \end{bmatrix}$ d $\begin{bmatrix} -43 \\ -51 \end{bmatrix}$

e $\begin{bmatrix} 3\frac{3}{10} \\ -\frac{11}{60} \end{bmatrix}$ 15 $x = 5, y = -9$ 16 a $x = 1, y = 2$ b $x = -1\frac{2}{3}, y = 1\frac{1}{2}$ 17 b He spends 420 min on cleaning cars

and 285 min on selling newspapers 18 a $S = (8, 7)$ b $\overrightarrow{PR} = \begin{bmatrix} 11 \\ 1 \end{bmatrix}$ 19 a $x = 1, y = 2$ b $x = -3$ $y = 1\frac{1}{2}$

20 a $\overrightarrow{AC} = \begin{bmatrix} 9 \\ 7 \end{bmatrix}$ b $\overrightarrow{DC} = \begin{bmatrix} 8 \\ 2 \end{bmatrix}$ c $\overrightarrow{BE} = \begin{bmatrix} 6 \\ -7 \end{bmatrix}$ d $\overrightarrow{EC} = \begin{bmatrix} -3 \\ 12 \end{bmatrix}$

INDEX